W9-CRC-717

PRAISE FOR *THE NEW COLD WAR*:

"Lucas is a fine writer, and his prose has all the verve and punch that the best of his magazine, *The Economist*, has to offer."

—*Foreign Affairs*

"A matter of huge importance to the West . . . I can unreservedly recommend Edward Lucas. *The New Cold War* is about the fate that has yet again befallen the unfortunate region of Europe that lies on the borderlands of East and West."

—Daniel Johnson, *New York Sun*

"Powerfully argues that America and Europe's excessive focus on Iraq and Afghanistan has blinded them to a threat closer to home . . . Offers one of the best briefs on how Yeltsin's Wild West became Putin's chilly petrofascism, detailing the return of rigged elections, forced psychiatric medication, the use of natural resources as foreign-policy bludgeons, and the rogue nations that are once again Moscow's best friends."

—*Philadelphia Inquirer*

"Vivid, highly readable."

—*Bloomberg.com*

"An invaluable primer for students of the Russian situation and a cautionary tale for [the West]."

—David Satter, author of *Darkness at Dawn: The Rise of the Russian Criminal State*

"A chilling account that needs to be taken seriously."

—Richard Pipes, author of *The Russian Revolution*

"An authoritative analysis of the disturbing events in Russia today. Thoughtful, thoroughly researched and brilliantly written . . . deserves the widest possible readership."

—Robert Gellately, author of *Lenin, Stalin and Hitler: The Age of Social Catastrophe*

"Highly informed, crisply written and alarming . . . Wise up and stick together is the concluding message in Lucas's outstanding book."

—Michael Burleigh, *Evening Standard*

"A devastating but apt critique of Vladimir Putin's domestic repression and increasingly aggressive foreign policy. Stark and clear-sighted . . . [and] an excellent read."

—Anders Åslund, senior fellow, Peterson Institute for International Economics, Washington, D.C.

"A brilliant and profoundly disturbing study of modern Russia. It is difficult to overstate the importance of Edward Lucas's latest work for U.S. and European policymakers."

—Bruce P. Jackson, President, Project on Transitional Democracies

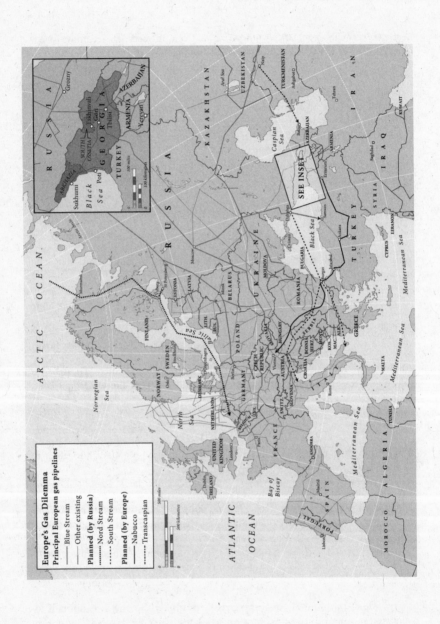

Europe's Gas Dilemma

Principal European gas pipelines

—— Blue Stream
—— Other existing

Planned (by Russia)
—— Nord Stream
······ South Stream

Planned (by Europe)
—— Nabucco
-·-·- Transcaspian

THE NEW
COLD WAR

Putin's Russia and the
Threat to the West

Edward Lucas

palgrave
macmillan

First published in hardcover in 2008 by PALGRAVE MACMILLAN® in the
US—a division of St. Martin's Press LLC, 175 Fifth Avenue, New York, NY
10010.

Where this book is distributed in the UK, Europe and the rest of the world,
this is by Palgrave Macmillan, a division of Macmillan Publishers Limited,
registered in England, company number 785998, of Houndmills,
Basingstoke, Hampshire RG21 6XS.

Palgrave Macmillan is the global academic imprint of the above companies
and has companies and representatives throughout the world.

Palgrave® and Macmillan® are registered trademarks in the United States,
the United Kingdom, Europe and other countries.

ISBN-13: 978-0-230-61434-5
ISBN-10: 0-230-61434-5

Library of Congress Cataloging-in-Publication Data is available from the
Library of Congress.

A catalogue record of the book is available from the British Library.

Design by Letra Libre, Inc.

First PALGRAVE MACMILLAN paperback edition: March 2009

10 9 8 7 6 5 4 3 2 1

Printed in the United States of America.

CONTENTS

Acknowledgments   vii
Preface   ix
Foreword to the Revised Edition   xiii

Introduction   1

1. Putin's Rise to Power   19

2. Putin in Power   37

3. Sinister Pretense   57

4. Why Money Is Russia's Greatest Strength and
    Our Greatest Weakness   87

5. The "New Tsarism"   101

6. How Eastern Europe Sits on the Frontline of
    the New Cold War   129

7. Pipeline Politics   163

8. Saber-Rattling, or Selling Sabers   189

9. How to Win the New Cold War   207

Notes   217
Index   250

To Cristina

ACKNOWLEDGMENTS

My thanks go first to my editors at *The Economist* for giving me a sabbatical to write this book. But its arguments are mine alone, and do not necessarily represent the newspaper's editorial line on Russia or anything else.

I am particularly grateful to my friends who commented on, and vastly improved, the manuscript. They include Martin Dewhirst, Jeff Myhre, Greg Pytel, James Sherr, and Zinovy Zinik. During my time in Moscow, Yevgenia Albats, Konstantin Eggert, and three Mashas—Gessen, Lipman, and especially Slonim—helped me greatly. Foreign correspondents' best sources, and best friends, are often colleagues: Kadri Liik and Christian Caryl as well as Isabel Gorst, Nina Khrushchera and Ana Uzelac all offered unstinting helpings of both friendship and their far greater knowledge of Russia; so did Marc and Rachel Polonsky. Without Claudia Sinnig I would have never done more than scratch the region's surface.

Two decades' worth of friends in what is now the ex-communist world have my deepest gratitude and affection: Tarmu Tammerk and my other colleagues at the former *Baltic Independent,* plus Kersti Kajulaid, David Mardiste, Eve and Mihkel Tarm, and Tiia Raudma in Estonia; Baiba Braže, Nils Mužnieks, and Pauls Raudseps in Latvia; Daiva Vilkelytė, Virgis Valentinavičius, Mirga Šaltmiras, and the Dvarionis family in Lithuania, Paweł Dobrowolski, Marek Matraszek, Paweł Żak, and most of all the Jabłońska family in Poland; in the Czech Republic Alena Doležalová, Andrei and Marta Ernyei, and Jan Urban; Ingrid Bakše in Slovenia and Edward Serotta in Vienna; as well as Bill Hough throughout the Baltic independence struggle. In Britain, Chris Cviić and Timothy Garton Ash first encouraged me to head east in 1988; the late Kari Blackburn, Steve Crawshaw, Daniel Franklin, and Ed Steen gave me my first big breaks in journalism. Michael Bordeaux, Paul Goble, Vladimir

Socor, Peter Reddaway, and David Satter have provided historical, moral, and strategic perspective over many years.

Government officials have been staunch allies too. Tomas Bertelman, Dag Hartelius, and Lars Freden from Sweden; Laura Kakko, Markus Lyra, and Rene Nyberg from Finland; Emma Baines, Janet Gunn, Richard Samuel, John and Judith Macgregor, and Elizabeth Teague from Britain; and John Kunstadter have all shared their thoughts generously and warmly, as did those whose talents are cloaked in anonymity, protocol, or shadow.

Ruthlessly though I have taken advantage of the help of these and many others, the mistakes of fact and interpretation in this book are mine alone.

This book was conceived and written over one summer, requiring exceptional efforts from my literary agents, Zoe Waldie in London and Melanie Jackson in New York, who grasped the urgency of the idea and found publishers willing to bring it out at breakneck speed. Stephen Edwards and Laurence Laluyaux sold the foreign language rights with exemplary efficiency. Bill Swainson and Emily Sweet at Bloomsbury, and Luba Ostashevsky and Yasmin Mathew at Palgrave, tolerated the questions and blunders of a first-time author with endless patience, while effortlessly cramming work that normally takes a year into barely three months.

My parents, siblings, and children have tolerated the absences, arrests, and assaults of a foreign correspondent's life with extraordinary stoicism and have given me unquestioning love at all times. My sister Helen was a fount of sanity and support in the most difficult years of my life; my brother Richard's wisdom and humor over the past two decades on the subjects of planned economies and postcommunist business have been invaluable.

Without the Odone family, this book would not have been written; Francesco lent his house. Most of all, Cristina gave her love and inspiration. The book is dedicated to her.

PREFACE

Russia's recent invasion of Georgia took most Western leaders by surprise. It inspired comments about "a fresh tack in Russian policy," of an unexpected crisis in post-Soviet East–West relations, and of an unwelcome "return to Soviet-era methods." As Russian tanks rolled into the territory of a neighboring democracy, speculation was rife about a firm Western response, and, not very originally, about "a new cold war." The assumption seemed to be that the Kremlin under President Medvedev had adopted a harder and harsher line than was followed during the preceding decade of Vladimir Putin's presidency.

Nonetheless, even though most comment was critical, there was no shortage in the Western media of views echoing the Kremlin's own pronouncements. Russia had been provoked. NATO had been meddling in "Russia's backyard." Russian forces had only been sent to defend Russian citizens. The "true aggressor" was the wild and irresponsible Georgian president, Mikheil Saakashvili. And Russia had an absolute right to "self-defense."

Numerous parallels were drawn between Russian actions and attitudes toward Georgia and Western policy toward Kosovo. The most common judgment can be summed up in the phrase "tit for tat." NATO bombarded one of Russia's friends, Serbia, and has offered recognition to breakaway anti-Serbian separatists in Kosovo. So Russia has now attacked one of NATO's friends, Georgia, and has offered recognition to breakaway anti-Georgian separatists in Abkhazia and South Ossetia. What could be simpler? A plague can descend on both their houses. The blame game takes hold. And sensible analysis goes through the window.

Despite Russian policy in the Caucasus being the matter in hand, few commentators have cared to draw the more telling parallel with the sad fate of Chechnya. For ten years after the collapse of the Soviet Union, Russia had played cat and mouse with the Muslim

Chechnyan separatists, whose homeland lies only a couple of squares from Ossetia on the Caucasian chessboard. Then, after one inconclusive Chechnyan war, President Putin launched a second, and used overwhelming force to crush the viper in his nest. Tens of thousands were killed. Hundreds of thousands were driven into exile. The capital, Grozny, was devastated, and a puppet regime was installed. The conclusion should be self-evident. When separatists dare to operate within Russia's frontiers, they are to be extirpated without mercy. When they surface on the territory of Russia's neighbors in the so-called "Near Abroad," and especially in the vicinity of vital pipelines, they are to be encouraged.

The Georgian crisis has demonstrated once again that Russian officials are masters of political games, where few Western leaders can compete. President Medvedev declares brazenly that Russia has an obligation to protect Russian citizens in South Ossetia, and most of the world assumes without question that the Ossetian minority in Georgia must be Russian. In reality, the Ossetians are ethnically distinct and culturally have more in common with the Georgians. They descend from Persian tribes, speak a language that's a close cognate to farsi, and, like the rest of the Caucasus nations, were conquered by the Russian Empire in the nineteenth century. They adopted a form of Orthodox Christianity in order to distinguish themselves from the neighboring Muslim Ingush—another ethnic group now inhabiting the Russian republic of Ingushetia—and Chechens. Since the establishment of Georgia as a sovereign member of the United Nations, they may best be described as Georgian citizens of Ossetian nationality. Their most famous son is Joseph Stalin, whose father was Ossetian and mother Georgian.

President Medvedev failed to mention that the Russian peacekeepers who arrived in 1992 have been steadily handing out Russian passports to Ossetians in North Georgia. Their hand-picked leaders have been schooled to appeal to Moscow for help. The sleight of hand is carried off with a skill that has many precedents in Russian history, but that few Westerners ever notice. For it is accompanied by a show of righteous indignation which could not be greater if Georgia had attacked Russia instead of Russia attacking Georgia. The invasion force, which raced through the Roki tunnel into Georgian territory on the night of August 7–8, was labeled as a mission of *mirotvortsy,* or "peacemakers." They were sent to rescue the Russian-backed South Ossetian militiamen who had started the initial shooting and had set the trap for President Saakashvili. They could not possibly have reacted with such speed if their operation had not been premeditated. As President Medvedev ingenuously explained, they had been sent "to coerce the Georgians into making peace." Yet they did not stop after completing the stated purpose. They were soon observed ransacking the vital oil port of Poti, sinking Georgian ships, demolishing important road and railway bridges, and occupying Georgian towns well beyond the combat zone. And, lo and behold, long before an international meeting could be convened to discuss the future of Abkhazia and South Ossetia, Moscow rapidly recognized the breakaway republics. Their South Ossetian puppet announced that his country would soon be joining Russia.

Of course, it is not enough to chronicle the combination of force and fraud by which Russian policy has habitually been pursued, or to bemoan the revival in recent years of Soviet-style politics. Though Vladimir Putin stood symbolically in Stalin's place at the fiftieth anniversary of the victorious "Great Fatherland War," he is not a new Stalin. And, though he has described the fall of the USSR as the "greatest catastrophe," he is very unlikely to be aiming at a full restoration of a Soviet party-state. In order to understand present-day developments, it is necessary to calibrate one's assessments of the many factors in play. Here, Edward Lucas's study *The New Cold War* is a first-class guide. Published early in 2008 after careful observation of Putin's rise to power, it applies great subtlety to the principal issues, and it suggests that under the Putin regime's new figurehead the Russian Federation will continue to finesse its own strategic and regional solutions.

For example, while having no illusions about Moscow's readiness to use brute force on occasion, Lucas does not believe that the tanks will roll on a broad front, that numerous countries will be swallowed whole, or that nuclear muscles will be flexed. Rather, he argues that Russia's neighbors will be bullied, undermined, infiltrated, disarmed by cyberattack and internal subversion, wracked by energy dependence, and generally entangled in a web of Russian-pulled strings. In the end, like Finland in the Soviet era, they will be reduced to a condition that remains nominally independent but effectively subservient. After its recent ordeal, Georgia will be lucky if half the country isn't permanently occupied by Russian forces.

Similarly, on the domestic front Lucas is not predicting a renaissance either of Stalinist totalitarianism or of a centralized command economy. Even if Russia's infant democracy has already been muzzled, Russia needs to stay open to the world in order to wield its chosen instruments of pipeline politics and authoritarian capitalism.

For this reason, the Kremlin will endeavor to maintain the mask of normality, to practice the "sinister pretence" that the strongarm methods of the past have been dropped for ever. Better, in other words, to murder the occasional journalist or to kill one man in a blaze of sensational publicity than to embark on a campaign to lock up all the dissidents in sight. Threats can be more useful than shots. Russia badly needs foreign investors and partners in global trade, and nothing too drastic is likely to happen to frighten the horses.

Some things, however, do not really change. One is the essentially predatory nature of Russian statehood, which has always preferred squeezing foreign countries to patient construction at home. Another is the gullibility and lack of imagination of all too many Western leaders.

In this regard, Lucas does not just engage in rhetoric. He makes positive proposals concerning an appropriate response from the rest of the world. He stresses the necessity of a common purpose between Europe and America, and between individual members of the EU and of NATO. At the same time, he draws attention to the special vulnerability of the countries on Europe's front line. Consistent support for the Baltic states, for Ukraine, and for the republics of the Caucasus is essential, as is a watchful eye on developing tensions in Central Asia. The West was foolishly persuaded to drop its guard when the "End of History" was announced nearly twenty years ago. And it is time for the guard to be erected again. After all, Russia has clearly not abandoned its perceived right to control the "Near Abroad." And from Moscow's point of view, what we call "the Middle East" has traditionally been seen as Russia's "Near South."

The New Cold War first published before the crisis in Georgia came to a head. But all the sound bites that issued from the world's media in the wake of the invasion are here set out in careful and logical argument. Those who did not read Lucas at the first opportunity can think themselves accursed. Fortunately, thanks to a new edition, they can easily catch up, and be better prepared for the next round and the next "surprise."

Norman Davies
Oxford, August 30, 2008

FOREWORD TO THE
REVISED EDITION

Since the first edition of *The New Cold War* was completed in September 2007, events have underlined its central theme: repression inside Russia and aggression abroad, and the West's alarmingly feeble response. Hopes that Vladimir Putin was preparing to leave power, or allow a fair contest between freely chosen candidates for the presidency, were dashed. With a few tweaks, the old regime of ex-KGB men and their business cronies has stayed in power. Abroad, Russia's behavior has turned concern into outright alarm. Perhaps the only reason for optimism in the late summer of 2008 is that many in the West seem to be waking up to the problem on our doorstep.

In the light of Russia's invasion and—at the time of writing—continued occupation of Georgia, the contentious use of "cold war" in the title now seems, if anything, an understatement. The Kremlin has shown that it is quite prepared to use armed force; the West has shown that it is not. That creates an asymmetrical relationship in which Russia, militarily weak but mentally decisive, can expect to get almost anything it wants. The war in Georgia, the *de facto* annexation by Russia of two of its provinces, and the West's humiliation are described in more detail in the revised version of Chapter Six.

Recent events have also proved the Kremlin's will to power. Putin's party, United Russia, won 64 percent of the vote and 315 of the 450 seats in the Duma elections in December 2007. In the March 2008 presidential elections, where Dmitri Medvedev won an almost uncontested victory with more than two-thirds of the vote, top U.S. and British papers ran articles about voter coercion at every social level—such as heads of factories strongly advising their employees on their election choices. Yet Medvedev rode in on a wave of democratic rhetoric: he made speeches denouncing "legal nihilism" and calling freedom better than non-freedom The months before his election provided plenty of examples of the latter, while his record in office provided only flimsy evidence of a change of course.

Psychiatric abuse remains the single most shocking echo of Soviet-style repression in modern Russia. In addition to the incidents cited in the book, the State Department's annual report[1] on human rights, published in March 2008, highlighted three further cases.[2] In February 2008 Roman Nikolaychik, an opposition activist from Tver, spent nearly a month in a mental hospital against his will, partly in solitary confinement. The use of psychiatrists as an intimidatory factor during questioning by the police and FSB, or even in private commercial disputes,[3] continued.

Most of the political prisoners identified in the book remain behind bars. Oleg Kozlovsky, the leader of the Obrona anti-Putin youth movement, was illegally (albeit briefly) conscripted into the army, despite his exempt status as a student. In May 2008 he spent 13 days in prison on an implausible charge of "troublemaking," after he tried to take part in an opposition demonstration. The Russian blogger Savva Terentyev was sentenced to a year in prison (suspended) for writing abusive material about his local police. Other bloggers who criticize the government, such as Oleg Panfilov, the director of a media freedom group, have experienced cyberattacks. In July 2008, Ilya Shunin, a National Bolshevik activist, was arrested on charges of running his (allegedly extremist) party's website. In the mainstream media, even quoting the views of those that the authorities regard as extremists risks prosecution. The authorities also used the extremism law to open a prosecution of the Sakharov Centre in Moscow over an art exhibition. Equally ominous is the developing blind spot toward truly extremist activity, such as the thriving "Movement against Illegal Immigration." The pro-Kremlin press now tends to report this outfit's loaded and inflammatory statements uncritically.[4]

The media remains muzzled, while those who try to present a different view struggle to survive. Among the most conspicuous infringements of press freedom was the treatment of Natalia Morar, a young Moldovan-born investigative journalist with the *New Times* magazine run by Yevgenia Albats. Morar had exposed a series of Kremlin corruption scandals, including, interestingly, links to an Austrian bank. She was stripped of her permanent residency in Russia and deported, on the grounds that she was allegedly threatening national security.[5] She has filed an appeal against Russia at the European Court of Human Rights. Marina Aslamazyan, whose arrest at

Moscow airport on a technical currency irregularity in 2007 led to the closure of the Educated Media Foundation, Russia's main independent-journalist-training outfit, was vindicated in a ruling by the Constitutional Court in June 2008. But the man who masterminded the case, Igor Tsokolov, became a presidential adviser on anticorruption issues.

Mikhail Trepashkin, the lawyer and former FSB officer who feared that he would die in prison, was released in November 2007. His replacement as Russia's most prominent political prisoner came not from the thinning ranks of the country's beleaguered opposition, but from inside the government: the deputy finance minister, Sergei Storchak, was arrested the same month on unlikely sounding embezzlement charges. Despite emphatic support from his boss, the finance minister Aleksei Kudrin, he has spent months in jail in what seems to be part of a turf war between ex-KGB men and economic reformers. Later, the prosecutor who led the investigation into his alleged misdeeds, Dmitriy Dovgiy, was arrested, too.

None of this seems to bother the Russian public. A striking sign of the mood within Russia was that in the summer of 2008, Joseph Stalin, the greatest mass murderer in the country's history, was running neck and neck with another disastrous ruler, Tsar Nicholas II, in an internet poll designed to choose the "Greatest Russian." That was not the result of a properly conducted piece of opinion research, yet it was still sad that contenders such as Andrei Sakharov polled dismally.

That reflects the Kremlin's success in entrenching its ideology in the public mind. Though explicit talk of "sovereign democracy" has waned, the idea that Russia is different and that Western ideas of political freedom don't apply is now entrenched. The latest notion pushed by the regime's spin doctors is truly bizarre: that the "Byzantium" of six hundred years ago was a model for contemporary Russia.[6] This fits neatly with the idea that Russia is a different (and higher) civilization, that it is under attack both from the east (the Ottoman Empire, nowadays Islamists) and from an ignorant and arrogant West (the Fourth Crusade then, NATO now). The rewriting of history continues apace. School history texts contain a deplorable blend of amnesia and nostalgia that impedes a proper understanding of Russia's tragic past, and they are criticized by professional historians.

Putin's supporters like to say that Russia is now free of ideology. The country simply pursues a commendably hard-nosed *realpolitik*.[7] From this point of view Putin is just a tough patriot doing a good job

xvi THE NEW COLD WAR

for his country, who dislikes the dominion of the Western-run international order. Optimists in the West even agree—maintaining that Putin does not represent a threat. Instead his abrasive personality aggravates western sensibilities. They say Russia is on track to democracy—but it's bumpy ride.

This argument ignores the explicit rejection by the Russian regime of Western values such as political freedom, the rule of law, the separation of powers, a free press, and individual rights. The attack on Georgia, and the menacing of Ukraine, is in part the result of the profound ideological challenge that these ex-Soviet states pose to the Kremlin. If Ukraine or Georgia can have a true multi-party system, an open economy, and a free press, why can't Russia have the same? Just as the Prague Spring in Czechoslovakia in 1968 presented a profound ideological challenge to the authoritarian communism of Leonid Brezhnev, the success of Georgia (and to a lesser extent the Ukraine) challenge the authoritarian capitalist model of Putin and his colleagues.

Some Westerners even find Putin's politics rather attractive. For the conscience-free and well-connected businessman, the idea of a kind of capitalism where success is determined by good connections rather than competence is appealing. That may explain why some Continental European energy companies, used to doing business in the shady glades of corporatist economic systems, are happy conducting business in Russia. Others like what they see as a robust economic nationalism. For xenophobes who find the whole idea of international economic integration threatening, the sight of a strong state that pushes multinationals around and bucks the will of the market is empowering.

This view overlooks the fact that Russia's success is based on a remarkable and unforeseen spike in the oil and gas price. And it fails to see that the Russian regime is overall a strong supporter of globalization. It is the global economy that allows Russian commercial entities to buy assets abroad, diversifying their own personal portfolios, and also extending Russia's reach in a way undreamed of by the Soviet leadership. It is the world's capital markets that turn what are still in effect government departments such as Gazprom into hugely effective money-making machines. You boost revenues by awarding quasi-monopolies, then make money listing the shares. Then you make more money from insider trading. Then you siphon off the revenues through inflated costs. Lastly—and this has yet to happen—you may loot the whole company, along the lines of Yukos, leaving the foreigners holding a worthless shell.

If you regard multilateral organizations such as the United Nations, the European Union, and NATO as ineffectual or sinister plots by Germany and America to conceal their interests, then Russia's defiance of international rules and norms is highly appealing. The sooner we go back to a nineteenth-century concept of bilateral relations between the great powers, when Great Britain ruled the roost and France and Germany had colonies and satellites around the world, the better. Poland, the Baltic States, the Balkans—all can go back into the Russian sphere of influence where they belong. Better the stable and predictable world of great power politics than the current combination of phony moralizing, bureaucracy, and illegal military intervention.

That approach has the virtue of consistency. But it is not what Russia stands for. If you dislike the West's behavior in Kosovo or Iraq, it is hard to see anything in Russia's action in Georgia to applaud. Medvedev wants a new European security organization, specifically based on international law. The idea is to tie the West in legal knots. But that is a long way from the world of the Congress of Vienna, the paradigm of great power politics, in which the victors of the Napoleonic Wars redrew the map of Europe at their convenience, ignoring the wishes of smaller nations. Moreover, supporters of old-style power politics should be careful of what they wish for. In a world where only size matters, the venerable countries of "old Europe" are vulnerable, too. For all their faults, multilateral organizations, international law, and collective security have served the world well. Those who yearn for their downfall may wish to polish up their knowledge of Chinese.

But perhaps the biggest flaw in all the pro-Putin arguments is the implied idea that the ex-KGB regime has been good for Russia. This could not be further from the truth. If the people running Russia resemble their nineteenth-century predecessors at all, it is the corrupt, paranoid, and incompetent ones, rather than the visionary reformers such as the murdered prime minister Piotr Stolypin, the man whose efforts nearly saved the Tsarist empire by creating a prosperous peasantry to defuse revolutionary sentiments. The Putin regime has squandered tens of billions of dollars while failing to modernize Russia's creaky infrastructure and dire public services. Corruption, even by Medvedev's own admission, is colossal, the fusion between state and business power almost total. The closest Western counterpart would be Italy's Silvio Berlusconi. Is that really a model which old-fashioned patriots in countries like Britain wish to emulate?

The dismal record of Putinism, missing a once-in-a-generation chance to modernize Russia's infrastructure and public administration, was highlighted in a comprehensive attack from two former insiders, Boris Nemtsov and Vladimir Milov. Nemtsov is a former deputy prime minister; Milov, quoted extensively elsewhere in the book, is a former deputy energy minister. Their pamphlet is almost impossible to obtain in Russia in its print form, though it is easily available on the internet in Russian and English.[8] Its approach is echoed by another pamphlet produced by Igor Yurgens, a businessman closely linked to Medvedev. "Russia's Future under Medvedev"[9] also highlights, albeit tacitly, the economic and political limits of the authoritarian model.

The latter pamphlet notes, rightly, that eight years of economic growth have defused some of Russia's most urgent problems. In 1999, non-payment of salaries, pensions, and benefits was the public's most pressing concern, mentioned by 55 percent of those polled. By 2007 that had dropped to 17 percent (still strikingly high, some might feel). But other issues have become more pressing. Inflation for example, rocketed to 15 percent in 2008, with food prices up by 25 percent. That seems to be reversing the sharp declines in poverty measured during the Putin era. Top priority, at least in 2007, was fighting corruption, mentioned by 45 percent of those polled.

Medvedev, on the face of it, agrees. He repeatedly mentions corruption as a big problem, while demanding less state influence in the economy. In March he lambasted the way in which predatory state officials extort money from small businesses.[10] He has set up a new anti-corruption office and has denounced the practice, endemic under Putin, in which lucrative jobs in the public administration are auctioned off to the highest bidder, based on their potential for bribe-taking and rake-offs.

But it is hard to see that such efforts can be credible when the most powerful people in Russia benefit so conspicuously from the old arrangements. Nor can such efforts be effective if the media is not free to ask embarrassing questions. The lesson of the past ten years in ex-communist countries is that unless the people at the top set an example, anti-corruption efforts simply turn into score-settling squabbles among the rich and powerful, rather than changing the system in which they operate.

Russia has continued to use its energy weapon, with increasing adeptness. The crucial imbalance is that the Kremlin does not need to worry about small East European countries as gas or oil customers. But those countries do need to worry about Russia as a supplier. The sharpest example in this was the temporary cutback in oil supplies to the Czech Republic in July 2008, after that country signed a deal with the United States regarding the basing of a missile-defense radar. As with the oil blockade of Lithuania, Russia blamed unspecified technical problems. The Czechs chose not to complain too loudly; luckily their country, almost alone in the ex-communist world, is linked to the Western pipeline system and can therefore import supplies from elsewhere.

It is on this front, of energy blackmail, that Russia has been most active. The attack on Georgia was probably a mistake from the Kremlin's point of view, stirring even the most comatose Western politicians into a dim awareness of what is afoot in the east. Far more effective is to push ahead with the boring but vital business of energy. Russia has continued to try to stitch up an international alliance of gas producers: not exactly a cartel on the OPEC model, but something that would limit competition between producers and, in particular, frustrate Western attempts to diversify supply. In January 2008, Russia (under the label of Gazprom) made an offer to buy Nigeria's entire natural gas production; in March it signed a deal with Bolivia, in April one with Vietnam. In July it offered Libya a deal to buy all that country's additional gas production and finalized an agreement with Hugo Chávez of Venezuela, who was visiting Moscow for another meeting marked by acclamations of friendship on both sides.

Russia's pincer movement on Europe, with the planned Nord Stream and South Stream pipelines through the Baltic Sea and Black Sea respectively, has highlighted the EU's own weakness and disarray. South Stream, a rival to the EU's own Nabucco pipeline, now has the support of Bulgaria, Austria, and Hungary, all of which were supposedly backing Nabucco. America has made some limited progress in trying to persuade Turkmenistan to sell its gas westward rather than to Russia, but with no practical result. Now that Russia has its thumb close to the crucial oil and gas pipelines across Georgia, Europe faces a bleak choice between accepting dependence on Russia, or making a huge, costly, and unpopular switch away from fossil fuels.

A Russian veto at the UN Security Council, exercised jointly with China, opposing sanctions against the regime of Robert Mugabe in Zimbabwe showed the continuing hostility of the Kremlin to Western concerns about political freedom and the rule of law. Sabre-rattling reached a new pitch with a proposal, leaked to the Russian newspaper *Izvestiya,* to base nuclear bombers in Cuba or

Venezuela. That makes no sense in military terms: the nuclear-armed missiles carried by Russia's strategic bomber fleet can be fired from thousands of miles away from America's shores. But as with other moves, it is indicative of an ingrained desire to tease, provoke, and menace the West that augurs badly for the future.

Yet the idea that Russia is a global threat is still a mirage. Plagued by equipment breakdowns and bad planning, the Russian military initially struggled to beat even the far smaller Georgian armed forces. It would have no chance against a serious adversary. Despite the billions of rubles being spent on rearmament, the results remain puny. Even getting spare parts for the most modern nuclear bombers remains a problem. The much-touted alliance with China remains vague, as does a real rapprochement with Islamic countries such as Iran.

By contrast, the idea that Russia is a political and economic threat to both its ex-communist neighbors in particular and the European Union in general has become a mainstream one. The "Power Audit of EU–Russian Relations" published by the European Council on Foreign Relations, a think tank in New York, argued presciently that:

> Russia has emerged as the most divisive issue in the European Union since Donald Rumsfeld split the European club into "new" and "old" member states. In the 1990s, EU members found it easy to agree on a common approach to Moscow. They coalesced around a strategy of democratizing and Westernizing a weak and indebted Russia. That strategy is now in tatters. Soaring oil and gas prices have made Russia more powerful, less cooperative and above all less interested in joining the West.
>
> Although the EU has failed to change Russia during the Putin era, Russia has had a big impact on the EU. On energy, it is picking off individual EU member states and signing long-term deals which undermine the core principles of the EU's common strategy [. . .]
>
> Russia's new challenge to the EU runs deeper than the threat of energy cut-offs or blockages in the UN. It is setting itself up as an ideological alternative to the EU, with a different approach to sovereignty, power and world order. Where the European project is founded on the rule of law, Moscow believes that laws are mere expressions of power and that when the balance of power changes, laws should be changed to reflect it. Russia today is trying [. . .] to establish a relationship of "asymmetric interdependence" with the EU. While EU leaders believe that peace and stability are built through interdependence, Russia's leaders are

working to create a situation where the EU needs Russia more than Russia needs the EU, particularly in the energy sector.[11]

The report categorized the EU countries according to their relations with Russia. They ranged from "Trojan Horses," willing to sabotage EU positions outright, through "Strategic Partners" whose commercial ties with Russia trumped any allegiance to common EU positions, "Frosty" and "Friendly" pragmatists who maintain practical relations with Russia but have varying willingness to speak out on human rights issues, and, lastly, "New Cold Warriors," who are prepared to use their EU veto in an overtly hostile relationship with Russia.[12]

The central question dividing these camps for the first half of 2008 was the arrival in the Kremlin of Dmitri Medvedev, who on the surface appeared to be the most liberal, tolerant, and modern leader in Russian history. His supporters noted that he has no background in the KGB; his tastes and hobbies, such as rock music and browsing the internet, are "Western" (whatever that means); he is a lawyer from Russia's most European city, St. Petersburg, and from a generation that spent its formative years in freedom, not fear. On the most optimistic reading of events, Putin was a selfless, clear-sighted patriot who had seen the limitations of his approach, and was prepared to back someone to build on his legacy of stability and prosperity, and add the missing extra ingredients of freedom and legality. That would complete Russia's transformation. (Cynics at once added that such a change would dismantle large chunks of what he had created.) The theory assumed that the people around Putin were similarly ready to let that happen and that Medvedev was indeed what he seemed to be.

But it was impossible to dismiss this theory of a liberalizing trend in Russia out of hand, so well-wishers such as Germany's chancellor Angela Merkel argued pressingly that it was necessary to give change a chance. In practice, that meant hanging back on the enlargement of NATO, and keeping talks going on a new EU treaty with Russia.

For a few months, the argument was inconclusive. Medvedev spoke publicly in favor of reform and legality; Putin—at least in domestic affairs—proved to be an inactive prime minister who has largely withdrawn from the day-to-day business of government. Some Kremlinological clues pointed in an encouraging direction, too. A limited reshuffle took place when Medvedev arrived in office, in which some of the most notorious ex-KGB industrialists were shifted sideways.[13] The fourteen-member inner cabinet convened by Putin, of the seven first deputy and deputy prime ministers, plus seven key ministers, has no representative of the FSB or any other intelligence organization. As the Russia-watcher Gordon Hahn points out, "even if more power now resides with Putin than Medvedev by virtue of his control of both the government and the ruling party, the Sechin clan failed to convert its former weight within the presidential administration in full to the White House [Russia's seat of government], while being deprived of all but one ranking post in the Kremlin."[14] Yet the new head of the FSB is Alexander Bortnikov, formerly Patrushev's deputy and a man rooted in the Putin era; no sign of a change of regime there. Konstantin Chuichenko, an old university friend of Medvedev's and a former KGB man, is the new head of the Kremlin's control department (Putin's old job). Chuichenko is a director of RosUkrEnergo, a company which epitomizes the politically well-connected but commercially questionable style of business that has flourished under Putin. And Vladislav Surkov, the author of the idea of "sovereign democracy" that Medvedev seemed to despise, is a deputy head of the presidential administration.

These shuffles could be interpreted as clever personnel politics by Medvedev, easing some of Putin's most sinister cronies away from the levers of power. Or it could be just that Putin himself decided that some of his former colleagues from the KGB were getting too uppity. It may no longer be the most accurate description to say that "Russia is run by ex-KGB men," but the ex-KGB legacy still clearly shapes Russian politics. If the "Chekists" are no longer in the most prominent positions of power, that is probably because they do not need to be. Russia now runs as they like it.

The real politics of the Putin succession are still as unclear as they were when *The New Cold War* was being written in July 2007, but there now seems little chance of Putin leaving the stage. When the two men appear together, he appears to dominate the sometimes hapless-seeming Medvedev. A top Westerner who visited Russia during the war in Georgia met with both men. Putin did the talking, he recalls. Medvedev sat quietly taking notes. Putin remains Russia's most popular and effective politician by far; Medvedev's own glory, such as it is, is a reflection of his predecessor's.

It may be that Putin wanted to leave power, but then found that he could not safely depart with his laurels. Once he is out of power, what is to stop someone raising dangerous questions about mass murder in the autumn of 1999 in the mysterious blowing up of apartment buildings, or the acquisition of billions of dollars by

firms such as Gunvor and RosUkrEnergo that in other circumstances (to put it mildly and non-libelously) might have flowed to
Russian taxpayers and shareholders? Just imagine the television
news in a post-Putin Russia carrying a small item that prosecutors
in Ryazan had decided to reopen their investigation of the "non-
bomb" there (covered in Chapter One); or that Swiss police, acting
on a tip-off from their Russian colleagues, had raided the offices of
Gunvor and questioned staff there about money-laundering. From
such minor sounding events, it would be a very short step indeed to
questions that lead to the heart of the Putin presidency.

If Putin wants to return to formal possession of the top job, it is
clear that nothing stands in his way. His ascension to the leadership
of the party he created, United Russia, in May 2008, hardly suggested a desire to leave the stage. If, however, he wants to move a bit
further behind the scenes—perhaps as chairman of Gazprom—that
will be perfectly feasible, too. An intriguing possibility remains that
the Russian-Belarussian Union, an empty shell for more than a
decade, may be the vehicle that provides him with the right kind of
sinecure: in March he took on the notional post of prime minister
of this as yet non-existent state. Yet as the war in Georgia showed, it
is Putin who runs Russia. Medvedev's job seems little more than
being the occasional soft cop to his prime minister's hard cop.

The crudest interpretation of events is that the Putin regime decided in 2007 that they risked overdoing things, and that a smoother
public face would help them achieve their objective better:
Medvedev was the perfect solution. He would vent some of the dis-
satisfaction with the shortcomings of the past eight years and talk
nicely about the future, while doing nothing. The West would wait
for its honeymoon with the new Russian leader to prove conclu-
sively disappointing; meanwhile, the chauvinist and greedy rulers of
Russia have more time to entrench their position. If so, that did not
survive the decision to occupy and, in effect, dismember a neighboring state. The West may be unable or unwilling to react as it
should, but few still argue that Medvedev is the harbinger of a new
era of reform, legality, and cooperation.

Yet Western policy remains paralyzed. Russia's most threatening
behavior—bullying neighbors, stitching up the energy market,
turning money into power in Western Europe—remains, in effect,
unchecked. The echoes ought to be deafening: with every new Russian leader since Gorbachev, the West ended up sacrificing principles
in the vain hope of helping supposed allies against supposed adversaries. In each case, the results have been negligible, the cost huge,

and the disillusion painful. Now we have done it again. If Medvedev did nothing else, he duped big European countries into derailing Georgia's chances of gaining a clear path to NATO membership at the Bucharest summit. European countries could see little reason to help a lame-duck American president and his dodgy protégé, and plenty of reason not to jinx their chances with the new leader of their most powerful neighbor.

During the time that the West has been asleep, many of the weapons that we could have used to defend ourselves have become blunt. Russia now no longer cares if it is excluded from clubs such as the Council of Europe or the G8, or if negotiations to join the World Trade Organization or Organization for Economic Cooperation and Development are frozen. Indeed, such "punishments" from the West will only reinforce the Chekist message to the Russian people: that their country is surrounded by malevolent hypocrites. That does not mean that the West should back away from these steps, but we should not expect them to have any great effect. The message from the Kremlin is a cold and confident one: you need us more than we need you. A few years ago, being frozen out of the developed world's capital markets would have been a real threat to the Russian elite. Now, if they find London, New York, and Frankfurt unwelcoming, they can turn to the thriving (and less pernickety) exchanges in Dubai, Mumbai, and Shanghai.

Far more than the assault on Georgia, it is Russia's divide and rule tactics that have proved most effective. They created turmoil at the NATO summit in Bucharest. They have crippled the European Union, which on paper is far stronger than Russia: three times bigger in population terms, and around ten times larger as an economy. For many of the vulnerable countries in Russia's shadow, the only hope now is a direct security relationship with America. That is what Poland and the Czech Republic have achieved, albeit at the cost of being explicitly added to Russia's list of nuclear targets.

Yet it is not too late to act. The real need now is for a two-speed NATO. Some countries—Italy and Greece, for example—no longer have the will to be in a military alliance that makes serious plans to defend its neighbors against Russian aggression. Other countries—America, Britain, Poland, the Baltics, Romania—still wish to defend themselves. So do countries such as Sweden and Finland, which are not members of NATO but deeply worried by their eastern neighbor. But the hard-headed, stout-hearted countries are hamstrung by those members of the alliance that regard confrontation with Russia as a disaster.

Misguided political considerations have prevented NATO, for example, from making proper contingency plans. Poland, for one, is allowed to discuss with NATO how to defend itself only against the preposterous notion of an attack from Belarus (a country one-quarter of its size)—but not one from Russia. Contingency planning that explicitly mentions Russia is seen as too provocative by big European members of NATO that place great weight on not offending the Kremlin. Still more lethally, NATO has no contingency plans on how to protect the Baltic states.

That must now change. It may be too late to save Ukraine—only the Ukrainian people themselves can do that. Paradoxically, a strong NATO response to Russian meddling in Crimea or elsewhere may make things worse, not better. Whereas Georgia's population strongly supports both EU and NATO membership, opinion in Ukraine is more divided. Though some Ukrainians are staunchly anti-Russian, the east of the country, as well as the Crimea peninsula, is heavily Russified. The population in these regions is skeptical of NATO membership, seeing it as likely to sever close family and business ties between Ukraine and Russia. Other Ukrainians simply want to postpone the question, seeing it as too internally divisive. As a result, the West needs to tread carefully. What may be seen by some Ukrainians as welcome gestures of support (such as joint military maneuvers) could strike others as menacing and provocative.

But the Baltic states are different. Estonians, Latvians, and Lithuanians have decided with heart and soul to throw in their lot with the West. We must not let them down. So far, the NATO military presence in the Baltic states has been a token squadron of fighter aircraft, plus a state-of-the-art radar and a new cyber defense center. That is not enough to show Russia that we mean business. NATO members need to send warships to protect the Baltic sea lanes. NATO soldiers must be a permanent presence on Baltic soil. It goes without saying that Estonia, Latvia, and Lithuania must increase their own defense spending, too.

Western countries can also be a lot tougher on others forms of security. Russian spying has reached unprecedented levels—and is probably more dangerous and destructive to Western interests than it was during the more cautious days of the old Cold War. A coordinated wholesale expulsion of Russian intelligence officers and their hangers-on would send a powerful message to the Kremlin that the days of dreamy optimism are over. Western countries also need to restore the tough vetting procedures for sensitive posts that were so unwisely dismantled during the 1990s.

The West can also use its soft power far more effectively. It is astonishing that Europe was for most of the past few years using its visa policy in a way that made holding a Russian passport more attractive than holding a Ukrainian or Georgian one. That must change. It will be sad for Russians if their visa applications become slower and more heavily scrutinized. But for that they can blame the politicians who have willfully and cynically turned their country into an international pariah, scorned and feared by those it does not dominate.

INTRODUCTION

It is chilling to see a friend's name on a death list.

It was October 7, 2006. I had been meaning to phone Yevgenia Albats, a gutsy Russian journalist colleague, since I had seen her name on an extremist Web site a few days earlier. A page (now defunct) on the site, www.russianwill.org[1], denounced as "enemies of the nation" some of the country's finest activists, lawyers, and journalists—all of them vehement critics of President Vladimir Putin's Kremlin.[2] It gave their home addresses and phone numbers, and their dates of birth—plus ominous question marks for the dates of death: in effect, a brazen incitement to murder.

But it was Yevgenia who called me first, to say that our mutual friend Anna Politkovskaya had just been gunned down in the entrance to her home. Politkovskaya was not just Russia's bravest reporter. She was the foremost critic of the Kremlin's savagery in crushing the rebels in breakaway Chechnya, scathingly depicting the authoritarian, cruel, and wasteful turn that her country had taken under Putin's leadership.[3] The murder took place as the president turned 54; many of her friends assumed it was a macabre birthday present. Regardless of the timing, Yevgenia was scared. She, like Politkovskaya, had been listed on extremist websites. Within hours of the shooting, the site's managers had added the date of death. Who would be next? But the official reaction was even more chilling than the murder.

Politkovskaya's murder should have been a national tragedy. But no senior Kremlin figure attended her funeral, and Putin took three days to comment on her death; though he condemned it, he dismissed her as a person of "marginal significance."[4]

Politkovskaya's death was a grisly reminder to those inside Russia of the threats faced by those who criticize the authorities, and highlighted the decline of press freedom there. But only weeks later came a wake-up call to the West,[5] delivered in the heart of London. On November 1 Aleksandr Litvinenko, a former officer of Russia's internal security force—the FSB (*Federalnaya Sluzhba Bezopasnosti,* or Federal Security Service)—who had fallen out with the authorities and fled to London, was poisoned with a rare radioactive isotope, polonium–210. After three weeks of agonizing suffering in a central London hospital, his last words directly blamed Putin for his murder.[6]

Certainly it was no ordinary assassination. Almost all the world's polonium is produced in Russia; there, as in every country, it is subject to strict legal controls in large quantities.[7] It also decays quickly. Ordinary criminals would have no chance of buying a lethal dose of polonium on the black market. British officials became convinced that the FSB itself had a hand in the murder. But Russia scoffed at requests for help, contemptuously blocked the British authorities' investigation, and then rejected the request to extradite the alleged killer, another former FSB man named Aleksander Lugovoi.[8] He had met London-based Russian officials both before and after the assassination, leaving a trail of polonium on his travels from Russia to Britain and back.[9] Mr. Lugovoi denies all wrongdoing, but whatever the rights and wrongs of his involvement, the affair amounted to nuclear terrorism in the heart of London, resulting in the murder of a British citizen and putting countless scores of others in danger.

༄

The two murders, and the Kremlin's reaction to them, are symptomatic of the subject of this book: the direct menace that Russia now poses, not only to its own citizens, but also to outsiders. Twenty years after Mikhail Gorbachev started dismantling communism, Russia is reverting to Soviet behavior at home and abroad, and in its contemptuous disregard for Western norms. Yet the outside world has been inattentive and complacent, partly due to greed and wishful thinking, and partly because of serious distractions elsewhere. Western public opinion and policymakers alike find it hard to focus on more than one or two problems at a time, which proved a costly mistake in the 1930s.[10] Ignoring the links between Stalin and Hitler; the West regarded the Soviet Union as a useful bulwark, and ultimately a key ally, against fascism.

The "war on terror" is leading to a similar mistake now. After the attacks on America on September 11, 2001, Putin hurried to offer cooperation, which the West gratefully accepted with little regard for the cost: A free ride for the Kremlin as it tightened the screw at home and bullied its neighbors abroad. Russia gained again in another way too: The war on terror weakened the Atlantic alliance. European countries were so preoccupied with their distaste for President George W. Bush that they all but ignored the direction that Putin was taking Russia. Even those that were prepared to stand by America's side, to join the "coalition of the willing" in Iraq and to allow "extraordinary rendition" of suspected terrorists, soon wished they had stood back. The bungled and blood-soaked aftermath of the invasion of Iraq, the legal black hole of Guantánamo Bay, the mistreatment of prisoners at Abu Ghraib and their systematic torture elsewhere, were not just unpopular among the public in the West and elsewhere. These abuses and blunders became the Kremlin's most potent propaganda weapons against America and its allies. During the 1990s, such a Russian stance would have been inconceivable: In the aftermath of victory in the Cold War, the West's moral stock was high, while the Soviet Union's anti-Westernism seemed a laughable historical relic. But as that period has passed, Russia's public rhetoric has become increasingly caustic. In 2007 Putin denounced America as a "pernicious" force in world politics.[11]

My shorthand term for the new era of uneasy confrontation between the West and the Kremlin is "the New Cold War." Despite all the bad news from Russia since Putin took power, this description is fiercely contested by those who find it exaggerated, senselessly provocative, or historically illiterate. Indeed, many who claim to be experts on Russia dismiss it as outright nonsense. In their own terms, they are right. For anyone who remembers the first decades of the old Cold War, and the years of stony détente that followed them, even the stormiest spats with the Putin Kremlin seem like minor squabbles. That, after all, was a time of global confrontation, when a surprise conventional attack in Europe by the Warsaw Pact could have reached the Rhine within three days, forcing the West to choose between conceding surrender and starting a nuclear war. Half the continent was under the ice cap of communism,[12] with even the most fleeting human contacts constrained by the climate of fear. Inside the Soviet Union, the Communist Party and the KGB (*Komitet Gosudarstvennoy Bezopasnosti*, or Committee for State Security) controlled almost every facet of daily life, from housing to the workplace, from holiday plans to schooling, from every published word to the most banal public organization or association. Practicing religious belief was risky, homosexuality illegal. Private enterprise was outlawed; every job depended on the state. Foreign travel was a rare and coveted privilege, not a right. For those outside the *nomenklatura*,[13] the communist state's charmed circle, finding out what was going on meant painstakingly parsing the leaden prose of misnamed propaganda sheets like *Pravda* [Truth] and *Izvestiya* [News].

Now Russia is no longer a closed society. Those determined to tangle with the authorities risk trouble, but people can largely say what they like and read what they like.[14] If they don't like life inside Russia, they can (almost always) easily go abroad. Such safety valves would have seemed inconceivable freedoms for most of the twentieth century. Paradoxically, now they exist, they are not greatly needed. Unlike the Soviet Union, Russia is not riven by economic discontent and failure. On the contrary, investment is pouring in and living standards are rising. Most Russians have never had it so good, and Putin's approval rating is consistently over 80 percent. Russians are delighted both with his hand-picked successor, Dmitri Medvedev, and Mr. Putin's promise of a continuing behind-the-scenes role.

Nor is Russia a global adversary. Indeed, it often looks like a partner. Russia is a member of the G8 club of big, rich, Western countries and of the Council of Europe, a talking-shop that also guards the continent's human rights conventions. It is part of the quartet that tries to broker peace in the Middle East; it says it is an ally in trying to check Iran's nuclear ambitions; it tries to bring sense to the megalomaniac leadership in North Korea. It takes part in peacekeeping in ex-Yugoslavia. Russia has allowed nearly a dozen of its former satellites to join not only the European Union (EU) but also the North Atlantic Treaty Organization (NATO). Kremlin complaints about NATO's eastward enlargement strike many as understandable geopolitics, not a neo-imperialist revanche. How would America like it if history had gone differently, if the Soviet Union had won the Cold War and persuaded the states of New England to declare independence and join the Warsaw Pact? That is, some argue,[15] pretty much what happened to Russia, which was reduced from superpower to a state of shrunken weakness in the space of less than two years.

Even under the newly assertive regime in the Kremlin, Russia has not become a military menace to the West. It cannot manage even to subdue fully the remaining separatist fighters in Chechnya, a province of barely 600,000 people in a place the size of Connecticut. In its decrepit, drunken, demoralized military, bullying (hazing) is endemic. On average 12 Russian soldiers commit suicide every month. Russia's newest warplanes are formidably maneuverable, its submarines super-silent, its torpedoes terrifyingly fast; but it has not—yet—been able to produce these brilliantly designed weapons in any quantities. Those in service are under-deployed. Only the strategic nuclear arsenal gives Russia the right to call itself a military superpower. But two-thirds of its missiles are obsolete. The Kremlin's ability to launch a disabling nuclear first strike on NATO has disappeared into the history books. So has its capacity to project military power around the globe, or even to launch a crippling conventional attack on Europe. In so far as a nuclear threat still exists, it is that paranoia and incompetence might lead to an accidental conflagration.

The old ideological conflict is over too. Radio Moscow no longer pumps out lectures on Marxism-Leninism; far from wanting to overthrow capitalism, Russia embraces it. The Kremlin's own ragbag philosophy of "Sovereign Democracy" (see Chapter Five) has replaced the jargon and dogma of communist ideology. The main aim is not world revolution, but self-justification: to explain why the Kremlin's overweening political and economic power is part of the natural order, not an aberration from the European mainstream. That may have more to do with psychology, in the form of an ingrained inferiority complex about the West, than with political philosophy. At any rate, the new ideology's main ingredients are unexceptional: an edgy sense of national destiny, a preference for stability over freedom, and a strong dislike of Western hypocrisy and shallowness. It is the combination and intensity that are unusual; similar views are held in many countries outside Russia.

All that is true and only a fantasist would claim that nothing has changed since 1991. The old Cold War is indeed over: I remember it when it was alive; I was there at its funeral. I grew up in an Oxford academic household deeply committed to fostering freedom of thought behind the Iron Curtain. My father smuggled Plato's *Republic* and the Greek *New Testament* into communist-ruled Czechoslovakia for fellow-philosophers who had been banished to jobs as stokers and window-cleaners. In the early 1980s I campaigned for Poland's Solidarity trade union. I studied German in divided Berlin, Polish in communist Poland. I covered the death throes of the so-called GDR (the "German Democratic Republic" was, in truth, simply the Soviet-occupied zone of Germany) for the BBC. In 1989 I was the only Western newspaperman living in communist Czechoslovakia, and watched as the Velvet Revolution swept away that dreary grey regime. As the Baltic States struggled to regain their independence, I was deported from the Soviet Union by the KGB, having entered Lithuania "illegally" with the first visa issued by the reborn but unrecognized authorities in Vilnius.[16] As Gorbachev's *perestroika* [restructuring] and *glasnost* [openness] flared and faded in the Soviet Union, I saw that wretched country crash into pieces. The week of the evil empire's collapse was one of the happiest of my life. It is closely followed by the day when the last remains of the Red Army occupation forces finally left the Baltic States that they had crushed five decades previously.

So the old Cold War will not return, and analogies with it are outdated. But so too are the rosy sentiments that succeeded it. The most catastrophic mistake the outside world has made since 1991 is to assume that Russia is steadily becoming a "normal" country. From this Panglossian point of view, any problems that arise are mere bumps in the road that will be left behind in the inexorable progress toward Western-style freedom and legality. That idea always seemed optimistic, but now it looks downright fanciful; those who still advocate it are deluding themselves and those who listen to them.

The gloomy signs started under President Boris Yeltsin, Russia's first democratically elected leader and in some ways one of greater stature than Gorbachev, who had dismantled Soviet terror at home and abroad. For a few brief months after the failed coup of 1991, the power of the KGB indeed seemed to be broken, and Russia showed glimmerings of wanting integration into the civilized world without ifs, ands, or buts. Though the Communist Party never returned to power, the damage it had inflicted proved too deep, the forces of darkness in Russia too strong, and the task facing Yeltsin and his allies too great. For all their brains, charm, and bravery, the "reformers" proved incompetent, weak, and ultimately venal; as they failed, Russia fell into the hands of those driven by selfishness for money and power, not idealistic desires to make their country prosperous and free. These swashbuckling tycoons called themselves "oligarchs."[17] Financial and political corruption became endemic. The ex-KGB came creeping back from the shadows, bringing their own values and habits: authoritarianism and xenophobia. Further, the means Yeltsin and his advisers used to stay in power were lethal to Russia's attempts to establish a system based on legality and freedom. In 1993 he used artillery to dislodge Soviet-era hardliners holed up in the Russian parliament. That was followed by a rigged referendum on a new constitution,[18] matched in 1996 by a presidential election in which a gravely ill Yeltsin trounced his Communist challenger thanks only to flagrant manipulation of both the media and the election count. The greed and influence-peddling of the clique around Yeltsin discredited pro-Western policies, the multi-party system, and the market economy.

Given what came next, the Yeltsin years don't look so bad in comparison. Though the state sorely lacked credibility, at least it was not feared. The 1990s had distributed wealth and power with chaotic unfairness, but nobody had full control of either. Russia's rulers were imperfect, but at least they were under constant, even debilitating, challenge. Every point of view was represented on television: Even when his advisers urged him to crack down on the media, Yeltsin demurred. Only a return to totalitarian rule was out of bounds. In the regions and republics of Russia, local rulers did as they wished, for better or for worse. But after the calamitous financial crash of August 1998, when Russia defaulted on a large chunk of its debts and devalued the ruble, the sense of failure surrounding the Yeltsin clique and its tycoon-friendly rule was absolute. The banking system collapsed overnight, wiping out the savings of the new middle class. Russia was ridiculed as the sick man of Europe, seemingly destined to survive on transfusions of Western credits and expertise. Words such as *Afrikanisatsiya* [Africanization] became fashionable.[19] As the lower house of parliament, the Duma, in those days still a rumbustious and powerful body, tightened its grip, the members of the presidential "family" started looking for an exit.

Their preferred candidate was a little-known bureaucrat: quiet, efficient, and above all loyal. He seemed the ideal guarantee for their continued wealth and safety. Vladimir Putin indeed honored that part of the bargain. But when Yeltsin named him unexpectedly as prime minister in the summer of 1999, few imagined that he would soon be dispatching Russia's political freedoms to the cemetery. The means were simple: He matched the public's disgust at the chaos and greed of the Yeltsin years with fear of the immediate present. Within weeks, mysterious bombings of apartment blocks in Moscow and elsewhere stoked a panicky public appetite for more security and less freedom. War restarted in Chechnya. His ratings rocketed, turning Putin from backstage zero to national hero in four months. At the time, the bombings seemed to most people to be genuine terrorist outrages, the clear consequence of Russia's past weakness in dealing with separatists and militants. In retrospect, they look like a cynical plot to panic the public into supporting the country's new rulers: the ex-KGB.

When Yeltsin stepped down on New Year's Eve 1999, Putin automatically switched jobs to become acting president. Russians liked his clipped, businesslike manner, his sobriety and physical fitness, his aptitude for hard work, and the glamorous aura surrounding a veteran of the Soviet Union's elite foreign intelligence service. But "Who is Mr. Putin?" was a pressing and unanswered question. As Chapter Two shows, Russians and outsiders alike were soon to get to know him a lot better, as a political squeeze began within months on the presumptuous tycoons, lawless regional barons, and out-of-control bureaucrats who had flourished during the later Yeltsin era. Some sort of clean-up was certainly overdue, but Putin also betrayed the positive legacy of the Yeltsin years; a Russia committed to friendship with the West, to pluralism in politics and the media, and to keeping the old KGB corralled, away from the heights of power. Though the swaggering cronies of the Yeltsin era left office unmourned, they gave way to a new ruling class: quiet, grey KGB veterans, mostly from St. Petersburg. An unwieldy new word appeared in the political lexicon: *efesbefikatsiya* [FSB-fication]. The FSB, the successor to the KGB's domestic wing, was back in business.[20] Under Yeltsin it had been just one government agency among many, using its powers to bug and blackmail, chiefly for the self-enrichment of its employees. Now that its former chief, Vladimir Putin, was in the Kremlin, the FSB was, in effect, running the country.

The trend was unpromising. Yet Putin has been highly popular in Russia, and, at least initially, abroad. From the start, Russians have been pleased that after the shocking muddle and moral emptiness of the Yeltsin years, someone was finally bringing order to their country. As with Benito Mussolini's Fascist rule in Italy, people were pleased about the superficial appearance of stability, and did not look too closely at the arbitrary exercise of power that lay behind it. Yet the Kremlin, and the mighty state bureaucracy below it, uses the law in its own interests but is not bound by it. As I show in this book, Russia has first tacitly and then explicitly abandoned the aim of becoming "normal"—an advanced industrialized country marked by political liberty and the rule of law, whose people could stand on equal terms with their counterparts in Western Europe and America. In the view of Russia's rulers now, Western values were tried during the Yeltsin era and found wanting. At best they were simply unsuited to local conditions. At worst they were part of a dastardly plot to weaken Russia and promote Western hegemony.

Now, for better or for worse, Russia is seeking its own way, based on a controlled political system, a strong presidency, and a tough stance toward the outside world. The result is a menace both to Russia, which now stands little chance of avoiding long-term decline, and to the West, which is struggling to cope with the Kremlin's bombast, bullying, and bribery.

In the 1990s, any such attempt to find a home-grown future would have been doomed by Russia's economic weakness: It was dependent on billions of dollars in outside loans and grants to pay for imports and to plug the government's deficit. When sky-high interest rates tempted a flood of hot money into the government-bond market in the late 1990s, it merely highlighted the economy's humiliating vulnerability to any outside loss of confidence. As Chapter Four shows, that red ink has now turned black. Russia's economy is booming. The first and biggest reason is high prices for oil, gas, and other raw materials—the best possible environment for a country rich in natural resources. That has sent tax revenues and exports soaring. The second reason is political stability. Investors, foreign and local, may find Russia's rules for business tough. But unlike those in the Yeltsin era, they stay fairly constant. In most of the economy, conditions do not change overnight. The result of this entire economic bonanza is that the Kremlin can afford to do what it likes. It no longer fears its foreign creditors: It has paid them off. It no longer fears the capital markets: Investors have been queuing up to buy shares, lend money, and start businesses. Greed has overtaken fear. Optimists hoped that financial security would give Putin the confidence to liberalize. They could hardly have been more wrong. Not only have the limited economic reforms of his early years have come to a halt; the Kremlin has adopted a tougher stance both at home and abroad. Russia wastes much of its windfall because of the lack of reform, while using money freely on stifling criticism abroad.

The biggest victims have been the freedoms of speech and association. The independent media has shriveled, with television in particular coming almost completely under the authorities' control. A forced change of ownership is the main tactic; a new law on extremism intimidates the rest. Critics of the Kremlin are not just muffled in the media but shackled at the polls. New electoral rules mean that independent candidates and small parties are in effect completely excluded from parliamentary elections. But the true test of political freedom is not elections, but what happens in between them. Here the verdict is depressing. Almost every possible channel for complaint and dissent is blocked. Enough individual activists have experienced judicial and bureaucratic harassment, as well as physical threats, to deter all but the bravest from speaking out or getting involved. My friends are increasingly unwilling even to talk on the phone. Foreigners with a record of criticizing the Kremlin have been finding it hard to get visas. Even small opposition demonstrations have to surmount exhausting bureaucratic obstacles. Rallies that go ahead anyway are violently dispersed by the police and security forces. Putin and others publicly denounce not-for-profit organizations as covers for foreign espionage. The judiciary's brief flirtation with independence has ended. The message to outside critics is simple: Putin is popular. Russia is doing well. Mind your own business.

Repression at home is matched by aggression abroad. Russia has suspended arms control agreements and started sending its warplanes to probe the airspace of NATO countries: both nearby ones such as Estonia, and even those farther away such as Britain. It has announced ambitious rearmament plans, including a return to a naval presence in the Mediterranean. It has restored the Soviet-era practice of keeping a fleet of strategic bombers (which can launch nuclear missiles) permanently airborne. It has threatened to target its nuclear missiles at European countries—a practice dropped in the Gorbachev years. Such military maneuvering may recall the confrontation of the old Cold War. But the real threat is a different one. When it comes to military might, Russia is still too poor and too weak to do more than posture: The nuclear arsenal and conventional forces are more a background psychological factor than a physical one. Instead of menacing the other side with high explosives, hardened steel, and enriched uranium, the New Cold War is fought with cash, natural resources, diplomacy, and propaganda.

Cash is the key. For those prepared to take the risks, pay the bribes, and ignore the dirt, Russia is a tempting business environment. At least at first, Westerners there feel that they are in a bigger, brasher, brighter version of their own countries. The profits are colossal and the people seem to be glamorous go-getters with a whiff of intoxicating Slavic charm. It is easy to ignore the blithe contempt with which the new Russian friends treat external constraints. And it is hard for foreigners to make a fuss about human rights questions when such issues do not seem to bother the locals. Russian patriotism may be prickly and irrational, but the wise outsider does not let such considerations get in the way of profit. That is shortsighted, for Russia is no ordinary trading partner. The New

Cold War is in part a struggle for market share. Russia is building up its clout as an energy supplier, while diversifying its customer base. In the coming years, Europe, and maybe even North America, will experience growing dependence on scanty and expensive Russian gas, with little chance of alternative supplies. Russia wields the energy weapon to bully its enemies and bribe its allies, and uses its financial clout to buy friends and influence. The big strategic worry used to be the Soviet navy's capacity to blockade Europe's sea lanes. Now it is the Russian gas company Gazprom's ability to blockade its gas pipelines. Once it was the Kremlin's tanks thundering into Afghanistan that signaled the West's weakness; now it is Kremlin banks thundering through the city of London.

Behind the scenes Russia's behavior is even more confrontational. The Kremlin's representatives throw habitual tantrums in international organizations such as the European Bank for Reconstruction and Development, the Organisation for Security and Co-operation in Europe, and the United Nations Development Programme. They obstruct programs in countries they don't like, and demand hefty pay-offs and concessions in return for their consent. Russian spying exceeds even the heights of the old Cold War.

The battle lines of the New Cold War are increasingly clear: America, Britain, and some European countries, mostly ex-communist ones, are trying to stand up against the Kremlin. In the middle are countries such as Germany that want close business ties with Russia but hope, probably in vain, to keep their political distance. The Kremlin's close friends are a rogue's gallery: Syria, Venezuela, and Iran, plus a handful of ill-governed ex-Soviet republics such as Belarus and Tajikistan. Increasingly, it shares positions with China, with which it is linked in a security organization of growing importance called the Shanghai Cooperation Organisation. Albeit at a price, this, if it develops further, will provide Russia with a global weight not seen since the 1950s.

Even seasoned Russia-watchers who flinch at the geographical and historical connotations of the New Cold War still agree that something pretty bad is going on: A favored phrase is a "sharp strategic conflict." Like the old Cold War, it is being fought chiefly in Europe, though this time the battleground has shifted east, to the once-captive nations that lie between Russia and the rich half of the continent. Russia makes no secret of its desire for a *droit de regard* in its former empire: It wants to know everything that happens and to have the power to stop what it does not like. That means a tussle in central Europe, the Balkans and the Caucasus, and particularly in the Baltic states of Estonia, Latvia, and Lithuania. They are the Soviet satellites whose loss the Kremlin resents most sharply. Their thriving economies and lively open societies are a constant and glaring contrast to the authoritarian crony capitalism across the border. Russia is putting the Baltic States under an energy squeeze, cutting off oil supplies to Latvia and Lithuania.[21] It has incited riots in Tallinn, the Estonian capital.[22] It has abandoned Yeltsin's policy of historical reconciliation. The Kremlin's line now is that the occupation of the Baltic states in 1940—part of the Hitler–Stalin pact—was legal. That should come as no surprise: Putin, who says the collapse of the Soviet Union was the "greatest geo-political catastrophe" of the twentieth century, believes the history books written in the Yeltsin years paint the past in too bleak a light. Although the Balts are small in population terms,[23] they are members—and loyal and active ones at that—of NATO and the EU. The West has, so far, defended them loyally in return. When Estonia came under attack in May 2007, George W. Bush promptly invited its president, Toomas Hendrik Ilves, for a high-profile visit to the White House. Rather like West Berlin in the days of the old Cold War, the Baltic States are militarily indefensible but symbolically vital: if they succumb to Russian pressure, who will be next? That has not deterred the Kremlin, which is determined both to divide them and to isolate them. As it strikes bilateral deals with other European countries one by one, it hints hard that the arrogant, troublesome Balts are standing in the way of mutually beneficial (and still more lucrative) ties.

The less resistance Russia meets, the more assertive it becomes. Language and behavior, such as justifying the Hitler-Stalin pact, that would have once seemed unimaginable crop up, first as something that can be dismissed as for internal consumption only. Then, it is a regrettable exception. Shortly after that, the world gets used to it. The limits of the tolerable are constantly changing—and in one direction only. The uncomfortable but unavoidable question is where this ends. If Russia gets what it wants in the Caucasus or the Baltics, the Balkans and Central Europe will be next. And what then? The Arctic? Western Europe? Slice by slice, the Kremlin is adding to its sphere of influence.

Russian tactics can also be more subtle. The Kremlin wants to build up its influence not only *on* the West, but also *in* the West. The growing business lobby tied to Russia represents a powerful fifth column of a kind unseen during the last Cold War. Once it was communist trade unions that undermined the West at the Kremlin's behest. Now it is pro-Kremlin bankers and politicians who betray their countries for 30 silver rubles. Western investment in Russia has already created a lobby for good relations with the Kremlin in the city of London, in German big business, and in the energy industry across Europe. That is reinforced by the billions of dollars of Russian investment pouring into Western Europe and North America. When Russian tycoons—who these days run their businesses at the Kremlin's bidding—own big stakes in the West's biggest companies, they are no longer outsiders, but insiders. Russia is becoming a giant, nuclear-armed version of Saudi Arabia, a country so rich and powerful that even what looks like semi-official support for terrorism has not brought Western disfavor.

The ideological clash behind this has changed, but it has not disappeared. Instead of an explicit argument between Marxist-Leninists and the supporters of welfare capitalism, both sides seem to endorse the same capitalist model. But it would be a mistake to think that the Kremlin is just aping the west. That was the mistake Russia made in the 1990s, when it tried to adopt standard templates for the market economy and political freedom wholesale, with what now seem, at least from a Russian viewpoint, like disastrous results. Far from copying the rules of the Western game, it has rewritten them. The first and simplest rule is: The Kremlin is always right. At home, any challenge, any resistance, will be crushed by brute force of money and the levers of state power. No court, no law, no appeal to good manners or ethical principles will help: Just as a back-woodsman knows not to get between a bear and his lunch, anyone dealing with Russia knows not to get between the Kremlin and its profits. Russian oligarchs have learned that bitter lesson. So have even the mightiest western investors, including oil giants such as BP and Shell.

The difference between Russian and Western models of capitalism can be deceptive, for respect for the law is so central to the Western approach to life that many of those who benefit from the security and predictability that it brings hardly think about it. But in the background, the idea that contracts are to be respected; that judges cannot be bribed; that court rulings must be upheld are all part of daily life. That is not the way it looks in Russia. The law is a tool for the powerful against the weak. Appeals to legal norms are dismissed as just disguised political pressure. The separation of powers, ethics codes, human rights treaties, and multilateral obligations are nothing more than convenient fictions, easily brushed aside when real considerations are at stake. If the West cites them in argument, it sounds hypocritical and insincere to Russian ears.

Don't Western countries break the law in pursuit of their national interests? Don't their politicians take bribes? Don't their officials help their business chums?

Indeed they do, deplorably. But such behavior is not the founding principle of the Western system but a blemish upon it. Multilateralism is frayed by self-interest and exceptionalism, but it is still the governing principle of the world legal order. The EU in particular (to the mystification of many Russians) truly does work as a sophisticated multilateral institution in which common rules and interests can trump national ones. So, to a more limited extent, does the World Trade Organization in its rule-based approach to international commerce and investment. (Russia has yet to join this body.) Similarly, when corruption is exposed—in most Western countries at least—it is condemned and punished. In Russia, by contrast, it is little exaggeration to say that bribery and corruption are not part of the system; they are the system. The fortunes of senior politicians are measured in billions of dollars. Kremlin officials run state-owned companies as sidelines. Nobody complains or asks about conflicts of interest. The most telling indicator of corruption is not Russia's low standing in the corruption rankings published by outfits such as Transparency International (see Chapter Three), but the lack of a public fuss about official crookedness. No senior official ends up in court unless he has first fallen foul of his political masters. The ideological conflict of the New Cold War is between lawless Russian nationalism and law-governed Western multilateralism.

The strangest feature of all this is the West's unwillingness to admit what is happening. This is only partly because of a pro-Russian business lobby that has beguiled the foreign-policy establishment in countries such as Germany. It is also because of an unwillingness to confront the uncomfortable consequences of Russia's new direction. Officials and politicians ask haplessly: "If Russia is a political menace again, what on earth are we supposed to do about it?" The old Cold War imposed a demanding regime of mental and moral toughness on the countries of Western Europe, for they knew that if they did not hang together they would hang separately. Now the Kremlin's central tactic of "divide and rule" has an almost free run. Western security rests on multilateral agreements; the idea that pooled sovereignty, shared security, and joint decision-making are the best way to defend free societies. But memories of that vital principle have faded and loyalty to it has frayed. Greece and Cyprus dependably lobby on Russia's behalf. Silvio Berlusconi, the Italian prime minister, once went so far as to describe himself as Russia's "advocate" in the EU.

During the old Cold War, no NATO member would have considered doing private deals with the Kremlin: Any overtures from the Soviet Union encountered hard-headed scrutiny, while few in Western officialdom made a career out of being nice to the Soviet block. Anyone in the business world who made a profit out of dealings with communist countries was an instant target of suspicion and risked ostracism. In the New Cold War, such deals are commonplace: Austria (which is not in NATO but is in the EU) plus Bulgaria, Cyprus, France, Greece, Germany, Hungary, Italy, Latvia, the Netherlands, Portugal, Turkey, and Slovakia, to name but a few, all have succumbed in recent years, in differing degrees, to the temptation to be "special friends" of the Kremlin. Sometimes this involves flattery: the Kremlin sweet-talks foreign politicians, complimenting them on their understanding of Russia, and contrasting this with the ill-informed and biased stance taken by others. Sometimes the private commercial interests of senior politicians and officials play a role. Typically, the first stage is characterized by an acceptance, and then a dependence, on gas supplies delivered along Russian-controlled pipelines. Next the country may allow Russian energy giants to buy assets such as refineries and distribution companies. That soon creates a powerful local lobby for good relations with Russia, and unwillingness to defend those being bullied or browbeaten elsewhere. Germany, for example, has been notably unwilling to stick up for Georgia or the Baltic states. The effect of such policies on their allies elsewhere—and in the long term on their own security—has barely been considered.

Fear of the Soviet Union cemented not only mutual solidarity in Western Europe, but also the Atlantic alliance with the United States. However much some Western Europeans distrusted Richard Nixon, despised Jimmy Carter, or flinched at Ronald Reagan's cowboy rhetoric, the bottom line was clear: It was the American nuclear guarantee that kept Europeans of all kinds safe and free. Keeping those psychological muscles toned once the old Cold War ended has proved too strenuous for many. Complacency is much more comfortable than vigilance. Trust is nicer than suspicion. And remembering the grim grey days of the past is hard. Memories of Russia now are shaped by the optimism that surrounded the end of the Cold War, not the realism of the previous four decades.

Those old reflexes would be useful now. Putin is heir (see Chapter One) to a scary and barely remembered figure from the Soviet past: Yuri Andropov, a former KGB chief who took power briefly when the geriatric Leonid Brezhnev finally died in 1982. Like Andropov, Putin believes that ruthless discipline is the key to economic recovery. Like Andropov, he places great weight on the use of the secret police, both to collect information and to intimidate opponents and backsliders. Like Andropov, he believes that the West is both weak and hypocritical and can be easily faced down with a mixture of threats and selective arm-twisting. The Andropov era was doomed to failure; it was trying to revive a country was crippled by the Communist Party's desire for total control, which calcified every part of life and restricted innovation. When Andropov took over, the Soviet Union was already groaning under the cost of maintaining its status as a military superpower, made all the harder by the preposterous economic system bequeathed by Lenin and Stalin. Central planning consumed colossal amounts of raw materials and provided a pitifully low standard of living for the population. A country in which condoms were so crude that they were called *galoshy* [galoshes], in which contraceptive pills, blue jeans, and sanitary towels were coveted luxury items, in which foreign travel was an all but unimaginable privilege, was a beacon only to the most masochistic socialist. The Soviet way of life was a combination of economic backwardness with repression at home and abroad. That was a hard sell.

Now the Kremlin has stopped wasting time, money, and people in trying to make a flawed economic system work and in pursuing an unworkably utopian political idea. Instead it has adopted the trappings of a Western system—laws, elections, and private property to conceal a lawless, brutal, and greedy reality. That is not only a problem for Russians. Though the country is still too weak militarily and economically, and too dependent on the outside world, to use brute force against the West, it has plenty of other tactics that are just as effective. Chiefly, it can menace and subvert the weaker and smaller countries in the ex-Soviet neighborhood. For them, Russia is like an aggressive man on crutches—no threat to the able-bodied, but still a menacing bully for someone in a wheelchair. It uses the Soviet Union's most powerful legacy, the monopoly hold on gas and oil pipelines running from east to west, to blackmail and bribe its former satellite countries. In response, the West not only fails to support its allies, but is also succumbing to pressure itself. The Kremlin uses its limited economic and diplomatic weight to paralyze its opponents' decision making, playing "divide and rule" with extraordinary success. Against irresolute opponents, clever maneuvering and posturing has proved remarkably successful. As in Soviet days, the Kremlin uses *dezinformatsiya* [disinformation] to camouflage its policies and discredit its opponents. Yet above all, money remains the West's greatest weakness. Having cast off the dead weight of ideology, the ex-KGB men in the Kremlin are presiding over a Russian Klondike, a source of irresistible temptation for greedy outsiders. When all else fails, Russia uses the methods of terrorists and gangsters, epitomized by the murder of foreign citizens and in the cyber-attack unleashed on Estonia in May 2007.

In short, the West is losing the New Cold War, while having barely noticed that it has started. Putin and his Kremlin allies have seized power in Russia, cast a dark shadow over the eastern half of the continent, and established formidable bridgeheads in the main Western countries. And the willingness to resist looks alarmingly feeble. It is that which has prompted me, after more than 20 years of covering the region, to write this book.

I start by showing how Putin and his ex-KGB colleagues captured a country exhausted by economic upheaval, disgusted by corruption, and yearning for strong and competent leadership. What it got was a cynical putsch, which used what looked like mass murder to create the public panic necessary to seize power. Chapter Two shows how, after a hesitant start, Putin consolidated his control of Russia. It explains how he built a political base among the winners and losers of the past 15 years, and attacked the most unpopular people in the country: the oligarchs. Chapter Three depicts the result: a sinister sham in which dissent is punished by arrest, forcible psychiatric medication, and bureaucratic harassment, in which elections are rigged, politicians tamed, the media muzzled, and the institutions of state hollowed out. Chapter Four examines the Russian economy— superficially strong but weak underneath. Chapter Five deals with outsiders' most common misunderstanding of modern Russia; that is, that there is no ideology. It explains how "sovereign democracy" includes powerful criticisms of Western shortcomings but is used to justify the xenophobic and authoritarian style of government in Russia. Chapter Six introduces the main battleground so far of the New Cold War: the ex-communist countries of Eastern Europe. Weak and badly governed, they offer easy pickings for the Kremlin's mixture of bribes and bullying. Chapter Seven explains the Kremlin's most potent weapon: energy. It shows how the Soviet-era monopoly on east-west oil and gas pipelines allows Russia to dictate terms to customers and penalize those who resist. Chapter Eight deals with the military and security dimension to the New Cold War. It shows the hollowness of the Kremlin's aims to become a military superpower, but shows how much more damaging and threatening are its activities in arms sales and in building strategic ties with China. Finally, Chapter Nine explains how the West can win the New Cold War: First by resurrecting collective security to deal with Russia's "divide and rule" tactics, and second by restoring the moral self-confidence that fuelled our victory in 1989.

CHAPTER ONE

PUTIN'S RISE TO POWER

How the KGB Seized Power in Russia

Vladimir Putin hardly seemed worth a footnote to Russian political history when an ailing President Boris Yeltsin made him prime minister on August 9, 1999. The fifth prime minister in less than a year,[1] he looked like a run-of-the-mill Russian bureaucrat: dull, unappealing, and all too likely to end up as another casualty of the country's unmanageable economic troubles and chaotic politics. Initially, little was known about him, personally or professionally. He liked judo and spoke German.[2] After working as a KGB officer in the former East Germany, he had returned to his home city of St. Petersburg[3] and quietly worked his way up the bureaucratic ladder. From the university's foreign relations department, he moved to a job dealing with foreign investors[4] and then to the Kremlin, where he worked in the presidential property department, a huge business empire based on the assets of the former Communist Party. After a brief stint overseeing the ties with Russia's regions, he became head of the FSB.[5]

But even then, a closer look suggested his appointment was more important than it seemed. A KGB career was a red-hot sign of distinction in the Soviet Union. Apart from the Communist leadership itself, the KGB had been the country's most knowledgeable, efficient, and privileged organization. It not only attracted the brightest people; it gave them a formidable training and an unbeatable network of contacts. They harbored a sense of great superiority over the shabby, humdrum, and ill-informed lives of the ordinary citizen. For many, that sense was stoked by special training in psychological tricks—how to manipulate strangers, to gain their trust or break their resistance. The result was more like a cult than a government bureaucracy. In a perverse sense, KGB officers felt themselves to be almost a lay priesthood: omniscient, omnipresent, and omnipotent. Being uniquely well placed to see its shortcomings, many harbored private doubts about the workability of communism. But they compensated both with a passionate patriotism, and an unbending loyalty to their fellow-officers.

The presence of any KGB veteran at the head of government would have been significant. But Putin was not just a run-of-the-mill KGB officer. He had served abroad. The First Directorate of the KGB, which handled external espionage, was an elite group within an elite group. Its members were specially selected and trained to withstand the temptations they would be exposed to during foreign travel—something that was an almost unimaginable luxury in the closed society of the Soviet Union. It is still unclear what exactly Putin did while he was in Dresden. The files of the East German secret police, the *Stasi*,[6] are curiously sketchy on his career there. Some believe that he was a lowly counterintelligence officer whose job was checking up on more glamorous frontline operatives. Others think he was given, but botched, an important job in managing the survival of Soviet intelligence networks as communism crumbled in East Germany. Both versions may be true. At any rate, Putin was handpicked for his loyalty, brains—and toughness.

An early sign of how his background might influence his behavior in political office came during his brief stint as prime minister, when Putin spoke to his former colleagues: "A group of FSB operatives, dispatched, under cover, to work in the government of the Russian Federation, is successfully fulfilling its task."[7] At the time, many thought that was a tasteless joke. In retrospect, it seems pretty close to a statement of fact. Since 2000, veterans of the Soviet intelligence and security services have taken control not only of the Kremlin and government, but also the media and the commanding heights of the economy. Olga Kryshtanovskaya, a sociologist at the Russian Academy of Sciences, estimates that as many as three-quarters of the top posts in Russia may be held by *siloviki*, an untranslatable term for current and former intelligence and security officers, derived from the Russian word *sila* [power].[8]

The rise to power of Putin and his friends is the culmination, accidental or deliberate, of a process that started in the early 1980s, when the KGB became frustrated by the gerontocracy surrounding the increasingly senile Leonid Brezhnev and the Communist Party leadership. Under communism, even the KGB was not all-powerful.

The KGB was not allowed to spy on the Soviet military intelligence service, the GRU,[9] or on the Communist Party, which regarded its "sword and shield" with a mixture of awe and contempt. Like its terror-inducing secret-police predecessors—the NKVD, the OGPU[10], the *Cheka,* and before them the Tsarist-era *Okhrana* and even the black-cowled monks of Ivan the Terrible's *Oprichniki*—the KGB could terrorize the powerless but only advise the powerful: it had no political authority of its own.

That came close to changing in November 1982 when Brezhnev died and the KGB chief Yuri Andropov was elected General Secretary in his place. For 15 months, the KGB was at the summit of power. The austere, scary Andropov tried to restore the Soviet system in both economics and politics. He had little success, partly because the Soviet Union was inherently unsalvageable, and also because his diseased kidneys gave out within months of his taking power; when he died, stagnation returned under his successor, a doddery Communist Party hack named Konstantin Chernenko who lasted only 18 months. Resigned to the inevitability of change, the KGB then became a strong supporter of Gorbachev's reforms—at least until they seemed to be leading to the country's disintegration.

This may seem a paradox. Certainly the main aim of many liberals and reformers in the Soviet Union's provinces in the Gorbachev era was to outwit the central institutions of power: the Kremlin, the armed forces, the bureaucrats who ran (or mis-ran) the planned economy, and most of all the cold grey men of the KGB. The two main levers of Soviet power, economic planning and the one-party police state, seemed one and the same thing. What nobody realized was that collapse of state planning would soon give the savviest people in the former Soviet Union—the ex-spooks—a chance to beat the West at its own game: capitalism. Political freedom and human rights, which seemed to be at the heart of public life, were just optional extras. They were dispensed—and then dispensed with.

It is Andropov who is Putin's role model. In July 1999, while still head of the FSB, Putin laid a wreath on Andropov's grave. Later, he had a wall plaque restored on the wall of old KGB headquarters, the Lubyanka, and praised Andropov as an "outstanding political figure." Since Putin's rise to power, the FSB has achieved something that the KGB never quite managed: Its members, current and former, are running the country. The difference between the two types is largely cosmetic. Shortly after becoming prime minister in 1999, Putin told

Russian television that "there is no such thing as an ex-Chekist."[11] Viktor Cherkesov, a close Putin ally (who, as the KGB chief in St. Petersburg, in 1988 ordered the last political repression in the Soviet Union and now runs Russia's drug control agency), wrote in 2004: "We [siloviki] must understand that we are one whole. History ruled that the weight of supporting the Russian state fell on our shoulders. I believe in our ability, when we feel danger, to put aside everything petty, and remain faithful to our oath."[12]

In the book on judo that he co-authored, published in 2004, Putin repeatedly makes the point that success is achieved with "minimum effort, maximum effect." [13] That is a salient feature of both his foreign and domestic policy. Trying to control everything, as his communist predecessors in the Kremlin did, makes the grip on power rigid and brittle. Much more effective, then, to concentrate not on crushing opponents crudely, but on keeping them unbalanced—and therefore vulnerable to a deft throw and armlock. Although the FSB has in effect mounted a successful putsch, recreating an authoritarian political system, it shuns total control. Instead, it has retained the outward appearance of political pluralism, in a way that still fools outsiders and wishful thinkers.

At first sight, the story seems simple. Russia was already in a terrible mess when Putin became prime minister. Then a spate of deadly and mysterious terrorist attacks, costing some three hundred lives, put the country in a state of national panic. Putin's response, of tough talk and still tougher deeds, made him the nation's most popular politician within weeks. He was therefore the logical and popular choice to succeed Yeltsin as president. Since then he has reversed the abuses of the Yeltsin years and made Russia strong and prosperous. For many Russians and outsiders, that is still the essence of the past seven years. Later chapters will deal with the abuse of power. But the means used in Putin's ascent to the presidency should dispel any illusions about the real nature of his regime once in office.

The story started with an obscure news item, barely covered outside Russia. Fighters from the breakaway province of Chechnya raided villages in neighboring Dagestan in August 1999.[14] A few days later, on August 31st, a seemingly unrelated bomb exploded in Moscow in an underground shopping mall—a glorified term for what is actually a warren of kiosks around the entrance to a subway station. One person was killed and 40 injured. Many blamed a mafia feud, though a previously unknown anarchist group left a note claiming responsibility. On a much bigger scale was the outrage on September 4, when a car bomb outside a military apartment block in Buinaksk, a town in Dagestan, killed 64 people and wounded dozens. Russia blamed separatists from Chechnya. Putin authorized attacks on what he called "illegal military units" there. It was not until four days later, when a large bomb planted in the basement blew up a nine-story apartment building in southeast Moscow, killing 94 people and wounding 150, that Russians began to think that they were under a sustained attack by terrorists. That impression was confirmed by two more mass murders. On September 13th, the day of mourning for those victims, another bomb blew up an eight-story building, also in southern Moscow, killing 118 and wounding 200. Three days after that, a truck bomb in Volgodonsk, in southern Russia, killed 17 more people.

The atmosphere created by this sustained assault was frantic. At night, vigilante groups patrolled the back streets of Moscow. The Chechens had long been Russia's least-popular ethnic minority and the attacks demonized them further. Putin immediately authorized a military operation against the "terrorist" republic. Russia would "wipe out" the culprits, even "in the shit-house," he said. That was a shocking piece of gangster slang that no previous Russian leader would have dreamed of using in public.[15] Some educated Russians winced; but it caught the national mood. The time for being nice was over.

But still puzzling questions remained. The Chechens had no record of attacking such targets, or using such means. The bombs had been expertly planted in buildings whose construction made them most vulnerable to attack. But the Chechens had previously shown no sign of having the organizational clout needed to get hold of big quantities of explosive, nor of the knowledge to use them so professionally.[16] The bombings had been well planned, probably months in advance, yet the fighting in Dagestan was quite recent. Chechen terrorist tactics in the past involved taking hostages and making practical demands: for the release of prisoners, or for negotiations with the Kremlin. This time, the supposed perpetrators had no motive. The inevitable result of the attacks was a war in which their already ruined republic would be obliterated.

The real beneficiaries were in Moscow. Rumours had been swirling around the Russian capital for a year that senior figures in the Yeltsin Kremlin were planning to use violence to head off what seemed like their impending downfall. The country's most powerful tycoon-politician, Boris Berezovsky, was under investigation for diverting foreign cash revenues from the national airline, Aeroflot. Another controversy surrounded Pavel Borodin, the head of the presidential property department. He had commissioned a controversial Swiss firm, Mabetex, to carry out richly priced renovations on the Kremlin's historic buildings. In September 1999, the Yeltsin family came under renewed scrutiny when Swiss investigators claimed to have found documents confirming that Mabetex had paid $15 million in bribes, including by providing credit cards for the president and his two daughters. The Yeltsin family has consistently maintained its innocence.[17] Only the blatant bribery of deputies postponed an attempt in the Duma to press ahead with Yeltsin's impeachment. Another seemed certain to succeed sooner or later. Yuri Luzhkov, the powerful mayor of Moscow, had thrown his political and financial weight behind former foreign minister Yevgeny Primakov's presidential candidacy. Elections were due in 2000, but they could happen even earlier were Yeltsin impeached. Appointing Putin and giving power to the "Chekists," was, in effect, the Yeltsinites' last desperate throw of the dice. The bombing campaign and fighting in Chechnya gave the move all the more impact: Attention shifted from the shenanigans about official corruption to the authorities' commendably tough response to a terrorist onslaught on Russia. Few wanted to make the accusation outright, but the bombing campaign was certainly a remarkably convenient coincidence.

Such theories would have remained at the fringes of discussion, except for the "bomb" that didn't go off. On the night of September 22, Aleksei Kartofelnikov saw a white car parked outside his 12-story apartment block at 14/16 Novosyolov[18] Street in Ryazan, about 120 miles (200km) from Moscow. An unusually observant man, Kartofelnik noticed that the license plate had been doctored to look like a local registration. He looked more closely, and saw three people carrying sacks into the building's basement. So, he called the police. Experts investigated what appeared to be a bomb and removed the sacks, a detonator, and a timer that had been set for 0530. Hundreds of people living nearby were evacuated; eventually a nearby cinema was opened to take them in. A local police explosives expert, Yuri Tkachenko, used a gas analyzer to examine the sacks' contents: yellowish granules, resembling pasta. The machine identified them as hexogen, a powerful explosive. The detonators were real and correctly wired. The police immediately put checkpoints on main roads. The car spotted by Mr. Kartofelnikov was found; it turned out to have been stolen.

On the evening of September 23, the head of the FSB's public relations division, Aleksander Zdanovich, appeared on a top talk show, *Geroi Dnya* [Hero of the Day]. Though happy to take the credit for the foiled bombing, he seemed oddly confused about what had happened, perhaps because he was ill-briefed, or perhaps for some other reason.[19] The interior minister, Vladimir Rushailo, speaking at a conference the next day, nearly 48 hours after the "bomb" was discovered, criticized the law-enforcement agencies for lack of vigilance and praised the public for theirs. The next day, September 24, Putin praised the air strikes on the separatist capital, Grozny. On Ryazan, he said:

> If the sacks which proved to contain explosive were noticed, that means there is a positive side to it, if only in the fact that the public is reacting correctly to the events taking place in our country today. I'd like . . . to thank the public . . . This is absolutely the correct response. No panic, no sympathy for the bandits. This is the mood for fighting them to the very end. Until we win. And we shall win.[20]

Neither he nor any other official source made any suggestion at this stage that the discovery had been anything but another terrorist plot. Then the head of the FSB, Nikolai Patrushev, stunned Russia by saying that the whole thing had been merely an exercise. He congratulated the residents of Ryazan for their "vigilance." The sacks had merely contained sugar and had been planted as part of a series of exercises.

The Ryazan FSB reacted with fury to the news that the bomb was a hoax. They issued a statement saying:

> It has become known that the planting on 22.09.99 of a dummy explosive device was part of an ongoing interregional exercise. This announcement came as a surprise to us and appeared at a moment when the . . . FSB had identified the places of residence in Ryazan of those involved in planting the explosive device and was preparing to detain them.[21]

One reason for the Ryazan FSB's anger was that on the night that the "bomb" was planted, Nadezhda Yukhanova, a telephone operator in Ryazan, reported overhearing a suspicious fragment of a trunk call to Moscow that she had connected: One caller said that his group had been noticed and needed to leave town quickly. The other replied: "Split up and each of you make your own way out."

When the local FSB traced the number dialed, it was registered at the FSB headquarters in Moscow. Patrushev claimed that his men "were among the residents who left the building in which an explosive device was supposedly planted. They took part in the process of producing their own photofit pictures, and held conversations with employees of the agencies of law enforcement." That was not the case. In fact the Ryazan authorities had arrested two suspects who then produced FSB identity cards. A high-ranking officer from the agency's Moscow headquarters came and collected them.[22]

Even by the Russian bureaucracy's bumbling standards, the initial explanation seemed unconvincing. The newspaper *Noviye Izvestiya* [New News] questioned Patrushev's sanity, wondering if he also confused colors or failed to recognize his relatives. Others wondered if the bombing campaign might be the work not of Russia's terrorist enemies but of the authorities, cynically trying to manipulate public opinion. It seemed unlikely that the Ryazan experts had mistaken hexogen for sugar. And if the sacks contained only sugar, why had they been swiftly removed for "expert analysis" in Moscow? Was it perhaps to get the incriminating evidence away from Ryazan? The FSB added to the confusion by saying that the sacks' contents had been "tested" at an artillery range and found to be inert. Why would anyone bother to do that with sugar planted in an official training exercise? Why had the exercise used a stolen car—against all regulations—in a dummy drill when one of the agency's own vehicles would have done just as well?

The FSB appeared to be scrambling to produce evidence that Ryazan was indeed one of a series of planned exercises. Dozens of other "tests" took place, most so amateurish that they would have shamed the bumbling Inspector Clouseau from the Pink Panther films. (In Moscow, FSB officers left a dummy package marked "bomb" in a police station office where it was discovered two days later.) None showed the sophistication and extent of what seemingly had been mounted in Ryazan.[23] At a meeting with the apartment block's inhabitants, FSB chiefs struggled to explain what exactly was being practiced in the "exercise"; why no local authority had been informed; why no preparations had been made to look after the evacuated residents. Other details were even more puzzling. The building was an odd choice to test alertness, as it included an all-night supermarket; deliveries there would not arouse much suspicion. However, the flimsily constructed brick building would have been an ideal choice for a terrorist attack: Of similar construction to the one bombed in Moscow the previous week, it would have not only collapsed instantly, but the debris would have slid downhill and quite likely damaged a neighboring building as well.

In March 2000 an FSB officer told a television interviewer that he and other officers had found by chance an unlocked basement in Ryazan, had bought sacks of sugar at a local market and a gun cartridge at a firearms shop, and had then ostentatiously planted the mock bomb to test local residents' awareness. A senior retired FSB officer, Gennady Zaitsev, said that the instrument used for testing the "explosive" had given a faulty reading because it was dirty; an error for which its operators had now been punished. That was meant to clear things up, but the result was yet more baffling. He may have been genuinely mistaken in his assertion, but staging innocent-seeming activities such as the purchase of sugar at a market, and of a cartridge at a gun shop, could be seen as odd ways to test public vigilance. Why come all the way from Moscow in a stolen car to leave three sacks of sugar in an unguarded basement? Moreover, no disciplinary proceedings had been launched against Tkachenko: he and a colleague had been officially rewarded for their courage, as had Yukhanova, the telephone operator, for her alertness. If anybody deserved punishment, it would have been those responsible for such an extraordinarily inconsiderate, badly planned, and pointless exercise.[24]

The authorities reacted with outrage to any suggestion of official complicity. Putin said it was "immoral" even to raise the question. It would indeed be unwise to rely only on the Russian media: It makes mistakes, just as reporters do everywhere. Putin's enemies could have planted rumors and red herrings. All the Russian officials involved vehemently deny any wrongdoing, and insist that the conspiracy theory has been cooked up by their political opponents. Proponents of the theory that the bombing had official backing can produce considerable circumstantial evidence, but nothing that directly implicates Putin, senior officials or his political allies. But the Kremlin could have easily cleared up the story. Instead of doing this, it sealed all material relating to Ryazan for 75 years and repeatedly blocked investigations by independent-minded Duma deputies.[25] Two Duma deputies who pursued the issue, Sergei Yushenkov and Yuri Shchekochikhin, have since died in suspicious circumstances.[26] A journalist associated with their investigation, Otto Lacis,[27] was badly beaten. He later died in a car crash. The commission's lawyer, Mikhail Trepashkin, was jailed on charges of breaching official secrecy; Amnesty International campaigned for his release, saying that the charges are bogus.

The Kremlin's strongest arguments, if it cared to make them, would be that Russian officialdom simply excelled its usual capacity for bungling and secrecy. Perhaps planning for the "exercise" was merely irregular, callous, and incompetent. Maybe the right paperwork was never issued, or went unread. Instead of admitting that, the Kremlin denies that serious questions are raised by the events, and concentrates hard on depicting those who persist in asking questions as mouthpieces for Berezovsky, an able propagandist with a vested interest in making Putin's Kremlin look bad. The alternative version is supported not only by Putin's sworn foes, but also by the statements and actions of dozens of independent witnesses and participants who have no reason to portray their government as homicidal maniacs, and who in some cases run a considerable risk in sticking to their story. The official version does not properly account for any of the strange details: the people, the "bomb," the car, the evacuation, or the initial official explanation. The handful of "culprits" who were eventually caught, tried, and sentenced for the bombings had no convincing links to the crimes.

The biggest reason for disbelieving the conspiracy theory about Ryazan is that it is so energetically pushed by Berezovsky, who—at least by his own account—is Putin's archenemy. Given his controversial record (see page 47) while at the heart of power in Russia during the 1990s, Berezovsky's favorite causes certainly deserve careful and cautious scrutiny. His analysis of Russian politics is interesting but self-interested. It should never be taken at face value. But a theory may have dubious backers and still be true. And Berezovsky is clever enough not to promote a version of events that could easily be rebutted as fictitious. The weight of evidence so far supports the grimmest interpretation: that the attacks were a ruthlessly planned stunt to create a climate of panic and fear in which Putin would quickly become the country's undisputed leader, as indeed he did. It is a measure of how far opinion has shifted that the conspiracy theory has gone from being an outlandish hypothesis to something believed by serious opposition politicians such as Grigory Yavlinsky, leader of the main liberal party, Yabloko. It is as if mainstream contenders for the Democratic nomination in America's presidential election had publicly supported the contention that the terrorist attacks of September 11, 2001 were an inside job organized by Vice President Dick Cheney. Perhaps even more terrible than the murder plot itself is the thought that Russian public opinion may be so accustomed to official brutality and abuse of power, and so relieved to have a strong man in charge, that it prefers not to worry about what really happened.

At the time, most of the Russian public set aside any theories about official complicity in the bombings. Putin's popularity was soaring against the other contenders for the presidential election due the next year, in 2000. He was a straight-talking tough guy, visibly sober and well organized; the best-educated and best-traveled Russian leader since Vladimir Lenin. He was young, compared to one rival, the decrepit-seeming former foreign minister, Primakov. He was not burdened with the Soviet political baggage of another: the Communist leader Gennady Zyuganov. Unlike a third contender, the mayor of Moscow Yuri Luzhkov, he was not linked publicly to any controversial business dealings. Perhaps most importantly, he was hitting Russia's enemies hard.

Putin's taciturn competence looked all the better compared with his lame-duck predecessor. In the final years of his presidency, Yeltsin was the most unpopular politician in Russia, seen as an embarrassing drunk whose scheming family and tycoon friends had cynically looted the country. It was his toxic touch that helped make Russian politics seem so unmanageable. Yet in the Soviet Union ten years previously, Yeltsin had been hugely popular. A bear-like Communist party boss from Sverdlovsk, a big city in the Urals region (which has now regained its pre-communist name, Yekaterinburg), he was originally a strong supporter of Gorbachev's reforms. He moved to become the party chief in Moscow, but then clashed with the Soviet leader in 1988 and then shed his communist ideology, becoming an earthy populist politician. Elected the leader of Russia—in those days not a real state but one of the country's 15 republics[28]—he was Gorbachev's chief critic and rival. Russians admired his honesty and outspokenness, though the outside world worried that he was too nationalist, too unpredictable, and (some whispered) too drunk. The garrulous and indecisive Gorbachev might have his faults, foreign diplomats and politicians conceded. But undermining him by backing an unknown rival would be crazy.[29]

Such doubts evaporated, at least for a while, in a few hours in August 1991, as the world woke up to find that Yeltsin was leading the resistance to a hard-liners' putsch that had toppled Gorbachev and was trying to restore Soviet-style dictatorship. As Yeltsin defied the danger of snipers to stand on a captured tank outside his office building, Moscow's "White House," he embodied Russian and foreign hopes for a future free of fear. Within a few months, he had dissolved the Soviet Union and the Communist Party, put the KGB under civilian control, declared Russia to be a multi-party democracy, and appointed a team of radical economic reformers to run the government. The intentions were admirable: He sincerely wanted to make Russia good as well as great, ditching both the ruinous doctrines of economic planning and the murderous ways of the secret-police state. But the difficulties were even greater than the hopes. The human, physical, and economic legacy of the evil empire remained and poisoned what grew on its ruins everywhere, especially in Russia. Communism was more deeply ingrained than in the captive nations of central Europe and the Baltics, where the rule of law, capitalism, and in some countries even political freedom were living memories. If any elderly Russians alive in 1991 had childhood memories of the brief provisional government that replaced Tsarist rule in February 1917, led in its last months by the moderate lawyer Aleksandr Kerensky, they were in no position to act on what they remembered.

Under Putin, and among foreign critics of the Yeltsin era, the 1990s are now dismissed as an era of unalloyed failure. Yet it is hard to imagine a Russian leader who could have done better. Even the best policies in the world, implemented in the ideal sequence with unlimited outside support, could not have made up for the nightmarish problems that Russia's rulers faced. But Yeltsin certainly blundered. Woefully confused about economics, ignorant of the world outside Russia, and in the habit of promoting thugs and crooks, he aggravated the effect of three highly unpopular but inevitable developments: vanishing savings, jarring economic dislocation, and a growing gap between the rich and poor.

The loss of savings, contrary to popular belief, predated Yeltsin's presidency. In the collapsing months of the Soviet Union, the central bank had run the printing presses red-hot, destroying the value of the ruble, which slipped from a nominal parity with the pound to first 30 on the black market (in early 1990) and then 300 (by mid-1991). As inflation soared and the exchange rate plummeted, money began to lose its function. At the ridiculously low prices fixed by economic planners, goods mostly stayed out of the shops; for lucky foreigners, that meant that for a wad of rubles worth pennies you might pick up a pair of clunky cross-country skis or a noisy but effective coffee grinder. If you were an ordinary family needing the necessities of daily life such as sausage or soap (and toward the end, even bread) you would be staring at empty shelves, queuing for hours, swapping favors to get what you needed, or paying what seemed like sky-high prices on the black market. Wise Soviet citizens started saving in cash in hard currencies, and, if they could, they exchanged their rubles too—though this was hampered by crude stunts such as the cancellation under Gorbachev of the highest-value ruble banknotes. Many people's savings existed only as numbers on a bank statement, in banks that had no real assets to back their liabilities. Most people believed that the "shortages" were only temporary: Once prices returned to "normal" they would then be able to spend their savings. This situation created what economists call a "monetary overhang"—a mountain of unspendable money. When Yeltsin's government rightly, and belatedly, freed prices in early 1992, goods reappeared on sale, first hawked on the pavement or at informal markets, then in makeshift kiosks, and eventually in the shops. The ruble became money again. But the goods were on sale at prices far higher, sometimes hundreds of times so, than those of the Soviet days. For millions of households, the worthlessness of their savings was suddenly and pitifully visible. Many Russians have never forgiven Yeltsin and his team of young economic reformers for that, although in truth their anger should be directed at Gorbachev and his long-forgotten colleagues for printing too much money in the first place. After a few years of growing but still precarious stability, the currency devaluation of August 1998 added insult to injury. Under Putin, by contrast, the ruble's value has remained rock-solid against Western currencies in nominal terms, and appreciated sharply in real terms. The banking system has recovered. Russian households regard the ruble as real money. For all his virtues, that is something that Yeltsin never managed.

The economic dislocation of the 1990s was unavoidable too. In the Soviet system, giant factories produced huge orders on the instructions of bureaucrats in Moscow. Waste was colossal, quality abysmal, attention to customers' wishes unknown. Outside a planned economy, much of the production was worse than useless, worth less than the raw materials used to produce it. As Jan Winiecki, a Polish economist, put it: "The Soviet cow drank more milk than she produced."[30] Management disciplines such as product development, sales, or marketing were unknown. Most enterprises had enormous social obligations—running everything from workers' housing to schools to heating plants. Slowly and painfully, the penalties and incentives of the market began to bite. Russia's economy began to modernize, initially by shedding labor and ending production of useless goods. But the price was years of hardship and uncertainty for many. Again, that seemed to be Yeltsin's fault: It was on his watch that the economy was contracting and unemployment was soaring. Few thought of the real culprits: Lenin, Joseph Stalin, and Brezhnev. Under Putin, the economy (see Chapter Four) has grown month-by-month for more than seven years. Russians appreciate that; few ask how Putin would have fared had he taken over the ruined Soviet economy and low oil prices, or how much better Yeltsin would have looked had he taken charge of Russia ten years later.

Most Russians were ill placed to judge Yeltsin's policies. The market economy was a mystery, and one they had to unravel almost overnight. Nothing in their past lives had prepared the population for rapid economic change. Soviet-era survival skills consisted chiefly of stoicism, made endurable by alcohol and tobacco. Suddenly, drive, initiative, and adaptability were what counted. Many of the ordinary Russians who went into business found life tough: Selling pathetic assortments of second-hand goods at seedy markets provided pocket money at best, but not a living. Many didn't even want to try. They retained a lingering Marxist belief that one man's profit was necessarily another man's loss. For many in middle age or older, it was too late to learn new tricks. Worse, those who knew the new rules were poor ambassadors for capitalism: speculators, spivs, and outright gangsters, whose profits were dependent more on unscrupulous quick-wittedness rather than talent, effort, or ingenuity. For those suffering years of hardship and uncertainty it meant little that others were grasping the opportunities—literally—of a lifetime. Brisk commercial relationships and cutthroat competition seemed as disgusting as the string pulling and hypocrisy of the earlier regime. "Everything they told us about communism was false—but everything they told us about capitalism was true" was a common complaint. For those on public sector salaries, living standards plunged.

Manual workers fared particularly badly. Under communism their jobs had been arduous and even dangerous. But they had been secure, relatively well-paid, and often with privileges such as cheap holidays on the Black Sea—sometimes even a coveted jaunt to Bulgaria. Laziness and incompetence were unpenalized, just as talent and hard work were unrewarded. The informal motto of the Soviet workplace was "We pretend to work and they pretend to pay us." Now life had gone from predictable to precarious almost overnight. State-owned enterprises provided not just employment, but also housing, heating, education, and health care. When the parent business collapsed, so did everything else. As unemployment rocketed, many middle-aged manual workers wondered if they would ever find employment again. New jobs meant harsh bosses and arbitrary discipline. Social benefits were pathetically small and often paid late.

Chaotic economics was matched by chaotic politics. Though Yeltsin wished Russia to become a modern and prosperous industrialized country, he had only the haziest idea of what this entailed in practice. His three immovable principles were free speech, friendship with the West, and to keep Communists out of power. These were fine things, but not enough to run a country properly. Viktor Gerashchenko, for example, a Soviet-era holdover who ran the central bank until 1994, simply did not believe that printing money caused inflation. Jeffrey Sachs, a Harvard economist, said: "[He] may be the worst central-bank governor of any major country in history."[31] The state was all but powerless: It could liberalize, but not regulate. The laws and institutions needed for a market economy, such as tax administration, a land register, banking supervision, and courts existed either not at all, or only in distorted and inadequate Soviet versions. Reforms were also haphazard and incomplete because Yeltsin never had a reliable parliamentary majority. Indeed, for most of the 1990s legislative power lay in the hands of people who were determined to thwart change, not support it. The easy way around that was bribing legislators. That got things done—but at the price of entrenching the idea that political power was a commodity to be bought and sold, rather than a reflection of the will of the people. The Yeltsin-era Kremlin became an increasingly pungent illustration of the well-worn proverb that fish start rotting at the head. Not a notably greedy man himself,[32] Yeltsin proved quite unable to rein in the clique of family and friends who surrounded him. Their greed and ostentatiousness became a byword for the failure of his rule.

By the time of the 1998 financial crisis, the multi-party system and the market economy, along with Yeltsin's personal reputation, were deeply discredited. Russians talked of *dermokratsiya* [shitocracy] and *prikhvatisatsiya* [piratization] instead of *demokratiya* [democracy] and *privatisatsiya* [privatization]. Poor people wanted pensions and salaries paid on time; business people wanted stability. Patriots wanted their country to be respected. Almost everyone wanted the oligarchs to be cut down to size. It was the perfect setting for a quiet putsch by the heirs of the KGB.[33] At first hypothetically, then tentatively, and soon with confident enthusiasm, Putin was discussed as a future president. Then and thereafter, his leitmotif has

Gloomy Russians

Who more effectively and quicker than anyone else can bring order to Russia now?	%
Putin	41
The Communists under Zyuganov	14
Armed forces	9
Fatherland-All Russia	8
Yeltsin	1
How would you describe politics in Russia today?	
Rise of anarchy	63
Democracy building	9
Old system, new names	8
Approach of dictatorship	6
What phrase best describes the political situation in Russia today?	
Tense	60
Critical, explosive	29
Quiet	3
Good	0
What economic system would you prefer?	
State planning and distribution	48
Private property and the market	35
It would have been better if the country had stayed as it was before 1985	
Yes	58
No	27

Source: VTsIOM

© *The Economist 1999*

been that he represents a clear break with the past. This is certainly true in terms of his style of rule: well choreographed and disciplined, quite unlike his predecessor. His policies are sharply different. Yet it remains a fact that he first rose to high office in the period he now decries, starting as an unemployed ex-spy and ending up running the country's most powerful government agency. However much his supporters dislike the notion, Putin is a product of the Yeltsin years, and the handpicked choice of the Yeltsin "family" and their tycoon friends.[34]

As Putin moved smoothly into the acting presidency and then won a presidential election in March 2000, the big question be-

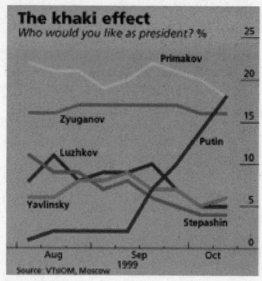

The khaki effect
Who would you like as president? %

© *The Economist 1999*

came not whether he would exercise power, but what kind, and over whom. Three possibilities were open. Putin might stay a mouse, timorously observing but not effectively influencing the workings of money and real power in Russian politics. He might be the longed-for magician who would get reform back on track, modernize Russia, and help it finally step over its post-imperial shadow. Or he might be a monster: an autocratic leader who would rule by fear, and who would return Russia to its xenophobic and authoritarian past.

CHAPTER TWO

PUTIN IN POWER

The Winners and Losers of the New Regime

I t was hard to tell at the beginning of President Putin's rule who would suffer and who would benefit. As the creation and creature of Boris Yeltsin's Kremlin, it seemed unlikely that he would be able to change the system that had taken root in the 1990s. How could he tame the oligarchs, whose private security services and bulging coffers made them more powerful than most institutions of state? And how would the center bring to heel the mighty tribal chieftains, bandit kings, mafia dons, strongmen, and warlords who ruled many of Russia's regions? At first it was hard to see how Putin could make a difference: A mere mouse seemed to be running round the Kremlin's endless corridors. The new president's inner circle was an uneasy mixture between the "family"—the Yeltsin cronies who had brought him to power—and two St. Petersburg clans, the *siloviki* and economic reformers. The president shifted indecisively between all three, seemingly agreeing with whomever had advised him last. "Putin jokes" were common, most of which had obscene punch lines.[1] Carefully staged photo-ops aside, the Russian leader cut an unimpressive figure in public: tetchy, foul-mouthed, and unsympathetic. If trouble brewed, he disappeared. When the *Kursk,* one of the most advanced vessels in Russia's nuclear submarine fleet, sank after a botched torpedo launch, Putin stayed on holiday for a week. When he was finally asked by an American television interviewer what had actually happened (Russian naval officials had blamed everybody and everything but their own incompetence), Putin seemed to find it impossible show sympathy, distress, or contrition. He grimaced and said simply "it sank."[2] Progress in the

Chechen war was slow, the casualties appalling. His popularity looked set to ebb as fast as it had flowed.

But the mouse had a taste for magic. Putin came out strongly for economic reform, saying that he wanted Russia to reach Portuguese standards of prosperity in a decade. His government pushed through a 13 percent flat tax in 2001; as in other countries where this has been tried,[3] the results were impressive. His ministers talked of setting up a "one-stop-shop" for registering small businesses, replacing the baffling and expensive trek between different state institutions that faced Russia's hardy would-be entrepreneurs. Then, as the months went by, the Putin-mouse's squeaks turned to roars. Stumblingly at first, and then more systematically, he began squeezing independent sources of political and economic power. For those who thought that the winners and losers of the 1990s were set in stone, it was time to think again.

The landscape of Russian society now is marked by three phases in recent history: the Soviet era, when political loyalty was at a premium; the Gorbachev/Yeltsin era, which prized talent and adaptability; and now the Putin era, which punishes only dissent. Each period has had its losers and its winners. The foundation of Putin's success is that so few have lost, and so many have gained. They include both those who have felt hard done by in the past and those who have done well through all three eras. Under Soviet rule, the biggest winners by far were the *nomenklatura*. Through a mixture of family connections, brains, and opportunism they reached, usually rather late in life, the best that the Soviet Union could offer: princely country houses, access to special shops where Western luxury goods were sold at knock-down prices, chauffeur-driven cars, prostitutes, and excellent health care. Only contact with foreigners was restricted: Distrust was so ingrained in the Soviet system that even the elite could not be allowed to mix freely with the enemy and his temptations.

The collapse of the one-party state and the planned economy suddenly made ideological purity and party connections matter less, while talent and flexibility were at a premium. The able members of the old power structures moved on, dumping their communist allegiances along with the gray plastic shoes and nylon suits of the Soviet wardrobe. Some moved into the private sector, setting up well-connected banks or import-export businesses. Others stayed in government service, such as the young Putin, handling municipal foreign relations in St. Petersburg, a city that some hoped might even eclipse Moscow in importance as Russia moved back to its European roots. Many KGB members moved to the "active reserve," working in the private sector but keeping their alumnus contacts alive, just in case.

For these able "apparatchiks," as the members of the communist establishment or *apparat* were known, Putin's rise to power was the best news possible. Their Soviet past gave them contacts and credibility; the new conditions offered them the chance to turn them into money. The best examples come from the top of the Kremlin: Sergei Ivanov, a career KGB spy who is now first deputy prime minister, has become chairman of the board at the new state-controlled aircraft manufacturing company, UABC. Igor Sechin, a deputy chief of staff in the Kremlin (whose Soviet-era job as a "military translator" in Africa strongly suggests a background in the Soviet Union's military intelligence service, the GRU) worked alongside Putin in St. Petersburg and is now chairman of Rosneft. Thanks to the bargain price at which it has acquired assets, Rosneft is now Russia's largest oil company. Sergei Naryshkin, a fast-rising deputy prime minister,[4] is a former colleague of Putin both from his St. Petersburg days and before that from the KGB, and is now his deputy there and chairman of the main shipbuilding company. Viktor Ivanov, a KGB veteran and a senior Kremlin figure who chairs the boards of Aeroflot and the air-defense systems giant Almaz-Antei, is setting up a state-run machine tool monopoly; he is expected to head it. Other former KGB officials also run, or are in powerful positions at, the ministries of economy, transport, natural resources, telecommunications, and culture. At least a quarter of Gazprom's management is made up of ex-KGB types. Aleksei Gromov, the Kremlin spokesman whose Soviet-era postings abroad strongly suggest a past career in the KGB, sits on the board of the main television channel. The railway monopoly, Russia's second-largest company after Gazprom, is headed by Vladimir Yakunin, a former diplomat and ex-KGB officer.[5] Soviet apparatchiks unable to make the transition, by contrast, disappeared like dinosaurs. Their last hurrah had been the failed putsch against Gorbachev. They could barely conceive a world without the institutions of Soviet power, much less operate in it. In a country where the male life expectancy had plunged below 60, many followed communist ideology to the grave. Few mourned them. Russia's new rulers regard with contempt the way that the old guard misruled the Soviet Union, turning it from superpower to basket case.

For different reasons, the old Soviet ruling caste is also despised by the chief losers during the communist era: the phantom middle class of principled and well-educated people who were deprived of the life they would have enjoyed in the capitalist countries. Advancement in any line of work was limited for those not prepared to swallow what Czesław Miłosz, the Polish Nobel Laureate, called the "Pill of Murti-Bing."[6] Some became scientists and engineers, professions largely uncontaminated by communist ideology. But many of the middle-class occupations that make up the bulk of employment in an advanced capitalist economy did not exist. The phantom middle class could not run small businesses because none existed. Professions such as medicine and teaching were of far lower status than in Western countries. The life of the mind was imprisoned by a system that prevented travel abroad and severely restricted access to the cultures and ideas of the outside world. Speaking out—which was almost unthinkable—risked severe punishment: The thought of being forced to move to a communal apartment, sharing a kitchen and bathroom with noisy alcoholics, was usually deterrent enough. The result was internal emigration. People retreated into drink, despair, and the intense friendships of their private lives, where in a narrow circle of trusted friends they could—they hoped—at least speak freely.

The Yeltsin years were good for many of this phantom middle class, at least initially. The professions boomed. Russian business needed commercial lawyers; Russian women wanted cosmetic surgery and decent gynecology and obstetrics; everyone wanted to learn English. Journalism went from being a closely guarded branch of Soviet propaganda to a profession open to anyone with a quick pen and a sharp mind. Occupations that had been unknown in the Soviet Union mushroomed: travel agent, realtor, salesman, tax accountant. Obscure hobbies turned into specialist businesses. Good things came in return; foreign travel went from unimaginable luxury to part of normal life in just a few years. People who knew London only from the pages of Dickens and Conan Doyle could see the real thing for the price of a coach ticket. Visa lines at Western consulates lengthened, first shamefully and then outrageously. Squalid and tatty Soviet apartments had a "*Yevroremont*" [Euro-makeover] and become gleaming and sometimes gaudy. Diet transformed: Vodka sales dropped; wine and beer consumption soared. Russians bought cars, to the point that big cities have now become unmanageably congested. Some started educating their children privately.

The Yeltsin years were also good for a second group of losers from the Soviet system: the commercially talented. The planned economy offered few openings for the ambitious, quick-witted, and sometimes less principled people who would have been the backbone of a capitalist system. A few got jobs running Soviet foreign trade, usually in close collaboration with the KGB. For the others, the only place for their talents was the black market. Denounced as "speculators" and subject to severe punishment if caught, they skulked on the margins of society, sometimes enjoying rich rewards if the KGB allowed them a little license in return for information about their clients.[7]

While offering both groups unparalled opportunity, capitalism also created some jarring juxtapositions. In the chaotic 1990s, even the most fastidious members of the country's intellectual and cultural elite found themselves rubbing shoulders with people they would have previously regarded with horrified distaste. Boris Berezovsky, a respectable Soviet-era mathematician, spotted an opening in the car business and became one of the richest men in Russia. Vladimir Gusinsky, a theatre director, used $1,000, his entire savings, to open a store selling women's clothing and copper bracelets. Ten years later he had the largest media business in Russia. Aleksander Smolensky, after years tussling with the Soviet authorities over his semi-legal business activities, set up one of the first cooperatives in the construction industry, and shortly thereafter a bank. Within five years he was one of the richest men in Russia. Others took a more direct route to riches. Hardened criminals were a natural basis for the newly emergent Russian mafia, whose ruthlessness and mutual loyalty outstripped a police force that had always relied on now-vanished political and KGB back-up. Their businesses ranged from looting state property, to establishing monopolies and cartels, to simple extortion.

For the dodgy and distinguished alike, the quickest gains came from goods that were portable and readily saleable, such as valuable raw materials.[8] Anyone crossing the former Soviet border into Poland would see roadsides dotted with signs offering to buy nonferrous metals. Wily middlemen began buying the most sought-after products of state factories and smelters, paying a nominal price to the nominal owner, plus a stiff "enabling payment" to the manager, and then selling the products on the open market. In the rudimentary post-Soviet legal system, it was not clear if any of this was illegal. The profits were even more fantastic for those who could run not only businesses, but also whole chunks of government. The most successful tycoons became the oligarchs, making multi-billion dollar fortunes by snapping up state assets at what seemed like knockdown prices, at a time when most Russians were struggling to keep their families fed and clothed. Perhaps that wasn't as bad as it seemed; in the mid-1990s, with the Communist Party seemingly on the verge of regaining power, few others wanted to buy these companies at all. But the auctions were strangely rigged, and, once in charge, the new owners proved better at stripping assets and diddling the other shareholders than building real businesses. The richer ones sent their offspring to the grandest English schools, such as Eton and Winchester, and bought bolt-holes in London's most upmarket districts. Russian good-time girls started shunning the foreign clients they had once chased so assiduously; the rewards for bagging a rich compatriot were so much better.

The tycoons set up institutions that they called "banks," but which would have been better described as a mixture of personal piggy banks, pyramid schemes, and bureaux de change. The boring business of making sensible loans to dependable borrowers, or competing for savers' cash by offering convenience and good service, was featured only for cosmetic reasons. In the 1998 financial crash, these "banks" mostly disappeared, along with their deposits. The nascent Russian middle class had lost their savings yet again: In 1991 it was to inflation, this time to fraud and incompetence.

Putin's single biggest achievement is that this crisis—against many expectations at the time—proved only a temporary setback. For all his attacks on other freedoms, he has preserved the ones that the "new Russians" most care about. More than ever before Russians can plan their lives: they can save, educate themselves, travel, and bring up their children as they like; they can buy anything they can afford, own property at home or abroad, worship (mostly) as they wish, read almost anything they like; they can even live according to their sexual preference (if not always publicly). Though they lack the freedom to choose their elected representatives, to organize publicly to influence their government, or to change their political systems, never in Russian history have so many Russians lived so well and so freely. That is a proud boast, and one that even those who dislike Russia's current path must honestly acknowledge.

The most significant changes are in the core middle-class preoccupations of travel, education, and entertainment. Private cars used to be a luxury in the Soviet Union. In 1993 there were 59 per thousand people. That figure has since risen fivefold. Around 15 percent of all Russians have been abroad at least once—something that would have been all but inconceivable in Soviet times. Indeed, Russians have become the ninth biggest spenders in the world on tourism. Hundreds of thousands go to Europe to shop, study, and relax. Russians took 1.47 million trips to Turkey in 2006; 900,000 went to Egypt (in both countries visas are available to Russians on arrival). Russians feel linked to the outside world in a way that their Soviet predecessors never were. Whereas once the international departure lounge of Moscow's Sheremetyevo airport was a sanctum for the elite, now dozens of airports all over Russia offer cheap and frequent travel abroad for any customer who can afford it.

For all but the very brightest in the Soviet Union, access to good education depended on parents' connections. Despite the communist system's egalitarian rhetoric, higher education in particular was highly elitist—well under a third of the 18-plus age group went to university. Now the figure is nearly 80 percent. At the good universities corruption is endemic both to get in and to get a good grade. Political connections (such as a job in a pro-Kremlin youth movement) may mean that you get higher education free of charge, or get in more easily. For those without such connections, costs at the best universities are soaring: Moscow State University used to cost $2,000 for a year's tuition; in 2007 it was $6,000. In some institutions, studying law or business can cost the equivalent of an American $40,000. Elsewhere, the quality of the teaching is often far lower than in Soviet days. The qualifications offers may be Mickey Mouse affairs such as diplomas in "marketing and international PR" involving often only part-time study. But the doors are not barred to anyone.

The life of the mind is still limited by politics, but only partially. Putin has not blocked the emergent middle class from outside intellectual life. It is true that the Kremlin's internal propaganda machine swamps most outside influences—but that reflects also Russians' own preferences. The Internet remains largely uncensored[9] for any Russian with the time to browse it (7% of Russian adults use it daily, 17% once a week and 22% at least once a month; in the last two years the number of Russian citizens with access to a computer at home has risen from 14% to 25%). Those that want to listen to foreign radio stations can still do so, at least on crackly, cumbersome short-wave receivers,[9] or online. If bookshops do not stock politically controversial material, it can be ordered from ozon, Russia's equivalent of Amazon. Small-circulation newspapers and magazines still write largely what they want; *Ekho Moskvy* [Echo of Moscow], the sole remaining independent domestic radio station, remains a symbolic trophy of media freedom.

The bourgeoisie that enjoys this lifestyle is small by the standards of advanced industrialized countries, in which a majority of the population typically describes itself as "middle class," but it is certainly growing. The Kremlin reckons that what it calls the middle class (those earning a monthly salary of $900-$1,100) will make up 35 percent of Russia's population by 2010. That is up from 20 percent in 2006, and from only 16.5 percent who identified themselves in this category in 2003. The consolidation of the middle class is creating a social force, albeit so far a politically passive one, that Russia has never had in its history, and its future political behavior is the biggest question facing the country. A big middle class may not be a sufficient condition for political freedom and pluralism, but it seems to be a necessary one. So far, Russia's new bourgeoisie strongly supports the status quo, but when (or if) it begins to chafe at lawlessness, corruption, and other ills it may demand more freedom and tolerance. The evidence so far, though, is that prosperity correlates with what might be called "soft nationalism"—the number of people who want "Russia for the ethnic Russians" is highest in the most advanced and prosperous cities: Moscow and St. Petersburg. Dmitri Polikanov, one of Russia's top pollsters, argues that as Russians become richer, they need something beside money to gain respect: that, he argues, increasingly seems to come from ethnic status.

While the middle class gets richer, the workers are not doing badly either. Not only has real disposable income doubled; unemployment, the great curse of Russia in the first 15 years of transition, is down to a largely fictitious 7 percent. Employers complain of labor shortages. It is no exaggeration to say that any Russian who is not a drunkard (and some that are) can find work. That appeals to the "old Russians": the losers of the 1990s, those senior in years, poorer in incomes, and more backward in outlook. Their wages and pensions are paid punctually. Employers have to offer better terms than ever before. A bloated public sector offers a safe, undemanding, and increasingly well-paid life for those prepared to stomach the necessary political compromises. For such Russians life has turned full circle from the Soviet era, for which they are thankful.

Russian capitalism is not Western capitalism: connections matter more, and laws matter less. Improvements have been infuriatingly slow and patchy. Many of the promises of Putin's first term have not been fulfilled. Public services are still dreadful, especially in rural areas. More out of fear than generosity, the governments have only trimmed the country's sprawling and inefficient network of social benefits, such as subsidized housing. But small businesses are still waiting for their "one-stop-shop." Interaction with the legal system threatens normal life, rather than safeguarding it. Despite cosmetic changes and paper reforms, bureaucracy remains a huge burden for households and businesses.[10] State ownership is growing not shrinking. But for such failings disgruntled Russians tend to not to blame Putin. Polls show most Russians think that the government is doing a bad job, while giving high approval ratings to the president.

For all that, modern Russia is a country in which it is possible for a private citizen to dream about personal fulfillment through brains and hard work. The promise of a prosperous and civilized life began in the Gorbachev and Yeltsin eras, but for many Russians, it has only become a reality under Putin. As a result, even the most self-consciously modern "New Russians" are proud of their country and mostly regard criticism with a mixture of irritation and bewilderment. Surely, they ask, this is just Western ignorance and hypocrisy? Why are we not being praised for our progress, rather than nagged about our shortcomings? Despite all the West's blunders, Russia has constantly extended the hand of friendship. It has cooperated with NATO on terrorism and closed down Russia's Cold War bases in Vietnam and Cuba. Not only are relations with many European countries (such as Germany) excellent, but Russia is respected and admired in much of the rest of the world for its ability to carve its own foreign-policy course. The criticism says more about the critics than Russian reality. If relations with America are frosty, the blame for that lies mainly in Washington, D.C., not in Moscow. It is the Americans' fault if they incite their puppet states such as Estonia, Georgia, and Poland to get on Russia's nerves. And it is Britain's fault if it harbors traitors, terrorists, and fraudsters. Modern-minded Russians regret the occasional chilly episodes in their foreign policy, but they do not take them too seriously. After all, they reason, what the West really cares about is business, and on that score Russia can't be ignored for long.

So much for the winners of the Putin years. But what of the losers? One clear category is the mafia. It was already retreating toward the end of the Yeltsin era. Now it has been squeezed out of the extortion business by a newly confident state. Amateur gangsters are no match for those who have the might of officialdom behind them. Small businesses still need to pay protection money to their *krysha* [protection; literally, "roof"] but this is far more likely to be to a powerful local politician or official than a swaggering thug in a shiny tracksuit and leather jacket. Clever gangsters have become respectable businessmen or public officials. The stupid ones have retreated back to the fringes of the economy. That change makes life more predictable, but not necessarily more comfortable, for legitimate enterprise. Instead of a rake-off from the profits, the new state-run mafia may demand a share in the business. If the owner refuses, he can lose everything overnight. For those with big businesses, the Putin Kremlin has brought more risk than reward. Prosperity means a larger cake—but only if you are entitled to a slice. The price of failure is now jail, exile, or assassination, while only total obedience to the Kremlin guarantees survival. The wise tycoon now portrays himself as a well-remunerated steward of the nation's wealth rather than its proprietor. The prime example of this is Oleg Deripaska, who interrupted his physics studies in 1990 to go into business. He became a billionaire in Russia's terrifyingly competitive aluminum industry and married a close relative of the Yeltsin family. "If the state says we need to give it up, we'll give it up," he said in mid-2007. "I don't separate myself from the state. I have no other interests."

The first victim of the Kremlin's squeeze was Vladimir Gusinsky, Russia's biggest media tycoon. His empire produced most of Russia's best-quality broadcast journalism—albeit under strong political direction from the top. Having strongly opposed the first Chechen war, Gusinsky's news coverage then swung unflinchingly behind Yeltsin in the 1996 election. This was the time when the newly free Russian media sold its soul: Believing that it was vitally important to keep the old communist guard out of power, the first generation of independent journalists in Russia's history produced—without much central direction—a public-relations blitz worthy of the most ardent Soviet propagandist. Though gravely ill, Yeltsin rose from seemingly hopeless unpopularity to beat his communist challenger, Zyuganov. The cause was perhaps noble. The means were anything but. Two years later, Gusinsky's main outlet, the television channel NTV, switched sides again, excoriating the Yeltsin Kremlin for weakness and corruption and supporting Luzhkov, who had his sights set on the presidency. (The Moscow mayor's energetic and hands-on approach to municipal capitalism made some term him an unlikely person to champion clean government.) Its punchy Sunday night political program, *Itogi* [Summary of Events] was often outrageously biased and sententious, although still an unmissable part of the week for anyone interested in politics. Its business coverage seemed to sway according to who was paying (or who was refusing to pay). Though it would have been too kind to call NTV independent in the full sense of the word, it was at least independent of the Kremlin. For those optimistic about Russia's future, NTV looked the most likely candidate to evolve eventually into a respectable channel where professional journalists would broadcast dispassionate news.

Though the Gusinsky media empire had disliked Putin from the start, few thought it would experience serious problems. Its satirical puppet show, *Kukly,* ridiculed him[11]—but every other politician in Russia, including Yeltsin, got similar treatment. Its commentators lambasted Putin over the authorities' response to the sinking of the *Kursk* submarine, and its journalists investigated the Ryazan bombing. But in a country where the state had enforced a monopoly on all information for seven decades, the freedom of even an imperfect media was treasured. That had been one of the few consistently commendable features of the Yeltsin era. Surely under Putin, the authorities would continue to be cautious in dealing with the country's top independent television station? Not a bit of it. Not only did the Kremlin order *Kukly* to stop making fun of the head of state, but, in the spring and summer of 2000, Gusinsky's offices were repeatedly raided by different law enforcement agencies on allegations that seemed either selective or invented. On June 13th he was arrested and spent several days in one of Moscow's most notorious prisons. A month later, he struck a deal with the government under which he would sell his media company to Gazprom. He then moved to Israel, eventually setting up a satellite channel, NTV+, that—for those able to watch it—is now Russia's only independent national broadcaster. Some of NTV's best journalists left; others were fired; a few switched sides. Some refugees from NTV moved to two small independent channels, TV-S and TV–6; both were shut down in the course of the next two years. Many of them now work at REN-TV, a channel with limited reach that has retained some independence. Now NTV, now named RTV, pumps out much the same mixture of apolitical entertainment and Kremlin propaganda as its supposed competitors.

Boris Berezovsky, the manic manipulator of Russian politics, was the second target. To many Russians he symbolized the looting and influence peddling that had characterized the Yeltsin era. Starting as a car dealer, he had acquired an oil company, a television channel, and control of the foreign-currency revenues of Russia's national airline, Aeroflot. He was so powerful in the late 1990s that for some time he had an office adjoining that of Chernomyrdin, the then prime minister. A close associate of the Yeltsin family, Chernomyrdin played a crucial (and still unclear) role in brokering

Putin's rise to power. But in the summer of 2000, Putin unleashed the prosecutor's office on him too. Berezovsky responded toughly, claiming that dictatorship was looming. Few wanted to listen. Within a few months, he had lost his most important assets. His television channel, ORT, was back in government control. Prosecutors and accountants were poring over the books at Aeroflot. His control over his oil company, Sibneft, had shriveled. Berezovsky moved to London where he gained political asylum. Some wondered why the British government allowed such a controversial figure to take up residence in the capital; that question was posed more sharply when the Russian authorities began demanding his extradition. The most likely answer is that it was a quid pro quo for Berezovsky's efforts in 1998 to bring about the release of two British citizens who had been kidnapped in Chechnya.

It was hard to sympathize greatly with Berezovsky. From a journalistic point of view he was an excellent source, often willing to chat in his rapid sibilant Russian, or his confident but eccentric English, at his ludicrously luxurious private club in downtown Moscow. But the fact remained that at every company he touched the other shareholders, employees, and customers tended to curse his name. He said he had fallen foul of a monster that fused political ambition and business greed, using the dirty tricks of the intelligence-service world. If so, could equally be argued that it was one that he had himself created and which he epitomized. Once based overseas, Berezovsky's mystique evaporated. His public pronouncements were increasingly shrill. He became politically toxic: An association with him might mean some extra cash but it spelled doom for anyone wanting a political future in Russia.

The other oligarchs dived for cover, offering fulsome political compliments to Putin and pledging to shun all involvement in political opposition. Only Mikhail Khodorkovsky, the founder and main shareholder of the Yukos oil company, was prepared to stand up to the Kremlin. His company was the best-run of all the Russian business empires. It had a controversial and even (some said) bloody start. Outside shareholders who had bought minority stakes in its production subsidiaries complained furiously that they had been cheated. Shareholders' meetings were shifted to remote locations at short notice, where the agenda and votes were rigged to produce decisions of outrageous unfairness. Some talked of more brutal means: A mayor and an oil refinery manager who had obstructed the company's rise had both met early deaths (Khodorkovsky vehemently denied involvement in either case). But the most interesting thing about Yukos was not its history—unexceptional by Russian standards—but the direction it was going. After the 1998 crash it had started cleaning up its accounts, brought in foreign managers and independent board directors, and replaced clunky and wasteful Soviet-era habits and technology with the most modern foreign expertise and equipment. At its peak, Yukos alone was producing 2 percent of global oil output. Compared to other Russian businesses, it was a model corporate citizen. Yukos paid $1.9 billion in taxes in 2000—more than the entire firm was worth at the time of privatization five years earlier. Khodorkovsky donated heavily to charities in both Russia and abroad, from Omsk to Oxford. For those who believed that Russia's robber barons were going to go from banditry to respectability in a generation, Khodorkovsky, the richest man in Russia and the 16th-richest in the world, was a shining example.[12]

Yet his strength was undermined by overconfidence. Khodorkovsky was not only publicly at odds with the Kremlin on issues such as the Iraq war (which he backed) and friendly relations with America (ditto), but his beneficence, official and unofficial, had begun to create menacing political clout. Hundreds of members of both houses of the parliament, plus senior officials and government ministers, were all heavily influenced in their decision making by the attentive generosity of the Khodorkovsky empire. By the standards of past years, that was nothing special. Every rich Russian had a payroll, and the bigger the coffers, the more impressive the help it bought. But this was a new era: Putin was not willing to tolerate any competitor for power, and particularly not one with grand plans in energy, foreign policy, and domestic politics. Khodorkovsky's preparations to build an independent export pipeline threatened the vital Kremlin monopoly on oil exports. The trigger may have been Khodorkovsky's plan to merge with Sibneft, another Russia oil giant, and then bring in an American energy company as a big strategic investor in the new firm. His company would gain not only expertise and commercial clout, but also heavyweight political insurance from America. If it went ahead, Khodorkovsky would be close to invulnerable. The Kremlin started firing warning shots, arresting a close colleague of his, and giving unmistakable signs of its discontent. Khodorkovsky countered with a well-publicized tour to meet regional leaders in eastern Russia. The Kremlin took that as a declaration of war. It was a war Khodorkovsky could only lose.

On October 25, 2003, Khodorkovsky's private jet landed for refueling at Novosibirsk airport in Siberia. Masked FSB agents stormed the plane, confiscated his bodyguards' weapons, and arrested him. He was taken to a prison in Moscow and charged with fraud and tax evasion. For Yukos's shareholders, including many Westerners, the bonanza of the past years turned to disaster. The company's share price tumbled as it was looted by its state-backed rivals, with its key assets sold off in order to pay gigantic tax bills. However fast Yukos tried to raise the money, the authorities increased the amount of tax due, while setting impossible deadlines for payment. On April 14, 2004, for example, the authorities insisted that Yukos pay $3.5 billion in unpaid taxes by the end of the day.[13] Bailiffs then froze Yukos' shares in Yuganskneftegaz, its main production unit. Yukos's assets were sold at knockdown prices to companies close to the Kremlin. On December 19, for example, the Russian authorities auctioned a 76.79 percent share in Yuganskneftegaz in order to recover what was now an alleged $28 billion in unpaid taxes. Western companies boycotted that auction, as Yukos had filed for bankruptcy in America and said it would sue anyone who took part in grabbing its assets. Only two companies took part, a Gazprom subsidiary and a previously unknown company, Baikalfinansgrup. The latter won, with a bid worth nearly $9.4 billion, barely half the $17 billion at which Yuganskneftegaz had been valued earlier in the year. Baikalfinansgrup had been registered only two weeks previously with a share capital of 10,000 rubles ($358.00) in a small office building in a provincial city. Despite this, it was able to borrow $1.7 billion from Sberbank, a state-owned financial institution, in order to pay the deposit needed to take part in the auction. Four days later, it was acquired by Rosneft.

In May 2005 Khodorkovsky was sentenced to a nine-year jail term[14] for fraud and other offences, which he is serving at one of the country's most remote prisons near the Chinese border in eastern Russia, an eight-hour drive from the nearest airport.[15] The fire sale of Yukos's assets has continued. Sometimes this involves the collusion of international energy companies who turn up to take part but not to win, or who win the asset only to sell it on to Gazprom. For smaller assets, the rigging is even more blatant. In July 2007, for example, Rosneft bought Yukos's transport subsidiaries, which chiefly owned leasing contracts on railway oil tankers, plus pumping stations and pipelines. The only other company at the auction, an unknown company called Benefit, pulled out of the auction after Rosneft's first bid. The next month, an unknown firm called Promneftestroi snapped up Yukos's overseas assets for $306 million in an auction in which only one other company, equally obscure, took part. Rosneft said before the auction that it was connected with Promneftestroi; afterward it said it had been misinformed and had no link with the company.

Any company that buys Yukos assets without Kremlin permission, by contrast, is asking for trouble. A salutary example of that came from the crushing of Russneft (confusingly named, but no relation to Rosneft), an oil producer controlled by Mikhail Gutseriyev, a pioneer of Russian business in the early 1990s with strong ties to Chechnya. After Russneft acquired, indirectly, some Yukos assets, a court froze all shares in the company. Gutseriyev became the subject of criminal proceedings and fled the country but vehemently maintains his innocence. His company, worth up to $9 billion, is set to be acquired for around $4.5 billion by Deripaska, the Kremlin's favorite oligarch, who will presumably pass it on to Rosneft. In a revealing moment, Gutseriyev denounced his "unprecedented hounding" by the Russian authorities, which included regulatory harassment of the company, a tax probe and criminal charges. "They made me an offer to leave the oil business, to leave 'on good terms.' I refused. Then, they tightened the screws," he complained. But within hours he had recanted, removing from the company's Web site the page bearing his protest and insisting that he was selling his company entirely voluntarily. After his son died in an unexplained car accident, Gutseriyev fled to Britain.

At the time, it seemed as though this assault on property rights would discredit Putin's style of Russian capitalism in the eyes of outsiders. But it proved just a blip. In the tussle between greed and fear, greed won. As the Russian stock market resumed its jet-propelled ascent, foreign investment, both direct and indirect, continued to pour in. Yukos was an "exception," seasoned Russia-watchers explained. This was what happened to a business whose boss made a direct political challenge to the Kremlin; nobody would be so foolish as to do that in future. The oligarchs were certainly a deserving target, and Khodorkovsky's past was packed with unanswered questions. But the attack on Yukos was outrageously selective. Its tax-avoidance schemes, based on the use of tax holidays awarded by regions trying to attract investment, were certainly ingenious. Any government would have been justified in scrutinizing them carefully, and probably closing them promptly. But other companies had used similar schemes without attracting official displeasure. And the calculations of unpaid taxes were exorbitant. The amount the government claimed it was owed for 2003 was, according to Yukos, 111 percent of the company's entire revenue. Companies that the Kremlin favors seem to get away with paying far lower taxes: Gazprom, for example, had revenues of $28 billion in 2003 and paid a tax bill of a mere $4 billion. The Russian state had other means of ensuring that citizens regained what they had lost in the looting and chaos of the 1990s. It could have renationalized the oligarchs' empires and paid compensation, or levied a stiff windfall tax when the oil price started rising. Investors would have whined, but they would not have squealed murder. Instead, the Kremlin used the legal system to get what it wanted, sending a double message: These are our enemies, and these are the means we will use to attack them.

So by 2004 Putin had the media and business under his thumb. But other strands of power remained outside the Kremlin's grip. The elected chiefs of Russia's regions and republics[16] could still cite their own electoral mandate in disputes with the "center." Their clout dated from the 1990s, when Yeltsin had once promised Russia's provinces "as much sovereignty as you can swallow." That experiment in ultra-federalism had been a disaster: in a strong Western country such as Canada or Germany, powerful regions such as Quebec or Bavaria may reasonably run their own affairs. But Russian officialdom's desire for extra revenues, private and official, multiplied with each layer of government. The single market became balkanized, with each region passing its own laws and regulations. At times of crisis, such as after the 1998 crash, some regions even restricted "exports" to the rest of Russia. In the Urals, there was even talk of a separate currency, supposedly to be more reliable than the ruble. The bigger and more powerful provinces, such as Tatarstan, started opening "embassies" abroad.

Putin had witnessed this—and disliked it intensely—while working in the Yeltsin Kremlin. As president, he moved swiftly to reestablish the center's political authority, thickening the sinews of power: the prosecutors, FSB, tax police, and interior ministry troops. After 2002 no regional leader challenged Putin head-on. But they could still ignore him. "Russia is big, and the Czar is faraway" is an old Russian proverb. Only under totalitarianism, it seemed, could the Kremlin reasonably hope to control life in the provinces tightly. But that changed in September 2004, when Russia suffered one of its worst terrorist attacks. Fighters proclaiming support for Chechen independence took hostage hundreds of children, parents, and teachers at a school in Beslan, North Ossetia. An anti-terrorist operation killed 334 of the hostages, including 186 children. In some countries, that would have prompted a bout of anguished official soul-searching. Chechnya clearly had not been "pacified" as the

Kremlin claimed. And why had the authorities proved so incompetent? They were unable, for example, even to cordon the school off properly. Many witnesses say they saw tanks fire shells into the school, contributing to the massacre; the hostage-takers' own explosives did not seem to explain the damage caused to the building. The authorities seemed unprepared to put out the fires that raged through the building after it was stormed. Most puzzling of all, the attack was launched *after* agreement had been reached between the then Chechen rebel leader, Aslan Maskhadov, and the North Ossetian authorities, on negotiations to end the siege. Those questions, posed only by the muffled voices of the liberal opposition, and lone journalists such as Politkovskaya, never gained a hearing. An icily angry Putin gave one of his most revealing speeches. It started with a bout of nostalgia:

> Today we live in a time that follows the collapse of a vast and great state, a state that, unfortunately, proved unable to survive in a rapidly changing world. But despite all the difficulties, we were able to preserve the core of what was once the vast Soviet Union, and we named this new country the Russian Federation.

It continued by equating the terrorists with Russia's external "enemies," not only in the East, but—for the first time—the West.

> [O]ur country, formerly protected by the most powerful defence system along the length of its external frontiers overnight found itself defenceless both from the east and the west . . . We showed ourselves to be weak. And the weak get beaten.
> Some would like to tear from us a "juicy piece of pie." Others help them. They help, reasoning that Russia still remains one of the world's major nuclear powers, and as such still represents a threat to them. And so they reason that this threat should be removed.[17]

Shortly afterward he announced new centralizing measures—planned some time previously—under which regional leaders would no longer be elected directly, but appointed by him and then endorsed by local assemblies. Every one of the special deals that Yeltsin had signed with 40 of Russia's 89 regions was cancelled.

The Kremlin is particularly nervous about the 20-odd republics that are the nominal homelands of the country's indigenous non-Slavic peoples. It remembers how "nationalism" in the Baltic states and elsewhere broke up the Soviet Union. A decade of separatist conflict in Chechnya raises the specter of the same in other parts of the Russian Federation.[18] Many of the country's minorities have ethnic cousins abroad, most of whom are Russia's historic or even current adversaries. The Tatars and other Turkic minorities for example, look to Turkey, once a superpower that reached deep into central Asia. Finno-Ugric minorities in places such as Komi, Mari-El, Karelia, and Mordovia have linguistic and cultural ties ranging from the strong to vestigial with Estonia (described by many Russians as their country's main enemy), Finland, and Hungary. All or any of these can easily be seen as a fifth column. Oil-rich Tatarstan, home of the country's second-largest ethnic group after Russians themselves, had reintroduced the Latin alphabet in place of Cyrillic for writing the local language, a close relative of Turkish. That makes linguistic sense (Cyrillic works well for consonant-rich Slavic languages, but mangles almost all others). But it was quickly prohibited by Putin.[19] It was not until 2007 that Tatarstan, after lengthy and expensive lobbying, won back some symbolic autonomy. A handful of other republics may now get the same treatment: limited self-rule in return for unflinching loyalty. In others, local activists expect only continuing repression and mergers with other local-government entities that will further dilute their already battered ethnic and linguistic identity. Pro-Kremlin local leaders in most of these places are therefore cutting back language teaching in the native tongues, discouraging ties with ethnic cousins abroad, and cracking down on anyone seeking even the mildest forms of autonomy. As in Soviet times, Russians see their language as the gateway to world culture for those unfortunate enough to grow up speaking gobbledygook from the boondocks. Few remember the genocidal effect of Russian rule as it spread east two centuries ago; nor do they remember the especial severity of Stalinist repressions on the Soviet Union's minorities.

Such historical amnesia is a hallmark of Putin's approach and part of the secret of its appeal. It pleases both the "new Russians" of the emergent middle class and the "old Russians" from the parts of society left behind by the wrenching changes of the past two decades. Though Putin's nostalgia for the Soviet Union strikes many outside Russia as baffling and offensive, many Russians feel that the Soviet Union was a time of great national achievement, and are baffled that anyone would object to it (even among young Russians, more than 60% agreed with their president that its collapse was a catastrophe). When they see their president being tough with the West, they feel proud.

It was possible to argue that all this was necessary. Only a tough leader could run Russia. After the anarchy of the Yeltsin years, it was time for discipline. The Russian people needed time to get used to a market economy and it was vital that they equated it with rising living standards and stability, not the looting and chaos of the 1990s. On foreign policy, the West could not expect Russia to be perpetually friendly and accommodating. Putin needed to act tough, at least for internal consumption, but this could be set aside as mere posturing: On all vitally important questions, such as in dealing with Islamic extremism or nuclear proliferation, the West and Russia were on the same side. In short, if Putin cut some corners, it was in a good cause. By 2008, the Russian political system would be "consolidated." Putin would step down and be replaced by a freely chosen successor, in accordance with the Russian constitution. But those corners have been cut not in a good cause, but a bad one. It is not only that the 2008 election showed not the slightest sign of being an open, fair, or free contest. The next chapter will examine the decline of political freedom in the Putin years in more detail and will show the mechanics of Russia's move from anarchy to authoritarianism— and how that trajectory is continuing.

CHAPTER THREE

SINISTER PRETENSE

The Kremlin's Use of State Power against Dissent

Vladimir Putin's personal popularity is by far the most important feature of Russian politics. It started high and has stayed there ever since. No Russian politician has ever enjoyed so much public support for so long. By the country's dismal demographic standards (the male life expectancy is 59), the president, who turned 56 in October 2008, is in tip-top condition, glad to strip to the waist to reveal his toned torso in carefully posed holiday pictures, or to appear in military uniform and in manly pursuits such as skiing. Unlike most Russian men, he is abstemious and uxorious. In 2002 an all-female pop group called Singing Together had a hit song with the revealing lyrics: "I want a man who doesn't drink, doesn't smoke and doesn't beat me. I want a man like Putin."[1] Though the personality cult is pervasive, it is also subtle and officially discouraged. Putin's daily doings may lead the evening news but the coverage is usually appreciative rather than outright sycophantic.[2] Even now, eight years after he first came to political power, no statues of Putin decorate Russia's squares; no streets or ships are named after him.[3]

Putin claims to be a democrat, comparing himself, seemingly without irony, to Mahatma Gandhi. Putin is certainly like the Indian leader in one respect: He enjoys his popularity, while feigning modesty. But the resemblance ends there. India's political system has put down deep roots since independence, not just in the formal business of counting votes fairly in freely contested elections, but in building the institutions and habits that make a country law-governed and its rulers accountable. Russia's attempt to create something similar, by contrast, has grown into a monstrous sham. The system is not avowedly dictatorial. Opposition parties are allowed to exist, albeit on the fringes of the political system. But they cannot demonstrate easily. They have no access to the media. In a free, law-governed country, the executive power is checked and balanced from all sides: by elected representatives, by the media, by public organizations, and by the judiciary. All these—almost everything that could constrain the power of the Kremlin—are broken or co-opted. So too are the most fundamental political rights: free speech and free association of individuals. These are guaranteed by the Russian constitution; they flourished during the 1990s. But under Putin, they have shriveled.

The most shocking form of repression is the forcible incarceration of critics in psychiatric hospitals. Along with the Gulag system of slave labor camps, the abuse of psychiatry was a hallmark of the Soviet system's degradation and intimidation of its own people.[4] Now it is creeping back. The authorities increasingly see dissent as a sign of impaired mental health: if most people are happy with their lives, and believe overwhelmingly Putin to be an almost godlike leader, surely only a mad person would challenge him—or, indeed, the system he heads. Albert Imendayev, a local politician in Cheboksary, a city on the Volga River, was planning to run in a local election in 2005. But, the day before he was due to register his candidacy, he was arrested and sent off to a psychiatric hospital for "evaluation." By the time he was released, nine days later, it was too late to register. Sometimes the authorities mix legal intimidation with psychiatric incarceration. Another politician in Cheboksary, Igor Molyakov, was serving a six-month sentence for libel in 2004. While in jail, he was sent to a psychiatric hospital on the grounds that his repeated complaints about corruption had made him insanely gloomy. On March 23, 2006 police raided the home of human rights activist Marina Trutko, breaking down her door, forcibly injected her with haloperidol (a antipsychotic drug), and taking her to a psychiatric hospital where she spent six weeks undergoing a daily regimen of injections and drugs to treat what doctors diagnosed as a "paranoid personality disorder." It was the third time that she had been forcibly treated. The first instance was in 2002 when she was incarcerated after a courtroom quarrel with a judge.

An anonymous Muscovite described by the pseudonym "Yelena" made the mistake of phoning a Duma deputy, Svetlana Savitskaya, at home, asking for her email address.[5] Savitskaya did not like this lesson in the duties of representative government and said that she would complain to the police or have the caller consigned to an asylum. Undeterred, "Yelena" dropped off a book by George Soros and a CD of Tibetan music with the concierge at Savitskaya's home address. She phoned Savitskaya to see if the package had been delivered. Savitskaya again complained about the phone call. "Yelena" then tried to deliver some more material, including articles from the press and her own thoughts about the KGB and Stalin. When she rang the doorbell, Savitskaya had the guards eject her from the building. Continuing a pattern of what might well be characterized as eccentric or even tiresome behavior, "Yelena" then wrote to Tatyana Dmitriyeva, the director of Russia's main hospital for psychiatric medicine, describing her experience with Savitskaya. She received a brush-off reply. She sent repeated emails and finally managed to telephone her at home. Dmitriyeva complained to the police, who visited "Yelena" and warned her to desist. No criminal case was brought. So far, so normal, perhaps: Important people everywhere dislike being pestered by the public and they may even complain to the police about it. But after "Yelena" attempted to approach Dmitriyeva at a public meeting, she found herself taken to the "acute section" of a psychiatric hospital. She told a doctor she was there against her will, but a judicial hearing ruled against her, and she spent the next ten weeks incarcerated. Indeed, Ms. Dmitriyeva says that 'Yelena' tried to attack her. But to be locked up and forcibly medicated looks like the application of a Soviet-era penalty in the twenty-first century.

The most alarming recent case came in mid-2007 in Murmansk, with the forcible incarceration and medication of an opposition activist, Larisa Arap. Arap was not only involved in the opposition group led by the chess champion Garry Kasparov, the United Civic Front, but had also campaigned against the sexual abuse of minors in psychiatric care. Arap wanted to renew her driving license, and—as is normal in Russia's bureaucracy-driven system—had to get a medical note confirming that she was in good physical and mental health. But when the doctor at her local clinic noticed her name, he asked if she had been responsible for an article in a local opposition newspaper claiming that psychiatric patients had been raped. When she confirmed this, he called the police, who took her to a psychiatric hospital 100 miles from her hometown. She was given medication against her will, and started a hunger strike. After 46 days, and following an energetic campaign by allies in Russia and abroad, she was released.

The legal framework that governs the use of psychiatry in law enforcement has been changed to a dangerous degree. Only psychiatrists from a special state-recognized register are allowed to give expert testimony. The rights of those forcibly consigned to psychiatric hospitals have been reduced. FSB interrogations of those with unusual religious beliefs increasingly include the presence of psychiatrists and involve medical-style questioning. The Moscow Helsinki Group, Russia's best-known human rights organization, says "everything is in place" for a return to Soviet-style punitive psychiatry[6]. So far, psychiatric abuse is not a carefully calibrated means of repression as it was then. Local officials and medical staff categorically deny any politicization of their actions and say that the treatment of these cases was in each case justified on medical criteria. However, if such practices are returning even occasionally, it is a dismal echo of a disgraceful past.

Far more systematic is the use of other forms of state power against political critics. Gorbachev freed the last Soviet political prisoners in 1988, starting an era of freedom that lasted barely a decade. Now Russia has at least a dozen. The best known was Mikhail Trepashkin, a lawyer and former FSB officer who bravely but unwisely tried to investigate the apartment bombings of September 1999. He had first come to public attention, along with Litvinenko, in a group of FSB malcontents that appeared on television in late 1998 to complain about corruption and murder plots within the organization. He was invited to start his investigation by Sergei Kovalev, a saintly ex-dissident who became the best-known human-rights campaigner in Russia's parliament. Trepashkin became convinced that the evidence surrounding the bombings was being doctored to divert attention from the real culprits: the FSB. But on October 22, 2003, a week before he was due to present his findings, he was arrested, and then in 2004 sentenced to jail for disclosing official secrets. Amnesty International made him a prisoner of conscience.[7] He was released November 2007.

Other political prisoners include two men accused of espionage: Igor Sutyagin and Valentin Danilov. Both men were academics who had passed information to foreigners, in Sutyagin's case to a shadowy and now-vanished outfit working out of rented offices in London that seems highly likely to have been a front for a foreign intelligence service. But in neither instance was it proved that any of the material was secret. Sutyagin admitted providing the information, which consisted of compiling a press review about military and foreign-policy affairs. After a closed trial, he received a sentence of 15 years of hard labor. Danilov had provided information that was declassified in 1992. He received a 14-year sentence. Both cases have been taken up by Amnesty International, as well as other international human-rights campaigners. Whether to count Khodorkovsky as a political prisoner is much debated,[8] but the persecution of Svetlana Bakhmina, a lawyer formerly working for him, is a clear scandal. A mother of two children then aged two and six, she was arrested early in the morning of December 7, 2004 and was sentenced to a seven-year term for embezzlement in a high-security penal colony. The company she supposedly defrauded, then a subsidiary of Yukos, said it has no complaint about her actions.

Unlike in Soviet times, the Kremlin does not need to jail all its enemies. The effect of cases like these is chilling. If you talk to foreigners, be careful: you risk being charged with espionage. If you work for a business that is at odds with the Kremlin, switch sides quick: otherwise you may end up like Mrs. Bakhmina. Many cases of harassment involve arrests after which charges are never brought, or petty fines for "hooliganism" and other charges. In mid-April 2007, for example, opposition activists tried to hold "dissenters' marches" in Moscow and St. Petersburg. The authorities reacted by restricting travel to and within both cities, breaking up the protests violently, and detaining hundreds of participants. Journalists were also arrested; 30 were beaten. Two months later, a court in Moscow fined one of the organizers, Kasparov, for "marching in a large group of people and shouting anti-government slogans." Two weeks later, the authorities confiscated 52,000 copies of an opposition newspaper's special edition on the protests.

In March 2007 a small group of human rights, environmental, and conservation campaigners tried to hold a "march of dissent" in Russia's third-largest city, Nizhny Novgorod.[9] Among their slogans were "Give Nizhny Novgorod back to the people!" and "Give us back freedom of speech!" The authorities initially said the march was illegal. When that tactic failed, they said the march would be considered trespassing. Then the organizers received home visits and phone calls from officials and unidentified figures telling them to cancel it. Journalists received similar warning phone calls telling them not to cover the march, and demanding that they share with the authorities any details they knew about it. People handing out leaflets advertising the march were arrested. Some were locked up for several days, and threatened with being put in cells with common criminals who would mutilate them. Students and teachers at local high schools were warned not to join the march.[10] From the authorities' point of view, the precautions worked well. A mere 200 people turned up, to find an estimated 3,000 interior ministry paramilitaries on the site, and many more flanking the outer rings of the city. Arrests started immediately, with participants being snatched from the crowd and dragged to the waiting police buses. Those roughed up included foreign journalists. Yet protests from the outside world were muted to the point of inaudibility.[11] Kasparov, a marginal figure who hardly presents a serious challenge to any candidate with Kremlin backing, fell foul of the authorities again when he tried to lead a protest at Russia's summit with the European Union (EU) in Samara in May 2007. He and his aides were prevented from traveling there, on the curious excuse that their air tickets might have been forged. Kasparov, a multi-millionaire who has lived for many years in America, immediately offered to buy replacement tickets. But this was not permitted. Instead, their passports were confiscated. They were returned only after the last plane had left.

Such simple bureaucratic harassment is often enough to disrupt protests and deter participants. But the most formidable weapon in the Kremlin's arsenal is charges of "extremism." In a parody of the rule of law elsewhere, Russia is steadily expanding the legal basis for state violence. On July 8, 2006, the Duma passed a law criminalizing extremism, giving the president the authority to secretly give orders to the FSB to assassinate "extremists" at home and abroad. But who is an "extremist"? The broad definition includes "those causing mass disturbances, committing hooliganism or acts of vandalism"; creating and distributing "extremist" material are criminal offences. So are "slandering an official of the Russian Federation," "hampering the lawful activity of state organizations," and "humiliating national pride." Criminalizing extremism is thus a useful tool for silencing both individuals and the media that report their doings: with a second violation of the law on extremism media outlets lose their license. A new version of the law in 2007 cast the net even wider, adding crimes driven by "political, ideological or social hatred." Once organizations have been designated "extremist," the media may not even mention them without referring to the ban. Conveniently, those even suspected of extremism are banned from running for public office.

The scope this law gives to officials wanting to intimidate the Kremlin's critics is huge. Despite being owned by Gazprom, the radio station *Ekho Moskvy* has maintained its feisty journalistic tone. Its editor, Aleksei Venediktov, says that he will fire any staff he sees practicing self-censorship. It broadcasts interviews with hated figures such as Toomas Hendrik Ilves, the American-educated president of Estonia, and opposition leaders such as Kasparov. It is a refuge for independent-minded journalists who would scarcely gain airtime elsewhere, such as Yevgenia Albats and Yulia Latynina. But in just two months in 2007, *Ekho Moskvy* received 15 letters from prosecutors invoking the extremism law. Why was the station carrying interviews with such provocative figures? Why were Latynina's commentaries so provocative? Even an editor as gutsy as Venediktov, a hippyish workaholic with a burning faith in press freedom, may not withstand such pressure for long.[12]

Ultimately, bravery in the face of threats may be futile. The authorities can also intervene more directly, by encouraging a media outlet's owner to change the editor. In 2007, Abros, a bank with close ties to the Kremlin, bought a majority stake in REN TV, a minor but independent-minded channel, and promptly installed a new editor who had previously worked at the state-run broadcaster, VGTRK.[13] Print media has maintained more freedom, at least for low-circulation outlets such as Albats's *New Times*,[14] and the sometimes scandal-mongering biweekly that Anna Politkovskaya used to write for, *Novaya Gazeta* [New Newspaper].[15]

The chilly climate is bad for institutions, and worse for individuals. Andrei Piontkovsky is one of Russia's best-known commentators: A vehement critic of Putin and savagely dismissive of Boris Berezovsky and most of Russia's political and business leaders. He takes regular swipes at U.S. President George W. Bush, at the leaders of the EU, and at many others. But he is no mere gadfly. He is one of a handful of Russia's real specialists on issues of nuclear strategy, familiar with the intricacies of arms treaties and the technological difficulties of missile defense. Eloquent, witty, and well informed, he would be instantly recognizable in any Western country as a punchy, heavyweight public figure (and he regularly spends time as a visiting fellow at American think tanks). It is hard to imagine any free country that would not cherish his involvement in public life. Yet in mid-2007, he received two letters from prosecutors inviting him for an "explanatory chat." The authorities in the southern Russian region of Krasnodar, again invoking the "extremism" law, had charged the local Yabloko branch with extremism. The inventor of the television program *Kukly*, Viktor Shenderovich, is probably Russia's best-known satirist. Like many others from NTV, he took refuge at *Ekho*

Moskvy and started a successful blog. In 2007, he too got an intimidating visit from the prosecutors, who warned him that he was "inciting hatred."

In theory, print media is still free. You can start a newspaper without too much bureaucratic trouble and try to sell advertisements and copies. But without a powerful sponsor, it will soon go out of business. Take the example of the *New Times,* pretty much the only truly independent weekly left in Russia. Its founding editorial staff included two of the remaining leading lights of serious Russian journalism: Albats, the country's best investigative writer; and Raf Shakirov, fired from the editorship of *Izvestiya,* once a top Russian daily, for his stark coverage of the botched anti-terrorism operation in Beslan. Its website, for example, carries footage of the Kremlin's bully boys beating up opposition demonstrators—pictures that Russian television will scarcely touch. The weekly's publisher, Irena Lesnevskaya (who in her previous incarnation helped found REN TV), was told by a top Kremlin official that hiring Albats was a "mistake." Almost any other magazine in Russia would have hurried to correct the "mistake." Lesnevskaya politely refused. The result is that nobody wants to advertise there. Doing so would be commercial suicide in a business climate where official disfavor means harassment by every state agency, followed usually by bankruptcy.[16]

The best-informed journalists are at the greatest risk if they step out of line. Elena Trebugova, a journalist who covered the Kremlin intimately, published two gossipy books that included embarrassing portrayals of Putin and his closest aides. She narrowly escaped assassination and moved to London in 2007. Similarly, high-profile individuals such as Shenderovich and Piontkovsky can also expect an appreciative welcome in London, Washington, D.C., or Brussels if they need it. But for more minor figures, tangling with the authorities means professional suicide—or worse.

Among what purport to be the world's advanced industrialized countries, Russia is one of the most dangerous places for journalists. Since 1992, a total of forty-seven have been killed. Under Mr. Putin the trend has slackened: according to the New York-based Committee to Protect Journalists, fourteen journalists have been murdered and eight suspicious cases are under investigation. The deaths in the Yeltsin years were more numerous, but less systematic. Shortly before his death in July 2003 Shchekochikhin wrote: "Do not tell me fairy tales about the independence of judges . . . until we have fair trials, documents will be purged, witnesses intimidated or killed, and those who try to investigate will themselves be prosecuted."[17] Two of the paper's staff have received death threats since they started to investigate Politkovskaya's murder. Another journalist, Ivan Safronov, was probably Russia's best-known reporter of military affairs: tenacious, scrupulous, and well informed. A former colonel in the Strategic Rocket Forces, he had exposed the repeated failure of Russia's most important new missile, the Bulava, and was investigating corruption in the state-run arms export business. On March 2, 2007 he fell to his death from a window in his apartment block. The authorities speedily pronounced it a clear case of suicide. His friends and colleagues could see no reason why a man in the prime of life, happy both at home and at work, should kill himself. A more likely cause of death, they said, was a big scandal that he was investigating about arms sales to Iran and Syria.

Other victims include Vyacheslav Ifanov, a cameraman at an independent local television station in Siberia. His mutilated body was found in his garage on April 5, 2007; the authorities pronounced it suicide. Paul Klebnikov, an American reporter who ran the Russian-language edition of *Forbes* magazine, was shot dead in 2004. Yevgeny Gerasimenko, an investigative business reporter, was killed in Saratov in southern Russia in 2006. His head was tied in a plastic bag, and his body was bruised. An unnamed homeless man was charged with the murder and the case has been closed. Ilya Zimin, a television journalist working for NTV, was murdered on February 26, 2006 after what appears to have been a violent struggle.[18] Another case is that of Fatima Tlisova, a reporter for the Associated Press and other news organizations in the Caucasus. Her reporting has prompted repeated beatings and attempted poisonings, as well as harassment from the authorities. She says that men identifying themselves as FSB extinguished cigarettes on every finger of her right hand, telling her it was "so that you can write better.[19]" In 2006 her 16-year-old son was arrested as a sympathizer with the Chechen rebels. With her colleague Yuri Bagrov, she has successfully gained refugee status in the United States.

The message of all this is "Be quiet." If you annoy the rich and powerful you face threats, beatings, or death. Even when the Kremlin is not directly involved, its reaction to the persecution of journalists sends a clear message: If you offend the powerful, don't expect the law to protect you. In almost all cases, the investigation has been as fruitless and lackadaisical as it was in the Politkovskaya shooting.[20] As the independent voices fade, the official view becomes ever more dominant. On national television, which 90 percent of Russians say is their main source of news, editors receive weekly or even daily instructions from the Kremlin on the "line to take" on important stories.[21] By far the majority of airtime is devoted to entertainment, sports, and anodyne feature programs. Criticism of the authorities is allowed—but only within limits. Putin likes to blame shortcomings on incompetent politicians and officials, while remaining beyond reproach himself.

The most telling consequence of all this is not that Putin is so prominent, but that his rivals are out of sight. The presidential party United Russia (known as the party of power) is the only one that matters. It is a stripped down version of the Communist Party of the Soviet Union (CPSU), modified for the new conditions of sham political pluralism. Its camouflage suggests that power is flowing from the bottom up, yet the real aim is to transmit power downward. Most senior officials belong to the party. It wins almost every election it contests, but unlike the CPSU, whose "leading role" was entrenched in the constitution, its power is guaranteed by informal and bureaucratic means.

Without a free media and real scrutiny of Russia's leaders and their policies, it would be rash to take public assent for granted. In any case, turning public opinion into political results requires a system that allows the opposition to challenge the powers-that-be. Russian politics is rigged to make sure that doesn't happen. The electoral system systematically discriminates against outsiders. A change in the summer of 2001 made it impossible for unaffiliated individuals and informal groupings to take part in elections, and sharply toughened the criteria for party registration. Instead of 10,000 members, they now needed 50,000, with branches at least 500-strong in at least 45 of Russia's 85 regions. The new law also abolished single-mandate districts in Duma elections and raised the threshold for election from 5 percent to 7 percent. That made life almost impossible for small parties, especially those without rich backers. If the authorities would prefer that a candidate does not run for election, the signatures are "checked" and enough can be ruled invalid to create a "breach" of the "rules."[22] The worst recent example of this came in the March 2007 regional elections when the liberals of Yabloko were chucked off the ballot papers in St. Petersburg, Russia's most European city. That was where the party stood the best chance of winning some seats—something that the authorities, evidently, were not willing to tolerate.

Yet Yabloko and the others are not outlawed. If their activists are arrested, it is for minor public-order offences, not for treason. They face at most a night in the police cells, not a decade in a labor camp. Their biggest weakness is not that the authorities crush them, but that they are so unpopular to start with. From a technical point of view, the elections are well administered. But they are neither free nor fair. The main international monitors said that the 2004 presidential election:

> did not adequately reflect principles necessary for a healthy democratic election process: essential ... standards for democratic elections, such as a vibrant political discourse and meaningful pluralism, were lacking. The election process failed to meet important commitments concerning treatment by the State-controlled media on a non-discriminatory basis.[23]

That bland bureaucratic language hardly does justice to the extraordinary charade of Russia's electoral system. Putin won an overwhelming victory, with 71.2 percent of the vote, after he grandly declined to fight a conventional election campaign. He didn't need to: the entire weight of the state apparatus was deployed to discourage his opponents, promote his image, and secure the maximum result consistent with the appearance of respectability. The two real challengers, the independent liberal Irina Khakamada and the leftist-nationalist Sergei Glazyev, found that local bureaucrats repeatedly interfered with their election meetings. Typical tactics were surprise bomb scares, power cuts, or other bogus safety issues. Two supposed contenders actually supported Putin. One of them, the speaker of the upper house of parliament, explained his candidacy thus: "when a leader who is trusted goes into battle, he must not be left alone. One must stand beside him."[24] Yabloko boycotted the poll altogether, saying it was a farce.

Perhaps the most dangerous candidate from Putin's point of view was Ivan Rybkin, a former speaker of the Duma backed by the exiled Berezovsky. Rybkin kicked off his campaign with a full-page advertisement in a business daily, denouncing Putin as "the biggest oligarch in Russia." He claimed that the Kremlin was a criminal conspiracy, in which Roman Abramovich, one of Russia's most shadowy tycoons, was managing Putin's ever-expanding business interests. It is worth repeating that it would be unwise to take Berezovsky or his friends as champions of political freedom and clean government, and the system they are denouncing is one that they helped create. But the questions are still interesting. What are the business interests of Putin and his family? It would be astonishing if he had spent the 1990s in high office without amassing a considerable fortune.[25] No definitive proof has been presented of any wrongdoing and it may well be that Putin's austere public image is matched by private rectitude. But what is clear is that none of the scrutiny that a Western country at least tries to give to its rulers' finances applies to Putin. The mass media studiously ignored Rybkin's allegations. Two papers owned by Berezovsky reported them, as did *Novaya Gazeta*. The Kremlin did not bother with a denial, let alone a rebuttal. Similarly, serious allegations by Khakamada about the authorities' cover-up of their botched handling of a terrorist hostage taking at a theatre in the Dubrovka district of Moscow in 2002 were ignored. Like so many other incidents that have stoked public panic, and thus Putin's power and popularity, the storming of the theatre in which the authorities used an anaesthetic gas to kill hostage-takers and hostages alike, is surrounded by questions that the authorities show no inclination to answer.

What happened next to Rybkin seemed more like a badly plotted political thriller than an episode in an election campaign. The planned centerpiece of his campaign was the war in Chechnya. After one abortive session of negotiations with the rebel leadership at a Moscow airport in 2001, the Kremlin has maintained the line that the separatist forces can be beaten by force alone. Rybkin wanted to highlight the war's cost to Russia, tapping into the growing resentment of conscription and the poor treatment of veterans. He slipped out of Russia to meet the underground Chechen leadership. The initial rendezvous was to be in the Ukrainian capital, Kyiv. But on the way there Rybkin vanished. He appeared again five days later, in a confused state, claiming first to have taken a brief vacation, and saying that he had been in difficult talks. But in London, he told Berezovsky's aides that he had been drugged, and had woken up four days later to be shown a video of himself "made by perverts." Shortly after, he withdrew from the race. His friends say he was given the psychotropic drug SP–117, part of the agency's blackmailing toolkit in the Cold War. Pro-Kremlin journalists were quick to denounce the incident as an attention-seeking stunt by a discredited loser. But Rybkin did not seem to be using it to promote his chances. In fact he seemed rather reluctant to come back to Russia at all. Had Berezovsky wanted to stoke his candidate's campaign by manufacturing a bogus threat, he could have found far more effective means of doing so.[26]

Rather than taking the risk of allowing genuine opposition, the Kremlin prefers something manageable. In the regional elections in

March 2007, it sponsored a new opposition party, Just Russia. On the surface, this seemed to be engaged in a fierce contest with the Kremlin's own United Russia party. Undoubtedly the personalities in both parties were keen to win: the spoils of victory are considerable. Real differences in outlook existed. Just Russia is anti-business, avowedly socialist, and also nationalistic in outlook. But the real story was different. Just Russia is not a serious contender for power, but a way of turning a potentially brittle monopoly into a more stable duopoly. Its real value is threefold. First, it crowds out real opposition, chipping away at support for Russia's Communist Party, the main left-wing opposition grouping. Second, the Kremlin dislikes any strong political institution, even those that it has itself created, and competition from Just Russia stops United Russia from getting over-confident. By allowing Just Russia to poll respectably—and win a handful of contests against United Russia—the Kremlin sends a message to the party barons: you may be rich, but you can still lose. It also sends a message to any regional politician with an eye to the future: sign up for one of the two main parties, or book your ticket to political oblivion.

The odd thing about this heavy-handed approach is that the Kremlin is not really facing any serious opposition. Liberal-minded opposition leaders may gain an appreciative hearing in Brussels and Washington, D.C., but their parties are mostly seen inside Russia as a shambolic collection of squabbling no-hopers, chancers, and freaks. Even in the Yeltsin years when it had a fair chance of winning, Yabloko got nowhere. The Communists, the only party with a claim to a real mass membership, have become a pathetic relic of a once fearsome predecessor. The party's incompetent and venal leaders consistently betray their elderly and embittered supporters.

The paradox is that so many Russians seemingly want to live in a system that curtails their freedom. Putin's approval rating is stratospheric; the difficulties that opposition parties experience meet with clear public approval. According to opinion polls quoted in a government newspaper in 2007, fewer than 50 percent of respondents agreed that Russia needed a political opposition at all; less than 30 percent believed the opposition had a right to push for alternative policies or take political power. Fully a third thought that the mere expression of opposition views constituted "extremism."[27] These figures may exaggerate the trend (it is certainly what the Kremlin hopes people are thinking) but it is not wholly invented. For many Russians, dissenting views and minorities of all kinds are not a vital ingredient of political pluralism, but a subversive and un-patriotic menace that is at best tolerated grudgingly, and if neces-sary squashed.

Such sentiments can be hard for outsiders to understand, but they make sense against the background of Russian history. When the rest of Europe was experiencing the Renaissance, the Reforma-tion, and the Enlightenment, Russia was still mired in feudalism, and ruled by eccentric tyrants. Brief spasms of reform and rebellion hardly dented the autocratic rule of the Czars. Only for a few months in 1917 under Kerensky did Russia have anything ap-proaching parliamentary government, before it was snuffed out by the Bolshevik putsch that later became known as the "October Rev-olution." Though the political pluralism of the Yeltsin era lasted for years, not months, it also failed to put down real roots. Many Rus-sians feel that multiparty politics failed them in the 1990s, and that their state institutions are too weak and corrupt to be trusted. Per-haps more deeply, they do not trust other Russians to vote sensibly. Handing power to a single strong leader may not be the best way of running Russia, but it may also perhaps not be the worst: at least it is easier to focus trust, attention, and criticism on one man, rather than on a bunch of greedy and self-serving politicians and bureau-crats. While that argument is flawed, as long as Russia's economy flourishes, it will be hard to refute.

Just as political parties have atrophied, so have the institu-tions of state that should keep the executive branch under con-trol. The Kremlin's human-rights institutions, for example, rarely cause trouble on specific cases, though they do promote human rights in the abstract. Vladimir Lukin, a retired liberal parliamen-tarian and ex-ambassador, has commendably denounced Russia's endemic ethnic and religious intolerance. When news broke in 2007 of what appeared to be the use of punitive psychiatry against Arap in Murmansk, he dispatched a team of independent psychi-atrists to investigate the case. His office publishes reports on the rights of disabled children and similar issues. He even lambasts the authorities directly about, for example, the bureaucratic ob-stacles they put in the way of public protests. But his reports get little airtime; the authorities respond politely or not at all. Noth-ing changes. Another outfit, the Presidential Council on Promot-ing the Development of Institutions of Civil Society and Human Rights, is headed by an ambitious pro-Putin politician, Ella Pam-filova. A third initiative is the Public Chamber, a consultative body consisting of a mixture of presidential nominees and nongovernmental organization (NGO) representatives. Such organizations are best seen as safety valves. A body like the Public Chamber can intervene, hold hearings, and wag its finger when public opinion gets really heated, for example, over the outrageous behavior of official motorcades—convoys of black jeeps and limousines that drive at high speed with flagrant disregard for other road users, sometimes killing those unlucky enough to be in their way. What it does not do is make laws or hold government ministers to account.

That job, in any free, law-governed state worthy of the name, should be done by the legislature. For those who remember the perestroika era, the Duma is a sad disappointment. In the years 1989–91 its Soviet-era predecessor, the Congress of People's Deputies, was a raucous, gripping spectacle of pluralist politics in action. To see it at work was to see totalitarianism crumble before your eyes. Millions of Soviet citizens would stop work to watch its debates. By contrast, the sight of the Duma (or the upper house, the Federation Council) at work is not merely catatonically boring; it is outright dispiriting. The proceedings are largely a charade. Duma deputies' main interest is in their lavishly subsidized perks, and in the enormous opportunities for bribes. These exist because Russian officialdom extorts predatory rents from every bit of human activity from birth to death, via imports, exports, taxes, and endless government inspections.[28] The prosecutor general recently estimated the total annual amount of bribes paid at $240 billion a year, around the same size as the national budget. Having a parliamentarian on your side can be a cost-effective short cut round these bureaucratic thickets. But it is one for which he will expect an appropriate reward.

A handful of independent-minded deputies, such as the beanpole-like Vladimir Ryzhkov, survived until the elections in December 2007. But aside from such eccentrics, no parliamentarian takes a stand on any matter of principle. They cannot afford to. Almost every member of Russia's legislature owes his (rarely her) seat to the Kremlin's whim. And accordingly they must sing the Kremlin's tune. Their task is to look enough like a parliament to maintain the pretence that Russia is run by a legislature with real power. They act as a sounding board, for example demanding economic sanctions on "fascist" Estonia, or any other country that has displeased the Kremlin. They can be a safety valve. In 2005, for example, amid a scandal about children adopted by foreigners who had been murdered or abused by their new parents, deputies called for a moratorium on foreign adoptions. They legislate—but only according to the script. Every law that the Kremlin backs gets through parliament. Nothing it dislikes stands a chance.

The Russian people seem unimpressed with the organs of power. Polls taken in 2007 give the Duma an approval rating of 27 percent (with disapproval at 52 percent). Only 5 percent thought that Duma members were working to improve the lives of the population; only 3 percent could name any positive qualities and 44 percent said that greed was the main motivation for those seeking election. Prospects for improvement are slight. Forty-five percent said they did not think that the parliamentary elections due in December 2007 would reflect the will of the people; only 8 percent thought the votes would be counted with complete honesty; fully a third said they would not regard the newly elected Duma as legitimate.

Definitions of democracy vary so widely as to be almost meaningless.[29] But the foundation of freedom is justice. For all the abuses and sleaze that disfigure the advanced industrialized countries of the West, honest judges and due process are the ultimate backstop, upholding the law and transcending politics. Not in Russia. Despite some spasmodic reforms, the justice system[30] is under the control of the Kremlin. Russian courts may offer a fair trial—but only in cases where nobody powerful has an interest. Otherwise the courts will just rubber-stamp the authorities' verdict. The problem is not just dishonest judges and pushy bureaucrats; it starts at the top. So long as the Kremlin itself is above the law, justice for anyone else is just a pretence. The International Bar Association, the Organisation for Economic Co-operation and Development (OECD), the International Commission of Jurists, the American State Department, and the anti-corruption group Transparency International, have all expressed concern about the fate of the legal system under Putin. Independent-minded judges have been dismissed, corruption is rampant. Even one of Russia's top judges, Valery Zorkin of the Constitutional Court, says that "bribe-taking in the courts is one of the biggest corruption markets in Russia."[31] A 2007 poll showed 40 percent of Russians did not believe that Russia was a law-governed state (30% thought it was); 38 percent distrusted the judiciary, and only 26 percent said they trusted it. Boris Jordan, scion of an émigré Russian family from America who has become one of Moscow's most high-profile, and normally enthusiastic, investment bankers, put it bluntly at a conference in September 2007: "Probably the single biggest thing that business in Russia today suffers from is that you can't really expect to get a proper court hearing."[32]

The most flawed part of the justice system is not the courts themselves, which few Russians use and fewer trust, but the prosecutors' service. This unreformed Stalinist relic is the engine of state illegality.[33] Prosecutors can freeze your bank account, putting you out of business; they can have you imprisoned in a disease-infested hell-hole; they can concoct evidence that will keep you there for decades; they can intimidate any witnesses, defense counsel, and even judges who try to stop them. With a few heroic exceptions, the prosecutor's office is the best friend of the authoritarian bureaucrat and the well-connected gangster. The most shameful tactic of all is intimidation of defense lawyers such as Boris Kuznetsov, whose client list is a *Who's Who* of the Kremlin's victims and adversaries. He has represented the Politkovskaya family, relatives of the crew of the *Kursk*, Sutyagin (the researcher jailed on espionage charges), and many others. In mid-2007 he fled Russia for his own safety, after being accused of leaking state secrets. His supposed "crime" was that he complained to the Constitutional Court about the FSB's illegal bugging of a client's phone conversations. Other lawyers who take on similarly high profile cases say they face similar harassment, in a way that recalls the treatment of dissidents' defense lawyers in the Soviet period. The prosecutors' office has asked the Moscow bar association to discipline Karina Moskalenko, a defense lawyer for Khodorkovsky who has won 27 cases at the European Court of Human Rights.[34]

Intimidating those lawyers willing and able to take a case to an international court is an ominous development. For Russians, the best chance of justice now is not in their country's own courts, but abroad; they make up easily the largest number of complainants in Strasbourg. The European Court of Human Rights there received a remarkable 8,781 complaints by Russians in 2005. In only two cases of the 110 that were accepted for trial that year was no violation found. In 2006, the number of complaints by Russians rose to 10,569, of which 151 were declared admissible; in only five was no violation found.[35] A recent nonpolitical case involved four people from the town of Cherepovets, a town on the Volga in central Russia, whose lives had been made miserable by pollution from a steel plant. The court ruled that their "right to respect for private and family life" had been violated by the contamination. The state should pay them compensation and either make the steel plant abide by environmental regulations or move them elsewhere. The Russian government paid the damages, but did nothing else. More typical are cases from Chechnya. In these, the Russian state has had to pay millions of euros in damages, and suffered repeated public humiliation for the theft, torture, false imprisonment, rape, and murder carried out in its name. Unsurprisingly perhaps, Russia has consistently blocked proposals—backed by almost every other country—to streamline the court's procedures and make it easier for citizens to use its services.[36]

So forget individual and collective protests, the media, elections, politicians, and the courts. What is left is "civil society"—a jargon term for public-spirited people and organisations[37] who make up the political subsoil in free countries. Far more than political parties, it is their protests and endorsements that focus decision-makers' attention on matters of public concern. They include everything from anglers' groups (strong lobbyists for clean rivers) to cyclists (road safety), parents (education, conscription), retirees, and disabled people. Such activity mostly operates somewhere under the official radar: Normal people only bother to engage with officialdom when they are seriously annoyed about something. It is very rarely the other way round in a free society: Only when, say, a mosque is infiltrated by terrorists, or when an animal-rights group turns to violence, does anybody in authority start interfering with voluntary organizations. One of the most encouraging developments of the 1990s in Russia was the growth of this kind of public-spiritedness. It was patchy, to be sure, and sometimes opportunistic and greedy—the term "grantsuckers" was coined for those activists whose main expertise was in cadging money for fashionable causes, rather than doing any good. But it was still a vast improvement on the Soviet past, when all independent public activity was banned. And it was a welcome reaction from the intense individualism and materialism fostered by the collapse of communist control. To visit tiny but inspirational charities and campaigns run from kitchen tables by devoted individuals was one of the clearest signs that Russia was slowly edging toward the European mainstream.

But now civil society in Russia is shriveling. It is not just that any political challenge to authority is instantly deemed suspicious. Even indirect criticism is either slapped down or left exposed to extremist violence. When skinheads chanting "death to homosexuals" attacked gay rights campaigners in Moscow in May 2007, for example, the police stood ostentatiously aside. The main weapon is to increase the burden of bureaucracy: The dull-sounding law "On Amendment of Selected Legislative Acts of the Russian Federation" that Putin signed on January 10, 2006 sets down tough registration and monitoring rules for NGOs. Even long-established outfits with headquarters overseas had to reregister with the Justice Ministry by mid-October; the documentation required included the home addresses and phone numbers of their founders. As with many Russian laws, the drafting is so vague that it is impossible to be sure what compliance means. Organizations can be asked to provide all correspondence with outside individuals and other bodies dating back several years, and to produce detailed budgets for their forthcoming activities, with explanations for any change from the annual "work plan." Among those that had temporarily to stop operations were Human Rights Watch and Amnesty International.

That gives the authorities, in effect, the power to shut down any group they like, without giving a reason. In January 2006 for example, the Ministry of Justice decided to close the "Russian Research Centre on Human Rights," an umbrella organization that includes some of the country's most distinguished campaigning outfits, including the Moscow Helsinki Group. Nobody in officialdom seemed to see the irony: A supposedly free country was now persecuting people who had withstood the onslaught of Soviet totalitarianism. Whereas the heroes of the Cold War dissident movement had to deal with the Soviet-era penal code, the new Kremlin tactic is to find minor infringements of the law: In the case of the human rights outfit, they had, supposedly, not filed proper reports of their activities over the past five years. The Russian branch of PEN, the most venerable international campaign for writers' freedom, had its bank account frozen, ostensibly because it had failed to pay taxes. (Russia is almost unique in the severity with which it regards NGOs' tax affairs, treating their income from foreign donors as if it was, in effect, commercial revenue.) The same tactic was used against the Centre for International Legal Defence. This organization helps Russians sue their country in Strasbourg. Even worse, the CILD is headed by Ms Moskalenko, the lawyer associated with Khodorkovsky.

Any organization that tries to represent Russia's ethnic minorities can expect especially harsh treatment. Those from Muslim regions, such as Tatarstan, are immediately painted as extremists and terrorists. Anyone showing the faintest sympathy for Chechnya is risking their freedom, if not their life. Boris Stomakhin, a campaigner for Chechen independence, received a five-year sentence in 2006 for inciting hatred against the army. The Russian-Chechen Friendship Society was closed after its head, Stanislav Dmitriyevsky, was convicted of inciting racial hatred. This closure immediately allowed the authorities to use a legal provision that makes it illegal for an NGO to be led by anyone with a criminal conviction. The society is now registered in Finland. Lower-profile causes with an ethnic dimension attract barely less vindictive treatment. The 600,000-strong Mari ethnic minority, for example, is a remnant of the Finno-Ugric tribes whose lands once stretched from Siberia to the Baltic sea. Unlike the Estonians and Finns, they have never had a state of their own. Around half live in the republic of Mari-El in northern Russia. After a brief national revival in the 1990s, they have now become the target of a vicious campaign of chauvinistic repression, spearheaded by the president of the republic, Leonid Markelov. The main aim of the Mari movement is to ensure the survival of the language, in theory officially protected, but now surviving chiefly among old people and in the countryside (around 20% of those calling themselves Mari admit to having no knowledge of the language whatsoever). However, the authorities seem to be determined to accelerate its decline. The local education authority's department for the Mari language has been closed. Television programs in the Mari language have been cut back; few books are published. Education in Mari is patchy and mostly stops at primary level. The Mari movement's leaders are denounced as "nationalists" and "separatists." Using such language is intended to associate them with the hated Chechen terrorists, and with the rebellious national republics such as Lithuanians and Georgians who broke up the Soviet Union in what many Russians see as an act of inexplicable ingratitude.

For some, that disapproval means physical violence. Vladimir Kozlov, the editor of the main Mari newspaper, was savagely beaten by unknown assailants in February 2005. Later that year skinheads from a group linked to the republic's pro-Kremlin leadership attacked and beat a group of Mari musicians. A film about Mari song festivals was banned. A particular source of suspicion is Mari links with Estonia. A handful of Mari students, along with those from other places with similar ethnic ties, have received scholarships to study there. Estonia is the headquarters of the world Finno-Ugric movement—in the eyes of Kremlin propagandists a vast revanchist conspiracy set on the break-up of Russia, but in fact run by a handful of volunteers from a shabby two-room office.

Any group that has taken money from any foreign source faces grave charges of espionage or treason. Yet one of the few good things that the outside world did in Russia in the 1990s was to spray money at anyone trying to form even a halfway credible public organization. It is true that this was often wasteful. It was sometimes even cynical: Western governments used such outfits as a way of collecting information about Russia, and even of influencing events there. But the Kremlin overstates the extent of this, and also regards it with paranoid suspicion. At a time when Russia could not guarantee the safe handling of nuclear waste, for example, it made sense for neighboring countries such as Norway to help environmental groups highlight the issue. That was not only good for Norway, but for Russia too. But according to the Kremlin's zero-sum logic, anything that was good for foreign countries must have been bad for Russia. The immediate victims of that type of thinking are state-financed foreign outfits that do not enjoy diplomatic immunity. The authorities' approach is highly selective. Germany's Goethe Institute, for example, is able to operate without difficulty, as are the Spanish Instituto Cervantes and the Institut Français. But the British Council, an organization better known for blandness than subversion, has had a remarkably difficult time. Its Moscow offices have been raided by the tax police on the pretext that the language lessons provided there are a tax-dodging commercial operation. In December 2006 its office in St. Petersburg was closed because it had broken unspecified "safety regulations." And in July 2007 the Council was forced to abandon its offices in Yekaterinburg on the grounds that it was not a proper department of the British Embassy. That sort of harassment of foreign cultural activity was a hallmark of the old Cold War: Its return is a striking feature of the new one. And given that most important NGOs in Russia accepted foreign money sometime during the 1990s, almost all are under suspicion. Even the most apolitical and harmless organizations are now facing the cold breath of official displeasure.

In 2007, the Educated Media Foundation, which has trained 15,000 Russian journalists since 1996, was forced into liquidation. In January its president, Manana Aslamazyan, accidentally broke the law by importing slightly more than the permitted amount of cash into Russia. That is an offence that normally goes unpunished. At most it attracts a minor fine; it is exporting undeclared cash that the authorities care about. But since then Aslamazyan's foundation has been harassed by repeated police raids, and threats of prosecution for money laundering; she fled to Paris. The foundation's plight prompted 2,000 Russian journalists, including dozens working in state-controlled media, to petition Putin in protest. He did not reply.[38] The foundation's real crime was not Aslamazyan's mistake over the cash, or even the technical accounting errors that the investigators claimed to have discovered. It was that over the years the American government had supported the foundation with around $8 million. That, in the Kremlin's eyes, is tantamount to treason. Putin has repeatedly described foreign-financed NGOs as being nothing more than fronts for foreign espionage and mischief making.

Such cases are not isolated examples of bureaucratic intransigence. They form a pattern. Having hollowed out real politics, the Kremlin fills the shell. An ironic shorthand term for the new phenomenon is GONGOs—"Government-organized nongovernmental organizations." Some of these are veterans' movements and religious groups that work closely with the authorities. But the most worrying development is the growth of phony popular movements that substitute for real public involvement. Their main role is to head off any repeat in Russia of the event that marked the nadir of Kremlin influence in the former empire in the past decade: the Ukrainian "Orange Revolution." This started in November 2004, with mass protests against a presidential election marked by corruption, intimidation, and unabashed fraud. Tens of thousands of photogenic youngsters in orange scarves set up a tent city in the center of the Ukrainian capital, Kyiv,[40] demanding a political change. After heavy diplomatic intervention from NATO countries to broker a deal, the standoff ended in a rout for the pro-Kremlin candidate and the triumph of his rival, Viktor Yushchenko. The celebrations were partly premature,[41] but the protests were deeply worrying for the Kremlin. The tent city seemed spontaneous, and certainly represented a large slice of Ukrainian opinion, particularly in the center and west of the country. Few asked at the time who was paying for the tents, flags, food, and sound systems. The truth was that the "Orange Revolution" was at least in part the result of detailed planning and energetic coaching by outside activists, seasoned by experiences in similar campaigns in Slovakia and Serbia. Initially dismissed by the Kremlin as empty nonsense, the combination of youth, idealism, and Western political techniques are a potentially lethal political weapon against corrupt and authoritarian regimes.

The danger of such a popular uprising in Russia may have receded now, but Kremlin officials remain convinced that American and European think tanks, with generous support from their governments, are planning something similar, or will do so sooner or later. The prime aim of the Kremlin's mass movements is to swamp any such attempt. Whereas the "colored revolutions" are fuelled with idealism for Western ideals, the Kremlin believes that Russian national values such as patriotism, deference, and a touch of xenophobia will prove an even more potent counter. The biggest such organization is *Nashi* [Ours], run by the Kremlin and sponsored by its associated businesses, including Gazprom. It can put thousands of uniformed young people on the streets at short notice. It has at least 120,000 members, ranging from the idealistic to the bored, from hooligans to opportunists. *Nashi* and its sibling organizations are partly a safety valve, giving at least the semblance of the excitement of a real political campaign: travel, new friends, and solidarity behind a common goal. But however much it tries to seem wholesome and patriotic, *Nashi* has other echoes. It recalls the perks-for-loyalty approach of the Komsomol, the Soviet Union's Communist Youth league. The unthinking nationalism and glorification of Putin lead some to call it the *Putinjugend* [Putin Youth], recalling the *Hitlerjugend* [Hitler Youth] of Nazi Germany. The 10,000 participants at the movement's 2007 summer camp at Lake Seliger, 220 miles (350 km) north of Moscow, wore electronic tags so that the organizers could check that they were attending the prescribed lectures and seminars. Shirkers were expelled. Some features of camp life were bizarre: Participants were told that the mammoths had become extinct because of their low sex drive and warned that the same could happen to Russia. Young women were encouraged to hand in skimpy underwear, which supposedly causes sterility, and accept more wholesome undergarments in exchange. Other features were outright nasty. Exhibits included defamatory material about Estonian politicians (depicted as fascists) and opposition figures (as prostitutes). The mass movements demanding freedom and justice in Ukraine and Georgia were described as American-led stunts, with no reference to the idealistic motives behind them, or of the authoritarian, corrupt, and bureaucratic regimes they targeted. *Nashi*'s manifesto includes lumps of regurgitated Soviet-era propaganda, praising Russians' communist-era courage, discipline, and strength. *Nashi*'s self-described "security service" conducts joint training exercises with the police in preparation for elections. A counterdemonstration by *Nashi* and other similar organizations can swamp anything that Russia's fragmented opposition can manage. Like the sheep chanting "Four legs good, two legs bad" in George Orwell's *Animal Farm,* it can intimidate through noise and numbers.

The two men who were at the time the frontrunners for the 2008 presidential election, Sergei Ivanov and Dmitri Medvedev, turned up at the camp to field questions and endorse the movement's goals and activities; later, a selection of *Nashi* members, plus others from similar outfits, had an audience with Putin himself. *Nashi*'s leaders insist that its only connection to officialdom is loyalty to the president, that its money comes from donors and that its leaders are independent patriots. Yet it seems remarkably well connected. In June 2006 the British ambassador, Sir Anthony Brenton, infuriated the Kremlin by attending an opposition meeting. For months afterward he was harassed by groups of *Nashi* supporters who interrupted his speeches, blocked his entry and exit from buildings, and kept up a chorus of catcalls and abuse wherever he went.[42] Yet how did they know his movements in advance? The Russian authorities have means of finding out that sort of information, but it stretches credulity that a mere unofficial youth movement would be so well informed.

In comparison with other Kremlin-sponsored groups, though, *Nashi* looks civilized, rarely getting involved in outright xenophobia and racism. In the summer of 2007 an outfit called *Mestnye* [Locals] started distributing flyers urging Muscovites to boycott non-Russian cab drivers. These showed a young blonde ethnic Russian refusing a ride from a swarthy, beetle-browed driver, under the slogan "We're not going the same way."[43] In September 2007, *Mestnye* members organized a sting operation to catch illegal immigrants, offering lucrative work to foreign-looking people in a market on the Yaroslavskoye Shosse in northeast Moscow, a favored location for migrant workers seeking casual work. Those who accepted the offer were driven not to the promised construction site, but to a migration service office for a document check, leading to 72 people being detained for immigration offences. Such unofficial xenophobia matches the official stance. On April 1st, for example, a decree explicitly backed by Putin banned foreigners from trading in Russia's retail markets. Unofficial and illegal migration is certainly a big problem in Russia: By some estimates, up to 12 million people are working illegally in Russia, compared to 1 million legal migrants. Other countries, including America, face similar problems. But it would be inconceivable that a youth movement backed by the White House would urge Americans to boycott nonwhite taxicab drivers, or that the American authorities would ban noncitizens from a whole swathe of business life.

Depressingly for those who hoped that the first generation of Russians to grow up with no memories of totalitarianism would be liberal, the evidence points to exactly the opposite. Although explicit support for extremist and racist groups is in the low single figures, support for racist sentiments is mushrooming. Slogans such as "Russia for the [ethnic] Russians," which was supported by no more than a third of those asked in the 1990s, now attracts the support of half of the population. A recent estimate in 2007 is that 500,000 young Russians belong to extremist youth groups.[44] The most worrying aspect is that the best-educated young Russians, far from being the tolerant cosmopolitans that Western wishful thinkers have predicted, have unpleasantly hard-line views. In a survey carried out for the Moscow Carnegie Centre think tank,[45] the most anti-American group of young people in Russia were university-educated male Muscovites. For now, those sentiments are still channeled into official public organizations. But the danger of teaching people political agitation is that they may decide to do it on their own. By sponsoring *Nashi* and other such movements, the Kremlin may be stoking something that it cannot always control.[46] A sign of how easily xenophobes can run amok came in August 2006 in Kondopoga, an unremarkable small town in northwestern Russia. A minor brawl, in which two Russians were killed, brought extremists from far afield who mounted a pogrom in which people of "Caucasian" (meaning swarthy, which in Russian, confusingly, is an adjective meaning from the Caucasus region, i.e., swarthy) appearance were beaten, sometimes severely, and chased from the town. The extremists torched shops and kiosks belonging to "outsiders." Similar movements in Moscow and St. Petersburg are increasingly brazen in attacking dark-skinned people on the street. The police, notorious for their own campaigns of harassment and extortion, seem unbothered about the violence, prompting sharp protests from African and other embassies. A similar example came in mid-2007 in Angarsk, a Siberian city where environmentalists have been campaigning against a local uranium reprocessor. A group of skinheads armed with staves and clubs attacked the protestors' camp, beating one man to death.

If all domestic constraints on the Kremlin have been removed, what about pressure from abroad? Its reaction to the Aleksander Litvinenko murder in 2006 shows how little the Russian leadership worries about the outside world. Litvinenko was at first sight an unlikely protagonist in an international incident. He had been a typical figure in the murky milieu between Russian business, organized crime, and the security agencies. Often wrongly described as a KGB agent, he was a military veteran who became a law enforcement officer for the FSB: closer to a special agent of America's Federal Bureau of Investigation or Britain's Serious Organised Crime Agency than an operative of the Central Intelligence Agency or the Secret Intelligence Service. During the 1990s he became disillusioned with the growing overlap between the FSB and organized crime. In particular, he was alarmed by a plan to kill Berezovsky—a man he knew slightly. Together with Trepashkin and some other FSB officers, he made his complaint public at a bizarre press conference in Moscow in 1998. Shortly after that he was fired and then served a short prison sentence. On his release he escaped from Russia, using a forged passport, and came to Britain via Turkey. Rather reluctantly, the British authorities gave him asylum.

Litvinenko was not a dissident in the normal sense of the word; nor, strictly speaking, was he a defector. At the time of his poisoning, his influence seemed minimal and his prospects poor. He lived a troubled life on the fringes of the Russian émigré community in London, dabbling in private security work, denouncing Putin with increasing vehemence, and striking up a close friendship with the exiled Chechen leader, Ahmed Zakayev.[47] A monthly stipend that he had received from Berezovsky since coming to England was cut back. The British authorities showed no interest in him. His limited English and extreme views kept him isolated. He stayed busy writing vitriolic articles for the Chechenpress website; in the summer of 2006 he denounced Putin as a pedophile.[48] He co-authored a book,[49] sponsored by Berezovsky, accusing the FSB of organizing the 1999 apartment block bombings. But the result was a densely written text: a challenge even for a specialist. The full details of his relationship to Berezovsky are still unclear. From the Russian authorities' viewpoint, Litvinenko was a traitor who received a justly deserved prison sentence for betraying official secrets and then fled abroad to work for a criminal and associate with terrorists. His defenders, such as the (genuine) defector and former KGB officer Oleg Gordievsky, say he was a hero who had seen the menace presented by Putin's Kremlin with prescient clarity.

What is not in doubt is that he was murdered in an elaborate but incompetent way. Litvinenko was poisoned with a rare radioactive isotope, polonium–210. Polonium–210 seemed to have been chosen because it would normally be undetectable. A rare radioactive isotope, it emits alpha particles, not the more common gamma radiation that standard radiological equipment would detect. Had Litvinenko died even a day earlier, the British authorities might never have identified the cause of his illness: that may have been what the assassins intended. The Kremlin did feel embarrassed enough to contest the allegation that it had ordered his killing (in contrast to its behavior after the 2004 car bomb assassination in Qatar of the exiled Chechen leader, Zelimkhan Yandarbiyev[50]). It instead pushed for another explanation; since the poisoning was bad for Russia, it must have been organized by Russia's enemies, with the most likely candidate being Berezovsky. Russia stonewalled the murder investigation. British detectives were not allowed to question the prime suspect, Aleksander Lugovoi, directly. The Russian authorities offered no help in clearing up other parts of the mystery, and instead they adopted a tactic familiar from the last Cold War: "admit nothing, deny everything, make counter-allegations." Why was Britain not handing over the terrorist Zakayev (the exiled Chechen foreign minister) and the fraudster Berezovsky,[51] they asked? Yet delivering either into the Kremlin's clutches was impossible. Russia's treatment of both Chechen insurgents and unruly tycoons had made it glaringly clear that neither man could expect even the semblance of a fair trial if they were sent back to Russia.

Exasperated, the British authorities began to focus on the FSB. They quietly expelled some London-based Russians who had been indirect contact with Mr. Lugovoi. When the Russian bombast continued, the authorities went public, declaring four unnamed Russian 'diplomats' to be persona non grata. These officials were in fact SVR officers who appeared to have been tasked with helping with FSB operations in Britain. Russia reacted by expelling four British embassy officials from Moscow. International support for Britain's stance was distinctly lukewarm. America's Secretary of State Condoleezza Rice counseled caution. German officials said privately that Britain had "overreacted." The Kremlin also made a blatant attempt to dissuade the EU from showing any support for Britain. A deputy foreign minister, Aleksander Grushko, gave warning: "Britain will appeal to EU solidarity. We hope that common sense will prevail within the EU and that its members will not give in to attempts to turn relations between Russia and the EU into a tool to achieve unilateral political goals. These have nothing in common with the EU's and Russia's real partnership interests."[52] As Britain persisted, Russia professed bafflement. "I don't understand the position of the British government," a foreign ministry spokesman said. "It is prepared to sacrifice our relations in trade and education for the sake of one man."[53] That seemed to sum up the gulf between the Kremlin's worldview and what counts as normal values in Britain. Litvinenko was perhaps not a hero. Maybe he was a nutcase, a fraud, or a pest. But he was entitled to the protection of the law. Britain had failed him, but it would not forget him. Meanwhile, Lugovoi became something of a media celebrity in Moscow, and was given second place in the election list for the Liberal Democrats, one of the handful of parties allowed to compete for seats in the December 2007 parliamentary elections.

That shows how feeble foreign criticism has become. The message from the Litvinenko affair is that Russia can get away with murder, metaphorically or even literally, and the response from outside will be to play down the argument and hope for better relations soon. That reflects not only Western pusillanimity, but also the removal of the final strand of outside influence on Russia: money. During the 1990s, Russia's financial weakness and desperate need for investment created at least a chance of encouraging legality and freedom. The World Bank and International Monetary Fund tried to insist on good government and reform as a condition for the billions of dollars they were lending to plug the holes in Russia's finances. That annoyed Russians, who recall (perhaps exaggeratedly) the Finance Ministry receiving faxes from Washington D.C., written in English, with instructions for their immediate implementation. Even if the policies were right, they were bought at a high price: Much of the money lent was looted instantly, finding its way to offshore bank accounts in Cyprus and Latvia (for the small fry) or Switzerland and Britain (where the serious money laundering happens). But private investors, gullible at first, began to bite too. The Kremlin knew that outsiders would risk doing business in Russian conditions only if at least some progress on property rights and enforcement of contracts was visible. The desire to please foreign shareholders and bondholders forced companies such as Yukos to mend their murky ways, clean up their corporate governance, and produce proper accounts. Now all that has changed. When oil was at $10 a barrel, Russia was pitifully weak. At $100 a barrel, it swaggers like a superpower. The crippling, humiliating debts that shackled the Yeltsin years have been paid off. Russia's books are not just balanced, they are bulging. Foreign companies are scrambling to open factories producing everything from cars to toothpaste. Even BP and Shell, whose prized gas fields were snatched by the Kremlin in 2007, are humbly hoping at least to be allowed to harvest some crumbs.

Russia's financial stability gives it the confidence to ignore other rules. It has sought for nearly a decade to join the World Trade Organization (WTO), the body that sets the rules for global trade. This would be a big step, at least potentially, toward bringing Russia into a law-governed international order. The WTO pushes its new members to chop back the thickets of protectionist legislation that shelter their home industries. Removing these barriers would have a big effect in Russia, which is notorious for both the tariff and nontariff barriers that its well-connected domestic manufacturers have erected to keep out foreign competition. It also offers a legal avenue of complaint to those outsiders whose business falls foul of predatory or politicized customs officials. That is sensitive in Russia too, where the customs agency is a great empire of state-run organized extortion. Membership in the WTO would also force the Kremlin to clarify its relationship with the puppet states it has created on its borders. Separatist statelets such as South Ossetia and Abkhazia (both in international eyes part of Georgia) and Transdniestria (a region of Moldova) enjoy customs-free access to Russia, with great potential for smuggling and money laundering. Joining the WTO does little for the raw materials industries. But it would be good news for importers of consumer goods, and for Russian manufacturers, who face penal tariffs in some of the world's most attractive markets. It is a sign of where the power lies in the Kremlin, and the mentality fuelled by Russia's energy riches, that WTO membership has become so low a priority: It would have given a hefty shock to the worst and least competitive bits of the Russian economy, and boosted the ones that will still be earning the country money when the oil and gas reserves dwindle. Russia is still trying to join in principle, but in 2007 talks seemed to be advancing at a snail's pace.

Russia's newfound wealth means that outside economic pressure on the Kremlin is minimal. The capital markets are awash with money, and Russia pays high returns. Russian companies can come to the London Stock Exchange and list their shares, regardless of whether their assets are stolen or mismanaged. Outside investors just hold their noses and explain that they cannot afford to miss out on a piece of the action. And Russia can pay for all the public investment and spending that it wishes. Moreover, the tables have been turned. Where the West once tried to use its money to speed reform in Russia, the Kremlin now uses its financial clout to subvert and weaken the political systems of other countries. As Julie Anderson, an American scholar, put it in a 2007 article:

> Chekists are in position to become extremely wealthy through not only economic policies that favor their own personal private interests, but through the extra-legal takeover of others' assets . . . with this immense wealth, they can, in turn, use their significant financial resources and international contacts to penetrate foreign governments, not only through financial-based recruitment of agents and other traditional intelligence

collection methods, but by gaining citizenship, starting or joining political parties, and running for political office in targeted
countries. This method to political influence is complemented
by the economic penetration of chekists, in league with not only
foreign nationals and political figures, but also organized crime,
in every region of the world, which enables them to move in and
exercise influence in elite circles.[54]

CHAPTER FOUR

WHY MONEY IS RUSSIA'S GREATEST STRENGTH AND OUR GREATEST WEAKNESS

Despite the savage economic downturn that hit Russia in the second half of 2008, Russians had still become more than six times richer in the period between Vladimir Putin's nomination as prime minister and the end of his second term as president. Russia's gross domestic project exceeded $1.3 trillion, more than six times greater than the figure in 1999. The average monthly wage climbed from a pitiful $65 in 1999 to more than $540.[1] In 1999 fully one third of Russians lived below the poverty line. Now it is one in six.[2] Russia was the twenty-second largest economy in the world when Putin took power. By the time he stood down it was the eleventh-largest. Investment bankers spoke of the "BRIC" countries—Brazil, Russia, India, and China—as the new powerhouses of the world economy.

Even Putin's most fervent supporters do not give him sole credit for this. The oil price soared from $18 a barrel to a peak of $147 in July 2008, bringing an extra $1.3 trillion in oil and gas revenues (hydrocarbons account for two-thirds of Russia's exports, half of government revenues, and around one-third of GDP). Prices for other commodities—nickel, steel, coal—rocketed too. That created a bulging war chest for politics at home and abroad. Russia's reserves (in the central bank and a separate stabilization fund) peaked at over $600 billion in the summer of 2008. The Russian state paid off its once crippling foreign debt.

Where outsiders once harried Russia over unpaid debts, now they are queuing for a place at the trough. For exporters, Russia was one of the most lucrative markets in the world both for investors (Russian shares rose by roughly $1 trillion) and exporters.

So Russia's finances looked dizzyingly good, especially for those who remembered the blizzard of bad news that marked most of the 1990s.

Foreign investment in 2006 was nearly $29 billion, up eightfold since 1999. Western investment has not played such a role in Russia since the late 1920s, when companies like General Motors and Ford piled into the Soviet Union to take advantage of the attractive conditions offered by Putin's distant predecessor in the Kremlin, Josef Stalin.

These outside investors brought not only money, but also ideas about management, governance, reporting, and accounting standards. Like managers everywhere, the people running Russian companies want to cut their cost of capital. That means persuading banks to lend cheaply, showing bondholders that their money is safe, and making shares attractive to outsiders. So Russian companies of all kinds smartened up their act: expanding abroad, spinning off subsidiaries, and trying to look like normal international companies in their corporate governance and accounting. Superficial financial transparency is the easy bit; having truly independent directors and clear ownership structures is much harder. It is easy to be rich; much harder to be respectable. In some places, another factor is at work too: Ambitious Russian managers want to be taken seriously, not sneered at as spivs in suits. The Kremlin does not help this process by providing slush funds from the state budget to favored companies. But it cannot stop it altogether.

But from the summer of 2008 that changed. As the oil price plunged, the Russian stock market slumped by three-quarters. Industrial production showed signs of collapse. Foreign reserves shrank by a quarter in the second half of the year, as the Kremlin tried to prop up the ruble. A series of small devaluations failed to calm the markets; Putin put his personal credibility at stake by insisting that no big devaluation was on the cads. Another raid on the rainy-day reserves for a $200 billion bailout of the financial system and politically favored industries had little effect.

It would be easy to say that the threat from Russia is over; the Kremlin will now have to adopt investor-friendly reformist policies to reassure businesses that the economy is in safe hands. That approach is woefully complacent. It is cronyism and arbitrary use of power that sustains the ex-KGB regime in the Kremlin. If they change that, they are destroying their own power. A real rule of law would end the climate of impunity on which the ex-KGB depends.

It would risk the development of independent centers of economic (and ultimately political) power. It would endanger the scams in oil and gas exports that provide billions of dollars for the regime's slush funds. It would encourage scrutiny of the grotesque corruption in public administration, such as in tax inspection, the security services, customs offices and the like.[3]

If real reform is not on the agenda, what is left for the Kremlin? One answer is the blame game: Putin and other leading figures in the regime have repeatedly attributed the financial crisis to greed and incompetence in America. Certainly there is plenty of such blame to go round, though had Russia's economy been less ill-run in past years, the country would be in far better state now to withstand the global turmoil. Blame can spread inside the country too: perhaps to rich Russians without political protection from the regime, perhaps to migrant workers, already abominably treated, who risk becoming the scapegoat for a population facing job losses and declining living standards. An extension of this may be default: those foreigners who hold Russian corporate debt may find the coming years a hard lesson.

Another possibility is to revive the tools of economic planning: controlling prices and directing credit. That is already going on to a limited extent, with price controls and subsidies for some goods. The banks are being ordered to provide loans to politically influential enterprises. The next step could be controls on foreign exchange transactions. But Putin and his associates have little enthusiasm for such a course. They remember how the failure of the Soviet planned economy fatally undermined the legitimacy of that state. They have no desire to repeat the experience.

The next option is repression: reducing still further the limited possibilities that Russians enjoy for public protest. Raids on human-rights groups and a wide-ranging new treason law suggest that is all too likely. The Kremlin has directly ordered media editors to cover the economic crisis in a "responsible" way.

The most worrying possibility is that the regime seeks another foreign adventure with which to distract the public from the failure of the domestic economic experiment.

Yet none of that solves the real problem, of Russia's distorted economic structure and bad policy mix. This should come as no surprise.

The failure of Putinomics was predicted by someone who used to sit at the heart of the Kremlin.

Andrei Illarionov is a lively minded free-market economist who used to be Putin's economic adviser and was the best advertisement for the Kremlin's reform credentials. He resigned in December 2005, saying "it is one thing to work in a country that is partly free. It is another thing when the political system has changed, and the country has stopped being free and democratic."[4] Since then he has become a fierce critic. From the safety of the Cato Institute in Washington, D.C., he says Russia is suffering from a synthesis of economic mistakes from other countries, involving flawed macroeconomics, political interference, and distortions caused by the natural resource industries.[5] One example is the "Dutch Disease," experienced by the Netherlands in the 1970s when booming oil and gas revenues led to an overvalued exchange rate and bloated state expenditures. High inflation and a stable ruble mean that Russia's real effective exchange rate has almost doubled since the 1998 crash, squeezing exporters of manufactured goods and stoking a boom in imports. Energy exports used to be a tenth of GDP; now they are a fifth, while the non-oil share in industrial output—which should be rising if the Russian economy were diversifying—is shrinking. Russia has also adopted a meddlesome industrial policy, rather like Argentina in past decades. The Kremlin is instinctively protectionist, and a chronic fiddler when it comes to tax regimes, import duties, special economic zones, and other legal privileges for favored industries and companies. That creates ample opportunities for kickbacks, but not robust, globally competitive companies. Since reform ground to an almost complete halt in 2003, the private sector has been eclipsed by the growth in the state's political and economic power. According to the European Bank for Reconstruction and Development (EBRD), the share of GDP created by private companies actually fell from 70 percent to 65 percent in 2006. Illarionov says Russia is turning into "a rent-seeking society, where weak and ineffective people are demanding subsidies and protectionism (and receive it), and the most talented, educated and entrepreneurial people are looking for possibilities to distribute and redistribute rents." Whereas private business used to be the preferred career choice of 78 percent of Russian young people in 1997, that has now fallen to 42 percent. A career in government administration and law was 30 percent then; now it is the chosen path of fully 51 percent.[6]

Another bad Latin American influence is the Venezuelan leader Hugo Chávez, a Putin ally and anti-American cheerleader who has been enthusiastically nationalizing his country's most important industries. History suggests that taxing foreign companies usually involves less temptation for corrupt officials than trying to run the industry themselves. Russia's cheerleaders like to claim that interference in the oil and gas industries was some kind of exception. After all, do not Saudi Arabia and other energy-rich countries also insist that their resources are developed by national oil and gas companies? But private ownership tends to bring more efficient management. In 1999, 90 percent of Russia's oil industry was in private hands. As investment poured in, production soared in Russia's clapped-out oil fields, which had been grossly mismanaged in the Soviet era and under state ownership in the early 1990s. That was a good trend, but it has stopped. Since the attack on the oil company Yukos, modernization has halted; annual growth in oil extraction has fallen from 13 percent to 2 percent. State-run giants like Rosneft spend their money on more interesting things: politics and acquisitions. After it snapped up the main Yukos asset, Yuganskneftegaz, the combined output of both companies actually fell: a case of one plus one equals 1.8. Admittedly, this is not just because of bad management: its geology is increasingly unfavorable too. But it is the same story in gas. Efficient independent gas producers have been gobbled up by the state-run behemoth, Gazprom; its production growth over the past eight years has been a measly 0.6 percent.

Stealthy renationalization has been one of the sharpest economic trends in Putin's second term. In 2004 the state controlled 11 percent of the voting shares in Russia's 20 largest companies; it now controls 39 percent. Sometimes owners voluntarily cede shares to the Kremlin's nominees at a cut price, hoping that they will at least be able to stay in business. Others simply have them taken. The tax code allows, in effect, the renationalization without recourse of any company that the authorities covet or are displeased with. All the tax authorities have to do is to claim that ownership has been transferred with intent to defraud. The result is to distort the economy: The gigantic profits that Russia offers for those who can use political power in their personal interests inevitably sucks investment and talent toward the state and companies associated with it, and away from knowledge-based industries offering advanced technology and sophisticated services.

The Kremlin has defined not only the hydrocarbon industries, but a total of 39 other industries, as "strategic." In banking, for example, an expanding state share is holding back modernization and the badly needed growth of lending to small and medium-sized businesses. The state's arms export company has taken over the largest car plant. It has effectively renationalized the aviation industry by merging successful small companies together with inefficient Soviet-era ones into a giant corporation with 75 percent of shares in state hands. Gazprom has bought the country's largest machine-building company. All such state interference ensures is that Russia's manufacturing industry is a weakling by world standards. Of Russia's ten biggest companies, all are in industries closely dependent on Kremlin decision making: mostly energy and mining, and in two cases telecommunications—which depends on the state handing out access to the radio spectrum. While such big companies are doing well, small and medium-sized businesses, the bedrock of an advanced economy, are struggling. In 2000, 1,200 companies produced 80 percent of Russian GDP. In 2006 fewer than 500 companies were producing that share. In America, 60 percent of GDP comes from small and medium-sized business. In Japan, 74 percent does. In Russia the figure is only 17 percent.[7]

The Kremlin's counterargument to all this is that the past 15 years show political freedom was bad for business, while authoritarian but stable rule now has proved much better. On the surface that looks true, but the claim requires careful analysis: How would Putin have fared when faced with Yeltsin's problems—and with the oil price of the 1990s? How different might Yeltsin's record have been if he had inherited an economy where private property was already entrenched, where businesses were restructuring fast to please foreign investors, and where a devaluation and high oil price were boosting growth? Businessmen themselves say the great boon has been a feeling of political and economic stability. It is partly phony: A truly stable system is also a transparent one, where people outside politics can easily see what is going on. In Russia, political decision making is shrouded in secrecy, and abrupt changes—such as the appointment of the unknown Viktor Zubkov as prime minister in September 2007—prompt agitated speculation about the Kremlin's real intentions. The stability is unpredictable in another way too: It conceals arbitrary and predatory behavior by the state. Still, many businesses feel even that is better than the wild swings and murky chaos of the Yeltsin years. The basic principles of capitalism—convertible money, property rights and enforceable contracts—may sometimes be breached in practice but are challenged in principle by no one.

What is clear is that the islands of prosperity and modernity are small compared to other countries, and still sit in a sea of backwardness. Though cumulative foreign investment in Russia was a creditable $150 billion in mid-2007, only around half of that is direct investment; the rest is in traded securities such as shares and bonds. The stock of foreign direct investment is a modest 7 percent of GDP, compared to 19 percent in Ukraine, 25 percent in Poland, 42 percent in Georgia, and a whopping 59 percent in Estonia.[8] Exclude investment in energy, and Russia's performance looks even less impressive. Few if any companies open up shop in Russia because they want to make things there for export. Bureaucracy and the appallingly bad transport system make the costs of doing business too high. That is in sharp contrast to the other big emerging economies: China, Brazil, and India. They are the workshops of the world, whereas Russia has yet to find a niche in any manufacturing export industry beyond weapons and aviation—both of which benefit from the investment and brainpower of the Soviet era.

Russia is still a tough place to live: in the UN Human Development Index it was at 65th place out of 177 countries examined in 2006, one place below Libya.[9] Since 1991, almost 10 million people have left the country.[10] The economy is still remarkably state-dominated and inefficient. Fully three-quarters of property in Russia (chiefly land) belongs to the state. Seventy percent of agricultural workers earn below the legal wage minimum (meaning that they work, in effect, as subsistence farmers). It is easiest to be middle class when you are single; families with children find life much harder. They are more dependent on Russia's abysmal public services, and exposed to the colossal price inflation of the housing market. The sharpest sign of Russia's underlying weakness is that decades of misgovernment have given the country one of the worst demographic profiles in the developed world, with just about the fastest-ageing population in Europe (other ex-communist countries such as Bulgaria and Georgia are in a similar mess).[11] For every 1,000 Russians there are 16 deaths and just 10.6 births. In the next decade, Russia's population will be shrinking by almost a million a year; at current rates, the UN says, it could fall by a third in 2050. The most glaring demographic problem, though, is not the birthrate but the extraordinarily high death rate, especially among men of working age—the 22d worst in the whole world—that rose from 10.76 per 1,000 men in 1989 to 15.45 per 1,000 in 2001. It has since declined only slightly, to 14.65 in 2006. (In America the comparable figure is 8.26, in the United Kingdom 10.13.) The causes are manifold: Russians smoke and drink more than almost any other people in the industrialized world. Drug abuse and sexual promiscuity are rampant among young people, which reduces fertility, as does pollution and the still habitual use of abortion as a means of birth control.[12] The plan is to splurge. The government wants to pay higher benefits to mothers of young children, raise spending on health care (both by raising salaries and building new hospitals), provide subsidized mortgages, build more public housing, establish two new universities and offer more scholarships.

Though a shortage of cash is no longer a constraint (with the state taking only 22 percent of GDP in taxes and other revenues, and a budget surplus of some 6 percent, Russia has one of the strongest fiscal positions of any economy in the world), progress on rebuilding infrastructure and improving public services is painfully slow. Russia has the worst health care in the industrialized world, for example. Chronic inefficiency and waste mean that big projects suffer from the same slow pace and cost overruns as their Soviet predecessors did. Russia's economy undoubtedly has great potential—maybe even enough to make people feel optimistic enough to have more babies. But so long as it is subject to the greedy and incompetent interference of the Kremlin, it will not achieve it. The distorted political economy is not just a sad waste of potential benefits for the Russian people. It also—like the fundamentalist feudalism of Saudi Arabia—has a pernicious effect on outsiders who engage with it. Western trade and investment in Russia has created a powerful pro-Kremlin lobby that distorts the outside view of what is happening inside the country. Just as when businesses are dealing with Saudi Arabia (or China or Nigeria), questions of justice and freedom in Russia are brushed aside. Every time the Kremlin shows its true face, foreign businesses lobby their governments not to "overreact." Western businessmen show no shame in following their pocketbooks. In the 1980s, it was communist trade union leaders who came to Russia to denounce Margaret Thatcher and Ronald Reagan as "warmongers" and to praise the "peace loving" Soviet leadership. Now the fellow travelers are capitalists, not communists. It was Britain's business tycoons who flocked to St. Petersburg in June 2007 to extol the pro-business policies of the Kremlin and to denounce the "emotional outbursts" of British former Prime Minister Tony Blair, who only a few days earlier, in one of his last statements as prime minister, had warned investors of the political risks of doing too much business with Russia.

Russia's heavy-handed rulers and their business associates are praised for the stability they represent, rather than denounced for their disregard for Western norms. Western bankers in Russia bring companies to the international capital markets, telling them just how much polish they will need to apply to attract the foreigners' cash. The world's top accounting firms make the books seem presentable; the most smooth-spoken foreign PR companies spread the word; renowned international consulting firms spruce up the management. Institutional investors in London, Frankfurt, Tokyo, and New York buy the shares and bonds. Just as communist trade unionists around the world once turned a blind eye to the appalling treatment of workers in the Soviet Union, foreign capitalists now ignore the way in which the Kremlin tramples on the property rights of both Russian and foreign businessmen. In fact, they do not just ignore it, they collude in it. Take, for example, the startling role of one of the world's "big four" auditors, PWC, in sanitizing the Kremlin's assault on Yukos.

Some questioned the alacrity which PWC showed in accepting the contract to audit the company back in 1995, when Yukos's image was about as bad as a Russian oil company's could be. But the commitment of the Yukos founders to cleaning up their act arguably vindicated that decision. By 2003, Yukos had the most transparent accounts of any Russian-owned oil company (incomparably better than, for example, Gazprom, which hides its costs, remuneration, acquisitions and revenues in impenetrable murk). But in June 2007, PWC said it had been mistaken, and withdrew its audit reports from the past ten years. 'PWC now believes information and representations provided . . . by Yukos' former management may not have been accurate,' it said in a statement.[13] That was a boon to the Kremlin, which used the decision as further evidence for its claim that Yukos was the Russian equivalent of Enron and that Khodorkovsky had embezzled tens of billions of dollars in company funds. The aim is to have Khodorkovsky sentenced to a further lengthy jail term for fraud before he becomes eligible for parole. Yet only a few months previously, PWC had been stoutly resisting Kremlin pressure, insisting that it stood by its audits.[14] But that stance was bringing a severe penalty. In March 2006 police and other investigators raided its office, confiscating computers and documents. It was convicted for underpaying taxes and for abetting Yukos in what the authorities called a tax-evasion scheme. PWC protested its innocence and appealed against the conviction. Prosecutors later said the firm had done no wrong.[15] As the pressure ratcheted up, the authorities seemed set on ending PWC's ability to operate in its operating licence in Russia. The merest whiff of official displeasure is bad business in Russia. Some companies, wanting to show their loyalty to the Kremlin, dumped PWC as their auditor. It even seemed as though the firm's lucrative contract to audit Gazprom was in doubt.

PWC justifies its change of position on two grounds. First, that it was misled by the Yukos management about the real state of affairs at

the company in the years 2002–4. Only in mid-2007, it says, did it receive new information that three trading firms that sold Yukos products were in fact owned by shareholders in the parent company. The
company's exiled management denies that: the schemes that the
Russian authorities are now criticizing were designed in explicit cooperation with PWC, to make sure that they were in compliance with
both local and international accounting standards, they insist.

PWC denies all wrongdoing and any suggestion of bowing to
government pressure.[16] That may indeed be the case, though it
leaves unanswered the question of how the supposedly fraudulent
Yukos schemes passed the scrutiny of auditors at the time. If highly
trained and highly paid people working for one of the world's top
accounting firms failed to spot a flagrant breach of the rules governing related-party transactions, they are open to charges of careless-
ness. If they did know, but did not object, they are open to the
accusation that they helped the company evade its taxes.

If the Yukos schemes were in fact not fraudulent but legal (at
least by the imprecise standards of Russian law), the explanation is
still more troubling. It would suggest that PWC was bullied by the
Kremlin into dumping its client. Certainly the last paragraph of
the statement issued by PWC when it backtracked has a strange
ring to it:

> In addition, PWC's decision to withdraw the reports was influ-
> enced by the fact that some former shareholders and manage-
> ment of Yukos are continuing to encourage others to rely on
> PWC's audit reports.

It is hard to see why an accountancy firm should have the slightest
objection to a company's former (or present or future) management
encouraging others to 'rely' on its audit reports. Audit reports are
meant to be reliable. That is why—in normal countries, at least—
they are required documentation for a public company.

This is not just about money: if the Kremlin case is manufactured, then innocent people are in jail; some of them may die there.
It is one thing for the authorities of a corrupt country to misuse the
legal system to grab assets and imprison opponents. It would be dismal indeed if they were helped in this by those who are meant to be
the guardians of financial integrity.

Even stranger than PWC's turnaround is when foreign businessmen connive in their own ill-treatment. Every one of the West-
ern-financed oil and gas projects developed in the 1990s has been

snatched in whole or in part by the Kremlin and its allies. Yet barely a squeak of protest can be heard. Shell and BP have both fallen victim to the Kremlin's idea that foreign capital and expertise is fine, but foreign control—and particularly foreign repatriation of sizeable profits—is not. In December 2006 Royal Dutch Shell sold a majority stake of its share in the giant Sakhalin–2 gas project to Gazprom, after the Russian government sued it for $30 billion in "environmental damages." It received $7.5 billion in a mixture of cash and shares—far less than the true value. The EBRD quietly walked away from the project. Yet Shell's boss, Jeroen van der Veer, thanked Putin for solving the problem and said his company would continue to invest in Russia. Western energy companies are so desperate for a share, any share, of Russia's hydrocarbon reserves that they will do anything rather than complain. Even the largest American companies are not exempt. Exxon is the largest shareholder in a highly successful neighboring project in Sakhalin but is also falling foul of the Kremlin. In 2006 it lost an appeal to extend its production license. In 2007 the Kremlin blocked its plans to sell gas to China. The Russian subsidiary of BP, TNK, had a license to develop the two trillion m^3 Kovykta gas field in eastern Siberia. That license committed it to producing 9 billion m^3 a year; around a third was for local consumers with the rest earmarked for export to China. But Gazprom, which has a monopoly on Russia's gas export pipelines, blocked that. Thus BP was forced to sell its nearly 63 percent stake for around $800 million, less than a third of its real value. Again, the Western company presented the news as positive. It has now become a "strategic partner" for Gazprom, and if it can help the Russian side make international investments, BP will be allowed to buy back a 25 percent stake in the project.

Perhaps the most delicious irony is that one of the Kremlin's greatest champions is not only barred from visiting Russia, but faces a criminal tax probe. Charming, eloquent, and dynamic, William Browder, an American-born British citizen, has defended Russia at countless investment conferences and other meetings. His persuasive argument is that outsiders must not be impatient; that economic modernization will come as Russian companies raise their standards to suit outside investors. His investment technique—highly successful—has been to buy shares in Russian companies and then kick up a noisy and usually effective fuss about the bad habits of the management. That has usually led to at the very least cosmetic changes but often to substantial ones. The "Browder treatment" might be uncomfortably bracing, but the result was almost always a higher share price for the victims. His targets included the mightiest companies in Russia, such as Gazprom and Sberbank, the state-controlled banking behemoth. Certainly investors in his firm, Hermitage Capital, have been delighted. Its value has risen sevenfold since Putin became president and it is now Russia's largest investment fund. For the happy investors, its hefty management charges seem more than justified. The investment he has attracted for Russia ought to have made Browder a national hero there. But in November 2005 he was turned back from Moscow's Sheremetyevo airport on undisclosed national security grounds: His campaign against cronyism and for investors' rights had clearly trodden on some powerful toes. Revealingly, Browder continued to insist that Russia was an El Dorado for investors and that his own plight was just a misunderstanding. Cheerfully extrapolating growth figures, he maintained that Russia is heading to become one of the most prosperous countries in the world. Even when 25 investigators raided his Moscow office in the summer of 2007, confiscating documents and computers, he was undeterred, claiming that the attack was politically motivated. Several of his top executives hurriedly left the country. To an outsider unfamiliar with the looking-glass world of Russian business ethics, his defense of it might seem odd. If a top foreign investor can be publicly humiliated by the law-enforcement authorities for "political" reasons, that should surely suggest that something is deeply wrong in the relationship between politics and the criminal justice system.

Moral myopia is not just bad for truth, justice, and fairness inside Russia. It weakens the outside world too. Western countries, for example, are belatedly waking up to the danger of allowing Russia to buy downstream gas assets such as distribution networks. Combined with the Kremlin's hold on all east-west gas pipelines, this would further strengthen Russia's potential energy stranglehold. Gazprom's deal with Germany's biggest energy company, E.ON, has given it great political clout in that country. Hoping to avoid the same fate, the British government has tried to discourage Gazprom from bidding for the country's main gas pipeline company, Centrica. But how will it be able to refuse such a bid if it is backed by Britain's own energy giant BP? It is as if a rape victim first thanks the rapist for not being too rough, and then goes into business with him. In personal relationships, such debasement would be possible only in a world where ethics and self-respect had lost all meaning. That is pretty much what has happened in foreign businesses' dealing with Russia. Rosneft, for example, is in effect the Kremlin's in-house oil company. Its boss, Igor Sechin, is one of the most powerful men in Russia. Rosneft has snapped up the assets of Yukos for peanuts in a series of bogus auctions. Yet when it listed a 13 percent chunk of its shares on the London Stock Exchange it raised $10.4 billion. Financiers such as American billionaire philanthropist George Soros urged Western institutions to boycott the offering; Illarionov called it a "crime against the Russian people." If a Russian crook turned up and tried to sell stolen Fabergé eggs on the streets of the city of London, it is hardly likely that the pin-striped captains of finance would be queuing up to do business with him: Handling stolen goods is a serious criminal offence. But that did not deter investors from buying Rosneft shares; or bankers from promoting them, or brokers from trading them. Their only worry—and probably a justified one—was that the political cronies and placemen in the company's top management seemed to have rather little idea about how to run a giant oil company.

Like water, money tends to flow downhill. More than 20 big Russian companies with a combined market capitalization of around $625 billion are now listed in London. Nine of those arrived in 2007. On the New York Stock Exchange, by comparison, where standards of disclosure are higher, only five Russian stocks are listed. London is also a center for Russian corporate bonds, with more than $33 billion raised in 2007, compared to only $11 billion in the whole of 2003. Britain is the second-largest source of foreign direct investment into Russia, and bilateral trade, at $16.3 billion in 2006, has nearly tripled since 2001. At least the influence of Russian dirty money in Britain is limited because so many other temptations are available. Russia's billions may seem colossal to a non-specialist but they are dwarfed by the influence of money from elsewhere: from China, from the Gulf, from the developed world. Although the Russian companies look big, most have only a sliver of their shares actually traded in London.

In Germany, by contrast, Russian influence seems proportionately stronger. Russia is a fast-growing trading partner: Exports rose from €15 billion in 2004 to €23.4 billion in 2006. Even the remarkably close personal and business ties that some top German public figures have with Russia arouse little censure. During the Cold War, Western politicians and officials who took money from the Kremlin risked professional disgrace and even prosecution. Now business is business.[17]

That approach may work well in the context of boosting profits and the share price for the next financial year. In the longer run, it is problematic: If you believe that capitalism is a system in which money matters more than freedom, you are doomed when people who don't believe in freedom attack using money. Russia has spotted that the weakest link in the Western approach to life is inattention to the moral and ethical basis of capitalism: If only money matters, then why is the Kremlin's money worse than anyone else's? The same Westerners who regard Russia as a playground where the political risk is "in the price" would be horrified if the same contempt for property rights and the public interest was displayed in their home countries. Yet that day is not far off. The creation of deep and liquid markets in energy is one of the best ways of countering the Kremlin's energy stranglehold in Europe. Germany's energy industries are firmly opposed to the European Union's (EU's) proposed liberalization partly because it would shake up their cozy cartels and partly because Russia, their closest trade and investment partner, strongly opposes it. The German government strongly endorses that line too. If this succeeds in derailing the EU's plans, that will mean less security, higher prices, and ultimately less freedom for the citizens of Europe—and higher profits and more political clout for the Kremlin.

It would be a mistake to see this as a triumph of mere opportunism. The Kremlin approach to the West, part-cynical, part-hostile, is based on an increasingly systematic way of looking at the world. In short, an ideology. Many thought that had died with the Soviet Union. As the next chapter shows, they were wrong.

CHAPTER FIVE

THE "NEW TSARISM"

What Makes Russia's Leaders Tick

When the Soviet Union's collapse ended the old Cold War, ideology seemed to have died with it. Seven decades of communism had left Russians highly suspicious of grand designs, and exhausted by the attempt to implement them. The radio broadcasts glorifying Marxist–Leninist ideas and the advantages of central planning to every corner of the map had already ceased under Gorbachev, while the stupefying mental gymnastics of dialectical materialism, once compulsory for every high-school student, had vanished from the curriculum. Though Lenin, Stalin, and Khrushchev remained etched in the national consciousness as notable leaders of the past, memories of Mikhail Suslov, the gray figure who for three decades served as the Politburo member responsible for ideology, disappeared like fog over the Moscow River. The reason was simple: Communist ideology had been a total failure, while the pragmatic welfare capitalism of the West seemed an unquestionably better bet. The empty shelves in Soviet stores matched the emptiness of the ideas. If the point of the system was a better deal for workers, why did they live so much worse than their supposedly slave-driven counterparts languishing in the capitalist hell-holes? Soviet-style ideology fared little better abroad, under those who did not experience it firsthand.[1] After 1991, even Russia's surviving communists shunned ideology, highlighting nostalgia, social fairness, and order in their manifesto and denouncing greed, unfairness, and chaos. Though they used the symbols and slogans of the past, few if any said they actually wanted to restore the planned economy and one-party state.

The result was that, through the 1990s, Russia was a political bazaar in which improvised kiosks offered everything from diluted communism to ultra-nationalism via theocracy, radical liberalism, and pragmatic politics based on the west European model. Proponents of the latter adopted the liberal, conservative, Christian, and Social-Democrat labels of their counterparts. But these embryonic Western-style parties had almost no members, and their ideas put down only shallow roots in Russia. Most remained mere fan clubs for particular personalities. Money came from "sponsors"—either powerful businessmen or rich elected officials. Still, these outfits called themselves political parties, advertised (usually lavishly) like political parties, and fought elections like political parties. Opinion polls showed their popularity rise and fall. They had anodyne names such as "Our Home Is Russia."[2]

It soon became clear that Western-style politics was not transplanting easily to Russia. Indeed, it was not transplanting at all. Working out what political ideas these parties stood for was hard. Most were in favor of more "social policy" (no hard thing when millions of old people were getting their pathetic pensions paid late or not at all). Varying degrees of prickliness and xenophobia enriched the mix, as the Russian population gradually lost its initial naïve enthusiasm for all things Western, and increasingly blamed its economic and social problems on "foreigners."[3] But it was clear on even cursory scrutiny that what these parties really believed in was getting into office and staying there. In the December 1993 elections to the Duma, the first party of a new kind broke on the scene, the "Liberal Democrats" of Vladimir Zhirinovsky who won a startling 23 percent of the vote. They were neither liberal nor democratic. Their public postures were extremist, sometimes nonsensically so. Zhirinovsky promised to provide free vodka if elected, and proposed building giant fans to blow radioactive waste into the Baltic States. He later proposed that America's Secretary of State, Condoleezza Rice, would benefit from being gang-raped by Russian soldiers.[4] It was hard to decide whether Zhirinovsky was a coarse clown, a real menace, a money-grabbing opportunist, or all of the above. Though his public positions were highly confrontational, his parliamentary deputies almost always voted to support the Kremlin. Some wondered if his party was a creation of the FSB; others thought it simply gave its support to the highest bidder. At any rate, Zhirinovsky's main role, by accident or design, was to break taboos: Most other politicians appeared reasonable in comparison.

Regardless of party or label, all Russian politicians wrestled with what mixture of pride and shame the Soviet past should arouse. Expressing nothing but disgust seemed a ticket to instant political oblivion, yet finding something to celebrate was hard. Some found solace in simple nostalgia, blaming Gorbachev and Boris Yeltsin for treachery and incompetence that had ruined a superpower. That went down well with older and less educated voters, but it was a hard sell to the rest. Pre-revolutionary Russia was the obvious alternative; pictures of the Romanovs and symbols of Orthodoxy mushroomed. But the Tsarist era resonated in so many discordant and contradictory ways: Should one sentimentalize Tsar Nicholas II, or idolize his hopelessly ineffective democratic opponents? Feudal and backward, Russia then was certainly not as bad as the Communists had said; without war and Bolshevism it would have probably evolved into something better—perhaps a constitutional monarchy, certainly freer and more prosperous than the tragic experiment that succeeded it. But it required great willpower to believe that the ruthless and incompetent rule of Nicholas II was in any way admirable.

The dilemma echoed from more than a century earlier. Was contemporary Russia picking up the threads from the 19th century Slavophiles, semi-mystical patriots who loathed Western materialism and individualism, or from the rationalist "Westernizers" who longed for Russia to import the best that the outside world had to offer? Amid this confusion, Soviet revivalism competed with somewhat naïve pro-Western liberalism, half-digested Tsarist nostalgia, and all manner of far-fetched ideas about Russia's unfulfilled spiritual and Eurasian destiny. The Russian pantheon stretched awkwardly from the Romanovs to Andrei Sakharov[5] via the cosmonaut Yuri Gagarin[6] and Lenin. The latter remains unburied, embalmed like a secular saint, in his mausoleum outside the Kremlin; he had, most Russians would say, been somewhat less bad than Stalin. Gulag victims could tell their stories—but guides at the FSB museum in Moscow insisted that the secret police had also suffered under Stalinism. The bombast about the Soviet Union's economic achievements vanished; lingering pride for its scientific and technological prowess remained.

Muddle was piled on twaddle, because the Soviet Union's own view of the past was so contradictory, both in terms of how to treat mass murder and its perpetrators, and in how to deal with Russian nationalism. In the 1920s, the official Communist line was that Russian imperialism had been a bad thing, just like Russian capitalism. Non-Russian cultures and languages such as Tatar, Mari, Komi, and the like gained official status and enjoyed a few years of modest cultural revival. Under Stalin, that switched sharply. Soviet communism and Russian chauvinism became almost indistinguishable. The words of the first verse of the 1944 Soviet national anthem are illustrative:

> Unbreakable Union of freeborn Republics
> Great Russia has wielded forever to stand!
> Created in struggle by will of the Peoples,
> United and Mighty our Soviet Land![7]

Under Gorbachev, Russia began to look at its past more critically. Subjects such as Stalin, the Gulag, and the great famine in Ukraine turned from taboo to hot topic within a matter of months. In terms of willingness to discuss history, a clear hierarchy emerged. Russian suffering could be discussed quite easily; that of other nations, less so. Not that painful topics from any side were in short supply. The Red Terror unleashed by the Bolsheviks after 1917 killed up to half a million people.[8] Collectivization in 1928–33 uprooted up to 4.5 million peasants. Up to 5 million people, in Ukraine and elsewhere, died of hunger. The Stalinist purges of 1937 to 1938 claimed up to 1.7 million victims, of which more than 700,000 were executed without trial. During the war, nearly 1 million ethnic Germans and 1.5 million Chechens, Crimean Tatars, and others, all of them Soviet citizens, were deported under the pretext that they were Nazi sympathizers. After the war, up to a million people were marched straight from Nazi prisoner of war (POW) camps to the Gulag.

Repression at home was matched by aggression abroad. The Bolshevik revolution quickly snuffed out the brief independence of the states of the southern Caucasus: Georgia, Armenia, and Azerbaijan. They were not to rejoin the family of nations for seventy years. In a cynical carve-up with Hitler in 1939, the Soviet leadership divided Eastern Europe into spheres of influence. When the Nazis attacked Poland, Stalin joined in barely two weeks later. After Poland had been divided up and wiped from the map, 22,000 Polish officers were murdered in Katyń. After the war, the Kremlin snuffed out any attempt to restore freedom in the countries of Eastern Europe. Having established brutal and ruinous systems of one-party rule and planned economies, it put down popular uprisings in East Germany (1953), Hungary (1956), and Czechoslovakia (1968). In 1979, the Soviet Union invaded Afghanistan, starting a war from which that country has never recovered.

If dealing with this history truthfully would be all but unbearable, trying to conceal it leads to an ingrained duplicity about both past and present. The Stalinist past still poisons political life in post-Soviet Russia; it is the source of both the Kremlin's xenophobia and its authoritarianism. The motto of the Ministry of Information in George Orwell's *1984* could hardly be more apt: "He who controls the past controls the future, and he who controls the present controls the past."[9] And as the Kremlin increases its power over public life, it is rewriting the past to suit itself. Although the ramifications are huge and the details complex, the principle could hardly be simpler. Russia is sanitizing the worst parts of its history, whereas other countries with a history of totalitarianism and empire tend to bemoan it. In Germany, for example, *Vergangenheitsbewältigung* is a word etched into that country's public life. A literal translation would be "overcoming the past," though a more common rendering is "coming to terms" with the past. Germany has been trying to do just that ever since the allied occupation forces in the western zones of the defeated Third Reich herded the population into cinemas to view newsreel footage of the concentration camps. The occupying powers' intention, enforced at gunpoint, was that nobody should be able to say that they "didn't know" about the mass murder of millions, or that Nazi dictatorship "hadn't been that bad."

It worked. Breast-beating about the past has been a hallmark of German policy ever since. The Federal Republic paid generous reparations to Israel and the countries of eastern Europe.[10] History textbooks in West German schools focus relentlessly on the Nazi era, its origins, crimes, and the disaster it had brought for Germany. The anti-Nazi resistance was glorified; Willy Brandt, who had spent the war on the Allied side, became the Federal Chancellor.[11] But at least Germany has only to deal with 12 years of Nazi dictatorship. That can be set against much more attractive bits of history: the founding of continental liberalism in 1848; the *Zollverein*, the continent's first customs union; and many other great cultural, literary, and scientific achievements in the 18th and 19th centuries. It is harder to find glorious moments in Russia's past. Germany's historical conscience may be unusually (and rightly) sensitive, but from a west European point of view, guilt about the past is pretty much the norm. Every big European country has had an empire, ran it badly at times (or always), and feels bad about it, sometimes perhaps excessively so. British guilt about imperial massacres and exploitation is so embedded in the school curriculum that pupils are genuinely surprised to find out that anyone argues that the empire had redeeming features at all. Americans and Australians feel a mixture of painful emotions about their forebears' treatment of those continents' original inhabitants. Whites in the West feel guilty about racism in their own countries. Political leaders apologize on behalf of their nations for acts that happened decades, even centuries, ago and over distant and recent crimes and shortcomings. Vietnam, apartheid, slavery, the allied bombing of Germany—all attract the deepest scrutiny of the finest historians, novelists, and playwrights. The threads—often muddled—of guilt, sensitivity, responsibility, and shame run so thickly through the Western way of looking at other countries and cultures that we hardly notice that they are there.

Blind spots still exist, of course. Until recently French discussion of Vichy was circumspect; Austria's view of its own history wobbles between remorse for the enthusiasm shown there for Nazism and the insistence that it was an alien import and that the country was Hitler's first victim; and many in Britain are still only dimly aware that their country's wartime role was not unalloyed glory, at least from a Polish or Indian point of view.[12] But the blind spots grow hugely as you go east. In contrast to the Federal Republic in the west, the Soviet-occupied zone of eastern Germany did not force its people to confront their past: Fascism was something imposed on Germany by outsiders (chiefly capitalists). The people of the "German Democratic Republic" were anti-fascists who had been liberated by their Soviet allies, not defeated. This type of revisionist history does little to make the East Germans love the rapists and looters of the Red Army. But it does stop them worrying too much about what had been done to the Jews, whose suffering was all but eclipsed in the official histories in favor of Nazi atrocities against communists and trades unionists.

Russia's new attitude to the Soviet past is summed up in Putin's infamous remark in his 2005 state of the nation address; in that speech, he pronounced that the collapse of the Soviet Union was the "greatest geopolitical catastrophe of the 20th century."[13] Some supporters try to put a positive gloss on this statement: What the great leader meant as catastrophic, of course, was the loss of swathes of historic territory such as Ukraine, Central Asia, and the Caucasus, plus the economic and social upsets. The latter were certainly personal catastrophes for many of the people involved. Yet a quick comparison with Germany shows the remarkable implications of the president's words. The collapse of Hitler's Third Reich also meant the loss of historic German territories such as East Prussia and Silesia. It brought colossal—indeed, catastrophic—suffering to the whole German nation. But no mainstream German politician would baldly call it a "catastrophe": first because it was the inevitable consequence of Hitler's demented policies; second, because Germany's suffering cannot be seen in isolation. Hitler's downfall meant liberation for the subjugated nations of Europe—and indeed ultimately for Germany itself.

Putin's statement was not a casual aside that can be dismissed as part of Russia's wider confusion over its history. The Kremlin is spearheading a new approach to the past that glorifies the Soviet Union, denigrates the West, and portrays the Yeltsin years as a period of disgraceful weakness and chaos from which Russia has now been rescued. The history books written in those days are therefore tainted—not least because they were published with the involvement of foreigners. "Many school books are written by people who work to get foreign grants. They dance to a butterfly-polka[14] that others have paid for. These books, regrettably, get into schools and universities," Putin said in the summer of 2007.[15] He demanded new history textbooks that "make our citizens, especially the young, proud of their country" and insisted "no one must be allowed to impose guilty feelings on us." Such textbooks are being produced; the ones he criticized are disappearing from the classroom.

The best illustration of this new approach is the way the Kremlin treats Stalin and Stalinism. Outsiders—especially those whose countries suffered at Soviet hands in the Stalin era—may reasonably expect that modern Russia, by its own account a friendly and civilized country, will distance itself from the barbarism of the past. Imagine the scandal in the Netherlands, Poland, or Israel if the German history syllabus presented Hitler and the Third Reich as anything other than a shameful stain on that country's past. Yet a new history teacher's guide endorsed by Putin, *A Modern History of Russia, 1945–2006: A Teachers' Manual*,[16] tries to shoehorn the greatest mass murderer of Europe's past century into a familiar yet ill-fitting role: the great leader forced by circumstance to take harsh decisions. It deserves detailed study.

For a start, it makes out that the greatest victims of Stalin's tyranny were not the patriots, peasant farmers, intellectuals, religious believers, and those tied to the past regime, but the Communist Party's bosses:

Practically all . . . Politburo members elected after the 17th Party Congress [in 1934] suffered from reprisals to a certain degree . . .

The ruling class was the priority victim of the repressions in 1930–1950. And it was all in a good cause:

The goal was to mobilise the leadership in order to make it effective in the process of industrialization ... political repression ... was used to mobilise not only rank-and-file citizens but also the ruling elite.

The purges created, it claims:

a new class of managers capable of solving the task of modernisation in conditions of shortages of resources, loyal to the supreme power and immaculate from the point of view of executive discipline.

In other words, it argues, Stalin was no worse than Otto von Bismarck, the German chancellor who united his country through *Blut und Eisen* [blood and iron]. The guide makes tangential reference to the extraordinary abuse of power that characterized the Stalin era, but only by putting him alongside other Russian leaders.

It is well known from Russian history how corrupting a long term in power is. Biographies of such outstanding rulers as Peter the Great and Catherine II prove it ... Stalin followed Peter the Great's logic: demand the impossible ... to get the maximum possible. So the worst that can be said about Stalin is that he was "controversial."

He is considered one of the most successful leaders of the USSR. The country's territory reached the boundaries of the former Russian Empire (and in some areas even surpassed it). A victory in one of the greatest wars was won; industrialisation of the economy and cultural revolution took place successfully, resulting not only in mass education but also in the best educational system in the world. The USSR became one the leading countries in science; unemployment was practically defeated.[17]

Stalin's success, by the crudest measure of industrialization and military victory, is indisputable. But the new history book skates over the colossal human cost: millions of forced laborers, the elimination of whole social classes, and the famines, both intentional and those caused by negligence It also ignores the fact that the Second World War was largely Stalin's fault. If he had not connived with Hitler in the 1930s, Nazi Germany would not have been able to attack. And had Stalin's paranoia not led him to kill the Red Army's best generals, and to ignore the warnings of impending Nazi attack,

Hitler's war in the east would have been far less successful. At any time since the collapse of Soviet totalitarianism in the late 1980s, such a revisionist approach would have seemed not just misleading but sinister. Now it is treated as bald historical fact, to be fed to Russian schoolchildren. The new party line is: If Stalin made mistakes, so what? Lots of people make mistakes.

"Problematic pages in our history exist," Putin conceded in mid-2007. But: "we have less than some countries. And ours are not as terrible as those of some others." He also strongly contests any attempt to put the two great mass murderers of the 20th century on a similar footing "I cannot agree with equating Stalin with Hitler. Yes, Stalin was certainly a tyrant and many call him a criminal, but he was not a Nazi," he said in 2005 in a joint interview with the then German leader, Gerhard Schröder, who signally failed to challenge the assertion.[18] Putin went even further, equating Soviet and Western crimes against humanity. He compared the Great Terror of 1937 to America's dropping of the atom bomb on Hiroshima. The comparison is strange. A strong argument can be made that the dropping of the atom bomb ended a war and saved countless lives, including many innocent non-Japanese who deserved to die least of all. It is also quite possible to argue that Franklin D. Roosevelt and Henry Truman were mistaken, callous, or reckless, overeager to see Japan defeated quickly, unwilling to consider other means of ending the war, and blind to the wider danger that nuclear weapons would pose. But, unlike Stalin, they were not the direct cause of the deaths of millions of people through execution, deportation, starvation, and collectivization.

In his use of "what about," Putin echoes, consciously or unconsciously, the favorite weapon of Soviet propagandists. Asked about Afghanistan, they would cite Vietnam. Castigated for the plight of Soviet Jews, they would complain with treacly sincerity about discrimination against American blacks.[19] Every blot on the Soviet record was matched by something, real or imagined, that the West had done. Hungary? What about Suez? Martial law in Poland? What about American-backed dictatorships in Latin America? But the contrasts even then were absurd. When the American administration blundered into Vietnam, hundreds of thousands of people protested in the heart of Washington. The authorities disapproved, but did not try to imprison the protesters. In a handful of cases the police or National Guard scandalously overreacted. The shooting of four students at Kent State University in May 1970 brought millions of students out on strike, closed hundreds of campuses, and remains a national scandal in America that is cited to this day. Yet when eight extraordinarily brave Soviet dissidents tried to demonstrate in Red Square against the invasion of Czechoslovakia in 1968, they were instantly arrested. Most were sentenced to exile or psychiatric hospital. Their names are all but forgotten.[20] The only person to protest publicly about the war in Afghanistan was Sakharov.

Russia now barely commemorates even the damage it did to itself, let alone the suffering inflicted on other people. Nothing like America's powerful and dignified Vietnam Memorial exists in Moscow for the tens of thousands of Soviet servicemen who died in Afghanistan. Russia's only museum dealing with the full horror of the Gulag is an excellent one, but it is in Perm, deep in the provinces 900 miles (1,500 km) from Moscow. The handful of museums in Moscow that try to highlight the Soviet past experience official harassment, not support. It is not just a remarkable silence; even to raise the question of the historical suffering of, say, the Poles or the Balts, arouses an instant and neurotically angry reaction. The official government newspaper, *Rossiiskaya Gazeta* and other mainstream media have even revived the Soviet-era lie that the murder of Polish officers at Katyń was actually a Nazi crime.[21] For Poles, who remember the combination of mass murder and official cover-up as one of the most shocking and painful episodes of the past century, that is akin to officially sanctioned Holocaust denial. Outsiders in these historical arguments often find this hard to understand. Most west Europeans tend to share Henry Ford's view that "history is bunk": Bemoaning your country's shortcomings in a vague way is de rigeur, but harping on about your ancient historical grudges is taboo, a kind of primitive vengefulness usually confined to the far-right of politics. So when the nations of eastern Europe say that Russia's revisionist version of history is so scary that it threatens their very right to existence, the response from their allies is usually polite bafflement, or outright irritation.

Why should it matter if Russia claims, for example, that the Soviet Union annexed Estonia legally in 1940? Why does it matter if the territory of the Moldavian Soviet Socialist Republic (SSR) included a bit of land that was (or wasn't) historically part of Russia? How badly did the Georgians behave in Abkhazia in 1991? Who does Nagorno-Karabakh really belong to? What historical and other rights do the Tatars, Russians, and Ukrainians have over Crimea? Yet such seemingly obscure questions were matters of life and death for countries and people, and may yet be again. They are part of the central front in Russia's new ideological war: The desire to rewrite history of both the distant and the recent past.

The heart of the problem is that the Stalinist version of the Second World War is now the most important myth in modern Russia's account of itself. Victory day celebrations are the highlight of the Russian patriotic calendar. To understand the Russian obsession with the "Great Patriotic War" (as the period from 1941 to 1945 was termed in Soviet parlance), it may help to imagine a highly concentrated version of English nostalgia for the Battle of Britain and the Dunkirk spirit, blended with America's most rose-tinted views of the heroism of the Normandy beaches and Guadalcanal, plus every continental European country's folk memories of united resistance to Nazism, all rolled into one. It recalls an idealized world when simple national virtues of solidarity and selflessness defeated an opponent who embodied evil. Against that background of sentiment and myth; to point out that the war was largely Stalin's fault; that the Red Army behaved little better than the Wehrmacht; and that the countries in between Russia and Germany wanted not to be "liberated" in 1944–45 but to regain their pre-war independence strikes many Russians as nothing short of blasphemous.[21] The idealization of the Stalinist war myth—the myth of unprovoked aggression, extraordinary sacrifice, and triumphant victory—absolves Russia of any guilt, responsibility, or even sensitivity about events before, during, and after the war. The secret protocol of the Molotov–Ribbentrop Pact, for example, was a justifiable tactical maneuver, and no great cause for shame.[22] History is rarely as simple as it seems, and it is quite reasonable to discuss both other pressures on Soviet policy—such as the fear of a war with Japan—and the mistakes made by Britain and France. A revisionist historian could make the argument that Stalin's deal with Hitler was no worse than Britain's betrayal of Czechoslovakia at Munich in 1938. But that would only be in the context of abhorrence, not justification. The Russian approach now lacks such crucial nuances. It blames the West for leaving Stalin no choice but to make a deal with Hitler. The scandalous practical consequences of that pact are skated over.

In the postwar period, the West and the Soviet Union are seen as moral equivalents: The Soviet Union no more "occupied" east Germany than the United States "occupied" the Federal Republic. NATO membership in eastern Europe now is comparable to the Warsaw Pact's role in the past. That may sound superficially balanced; but in fact it topples the entire edifice on which not only Europe's postwar history, but also the continent's current politics, is based. If the Cold War in Europe stops being a struggle between freedom and tyranny, instead becoming just an old-fashioned geo-political tussle, then values and voters' wishes count for nothing. The former satellites were not captive nations, enslaved by an evil ideology, but mere pawns on a chessboard. The Americans subsidizing the anti-communists of the Solidarity trade union in Poland is the moral equivalent of the Soviet Union helping the Sandinistas in Nicaragua. In short, communism as an ideology was a dead end, and the planned economy was a disaster; but the Kremlin's raison d'état survives. Just like any big country, Russia has the right to determine its neighbors' future: And they have no right to complain about it.

The Kremlin's historical revisionism catches the former satellite countries in a double bind. First, the Stalin era was not that bad: If these countries suffered, so did millions of Russians, who also bore the brunt of the struggle to defeat Hitler. Second, did not the heroic Red Army liberate eastern Europe from the fascist yoke? Any dissent must mean that one is not just ungrateful, but hotheaded, egotistical, revanchist, and a closet Nazi. During a row over a Soviet-era war memorial in 2007, the *Nashi* [Ours] organization waved placards outside the Estonian embassy, spelling the country's name "eSStonia," its president's as "toomaSS ilveSS." The idea that the Estonians might have good reason to regard the Soviet "liberators" as just another occupier is seen as an obscene historical slander.[24]

Indeed, Estonia is now one of the New Cold War's two hotspots (see Chapter Six). Estonia is where Russia's geopolitical ambitions, economic muscle, and historical amnesia overlap. It is also a country determined to defend itself. For that reason, it repays close study. If the Kremlin can crack Estonia, the chances for the rest of eastern Europe look bleak. At first sight though, it is hard to see why Russia would bother. Estonia's population is one-hundredth of Russia's. It is of pipsqueak significance in terms of economic weight—less than 0.2 percent of the gross national product (GDP) of the Euro-zone. A big Polish city such as Katowice is far more important. For Russians to identify Estonia as a serious enemy seems a little short of neurotic.[25] But Russia is right to take Estonia seriously, and the outside world should do so as well. The country may be small, but it is of symbolic importance to both Russia and the West. It is the best example of a post-communist success story, with a clean and modern public sector and hi-tech and service industries that contrast sharply with Russia's hydrocarbon-heavy economy. But just as that makes outsiders moist-eyed with appreciation, it makes Russia green-eyed with annoyance and envy. If Estonia—which has, however unwillingly, shared Russia's destiny for centuries—can succeed while playing by Western rules, it casts doubt on the Kremlin's central argument of Russian exceptionalism. Maybe it is possible after all to combine stability and prosperity with freedom and openness. If Estonia's success is so painfully embarrassing, then perhaps it would be better if it were not successful—or did not exist—at all.

The fight is rooted in contradictory views of history. The way the Estonians tell it, their prosperous, law-abiding country was more advanced than Finland before the war until Estonia, along with its Baltic neighbors of Latvia and Lithuania, was obliterated by the Hitler–Stalin Pact. Soviet troops marched in, under a series of preposterous excuses, including that a local foreign-language journal, the *Revue Baltique,* had published a provocative article.[26] The economy spiraled downward. Grotesquely rigged elections produced a parliament that "requested" to join the Soviet Union. Estonia was not to return to the world atlas until 1991. On two June days in 1941, around 10,000 of Estonia's best-educated people, including a tenth of the Jewish population, were deported to the depths of Russia—typically with a midnight knock at the door followed by a few minutes hurried packing. Of some 2,500 children, fewer than half were ever to return. In total, more than 50,000 people were either deported, executed, or conscripted into the Red Army. Communist terror had begun.

When Hitler attacked the Soviet Union a few days later, it is hardly surprising that many Estonians were glad to see the back of the Soviet occupiers. When they returned in 1944, many Estonians fought them. That was not because they liked the Nazis: Had it been American or British forces chasing out the Germans, the allies could have counted on resolute support and a warm welcome. Conversely, had the French or Dutch shared the Estonian experience of 1940–41, and then faced not Western but Soviet "liberators" in 1944, they too might have reacted like the Estonians. What happened next confirmed the Estonians' fears: Communist terror returned—literally—with a vengeance. The Soviet authorities ruthlessly hunted down those with connections to the prewar government. Deportations restarted, and intensified. In March 1949 they reached their peak, with some 20,000 people, the majority of them women and minors, deported to Siberia. In all Estonia lost around one-sixth of its population at Nazi and Soviet hands. In the name of "breaking cultural continuity" with the prewar republic, public and private book collections were purged of any material that might remind future generations of what they had lost. As a young man, Jaan Kross, later to become Estonia's best-known novelist,[27] remembers watching a Soviet functionary outside the country's main university library, chopping up books with an axe.

Russia's version of Estonia's history is rather different. It starts off not in 1918, with the birth of the Estonian republic, but earlier, with Peter the Great's push into the Baltic provinces previously conquered by the Teutonic knights and then Sweden. Estonia's two decades of independence was an aberration that counts for nothing against centuries of Tsarist rule. At a meeting with journalists in 2005, Putin put the Kremlin view as follows: Under the peace treaty with Germany in 1918, "Russia turned over some of its territories to Germany." In 1939, "Germany returned them to us, and these territories joined [*voshli v sostav*] the Soviet Union." There was, therefore, no occupation after the war, "as they were already a part of the USSR." He justified this approach by saying: "Whether this was good or bad, such was history. It was a secret deal, the small states being a currency of exchange. Such were the realities of life, regrettably."[28] This view of history allows no room to see the war from Estonians' viewpoint, while characterizing the decisions they made in the harshest possible terms; the Estonians who fought in German uniforms against the returning Red Army were Fascists, and those who praise their bravery and sacrifice are nothing more than nostalgic Nazis.

Estonia's tragic fate was shared almost exactly by Latvia and Lithuania.[29] The behavior of Soviet forces in Poland was if anything more scandalous. Not only did the Kremlin attack Poland in the rear in 1939, while it was already facing the Nazi war machine; they treated the population of eastern Poland so badly that many Jews chose to take their chance under the Nazis rather than face the murderous barbarity of Soviet rule.[30] In 1944, Stalin cynically ordered his troops to stand by while the Nazis crushed the Warsaw uprising. The elimination of the strongest parts of the Polish underground army, loyal to the lawful prewar government, would make it much easier for the Soviets to install their own puppet regime. But Poland is 30 times bigger than Estonia. For now at least, it is less of a target for the Kremlin.

The natural and civilized response to wartime Europe's catalog of impossible choices, brutality, and betrayal is to mourn the dead on all sides and vow "never again." That is the west European approach, refined over five decades of peace and cooperation. It is also now the approach in the ex-communist states that are in the European Union (EU) or heading toward it. Intense historical animosities between Hungary and Romania, between Macedonia and Bulgaria, and between Poland and Lithuania have been largely buried. It is far more important to have neighbors that are prosperous and free than to win arguments over history. Outstanding issues are buried in specialist committees of historians and museum curators, or discussed—for example—in the thickets of philology. A long wrangle that epitomizes the new style of argument is an intricate Polish–Lithuanian dispute over orthography. Poles of Lithuanian descent, backed by the government in Vilnius, want to be allowed to use letters such as "ė" and "ų" when spelling their surnames in official documents: These are part of the Lithuanian alphabet, but do not appear in the Polish one. Conversely, many Lithuanians of Polish extraction want to use their "ł" and "ż," which do not feature in Lithuania's official alphabet. Amid such minutiae, it is hard to remember that before the war, Polish–Lithuanian relations were at best icy, and at worst violent. A Polish military expedition in 1921 took Lithuania's historic capital, the mainly Polish city of Vilnius, and kept it until Stalin returned the city to Lithuania in 1940. For that entire period, Poland and Lithuania had no diplomatic relations; in 1939, as Poland was torn apart by totalitarian superpowers, Lithuania closed its frontier to Polish refugees. During the war, Lithuanian and Polish partisans took time out from fighting the Russians and Germans to keep their old enmity alive.

Russia's approach to its neighbors could hardly be more different. Committees of historians set up during the Yeltsin era are not only dormant; their foreign members, such as the Latvian historian Heinrihs Strods, are banned from coming to Russia. Commentaries in the Kremlin-controlled media completely rewrite the historical record. It is hardly surprising that less than a tenth of young Russians think their country need apologize to the Baltic states for the Soviet occupation.

Sanitizing Soviet history is one leg of the Kremlin's emerging ideology; another is rewriting the 1990s under Yeltsin. The new teachers' guide highlights anarchy, failure, and weakness, while almost wholly ignoring the successes of those years, such as the growth of a free media; open multiparty elections; a lively parliamentary culture; the end of central planning; and the growth of millions of small businesses. Far from being a period marked by unparalleled pluralism and political freedom, the Yeltsin years are now described as a series of disasters in which Russia's enemies tricked and humiliated the country, stoking disorder and undermining the state.[31]

It is reasonable to put the past under scrutiny, and nobody would argue that the 1990s were pleasant. But it is twisting the facts to portray, as the Kremlin does, the collapse of the Soviet Union as a disaster equivalent to the Versailles peace treaty imposed on Germany after the end of the First World War. In that case, military defeat and international censure[32] was coupled with crippling reparations. In Russia's case, not only did it suffer no military defeat, but it was deluged with international goodwill. Far from bankrupting Russia with demands for reparations, the West was pumping in billions of dollars in loans and aid. That the result was disappointing has more to do with Russia's own political weakness, and the inevitable consequences of ruinous economic planning, than with Western bungling. Perhaps the advisers should have been less ambitious or doctrinaire in their advocacy of price liberalization, monetary stabilization, and privatization. Some of them may have been too close to the investment bankers who profited from privatization and other transactions. But it is absurd to argue that they were actively malevolent. Even if Russians now think that they somehow had a raw deal, that the medicines were wrong, or would have been better prescribed in a different dosage and sequence, that is no reason for anti-Westernism. Germany and Japan suffered far worse, with outright military defeat and occupation, but became staunch Western allies within only a few years.

Such revisionist history shades right into politics; the youth wing of "United Russia," *Molodaya Gvardiya* [Young Guard] organizes marches under the slogan, "No return to the 1990s." From this viewpoint, not only was the West trying to weaken Russia, but the political leaders who worked with them were selling Russia down the river. The big historical turning point is not the collapse of the Soviet Union and birth of freedom, but the end of the Yeltsin era. The new history guide's chapter on the years from 2000 states admiringly: "We see that practically every significant deed is connected with the name and activity of President V. V. Putin."[33]

Patriotism and historical revisionism are two of the best means the Kremlin has found to fill what Sergei Markov, one of its top advisers, calls Russia's "ideological vacuum." The third element is xenophobia. According to Lilia Shevtsova of the Moscow Carnegie Centre, one of the most lucid analysts of Russia's drift to authoritarianism, "anti-Westernism is the new national idea."[34] Putin has swung from citing Western countries as examples to denouncing the West for hypocrisy and arrogance. It started as early as 2004 when he accused America of a policy on Chechnya that was designed to destabilize the Russian Federation. In the same year he likened America to an old-fashioned colonialist, a "strict uncle in a pith helmet" instructing others "how to live their lives" and punishing objectors with a "missile-bomb truncheon."[35] In his 2006 annual address to parliament, he referred to the United States as "Comrade Wolf," a figure who "knows whom to eat. He is eating and listening to no one."[36] Over time, the rhetoric has become harsher. America "has overstepped its national borders in every way . . . No one feels safe anymore," he told a security conference in Munich, Germany in February 2007.[37] Later that year he likened America obliquely to the Third Reich for its policy of "confrontation and extremism" and "its contempt for human life, the same pretensions of world exclusivity and diktat."[38] Criticizing American policy is no crime—many Americans have detested the Bush administration since the moment it took office. But the Kremlin's anti-Westernism creates a bogeyman that allows Russia's rulers to sidestep any criticism of their own authoritarianism. Put crudely, the argument goes like this: "Democracy equals chaos and is promoted by Russia's enemies." Putin's defenders, both in Russia and abroad, cite all manner of slights and policy blunders by America and Europe to justify this rhetoric, but it still seems bizarre to compare America that for decades has been a champion of freedom to Hitler's Germany.

For all its shaky logical foundations,[39] a sign of how well this approach is succeeding is that the overtly pro-Western camp in Russia has shriveled to insignificance. Beyond a small handful of journalists and people working at Moscow think tanks, almost no mainstream public figure is prepared to defend the EU, NATO, or the United States against the caricature that they are all menacing hypocrites out to destroy Russia. As Shevtsova notes, attitudes toward the West have become a "litmus test of loyalty to the authorities and the system."[40]

For all the anti-Western sentiment among Russia's elite, it is hard to see an appetite yet for real confrontation. Rich and powerful Russians buy their luxury goods in the West, educate their children there, take their holidays there, and stash their ill-gotten gains there. So far at least, anti-Westernism has had a mixed effect: according to polls in 2007, fully 70 percent of Russians see Europe as a partner of sorts, even though a similar number say they do not consider themselves European; fully 73 percent of Russians think that their country should aim for a mutually beneficial relationship with the West; and only 16 percent think Russia should distance itself. Almost half see the EU as a threat to Russia's economic independence; 67 percent say they have a good opinion of it; and only a third see a long-term relationship with the EU as desirable. Such ambiguous feelings toward the West are nothing new. As Russia's great Symbolist poet Aleksandr Blok wrote in his 1918 poem, *The Scythians:*

> *Russia is a Sphinx. Rejoicing, grieving,*
> *And drenched in black blood,*
> *It gazes, gazes, gazes at you,*
> *With hatred and with love!*

So far at least, anti-Westernism has been principally a political device, designed to keep power. But it may be hard to control; German intellectuals who claimed they had lost the First World War because of a "stab in the back" reaped a bitter harvest a few years later. As Shevtsova laments, "the ruling elite has let the genie out of the bottle and it will be very difficult to put it back again."[41]

The next element in Russia's nascent state ideology is religion, in the form of the moral and spiritual legitimacy provided by the leadership of the Russian Orthodox Church (ROC). Having been a dutiful servant of the Soviet regime that in the 1930s drove it almost to extinction, the ROC enjoyed a strong revival, at least in terms of numbers, in the post-Soviet era. In the Yeltsin years, its public posture was often ambiguous. Some leading figures flirted with Russian nationalism and anti-Semitism. Others seemed more involved in using the generous tax and legal privileges to build business empires—for example, in bottling mineral water, or in importing cars, tobacco, and alcohol.[42] Yeltsin's own attitude to the ROC was dutiful rather than devout. Under Putin, its influence has soared and its profile sharpened. Whether it is sincere or self-interested, Putin's own religious belief is certainly conspicuous. He regularly attends church services, and likes to show his interlocutors a crucifix that he rescued from a fire at his family home. With an approval rating of 54 percent, the ROC is the second most-trusted institution in the country (the presidency has 68 percent). Yet the numbers are puzzling. Russians are still more religious in belief than most Europeans: In a 2007 poll 58 percent said they believed in God, up 6 percent from the previous year.[43] However, 59 percent said they never attended church services, up 4 percent since 2005. Although church and state are nominally separate, the church's privileged legal status has become deeply entrenched. Indeed, Russian secularists and scientists are becoming alarmed by the teaching of religious dogma as fact in Russian schools, and the Orthodox hierarchy's increasingly vehement opposition to evolution. The connection is undisguised, even with the organs of power that most damaged the ROC in the past. The church next to the FSB's Lubyanka headquarters bears a plaque thanking the FSB for their help in restoration work. "All power is from God and so is theirs," says a priest who leads the service.[44] At least some of the *siloviki* seem truly to believe that they are chosen and guided by God.

In return for state protection, the ROC provides loyal support to the Kremlin's attempt to differentiate Russian and Western civilization. The central document of the church–state compact is a declaration issued in 2006 by the World Council of Russian People, an assembly of secular organizations that acknowledge the spiritual leadership of the ROC hierarchy. It adopted a "Declaration of Human Dignity and Rights," a manifesto that aims to counter the United Nations "Declaration of Human Rights," the founding document of universalist Western thinking on the subject. The head of the ROC, Patriarch Aleksei, said that the Western vision of human rights did not permit Orthodox faithful to live in accordance with their beliefs. Indeed, he said such an approach would lead to a "neo-pagan" revival. The council took particular exception to the focus on individual rights, which it blamed for both moral relativism and the deprival of the interests of others. "There are values that are no less important than human rights," the concluding statement said "These are faith, ethics, [national] sacraments, Fatherland."[45]

Reasonable people may disagree about the usefulness of human rights as a political concept. But that is not the argument at issue here: What unites both the ROC and the Kremlin is not just a shared past in the KGB but also the passionate belief that Russian civilization is based on unique values, quite different from those in the West—an idea that fits perfectly with the notion of "sovereign democracy." "*Pravoslaviye, Samoderzhaviye, Narodnost*" [Orthodoxy, Autocracy-Sovereignty, Nationality] was the motto invented in the 19th century by Count Sergei Uvarov to give a philosophical basis for the rule of the reactionary and xenophobic Tsar Nicholas I; worryingly, it seems to be as potent now, in the days of modern Kremlin authoritarianism, as it was in the days of Tsarist feudalism. The Orthodox hierarchy also shares the Kremlin's anti-Westernism, insisting that foreign religions, particularly Roman Catholicism, are determined to steal its flock. Vsevolod Chaplin, the spokesman for the patriarchate, complained recently: "After the breakdown of the Soviet Union a great number of people in the Roman Catholic Church decided that was the moment when it was possible to conquer these big territories and huge populations."[46]

Thus, a distinct Russian approach to politics has been taking shape. From the outside it seems clear that it is based on xenophobia, authoritarianism, historical revisionism, and exceptionalism. But how is it described inside Russia? Understanding that can be tricky for outsiders, because so many of the terms used have no easy equivalent in English (and sometimes, even in any non-Slavic language). Take the word *gosudarstvennik*, applied approvingly to Putin and most of his associates. A possible translation would be "statist," but that does not reflect the full meaning. Nor does the literal translation "man of state." The state in Western political culture is the servant of the people, and "statist" is a mildly derogatory term, suggesting unaccountable bureaucracy, interference, and a lack of accountability. But *gosudarstvennik* in Russian has a ring of patriotism about it. A *gosudarstvennik* cares about the state's prestige and strength; he believes it to be an expression, perhaps the highest expression, of society, culture, even of civilization. In other words, the Russian state exists not to serve the people, but as a project or mission with an almost supernatural basis.[47] "Culture is fate. God made us Russians, citizens of Russia,"[48] says Vladislav Surkov, a former advertising man who is now the Kremlin's chief. This is reflected in the idea that Moscow is a "Third Rome," inheriting the imperial, cultural, and spiritual mission of first ancient Rome and then Byzantine Constantinople.[49] Putin's desire to restore the supremacy of the Kremlin at home, and strengthen its reach abroad, has little or nothing to do with the will or welfare of the Russian people: Their applause is welcome—and indeed expected—but the motivation is a transcendent, not a practical one. The point is to promote Russia's "*derzhavnost*"—an untranslatable word meaning, roughly, "great power status." That means the state throwing its weight about both abroad and at home, with behavior sometimes called *derzhavnichestvo* [Great-powerishness]. The latter involves another crucial if misleading phrase: "*diktatura zakona*" [dictatorship of the law]. Much used by Putin in the early years of his rule, it sounded superficially like a plea for Russia to become a "*Rechtsstaat*," the German term for a state where the rule of law is supreme. That is certainly the case in other free countries in which the law is the servant of the people and not the other way round (elected representatives can, over time and with a big enough mandate, rewrite any law, and even the constitution). In Russia, however, *diktatura zakona* has turned out to mean not the subjection of the executive power to the abstract values of an independent judicial system, but the executive branch's untrammeled use of legal sanctions against its opponents—including, for example, defense lawyers.[50]

The final phrase in this short political glossary is the "*vlastnaya vertikal*" [power vertical]. Unfamiliar to outside ears, this has strong connotations of order and stability in Russia: Its partial Western counterpart might be the British phrase "joined-up government." But whereas that phrase in a Western country means different institutions working sensibly together, in Russia the idea is rather different: that is, that orders given at the top are carried out below. The first clear ideological element that emerged from the Kremlin was the need for Russia to be a strong centralized state. Putin himself says it is in the country's "DNA."[51] The decentralization of the Yeltsin years he dismisses as anarchy; something that gave comfort to those foreigners who want to break Russia up into more manageable units. The idea of vertically integrated power might seem unexceptional, as it is what happens in a well-organized bureaucracy anyway. But Russia does not have, and has never had, a well-organized state administration. It is riddled with not only incompetence, waste, and laziness, but also favoritism and special interests. In its 2006 report on Russia, even the normally cautious Organization for Economic Co-operation and Development (OECD) could barely restrain its language.

> The state bureaucracy is inefficient, largely unresponsive to either the public or its political masters, and often corrupt. It is cited by foreign and domestic investors alike as one of the principal obstacles to investment in Russia today. It poses a particularly heavy burden on small and medium-sized enterprises, which are often less able to defend themselves against the bureaucracy than are large companies. Moreover, the poor quality of the state administration impinges on structural reforms in almost every other field, since it limits the government's ability to implement any policies that require administrative or regulatory capacities of a high order. It also imposes significant costs on citizens engaged in such routine tasks as registering property transactions.[52]

This is not new. When fuelled by terror and slave labor in the Stalin era, the bureaucracy managed to industrialize the country quickly, though at enormous human and other costs. Since then, the Soviet bureaucracy reverted to something that would have been all too familiar to the great nineteenth-century Russian novelists like Gogol: functionaries paying lip service to their orders from above, while concentrating on the main jobs of shirking responsibility, dodging blame, enriching themselves, and helping their friends. That, ultimately, helped dissolve Soviet power. Left unchecked, the same misrule could also destroy Russia. A strong *vlastnaya vertikal* is the supposed antidote to the corrosive swamp of state administration: It is a culture of discipline and respect in which orders are carried out, money is accounted for, and the state's interests are served, not betrayed.[53] In Western countries that happens, more or less, thanks to the professional pride of bureaucrats, the scrutiny of the citizenry and the media, the pressure from other public institutions, and scrutiny from elected representatives. But almost none of these function in Russia. Indeed, the Russian language lacks a word for "public servant" or "civil servant"—the usual translation, *chinovnik*, would be better rendered as "placeholder."[54]

The practical result of the ideology of centralization is to concentrate power at the very top, where it becomes unaccountable, unpredictable, and inefficient. As Shevtsova points out, the system created by the Kremlin has four structural weaknesses. First, personalized power and the electoral calendar are inherently risky, as they require the regular manipulation of elections That is a potential source of popular discontent. Second, the regime wants both stability and to redistribute resources in its own favor. That undermines property rights and unnerves investors. Third, lack of legitimacy means that succession is fraught with difficulty: It involves regular disruptive purges, where the new placeholder, and his superior, blame the previous incumbent for all past failures. Finally, the destruction of political pluralism removes the main social safety valve. This last point may prove the most important. History suggests that highly centralized societies do not work very well, and Russia is proving no exception. The signature of the "First Person" (as Putin is sometimes known), or the lack of it, can make or break a career, a deal, or a life. As a result, taking initiatives is risky; hoarding information makes sense; obedience matters more than results. The Kremlin may not have consciously wanted to end reform, but it can be no surprise that the ideas of the brightest and best people in Russia have been sidelined, seemingly indefinitely.

Putin's fondness for at least the appearance of tight control may stem from his repeated difficulties in establishing it. For someone ostensibly so powerful and so popular, his grip has often seemed surprisingly fragile. The first year of his second term, for example, was ill-starred. It started in May 2004 with the murder of his hand-picked collaborationist leader in Chechnya, Akhmed Kadyrov. Kadyrov was hardly an ornament to Russia's political life: His notoriously brutal henchmen matched even their terrorist opponents in scandalous disregard for life, property, and the laws of war. But Kadyrov's assassination by separatist fighters was a somber reminder that the claims that armed resistance had been crushed were simply false. Then came Putin's one and only attempt to make a serious and painful reform to Russia's wasteful and obsolescent system of social payments. The idea was a simple one: to replace benefits in kind with cash. Instead of providing cheap housing, free transport, subsidized medicines, and so forth, the state would pay the recipients instead. That is the way most countries organize social welfare. Subsidized goods and services encourage monopolistic thinking among the providers, reduce choice, and cause waste. But in Russia, that is not the worst outcome. In any system involving cash transfers, the money can simply be stolen by anyone powerful enough to cover their tracks. Pensioners' right to free travel on public transport, by contrast, exists simply by virtue of age, which is visible and cannot be cancelled or stolen. As a result, Russians believed, probably with good reason, that they would end up paying full price for something that they had previously got for free. Spontaneous demonstrations mushroomed across the country, prompting a hurried and humiliating climbdown. Since then, serious reform has been a dead letter. The year got worse; the "Orange Revolution" in neighboring Ukraine in the late autumn showed "people power" at its most romantic and compelling—and highlighted the rigid and sterile politics of Russia, as well as the dispiriting apathy of the population there.

The Kremlin's response to that was not to loosen up, but to tighten still further. Russia was "at war" with its terrorist foes, Putin said. That justified almost any restriction on political liberty. The urgent need was to make Russia stronger, and therefore safer. Michael Yuryev, a businessman close to the Kremlin, in 2004 gave an illuminating list of what he regarded as truly essential freedoms on which the "national idea" should never infringe.[55] They boiled down to private enterprise and the right to travel around Russia. He explicitly excluded from the list the requirement to obey constitutional provisions on electoral terms, the right to form political parties, and the freedom of privately owned mass media. Yuryev used to be seen as an extremist eccentric who believed in an irreconcilable clash of Russian and Western values, who wanted Russia to be both isolated and explicitly imperial in outlook. His recently published book, *The Third Empire: Russia as It Must Be*[56] describes a world in 2053 when Russia has defeated America in a nuclear exchange. That may just be unpleasant fantasy, but Putin has repeatedly adopted both his phrases and his ideas.

The new ideology that has taken shape since 2004 has a name, the anodyne-sounding "sovereign democracy." This phrase elides two key concepts enshrined in the preamble to the Russian constitution. But "sovereign" clearly counts for more than "democracy." As Masha Lipman of the Carnegie Centre notes, the phrase conveys two messages:

> First, that Russia's regime is democratic and, second, that this claim must be accepted, period. Any attempt at verification will be regarded as unfriendly and as meddling in Russia's domestic affairs. And sovereignty also implies that outside (i.e., western) norms do not apply.[57]

The new ideology includes a surprising dose of what in Western countries would be called "new age" thinking. That might seem surprising at first sight: The tough greedy world of the Kremlin could hardly be more different from the herbs, healing crystals, and hogwash beloved by the devotees of the "Age of Aquarius" and similar types. But according to Surkov, "Russian cultural consciousness is clearly holistic [and] intuitive and opposed to [the] mechanistic [and] reductionist." He continues:

> Synthesis prevails over analysis, idealism over pragmatism, images over logic, intuition over reasoning, general over particular. This naturally does not mean that the Russians lack analytical thinking and people in the western countries [lack] intuition. The issue here is the ratio. Let's put it like that: the Russian person is more interested in the time than in the blueprint of an alarm clock.

So what stems from this "intuition" about how a society should best be organized? Surkov continues:

> First, it is the aspiration for the political wholeness through the centralisation of power functions. Second, idealisation of the goals, pursued by the political struggle. Third, personification of political institutions. All these phenomena exist in other political

cultures, however, their presence in our political culture exceeds the average level.[58]

That may sound vague to an outsider, but it has clear practical effects, which nudge Russia in the direction of what might easily be called fascism. The first and third ideas combined mean that no institutions matter outside the presidency. Power flows from the very top. That means that parliament, the judiciary, the police, and the civil service, the institutions whose complex interrelations guarantee individual freedoms, all are subordinate to the will of the man at the top.

Whether or not this should even be called an ideology is contested. Surkov is widely described as the Kremlin's head of ideology, a designation he does not reject. His colleague Dmitri Medvedev however, said he dislikes the term "sovereign democracy" and called it an "ideological cliché."[58] At any rate it is not the ideology of Suslov's day. Surkov is a lively minded figure with an easy, populist touch. Suslov was regarded as dull even by the narcolepsy-inducing standards of the Soviet politburo. Surkov uses little jargon; Suslov used nothing else. Surkov was a successful businessman in television, advertising, and public relations before he moved to the Kremlin in 2004 (his biography suggests he may have worked for the GRU in the 1980s); his career, spanning the worlds of high state office, media, espionage, and private business, is the embodiment of Russia under Putin. Suslov embodied the Brezhnev-era Kremlin; it is hard to imagine him in any role other than as a communist functionary. But the similarity is still striking. In both cases, the aim was to explain the difference between the ideal and the reality. Suslov had to explain why the CPSU (Communist Party of the Soviet Union) deserved to stay in power even though the utopia it promised showed no sign of arriving. Surkov has to give a justification for Russia's new political system, of authoritarian state capitalism. Like Suslov, he also has to explain why questioning the system is not just mistaken, but treacherous.

The big question for the West is how to deal with it. Some argue that this is all better than nothing. Vlad Sobell, a Russia expert at the London offices of Daiwa, a Japanese investment bank, says that Surkov is developing a "fresh, post-totalitarian application of liberalism."[59] Russia has its own political culture, so it needs its own political philosophy, the argument goes. Better to have something homegrown than import misunderstood ideas from outside, such as Marxism. In addition, Russia is also right in rejecting the idea that global stability depends on the United States playing the role of "global teacher-cum-policeman." Multipolarity will be more stable than a unipolar, U.S.-dominated world. Others simply want to rebut "sovereign democracy" in both its premises and its arguments. Certainly much of this is based on exaggerations and misapprehensions. The outside world was not trying to weaken Russia in the 1990s (indeed, one of the big fears of that era was that Russia might disintegrate, or prove too weak to control its nuclear weapons). The current U.S. administration has overstretched America's military power and shredded its reputation. But the idea that America is threatening the world is a bogeyman. Bogged down in Iraq and Afghanistan and scrambling to cope with the rise of China, the supposed global hegemon is too weak to fulfill the tasks it faces, not too strong. America's "democracy promotion" efforts may be ill-judged or hypocritical on occasion, but the isolationism that America-bashers seem to want would have a high price: It would mean, in effect, agreeing to leave the world in the hands of dictators.

Russia certainly has the right to its own political culture; every country does. And the aftermath of totalitarianism may mean tolerating some unpleasant and features, at least for a time (Germany in the 1950s was very different from the way Germany is now). Surkov is right on that. But he has not made a persuasive case for reinventing the wheel. The basic means by which a free country works are universal: the rule of law, separation of powers, independent media, and fair elections. And the clear sign from the Kremlin is that these elements of political life are not just optional, but outright undesirable.

The most telling point, though, is not to rebut the Kremlin's criticisms of the West, which may in some cases be accurate and merited. It is to point out that other countries' shortcomings do not justify Russia creating new ones of its own. Violent abuse of power by the state is bad, regardless of what other countries are doing. Whether it is snatching assets from well-run private companies, locking up opponents, stifling criticism, or hollowing out supposedly independent public institutions of state, the Kremlin is doing a disservice to the people of Russia, in whose name it supposedly governs. The novels of Fyodor Dostoyevsky include powerful criticisms of the West in the nineteenth century. But that did not mean that the rigid brutalities of Tsarist autocracy such as the knout, serfdom, censorship, and deportation to Siberia were a better way of governing the country.

So why does the Kremlin promote this ragbag ideology, which alienates outsiders and promotes misgovernment of the country?

The crudest reason is that it is an easy way of staying in control. Por-
traying Russia as a fortress besieged by malevolent hypocrites is a
handy way of explaining to the population why its sacrifice of freedom is necessary. Second, intimidating the outside world is a good
starting point for fending off their interference. Talking toughly was
a standard approach of Soviet negotiators during the old Cold War.
Terrifying rages and frosty silences would melt without explanation
with the prospect (usually illusory) that the thaw would continue if
only the other side would see reason and back down. But the most
worrying explanation of all is the simplest: The Kremlin adopts an
ideology based on Soviet nostalgia and xenophobic rhetoric because
it partly or even wholly believes in it. If this explanation is true, it
makes it all the more worrying that the outside world still seems so
unbothered.

CHAPTER SIX

HOW EASTERN EUROPE SITS ON THE FRONT LINE OF THE NEW COLD WAR

"A quarrel in a faraway country between people of whom we know nothing." That is how Britain's prime minister Neville Chamberlain dismissed Czechoslovakia's struggle for survival before signing the Munich Agreement in September 1938, which sealed that country's dismemberment by Nazi Germany. At that the fate of the continent was being decided in central Europe. Nearly 70 years later the story is similar, but the threat is from Russia, not Germany, and the victim is Georgia, not Czechoslovakia.[1] Following an ill-judged Georgian attempt to reconquer the Russian-backed puppet state of South Ossetia, Russian forces, overwhelmingly stronger and with superior airpower, won a quick military victory—defeating Georgia's army, regaining complete control of both South Ossetia and the other breakaway region of Abkhazia, and also occupying strategically vital positions within Georgia proper. The West protested, but proved ineffective.

The Georgian drama played out in the main theatre of the New Cold War—the countries bordering Russia, starting with those covered by the 1939 Molotov–Ribbentrop pact—the Baltic states, central Europe, and the Balkans—but reaching around the Black Sea to the Caucasus.

Yet this is a region where, until recently, the West was forging ahead thanks to both its strengths and its opponents' weaknesses. NATO won the last Cold War partly because it could outspend the Kremlin, and partly because planned economies and one-party states are inherently prone to decay. But the other ingredient—and perhaps even the most important in retrospect—was "soft power." Highlighting the contrast between the prosperity and freedom of the "capitalist camp" and the backwardness and repression of the "socialist camp" dissolved the totalitarian glue that held the Soviet empire together. In effect, the messianic communism of the 1920s, which believed that the masses in every country needed only to hear the message to support it, went into reverse. Fewer and fewer people in the capitalist world wished they lived in the communist one, and the more they learned about it the less they wanted it. By contrast, most people living under communist rule wished things to be different. The more they learned about the West, the more they liked it, and the less they believed their own rulers' propaganda. That process did not stop with the collapse of communism: After 1989, the same soft power consolidated the West's victory. Having thrown off dictatorship, the nations of eastern Europe soon decided that they wanted "Euroatlanticism."[2] That is convenient shorthand for the advantages offered by the American-backed security umbrella of NATO membership, and the good government and economic advantages associated with the path to membership of the European Union.[3]

Euroatlanticism is not an easy ride, but it is clearly a beneficial one. Joining the EU means a commitment to cleaning up and modernizing all the debris of totalitarian rule. It means everything from making the courts and police honest and efficient to ensuring solid property rights and strong anti-monopoly laws; introducing internationally recognized education and environmental standards; and sticking to the stable macro-economic policies necessary to adopt, eventually, the euro as a common currency. Admittedly, the details are often messy. It is easy to ridicule pedantic food hygiene standards and to complain about tiresome and costly regulations that protect inefficient farmers or clog up the labor market. The rules are not only sometimes silly, but may be applied hypocritically or inconsistently. Some countries are much better at promising reform than doing it. But the results speak for themselves. The expansion of the EU has been a great success. The new members are growing fast, spectacularly so in some cases. Even their often weak and incompetent governments do not affect foreign investors' confidence. And unlike Russia's distorted, petroleum-fueled economic growth, the new members' prosperity is based on manufacturing, services and—increasingly—high technology. The eastwards expansion of NATO has had a similar beneficial effect. Demoralized, sprawling, Soviet-style bureaucracies and excitable, amateurish militias in the former captive nations have reformed. In some cases, such as Poland, they are becoming modern and flexible armed forces.

While Euroatlanticism has continued a deep and seemingly irresistible advance, the story for the Kremlin for most of the years since 1989 was one of retreat and defeat. It is salutary to note what was regarded in 1992 as the irreducible minimum that Russia could accept. Igor Rodionov, then head of the military staff college (and later Yeltsin's defense minister), said Russia would insist on:

> The neutrality of East European countries or their friendly relations with Russia; free Russian access to seaports in the Baltics; the exclusion of "third country" military forces from the Baltics and non-membership of the Baltic states in military blocs directed at Russia; the prevention of the countries that constitute the CIS from becoming part of a buffer zone aimed at separating Russia from the West, South, or East; maintaining the CIS states under Russia's exclusive influence.[4]

That may read like an ominous wish list now, but for most of the past years it seemed like a catalogue of failure. All the Soviet Union's Warsaw Pact allies—Poland, the Czech Republic, Slovakia and Hungary, as well as Romania and Bulgaria—joined NATO; so too, in 2004, did the Baltic states, which Russia terms "ex-Soviet republics."[5] Even Georgia and Ukraine seemed to be on track to join NATO eventually; Russia cut its own access to the prized Baltic seaports in a failed attempt to exert economic pressure.

It was hard to see how Russia would recover. It lacked the Soviet Union's hard power—military muscle—and seemed unable to find a rival to Euroatlanticism. Russia's friends were a diminishing number of dictatorships: incompetent, unattractive, and unsuccessful. In Slovakia, for example, Russian security services and business circles cultivated close links in the 1990s with the strong-willed and heavy-handed prime minister, Vladimír Mečiar. That stoked intense opposition from most local opposition parties, strongly helped by European and American think tanks and activists. A cross-party anti-Mečiar movement stormed to victory in the 1998 parliamentary election, kick-started reform, and turned the country from an isolated backwater to a foreign investors' darling.[6] Similarly, the Serbian strongman Slobodan Miloševic enjoyed strong Russian support in his wars with Western-backed Croatian, Bosnian, and Kosovar adversaries. But the economic and political consequences of his nationalist rule, and the sanctions they brought, were ruinous; in 2000 he, too, was toppled.[7] In Lithuania, two politicians with close ties to Russia left office in disgrace. Rolandas Paksas, leader of the Liberal Democratic Party, served as president for 14 months. He was impeached in 2004 and banned from running for public office in the future after the country's security service complained publicly about his alleged ties (which he vehemently denied) to Russian intelligence and organized crime. The leader of Lithuania's Labor Party, Viktor Uspaskich, fled to Russia and successfully gained political asylum there in 2006. His personal bookkeeper had revealed to the Lithuanian authorities what appeared to be some Russia-linked irregularities in the party's finances. (Uspaskich, a wealthy businessman, strenuously protests his innocence and returned to Lithuania in autumn 2007—and to house arrest.) But these reverses proved only temporary: the two men's parties were set to poll strongly in the Lithuanian elections due in October 2008. The ruling Euroatlantic government coalition was perceived as so incompetent and corrupt that voters seemed willing to back populists, out of a mixture of despair and protest.

The colored revolutions in Georgia in 2003 ("Rose"), Ukraine in 2004 ("Orange"), and Kyrgyzstan in 2005 ("Tulip") were similar stories of joyous successes followed by dispiriting reality. At first, they highlighted the failure of Russia's approach to its neighbors. In each case they displaced a corrupt and authoritarian regime; in the latter two cases, one that the Kremlin had found easy to deal with. The seemingly obvious lesson from this was that people in the ex-Soviet region had a strong appetite for clean government and freedom, and found the Kremlin's diet of crony capitalism and secret police rule unappetizing. The Russian reaction was initially bafflement, but then renewed resolve to find better tactics. That determination has begun to bring results.

The Euroatlantic tide has stopped flowing westwards. Appetite for expanding the EU and NATO has waned, and disappointment with the new members has grown. Secondly, Russia's own power, hard and soft, has started increasing. The first examples came from Central Asia. The Uzbek dictator Islam Karimov, after a brief flirtation with America after 2001, is now one of Putin's closest and most dependable allies.[8] The Uzbek regime appreciates Kremlin help in its ruthless suppression of Islamist opposition forces, and in countering intermittent outside criticism of its deplorable human rights record (though the latter, at least from Britain and America, is muted: they, too, hoped to find in Uzbekistan a useful ally in the "war on terror"). The West has also lost influence in Kazakhstan, ruled by its president-for-life Nursultan Nazarbayev. Despite rampant corruption, the country is the most advanced and impressive in Central Asia. But Kazakh foreign policy is ultra-cautious, reflecting the president's domestic priorities: economic growth and education. Nazarbayev's regime is steadily building stronger relations with the West and with China, but it wants on no account to quarrel with Moscow. A glance at the map shows why: the Kazakh–Russian border is the longest land frontier in the world. Northern Kazakhstan is largely populated by ethnic Russians, roughly a third of the population. For now at least, Kazakhstan could only lose from a confrontation. Irresolution and division in the West make the Kazakhs despair: Why should they take a Euroatlantic option seriously, when it is not offered seriously?

The Kremlin's power is greatest in Tajikistan, a poverty-stricken narcostate wholly dependent on Russia for its financial and military survival. Russian troops ensured that Emomalii Rakhman, the country's leader, won a five-year civil war that ended in 1997; they have kept him there ever since. Remittances from Tajik migrant workers in Russia are an economic lifeline for the impoverished population. In Kyrgyzstan, Russia has bounced back. It flirted with an idealistic pro-Western orientation under its first post-Soviet leader, Askar Akayev, who said he wanted it to be the "Switzerland of Central Asia."[9] When his rule became mired in autocracy and corruption, a popular uprising in 2006 seemed to presage a Ukraine-style revolution. As in Ukraine, that proved premature. Kyrgyzstan is the uneasy host to both an American and a Russian airbase. The oddball of the region is Turkmenistan, the most mysterious of all the post-Soviet countries, with gas reserves second only to Russia's in the former Soviet Union. For the first 15 years of independence it was run by its former communist boss Saparmyrat Nyÿazow, an eccentric megalomaniac who renamed himself Turkmenbashi (Father of the Turkmen), closed down public services, and instituted a terror-based personality cult. His replacement, Gurbanguly Berdimuhammedow, has relaxed some of the most odious features of Nyÿazow's rule, but has also weakened the country's determined isolationist stance, which seems to be allowing Russia greater influence.

Specific conditions in the Kremlin's two European allies, Armenia and Belarus, have so far made them almost immune to the pull of Euroatlanticism. Armenia enjoys by far the most political pluralism of any of Russia's allies; it is also one of the biggest per capita recipients of American aid in the world. That makes it an unlikely member of the Kremlin camp. The main—and probably sole—reason is its need for support against neighboring Azerbaijan.[10] Belarus is, on paper, the Kremlin's closest ally. Heavily Russified in the Soviet era, it lacked the strong alliance between patriots and freedom-lovers that pulled neighboring countries such as Lithuania and Poland out of the Kremlin's orbit. After coming to power in 1994, the Belarusan president Alyaksandr Lukashenka[11] suggested merging his country with Russia to form a Russian–Belarusan Union, sometimes known as the union state. Seemingly the only foreign policy venture that might have worked, this has produced no practical benefit—except perhaps to Putin, who became its nominal prime minister in May 2008.

The main reason is that both sides' enthusiastic pan-Slavic rhetoric concealed wildly contradictory aims. The power-hungry Lukashenka saw the union state as a chance to strut on a much wider stage: in the declining Yeltsin years he was (and not only in his own eyes) a possible hard-line candidate for the presidency of the combined state. In the meantime, he hoped that the economic merger would mean continued supplies of gas for his country's old-fashioned industry at Russia's subsidized domestic price, and the chance to piggy-back the weak Belarusan ruble on the much stronger Russian one. Yeltsin disliked his Belarusan counterpart's dictatorial ways, but appreciated the convivial atmosphere of their meetings. Putin took a different view. He loathed the waffle associated with the union state as well as the boondoggles (for example, exploiting the lucrative array of loopholes created by the overlapping customs regimes). His suggestion was that Belarus should simply join Russia, with Lukashenka's presidency either being abolished or downgraded to a purely ceremonial position. He also drove a much tougher bargain on energy supplies. In January 2007, Belarus agreed to sell Russia half its national pipeline company, Beltransgas, for $2.5 billion; in exchange, Gazprom merely doubled the gas price, rather than quadrupling it as threatened. Belarus also gained a six-month delay in paying the new rate, and scrambled to try to borrow $1 billion on international markets to plug the gap.

Faced with Putin's visible disdain and repeated public snubs, Lukashenka has reinvented himself as a patriot, adopting the language of national independence and a distinct Belarusan identity. This was remarkable, given the sometimes lethal forms of persecution his regime had adopted toward the country's nationalist opposition in the past. He put out strong feelers in 2006 and 2007 about the possibility of a radical change of direction. The West, particularly America, is enthusiastic about this, but insists that a score of political prisoners be released first. After that it is prepared to discuss the restoration of political freedoms in exchange for a safe and dignified exit from power for Lukashenka and his close colleagues. This is already a big step, given that the regime has murdered at least four of its critics.[12] The regime seemed belatedly to be moving toward this in mid-2008.

The Kremlin has also revived the organizations Russia has set up in the former Soviet Union. The first of these was the Commonwealth of Independent States, which includes the 12 former Soviet republics (but not the Baltic states). In one sense, the CIS has been a startling failure. Of its dozens of documents and agreements on economic and political integration, almost all have proved entirely meaningless. A supposed free trade zone, to have been launched in 2005, has been repeatedly postponed. Even more limited attempts to promote cultural cooperation, or to free the movement of people, capital, goods, and services, are still bogged down by predatory customs regimes and bureaucracy. The main residual purpose of the CIS is as a source of sinecures,[13] for providing rival teams of election monitors to rebut outside claims of ballot-rigging, and as a means of scheduling meetings with ex-Soviet leaders whom the Kremlin might not want to invite for a bilateral visit to Russia. But it is still a useful backstop. Though Georgia, Ukraine, and Turkmenistan have all announced their withdrawal in whole or in part at different times, no member country has actually left.

Other, newer organizations have narrower memberships and more closely defined goals, chiefly in security cooperation. In 2001 Russia's most loyal allies in ex-Soviet Central Asia, Kazakhstan, Kyrgyzstan, Tajikistan, and Uzbekistan, joined along with China in the new Shanghai Cooperation Organization (SCO).[14] This was originally conceived as a coordination organization to deal with the evil trinity of post-Soviet politics: "terrorism, separatism and extremism." It was paralleled by the Collective Security Treaty Organization (CSTO),[15] a Kremlin-led version of NATO, with embryonic joint armed forces. In 2005 the SCO adopted a sharply anti-Western and anti-interventionist tone (see Chapter Eight) though in 2008 it took a more cautious approach. The much-touted Eurasian Economic Community and the Common Economic Space, both intended to be Kremlin-led rivals to the EU, have been conspicuously if unsurprisingly unsuccessful. Integrating open, law-governed economies is hard enough; doing the same for those run by closely allied bureaucrats, tycoons, and spooks is much harder. Having shored up its allies, Russia is now projecting its power into the enemy camp. The first and most conventional means for this is old-fashioned politics and diplomacy, involving a mixture of schmoozing, sulks, tantrums, and arm-twisting very familiar from the days of the last Cold War.

A big battleground for this is the Organization for Security and Co-operation in Europe (OSCE). This is the successor to the Conference on Security and Cooperation in Europe (CSCE), which played a big role in projecting Western soft power into the Soviet bloc in the days of the Cold War.[16] After two years of talks in Helsinki, countries on both sides of the Iron Curtain signed the "Helsinki Final Act" in 1975. The West accepted Europe's current frontiers.[17] In return the Soviet side agreed to respect universal human rights. The Soviet leadership thought this would be merely a paper concession. In fact it allowed campaigners in the East, such as Czechoslovakia's Charter 77 and the Moscow Helsinki Group, to complain that their governments were violating international commitments. That revived the dissident movement and proved a potent propaganda weapon. After the collapse of communism, the CSCE renamed itself the OSCE. Russia used to be a strong supporter, seeing it as a useful alternative to NATO. Now it treats it as a battleground. Russia is determined to throttle the OSCE's election-monitoring arm, the Office for Democratic Institutions and Human Rights (ODIHR, pronounced, aptly enough, "oh-dear"). For example, it has said that it will accept only the same level of election monitoring that the OSCE extends to countries such as Turkey and the United States. It repeatedly urges the OSCE to investigate the rights of Russians in the Baltic states (something that it has done, and pronounced satisfactory). More fundamentally, it wants the organization to return to its original mission, as a place for discussion between nation states, and to stop "interference" on its own behalf. It wants the secretariat to be strictly accountable to the member states—which, given the OSCE's consensus-based structure, means that it will be able to do almost nothing.

It is a similar story in other international organizations dealing with the ex-communist world. At the Council of Europe, which sponsors the European Court of Human Rights, Russia is blocking reforms that would streamline the submission of complaints. This would particularly benefit Russian citizens, who are the biggest group of plaintiffs. Russia wants the Council of Europe to change its priorities, moving away from human rights toward migration, cultural work, and crime-fighting. At the European Bank for Reconstruction and Development (EBRD), Russia is blocking projects in pro-Western countries, while insisting on extensive support for Russian companies and infrastructure projects, and the lending of respectability to Kremlin-backed banks that want to approach international capital markets. In the United Nations Development Program, it furiously objected to the hiring of Estonia's former prime minister and flat-tax pioneer, Mart Laar, as an adviser to Georgia.

The Kremlin does not find that any kind of multilateral diplomacy comes naturally. Its main political approach is to find bilateral differences and weaknesses and exploit them. It keeps alive, for instance, lingering disputes over ex-Soviet borders, refusing to clear up border disagreements with Estonia. Like Latvia, Estonia lost small amounts of territory during the Soviet occupation. Like Latvia, Estonia has renounced any claim to them now. But the Kremlin wants to confirm its victory by insisting that no reference be made to the country's pre-war existence.[18] The fiercest tussles are still in the darkest corners. The prime example of this is Moldova, the poorest, weakest, and probably most obscure country in Europe. It also has probably the weakest historical claim to statehood of any ex-Soviet country.[19] Some, like the Baltic states, had decades of independence in living memory. Others, such as Ukraine and Georgia, clearly existed as separate countries in the more distant past. But Moldova is an arbitrary creation of the Molotov–Ribbentrop pact, which annexed Romania's eastern provinces to the Soviet Union. After the war, the northern and southern extremities were handed over to the "Ukrainian Soviet Socialist Republic." The middle bit, plus a strip of mainly Russian-speaking territory on the east bank of the Dniestr River, formed the "Moldavian Soviet Socialist Republic," under wholly arbitrary boundaries. The usual Stalinist terror ensued. Well-educated people and anyone suspected of Romanian nationalist sympathies were deported to Siberia. The language was rewritten in Cyrillic characters, and declared to be not Romanian but "Moldovan" (although the spoken versions of both languages remained almost indistinguishable). When the Soviet Union began collapsing, opinion in Moldova divided three ways. A vocal minority simply wanted reunification with Romania, arguing that if the Molotov–Ribbentrop pact was illegitimate, then its consequences must be reversed everywhere. A second, larger group wanted independence for a multi-ethnic Moldova, including both the Romanian-speaking part and the Russophone region of "Transdniestria" (which happened to be home to all the republic's industrial enterprises). A third group, based in Transdniestria, were Kremlin loyalists and claimed that "Romanian nationalists" were planning discrimination and reprisals against local Russian-speakers.

With common sense and careful negotiation, the differences between the three sides could have been settled. But such qualities were in short supply in 1990–92. Transdniestria declared independence, and beat back (with extensive support from Russia) a Moldovan government attempt to re-establish control. Since then, the two sides have maintained an uneasy ceasefire. No other country—not even Russia—has formally recognized the Transdniestrian regime. Its narrow strip of territory has become a center for lucrative smuggling rackets and covert arms sales—businesses in which well-connected politicians in Russia, Ukraine, and even Moldova have developed lucrative interests. Russia maintains a force of "peacekeepers" in Transdniestria, who are also in charge of a colossal conventional weapons dump left over from the days of the Warsaw Pact. Russia was supposed to have withdrawn this by 2001 but claims, implausibly, that the local population will not permit it. It is true that "spontaneous" demonstrations have blocked the railway tracks near the barracks and depots, but it is hard to believe that the otherwise loyal and efficient Transdniestrian security service would not be able to disperse them if necessary.

In theory, five outside powers—America, the OSCE, Russia, Ukraine, and the EU—are trying to bring the Moldovan and Transdniestrian sides together, and promote the "three Ds": the demilitarization, democratization, and decriminalization of Transdniestria.[20] In practice, these talks, like those in other frozen conflicts, have proved unsuccessful. The Kremlin's bilateral efforts to persuade Moldova to accept a confederation with Transdniestria have come closer to success, though so far American and European intervention has managed to prevent Moldova actually signing up for any Russian peace plan. The real reason why the West is losing in Moldova is not military, however, but the country's own political and economic weakness: the product of corrupt and highly inexpert government. More than almost anywhere else in the ex-communist world, the Euroatlantic option lacks credibility and impact. Almost nobody in the current Moldovan government, for example (the foreign minister included), speaks English. Romania, which should be Moldova's bridge to Europe, is seen as an unpredictable and chauvinistic threat, not a helpful neighbor. On the economic front, Moldova's industry is mostly based on low value-added products such as cheap wine and unprocessed fruit. That makes it vulnerable to the trade sanctions imposed by Russia in 2006. Other ex-communist countries have responded to these by reorienting their exports to Western countries. Moldovan firms seem to lack the ability or willingness to do this. Russia has also squeezed the Transdniestrian economy by raising gas prices and cutting credits. That presents the Moldovan leadership with the tempting prospect of an immediate deal, if they will only drop their remaining ambitions for European integration.[21] If events proceed in this way, the result will be a striking defeat for the Euroatlantic forces in the post-communist world. A combination of timidity and inaction will have allowed Russia to use a mixture of economic, political, and military levers against an almost defenseless adversary. In return for sacrificing a few Transdniestrian pawns, Russia will have won back a country into its sphere of influence for the first time since the collapse of communism.

It is Georgia, however, that has turned out to be the hottest spot of the New Cold War. Reading news reports of the war in August 2008, it would be easy to assume, wrongly, that the fighting started with an unprovoked attack by Georgia on neighboring South Ossetia. The truth is a lot more complicated. It starts with Georgia's difficult rebirth as a modern state. Russia had ruled the Caucasus already for a century before the Bolshevik revolution. It snuffed out the infant Georgian Democratic Republic in 1921. In the 1930s, Stalin applied a reign of terror that the Baltic states and other Kremlin trophies would find all too familiar ten years later. Tens of thousands of people were deported or murdered. Unlike the Baltic states, Georgia regained its independence with no living memories of legality and statehood, and without the help of a well-educated and patriotic Diaspora.

As communist rule crumbled in the late 1980s, nationalist leaders such as the erratic philologist Zviad Gamsakhurdia, backed by enthusiastic nationalist militias, faced an almost impossible task: running a country with no secure borders and no tradition of statehood. They showed little interest in the mundane tasks that were occupying the Estonians, such as stabilizing the currency, attracting foreign investors, and establishing a modern civil service. Instead they fought civil wars with the country's two main ethnic minorities, the Ossetians and the Abkhaz. Both of these enjoyed a degree of autonomy under Soviet rule, and disliked the idea of

Georgian independence, particularly if based on Gamsakhurdia's swaggering and eccentric ethno-nationalism. The results were appalling. In the Abkhaz capital Sukhumi, anonymous arsonists torched the national library, museum, and state archive. It was as if Washington, D.C, lost the Library of Congress, the Kennedy Center, and the Smithsonian in one blaze. The Abkhaz,[22] with strong support from both Russians and Chechen extremists who disliked the Georgians even more than the Russians, beat the Georgians back. Two hundred and fifty thousand ethnic Georgians—around half the population—fled.

That difficult birth nearly proved fatal for Georgia. For almost a decade, it was written off by Western allies as a hopeless basket case. Gamsakhurdia was deposed in 1992 and Eduard Shevardnadze, who had been Gorbachev's foreign minister, took over. He brought stability, but no reform. Crony capitalism took root: the Shevardnadze family had an eye for profit, but no sense of how to build lasting economic growth. Russia maintained troops in Georgia, and occasionally used them. Reform was skin deep.[23] All that changed in 2003 when the Georgian population, almost Italian in its love of good company and dislike for organization, rose up against the incompetent and increasingly authoritarian Shevardnadze regime. That brought to power Mikheil Saakashvili, an American-educated, *Economist*-reading lawyer, determined to reform Georgia at warp speed, with Estonia as his explicit model. Though nobody would cite the country as the ultimate model of freedom and good government, progress was astonishing. Foreign investment poured in; tax rates flattened, government revenues and salaries soared, public services improved; the economy boomed. Whole government departments, such as the notoriously corrupt traffic police, were simply abolished. Tax rates were low and the system simple.

The result was, for a while, to turn Georgia into the region's most successful country, which attracted those it once repelled. The first region to shift allegiance was Ajaria, a semi-independent region that had become a magnet for international organized crime under its leader, Aslan Abashidze. His popularity—genuine in the early years of his regime—was based on having spared his people, Georgian-speaking Muslims, from the miseries afflicting the rest of the country. But as that chaos and poverty turned into economic growth, stability, and political freedom, his hold weakened. In a putsch in spring 2004, Abashidze was forced out by popular protests and fled to Moscow. Ajaria has become a Georgian showcase, attracting foreign investment and tourism from the whole

Black Sea region and beyond. Abashidze had been a strong supporter of Putin's, but his departure was a minor blow compared to the effect that Georgia's prosperity had on the weaker of the Kremlin's two puppet states in Georgia, South Ossetia and Abkhazia. The Ossetians' historic homeland straddles the Caucasus mountains. On the north side, the Ossetians, orthodox by religion, find themselves stranded in Russia's worst-governed region amid increasingly restive Muslim populations in the neighboring republics. South Ossetia was an autonomous region of Soviet Georgia; it did not need to declare independence. It was backed by the Kremlin, but formally recognized nowhere.

After a botched attempt in 2004 to retake South Ossetia by force, Saakashvili's main tactic was to regain his breakaway regions through soft power and repeated diplomatic initiatives.[24] He exploited the Kremlin's crude imposition of its own stooges in place of the native South Ossetian politicians who led the fight against Georgian nationalism in the early 1990s. These founding fathers formed a government-in-exile to promote reintegration with Georgia. Some of the 70,000 South Ossetian population even started commuting to work at jobs in Georgia. They found there not the autocratic ethnocracy depicted by Kremlin propaganda, but a thriving and tolerant society. Despite increasing levels of Kremlin subsidy, the South Ossetians' historic sympathies to Moscow seemed to be shriveling.

That was good news for Georgian citizens of all ethnicities and a sharp contrast to the position on the other side of the Caucasus mountains. But it was bad news for the Kremlin, which sees law-governed, prosperous, and stable neighbors as a problem, not a benefit. Saakashvili was not just a successful technocrat but also a torchbearer (albeit a sometimes hotheaded and blinkered one) for Western values. His aim is to anchor Georgia in the Euroatlantic economic and security structures that have served other countries so well. That presents a profound ideological challenge to Russia. Ex-Soviet countries that, despite a similar history and cultural background, adopt a different model of development raise embarrassing questions. If Georgia can have a lean, clean state bureaucracy, why can't Russia? If Ukrainians can have a lively pluralist media, why can't Russians? Though few would have predicted its ferocity, a counter-attack was inevitable.

Trouble started brewing in 2006, when from March to May Russia imposed an escalating series of import restrictions, first on Georgian exports of food and drink,[25] ostensibly because of hygiene worries (public health authorities in other countries found no cause for concern). Russia then closed the only border crossing with Georgia proper, allegedly for some construction work. That halted, in effect, all Georgian exports to Russia while stimulating trade through the South Ossetian-controlled Roki tunnel. On September 27, 2006, Georgia arrested four officers of the GRU, allegedly because they had been planning a coup, prompting a furious response from the Kremlin.[26] A more cool-headed Georgian leader might have quietly deported the men. But Saakashvili, whose charm is matched only by his temper, ordered them to be paraded in front of the television cameras as they were handed over to the Russian authorities. Russia recalled its ambassador, and cut postal, phone, and banking links with Georgia. Gazprom said it would double the gas price to Georgia, from $110 to $230 per thousand m³.

More sinisterly, other bits of Russian officialdom such as the tax police, immigration authorities, and school administrators started harassing people with Georgian surnames and deporting Georgian citizens, allegedly as illegal immigrants.[27]

Russia seemed to expect Georgia to buckle. But as so often with economic sanctions imposed by the Kremlin, the attempt to exert political pressure through Soviet-era trade ties proved counterproductive.[28] Georgian exporters raised quality and packaging standards and started to export to new markets. Saakashvili, who had long been urging his country's entrepreneurs to shed their dependence on Russian customers, said he was grateful. Georgia's growth rate lost at most a couple of percentage points as a result of the Kremlin sanctions. And the country's morale soared.

The economic warfare was matched by increasingly alarming military measures. In March 2007, a fleet of helicopters spent two hours firing cannon, rockets, and an anti-tank missile at three villages in the Kodori Gorge, a region of Abkhazia where the Georgian authorities had recovered control from a local warlord in July 2006 and set up a parallel administration. Luckily, the buildings hit by the rockets were unoccupied. Russia denied responsibility and stonewalled an investigation, declining to provide aviation logs or trace the origin of a missile whose parts were recovered after the attack. Yet no other country in the region has helicopters with night-fighting capabilities; the munitions used were Russian-made; more than 50 witnesses said they heard helicopters. Russia argued that Georgians were the likely culprits: after all, if the attack reflects badly on Russia, then Russia's enemies must be the most likely perpetrators.[29] Outsiders shrugged their shoulders.

Then, on August 6, 2007, a Russian-made Raduga Kh–58 anti-radar missile, fired by one of two Sukhoi Su–24 jets in Georgian airspace, landed in a village near Tbilisi.[30] Its 150 kg warhead failed to explode. Again, the facts point in one direction only: Georgia's air force has no Su–24s, while Russia's has hundreds. Georgian radar produced records showing that they had tracked the intruders entering the country's airspace from Russia. The most likely planned target was nearby, a new NATO-compatible radar station. The Baltic states and, later, Sweden, came out with strong statements supporting Georgia. Most other countries equivocated. So did the OSCE, blaming conflicting accounts from the parties concerned. The EU said the event was "dangerous and alarming" but did not assign blame.[31] If the aim was to test Western reactions, the message was clear: military adventurism in the former empire comes with no political price attached.

In September, Georgia marked what was probably the high-water mark of its efforts to solve the South Ossetia conflict with soft power, holding an international conference in Tamaresheni, one of many ethnically Georgian villages in the region controlled by the authorities in Tbilisi. Russia complained about the presence of foreign diplomats and international observers at the conference, which highlighted Georgia's efforts to promote its own loyalist South Ossetian administration. But this was soon eclipsed. In early November, the country plunged into a political crisis, as Saakashvili fought off an attempt by the opposition to topple him. He had less support than he would have liked. Many of the Georgian president's friends and allies had become increasingly alarmed by the hot-headed, heavy-handed, and cronyist features of his rule. "Misha," as his friends call him, relies on a small circle of advisers. Decisions come quickly and often in the small hours of the morning, after hurried conclaves and chaotic series of mobile phone conversations. The atmosphere can be exhilarating, not least thanks to Saakashvili's own personality. But the quality of policymaking is poor and public administration—for example, in the conduct of elections—has come to seem off-puttingly partisan. Some of the president's more sober allies began quietly distancing themselves from his court.

Yet the Georgian opposition, a mixture of moderates, eccentrics, and extremists, bankrolled in part by the billionaire tycoon Badri Patarkatsishvili, a close ally of the London-based Russian émigré Boris Berezovsky, seemed even more alarming: hysterical, intransigent, and with in some cases shady links to Russia and organized crime. Their demand for a parliamentary rather than presidential republic was a legitimate one. The way they pursued it verged on the insurrectionary. Yet it was hard to agree with the authorities' simplistic portrayal of a looming Moscow-backed putsch. Berezovsky, after all, is an arch foe of Putin's. Why would one of his closest friends be trying to do the Kremlin's dirty work in the Caucasus?[32]

Influential outsiders spent much time urging the authorities, with mixed success, to treat the opposition with respect. Suggestions that the opposition itself behave responsibly seemed to go wholly unheeded. Opposition demonstrations, ostensibly demanding early parliamentary elections, denounced Saakashvili as a "bandit" and "terrorist" and hanged him in effigy. None of that, however, excused what happened next. On November 7 Georgia imposed a state of emergency; riot police dispersed a demonstration using excessive violence and closed the main opposition television station, smashing equipment and intimidating its staff. Saakashvili claimed that he was forestalling a Russian-backed coup. Many of his friends thought he was crying wolf and came out with unprecedentedly sharp criticism.[33]

Against international advice, the Georgian president called early elections on January 5; though these were better administered than feared, they did not give the opposition time to campaign properly, and Saakashvili was returned to power with 53.4 percent of the vote. The opposition insisted that widespread fraud had taken place, but was unable to produce evidence of more than minor irregularities. International observers gave rather reluctant endorsement of the result, with a troubling number of complaints:

> While the election was in essence consistent with most OSCE and Council of Europe commitments and standards for democratic elections, it also revealed significant challenges that need to be addressed urgently. Although this election represented the first genuinely competitive post-independence presidential election, shortcomings were noted. The campaign was overshadowed by widespread allegations of intimidation and pressure, among others on public-sector employees and opposition activists, some of which were verified by the OSCE/ODIHR EOM. The distinction between State activities and the campaign of the ruling United National Movement (UNM) party candidate, Mikheil Saakashvili, was blurred. In addition, other aspects of the election process, notably vote count and tabulation procedures, as well as the post-election complaints and appeals process, further

presented serious challenges to the fulfillment of some OSCE commitments.[34]

The Georgian authorities certainly did not help their public image, or the health of their country's political system, with their approach. But for all Georgia's shortcomings, its political system was still in a far better state than Russia's. Without outside interference, it was entirely plausible that Georgia would continue on its bumpy path of political and economic development towards the EU and NATO. This in turn offered the admittedly distant prospect of reconciliation with the breakaway provinces. The goal was to show Ossetians and the Abkhaz that they had an alternative to stagnating in a kind of Russian Puerto Rico: integration into a dynamic and prosperous EU country.

But that process required both time and peace. Instead, a hideously botched NATO summit in Bucharest all but guaranteed a speedy descent into war. America, Georgia's strongest supporter, managed to leave its key European allies under the impression that it was not insistent on Georgia and Ukraine receiving a "Membership Action Plan," or MAP—the next stage for the two countries' admission to the alliance. Yet at the same time it gave the impression to the Georgians that a MAP was in sight. The result was a crashing disappointment. European countries such as Germany, backed by France, flatly refused to consider Georgia and Ukraine as candidates worthy of a clear path to membership. At a late-night meeting of foreign ministers, tempers flared. New members of NATO such as Poland watched in horror as countries from "old Europe" said bluntly that their relations with Russia mattered more than the interests of their nominal eastern allies—and particularly of the erratic and tiresome Saakashvili. At the heads of government meeting later, Angela Merkel of Germany patched up what seemed like a compromise: an unqualified promise of NATO membership—but with no date or time plan attached. In a savage performance the next day, Putin, visiting what many thought would be his last international gathering, threatened Ukraine with dismemberment if it persisted in trying to join the alliance. That prompted a sharp protest from Kyiv.[35]

NATO members had sent a lethal signal to the Kremlin. Even as they were packing their bags, and an upmarket Bucharest hotel was repairing the furniture smashed (it is said) by the disappointed Saakashvili, Putin had issued a decree ordering the Russian state bureaucracy to establish official ties with Georgia's breakaway regions.

Georgia responded by imposing, in effect, a veto of Russia's nearly completed talks to join the World Trade Organization. On April 20 a Russian warplane shot down an unmanned Georgian drone over Abkhazia. The drone's camera recorded the attack, which was widely posted on the internet.[36] Russia said that a NATO country had staged the attack as a stunt and accused Georgia of preparing an attack on Abkhazia from the Kodori Gorge. It sharply increased its military (ostensibly peace-keeping) presence in Abkhazia. In June it repaired a strategically important railway using "railway troops"—a military construction brigade whose curious name is a hangover from the days of the Soviet military. The West responded weakly and belatedly. Russia also pursued a diplomatic tack, offering to broker agreements between Georgia and the two separatist entities on the non-use of force. That sounds superficially sensible, but would have required the Georgian authorities to treat the Russian-backed puppet regimes as equal negotiating partners, as well as en-shrining the *de facto* partition of the country. Saakashvili tried in vain to strike up a rapport with Medvedev—at the time still seen as a possible harbinger of a thaw in Russian foreign policy. He got nowhere. Georgian attempts to reopen peace talks with the Abkhaz leadership proved similarly fruitless. Meanwhile, friction between Georgian and separatist police and soldiers, sometimes also involv-ing Russian peacekeepers, continued, with both sides trading accu-sations of brutality and illegal behavior.

The man who perhaps more than anyone else should have been dealing with this issue at a European level was Javier Solana, the for-mer NATO secretary-general who is the EU's foreign policy chief. Yet his record of involvement has been remarkably lackluster. De-spite his promise to put the issue of frozen conflicts[37] high on the agenda of the EU–Russia summit in Siberia in June, results were puny. Russia appeared to have succeeded in forestalling criticism, by linking discussion of this question with that of Kosovo. The parallel is superficially convincing, but falls down on several points. The Georgians are the victims of ethnic cleansing, particularly in Abk-hazia. In Kosovo, Milošević was the perpetrator. Russian peacekeep-ers have proved self-interested, to put it mildly. NATO forces in Kosovo strive to be impartial. The West has negotiated in good faith over the future of Kosovo for years; Russia's interest is in needling Georgia, not reaching agreement.[38]

As Russia's position hardened, the last chances to avoid a war crumbled. The Abkhaz authorities rejected out of hand a German-backed peace plan. A deal to build a new railway through Georgia, linking Azerbaijan and Turkey, provided another reminder of Georgia's importance as a transit corridor. It was to be the last piece of good news for a long time. In late July, Russian media outlets began carrying inflammatory reports about Georgian preparations for war in South Ossetia. On August 7, heavy Russian armor began entering South Ossetia through the Roki tunnel, while artillery bombardments of Georgian positions intensified. Only hours before, Saakashvili had offered a unilateral ceasefire.

What exactly happened next is still unclear. Russia claims that Georgia launched a violent assault on Tskhinkali, the main city of South Ossetia, causing hundreds of civilian casualties. That has not been independently confirmed, and later estimates are of scores of casualties, rather than the 2,000-plus originally claimed. Russia immediately accused Georgia of killing a number of its peacekeepers and perpetrating "genocide" against its citizens (90 percent of the residents of separatist-controlled South Ossetia had Russian passports). Together with its local allies, Russia launched a land, sea, and air assault against the Georgian forces in South Ossetia, against the Kodori Gorge, and against other parts of Georgia. The result was the fiercest fighting in Europe since the wars in ex-Yugoslavia. Hundreds of people were killed, mostly civilians; tens of thousands fled their homes.

The war itself was over quickly. On August 9, Russia sank a Georgian naval cutter and through its local proxies opened a second front in Abkhazia, attacking the Kodori Gorge, and began bombing targets inside Georgia. Georgian forces in South Ossetia began a retreat that turned into a rout. Saakashvili declared martial law. On August 10, Georgia declared a unilateral ceasefire, which Russia rejected. At the United Nations, Russia—according to the U.S. ambassador there—demanded "regime change" in Georgia. By August 11, Russian forces were pouring into Georgia, meeting little resistance and occupying military bases and the town of Gori, on the country's main east–west highway. Georgia said it was withdrawing from the CIS; an American plane carrying relief supplies was able to land at Georgia's main airport; and Ukraine said it would not allow Russian naval ships involved in the war to return to Sevastopol. But with Russian troops seemingly readying themselves for an attack on all-but-defenseless Tbilisi, Georgia had no cards left. A loosely worded ceasefire agreement brokered by the French president, Nicolas Sarkozy, ended the fighting—but not the conflict.

As the dust settled, intriguing questions began to arise. Pavel Felgenhauer, the well-connected Moscow-based military analyst, said that the whole thing had been planned by Russia from the start.[39] Plenty of evidence supports that: the pre-positioning of Russian troops, the systematic escalation of provocations, the slickly prepared media offensive. Yet certainly some blame for the start of the war must rest on the Georgian side, too. The much-repeated message to Saakashvili over the previous months from visiting Western friends had been "Russia will try to provoke you into a war. Do not respond." The thinking on the Georgian side appears to have been that the provocations were becoming intolerable, and that a quick surprise attack on South Ossetia might pre-empt an upcoming assault from Russia elsewhere. That was a risky and probably unwise approach that depended on two things: first that a Georgian attack could disable the Roki tunnel, preventing speedy Russian reinforcement of South Ossetia; secondly, that Russia would swallow its defeat and not use its overwhelming military superiority to attack Georgia elsewhere. If those were the assumptions, both were mistaken. A bridge leading out of the Roki tunnel was damaged but soon repaired. And Russia counter-attacked with complete disregard for the squawks of protest that began coming from Western capitals. As with the November crackdown, the Georgian leadership had completely failed to appreciate how easily their support in the West could be dented.

The result has been a catastrophe for Georgia. Russia moved quickly to give formal diplomatic recognition to South Ossetia and Abkhazia—ending once and for all its always flimsy recognition of Georgia's territorial integrity. Thousands of people fled the Georgian villages in South Ossetia in the face of Russian looting, rape, and purges. Vital parts of the country remained under Russian occupation. A Russian checkpoint controlled Georgia's main east-west highway. No full account of the damage was available as of the end of August, but the evidence of widespread and systematic destruction of military and transport installations was overwhelming. Though the Kremlin claims to have pulled out its combat troops, thousands remain under the fiction that they are CIS peacekeeping forces (the CIS does not appear to have been consulted about this). Georgia's armed forces, American-equipped and Israeli-trained, are licking their wounds. Saakashvili's own position was shored up during the war, with even political opponents rallying to his side in the cause of national unity. In the coming months it may be more precarious.

The effect of the war inside Russia, wildly popular, has been to end any talk of a "Medvedev thaw." The diminutive lawyer from St.

Petersburg slipped effortlessly into his new role as leader of a martial nation, denouncing Georgia and the West in almost equal measure. Russia, he said, was not frightened of a "New Cold War." Indeed, it does not seem frightened of a hot one, issuing stern threats to NATO not to build up a naval presence in the Black Sea.

The wake-up call to the West could hardly have been louder. Fears of a similar conflict in Ukraine or the Baltic states were stoked by bellicose statements from Russian politicians about Russia's right and duty to protect its citizens, wherever they might be. But it is unlikely that the Kremlin will continue in this vein, at least immediately. Though Russia is determined to face down criticism from the West (which it believes it can withstand through its economic muscle) it does not at the moment show any signs of wanting a wider conflict. Why should it? So many other fronts offer easy progress. Having discovered soft power in recent years, the Kremlin is most likely to continue using it.

The simplest feature of the Kremlin's rhetorical counter-attack against Euroatlanticism is an appeal to national self-interest (or, more accurately, the self-interest of national elites). Konstantin Kosachev, chairman of the Duma foreign affairs committee, terms it "absurd" that ex-Soviet countries should shun the benefits of cooperation with Russia and instead want to "enter the straitjacket of European institutions and fall under the diktat of Brussels."[40] In other words, countries that throw in their lot with the Western camp, far from gaining freedom, lose their sovereignty and are forced to accept an alien set of values. "Sovereign democracy" allows rulers to run their country as they like (so long as that broadly chimes with Kremlin interests).

The most effective manifestation of this is in the Kremlin's own version of "people power," both in the form of mass public movements and phony NGOs. Here the main asset is ethnic Russians, up to 25 million of whom were living in other bits of the Soviet Union when it collapsed.[41] Putin has given a sharp new edge to Russian concerns on this issue. As early as April 2000, he endorsed a new military doctrine that defined "discrimination" against its citizens abroad as one of the military threats facing Russia.[42] In his 2001 address to the upper house of parliament, the Federation Council, he widened that to include not just Russian citizens, but "compatriots," a loose term that can be used to include any Russian-speaker with a pro-Kremlin orientation. In 2002, in a speech to diplomats, he again underlined the importance he attached to the subject.[43] Russia set up new bodies to encourage migration back to Russia, to simplify the procedures for gaining Russian citizenship, and—most importantly—to funnel cash and other support to pro-Kremlin organizations outside Russia. Tougher visa regulations for Georgians, Azeris, and others accentuated the choice: without a Russian passport it became much harder for them to study, work, or trade. Unwittingly, the EU amplified that effect, giving preferential treatment to Russian visa applications over, say, Ukrainian or Georgian ones.

Elsewhere, Russia is using a new, subtler, and more effective weapon: NGOs. Financed by Western think tanks, charities, and (sometimes) government agencies, these have proved the most effective way of organizing and financing popular movements for political freedoms in ex-communist countries. In the Kremlin's eyes, they are little more than fronts for foreign intelligence agencies. The idea that the peoples of Eastern Europe might genuinely want to be in alliance with the world's largest free countries is dismissed as sentimental nonsense.[44] Now Russia is trying to use the same tactic. Kremlin-financed think tanks have been set up in Ukraine, the Caucasus, and Moldova, coupled with media outlets, internet websites, and networks of academics. A senior Kremlin official, Modest Kolerov, heading the department for "interregional and cultural ties with foreign countries," was in charge of this network, which includes phony news sites on the internet that peddle distorted or outright invented versions of events.[45] The most elaborate disinformation efforts are mounted in English, with a polished presentation that belies their origins.[46]

The exercises of Kremlin soft power in Moldova and Crimea have so far been mere sideshows, however. The big argument is in the Baltic states. In a narrow sense it is about history; more widely it rages over the right of these countries to determine their own cultural and linguistic future. The central issue is the fate of the Soviet-era migrants (mostly Russian-speaking but not all ethnic Russians) who were brought to Estonia and Latvia in the Soviet era to boost the industrial workforce and to dilute their national identity.[47] Deeply resented under Soviet rule, this became a central political issue once independence was regained. In Estonia's case, 88 percent of the population had been ethnic Estonians before World War II.[48] By 1989 that had shrunk to 61.5 percent. The Estonian language was pushed out of public life.[49] On regaining independence, Estonia said citizenship for occupation-era migrants and their descendants would be conditional on a basic knowledge of Estonian language and history.

That struck many as harsh. After all, around half of these people had been born in Estonia. They had not chosen to come there. It would be unfair to leave them as a stateless people, casting the shadows of suffering and injustice still wider. Still less would it be fair to discriminate against them in the workplace. Lithuania gave automatic citizenship to all Soviet citizens living on its territory at the time of independence: that included less than a tenth of the population who described their ethnicity as Russian, and a similar number calling themselves Polish. But Estonia's and Latvia's predicament was different. Migration, mainly of ethnic Russians, during the Soviet era had been far larger. Many of the "illegal immigrants" who had arrived during this period were deeply opposed to Estonian independence. They mostly spoke no Estonian and had no desire to learn. Indeed, if addressed in Estonian, they would object. If Estonia set no conditions for citizenship, the chances that the new arrivals and their descendants would integrate seemed slim. Estonia and Latvia gave automatic citizenship therefore only to the citizens of the pre-war republic and their descendants. In Estonia, Russians who had supported the struggle to regain independence were entitled to citizenship on demand. Everyone else had to apply for naturalization.

Many outsiders thought that was dangerously mistaken. The wars in ex-Yugoslavia showed how quickly newly independent countries could alienate minorities and prompt outsider intervention, with a terrible cost. But in the Baltics these fears proved groundless. One reason was that the local Russian leaders were a deeply unimpressive lot: Soviet has-beens and never-weres. Another was economics: the Baltic states were thriving while Russia was in chaos, meaning that few Russians decided to take advantage of resettlement grants and go home to the motherland. Some that did soon tried to return. In fact, Estonia's citizenship and language laws (like the broadly similar ones in Latvia) have proved successful. Although Russian remains widely spoken, the national languages have regained unquestioned prominence. By mid-2007, nearly 84 percent of the population held Estonian citizenship, up from 68 percent in 1991. As of mid-2007, around 8 percent were citizens of other countries (mostly Russia) and a similar number were still stateless. Several thousand people a year continue to receive citizenship by naturalization. Some international organizations make occasional suggestions about tweaks to the law—such as cutting the cost of language lessons—but in Europe and America the principle that Estonia and Latvia award citizenship to those who make a conscious choice and show the necessary effort seems established.

Russia, by contrast, contests the citizenship policy both in principle and in practice. From the Kremlin's point of view, all Soviet citizens living in Estonia at the time of independence deserve the same treatment. The Estonians' policy is discrimination, pure and simple, based on the crudest form of ethnic nationalism. The West's collusion in this is an act of gross hypocrisy. If true, that would be a grave charge. Estonia's counter-argument, though, is a strong one: citizenship is given on historical, not ethnic grounds. Nearly a tenth of the population of the pre-war republic were ethnic Russians. Any who are alive today, and any who can prove descent from them, get citizenship automatically. Furthermore, Estonia has now relaxed its citizenship law, creating exemptions for those who have finished an Estonian-language school, and for the elderly or mentally handicapped. Non-citizens were allowed to vote in local elections, and, assuming they spoke the national language sufficiently, were able to hold all jobs except those involving national security. But the Kremlin keeps up a constant barrage of criticism, claiming that the rights of Russians are being abused and demanding that the outside world do something about it.[50]

People power and conventional political pressure combined in late April 2007 in the Kremlin's reaction to an Estonian government decision to move a Soviet war memorial, and some nearby graves, from central Tallinn to a military cemetery. Though the memorial had become a magnet for extremists on both sides, creating a minor policing problem, it was not a national security threat and many in Estonia and abroad regarded the decision to shift it as precipitate and unwise. Although Estonians disliked the statue as a symbol of the renewal of a hated Soviet occupation, in the eyes of many Estonian Russians it was "Alyosha the Liberator" representing the heroism and sacrifice of the struggle against Hitler.

On the night of April 26, as the Estonian authorities cordoned off the statue and prepared to move it, a mob looted the center of Tallinn, breaking windows and torching bus shelters. Chanting "It's all ours," "Fuck Estonia," and "USSR forever," the mainly young and often drunken protestors were to many Estonians a sign of Russians reverting to type. The truth was less alarming: although the majority of Estonian Russians objected to the decision to move the statue, only a tiny minority of them expressed their views violently. What was worrying was that the Kremlin not only did not condemn the violence being perpetrated in the name of Russian patriotism, but endorsed it, praising the looters as youthful patriots who were protesting about Estonia's "fascist" vandalism of a sacred edifice. The Russian media portrayed those arrested as political prisoners; the one fatality of the night of April 26, an ethnic Russian stabbed in a fight over looted property, was reported as a victim of police brutality. Estonia initially found itself in perilous diplomatic isolation. Other countries mumbled excuses and banalities, saying that Estonia and Russia should sort out their differences peacefully. Only Poland, itself no stranger to the Kremlin propaganda machine, came out at once with forthright support.

Luckily for the Estonians, Russia grossly overplayed its hand. *Nashi* and other organizations attacked Estonia's Moscow embassy. They defaced the embassy's outside walls and placed loudspeakers against them, blasting round-the-clock military music from the Stalin era into the building.[51] They jostled the Estonian ambassador, Marina Kaljurand, when she tried to give a press conference (the child of a Latvian–Russian mixed marriage, she was hard to demonize as the champion of neo-Nazi revanchism). The pickets—without any legal authority and with the supine cooperation of the city's normally officious police—blocked the street, checked the documents of passers-by and organized the noisy and sometimes violent protests, including the threat to "dismantle" the embassy.[52] When the Swedish ambassador visited in a sign of belated solidarity, the pickets tried to turn over his car. All that was a clear breach of the Vienna Convention (something that the Kremlin insists be meticulously observed when Russian embassies attract protesters). A Russian delegation invited to Tallinn, echoing the language used by Stalin's emissary Andrei Zhdanov in 1940, demanded the resignation of Estonia's government and a criminal investigation into the repression" of "antifascists."[53] That was a big mistake. Had the Kremlin stayed in the background, Estonia would have suffered heavy damage to its reputation. Western pressure for a change of citizenship and language policies would have increased. Quite possibly the government would have had to resign. But by overplaying its hand, the Kremlin made even the exercise of soft power over an easy target ineffective and counter-productive. Any queasiness that the outside world felt about Estonia's seemingly cavalier treatment of a war memorial was counter-balanced by outright nausea at Russia's response. Statements of support began flooding in. Estonia's president, Ilves, was invited to the White House. In turn, the Russian media became almost hysterical. *Komsomolskaya Pravda* (Young Communist League Truth) printed an astonishing poem looking forward to the day when the Russian armed forces might retake Estonia by force. The final extract reads

> *The Pskov division is not far off,*
> *A short forced march and Tallinn falls.*
> *They may say public opinion will be against it*
> *Now that Estonia is in NATO.*
> *So what? Who in NATO cares?*
> *I will not hang on their every word.*
> *So what if they call it an occupation?* ·
> *They will grumble and grind their teeth*
> *Saying freedom's flame is doused again.*
> *But we will settle with those greedy swine*
> *Who would sell their mother and father for gas.*
> *I am not scared to tell you, Estonians,*
> *The EU will not be able to help you . . .* [54]

Even at the time that sounded sinister, and it is yet more ominous following the attack on Georgia. The Russian forces in Pskov, just across the border in Russia, practiced the recapture of the Baltic states in 2007. Details of the exercise are sketchy, but it seems to have involved an intervention to protect the rights of "Russian-speakers" threatened with violence by local "nationalists." The aim of the exercise was to see how easily the Russian invading forces could capture the airfields and ports, thus preventing NATO from reinforcing its allies. The Baltic states have no air defenses of their own and are dependent on a squadron of borrowed NATO fighters whose record in reacting to Russian intruders has been less than impressive.

The Kremlin's activities in its former empire are mainly organized from the shadows. As well as Kolerov, the mainstream external intelligence services have been given lavish resources and unlimited political backing since Putin came to power. In a speech in July 2007, he said the foreign intelligence service, the SVR,[55] should "permanently increase its capabilities."[56] The FSB, which was once restricted to dealing with security threats inside Russia, now has a full legal license to operate abroad. As well as promoting disinformation and manipulating public life, these two agencies and the GRU all try to penetrate the central institutions of state in the ex-Soviet countries. Counter-intelligence officers note with alarm their success in recruiting and placing agents and informants in the criminal justice system, the armed forces, the security and intelligence services, the foreign, defense and interior ministries, and elsewhere.

During the Estonia crisis, and in 2008 against Georgia, Russia opened a new front: cyber warfare. National security experts have been worried for years about the internet's potential for disruption, subversion, criminality, and espionage. Sometimes the perpetrators are gangsters, sometimes terrorists; sometimes they have the backing of a nation state. In Estonia's case, the attacks seemed to mix all three factors. The technicalities of cyber warfare are shrouded in jargon,[57] but the main effect was to disrupt Estonia's links with the outside world. Important government websites were unavailable— including those, such as the foreign ministry, that were most needed to counter the Kremlin propaganda offensive. The same happened in Georgia in August 2008. Tracing the source of the cyber attacks was tricky as the infected computers were in botnets composed of computers spread all over the world.[58]

The "bronze soldier" row is unlikely to be the last time that Russia tries to exert influence on the Baltic states. Russian speakers, particularly in Estonia and Latvia, are still dangerously unintegrated and open to incitement or provocation by extremist movements. In the 1990s, security services in all three Baltic states found links between local ultra-nationalists and Russia's secret services. Persuading local skinheads to attack Russian cultural, social, or historical landmarks would give the Kremlin the perfect excuse to demand that the rights of "compatriots" be protected. Another potential vulnerability is the transit agreements across Lithuania to Kaliningrad. Although Russia now transports most of the sensitive military traffic to its western bastion by ferry, it retains the right to send sealed trains across Lithuanian territory and also has an air corridor available on request. Lithuanian "extremists" blew up this railway in 1994 but luckily no casualties resulted. It could easily happen again. Sabotage to the power generation network could lead to blackouts in Kaliningrad, again giving the Kremlin the pretext to intervene to stop an economic "blockade." Russia has also been stoking discontent in Crimea. This region of Ukraine combines several potentially explosive elements. Sevastopol in particular is a naval citadel as dear to Russian hearts as Portsmouth or Plymouth are to the British, or Pearl Harbor to Americans. A Russian naval lease is due to run out in 2017. Ukraine would like Russia to leave early, and pay a higher rent. Russia shows no sign of wanting to leave at all. The population includes many ultra-loyal Russians, mostly holding Russian passports, who are wholly unreconciled to Ukrainian rule.[59] A further

threat is increasing Islamist sentiments among the region's indigenous, but now marginalized, Tatar population. That would allow
Russia to complain that terrorists were threatening the security of
its naval base, or attacking Russian citizens.[60]

But Russia's biggest chance now lies in the failure of the ex-
communist countries to make the most of the chances of the past
decade. Admittedly, their starting point in 1989 was intimidatingly
difficult. They had been cut off from the outside world, their
economies distorted by communist rule, and public-spiritedness
obliterated. The habits of how to live in a free society were distant
memories, not practical skills. They had to be relearned, and at a
time of wrenching economic change. It is easy therefore to see why
even some sophisticated foreign-policy thinkers in Western Europe
saw the collapse of communism not as a triumph, but as a tragedy.
By keeping the backward nations of the Soviet bloc locked up behind totalitarian bars, the way was clear for the more civilized and
advanced countries of Western Europe to consolidate their successful economic and political integration. The old EU could absorb occasional new members, but the difficulties presented by integrating
Greece, which joined in 1981, made many feel that the outer limits
had already been reached. The fall of the Berlin Wall turned the
comfortable life of the West Europeans upside down. "This is the
biggest catastrophe to hit my country for decades," a thoughtful
Finnish diplomat told me in 1991, just after Estonia had regained
independence. Little seemed left of the newly re-emerged country's
pre-war prosperity: it was all too easy to imagine its future as a
poverty-stricken gangster land, riven with ethnic conflicts and run
by strange bearded men with bad teeth and eccentric ideas. Finland
and Estonia shared a linguistic and cultural heritage—but little else.
"There is no way we can abandon them. There is no way we can
protect them. There is no way that we can civilize them," he
moaned. His worst nightmare, he explained, was that Finland would
sooner or later inevitably be drawn into a row with Russia on Estonia's behalf. For a more than a decade, that seemed unlikely. Now it
is all too plausible.

In the years after 1991, such sharp fears soon seemed passé. The
EU grudgingly decided that, in principle if nothing else, it had to expand to include at least those ex-communist countries that would
swallow the whole Union's voluminous rulebook. That set the stage
for a lengthy and often mind-numbing series of wrangles marked by
disingenuous behavior on both sides. Applicant countries would
sometimes actually meet standards in full, but more often merely

pretend they had. EU inspectors would fume and produce cross reports about the backsliders, always aware that their objections
might be overruled for political reasons.

By 2004, it seemed as though the ex-communist countries were
safely anchored in the Euroatlantic harbors of NATO and the EU,
stable, secure, and prosperous. But since 2004, things have started to
unscramble. The sacrifices and discipline needed to join a club are
usually greater than those required to stay in it, and the EU and
NATO are no exception. Reform stalled during the boom years.
Now, with a sharp economic slowdown looming, the East European
countries look less like youthful economic tigers and more like
moth-eaten old ones. The rule is weak governments, sharply polar-
ized politics, and a heavy diet of scandal, typically involving some
mixture of corruption, organized crime, and misbehavior by the intelligence services.[61] That is reinforced by sometimes sharply different ideas about social policy, such as equal rights for homosexuals,
conditions in children's homes, or treatment of the Roma (Gypsies).
West Europeans also worry about over-mighty spooks. In most ex-
communist countries (Estonia is a rare exception) the intelligence
and security agencies operate with a disrespect for the law and a
scandalous lack of political control.

Public services in the new EU members are still poor by European standards: healthcare, the criminal justice system, and public
administration are particularly unimpressive. But that has not produced strong political pressure for good government. People prefer
to vote with their feet rather than wait for their votes to be counted.
Millions have emigrated, for the short or long term, to Western Europe. The size of this migration is still hard to document, though it
is clearly the biggest in Europe since the end of the Second World
War. The motives for leaving are multiple. Wages may be two or
three times higher in the rich countries of Europe, though the cost
of living is high and separation from family and friends has its cost.
That benefit now seems to be eroding. Harder to bridge is the gap in
public services. It is difficult for people who have not lived in an ex-
communist country to understand the—literally—demoralizing effect of persistent rudeness and corruption in public services, which
leaves the user constantly feeling that he is a supplicant, not a client
(let alone a valued customer). Medical treatment typically involves a
series of carefully calibrated payments to doctors, nurses, anes-
thetists, and therapists. The education system is riddled with corruption, including both payments for "special lessons" from
teachers, incentives to secure admission to a sought-after university,

and even backhanders to ensure good exam results. Simply renewing a driving license or applying for minor bits of official paperwork can be lengthy and humiliating. Government bureaucrats have inherited the communist-era idea that the outsider is always wrong, his time is free, and arbitrary decision-making is the privilege of office.

It would be fanciful to say that the Kremlin is masterminding every hiccup and foul-up from the Baltic to the Black Sea. But it is certainly true that bad government and diplomatic isolation make it much easier for Russia to exert its influence. As Bulgaria, say, becomes isolated inside the EU for its failure to attack corruption, the openings for Russian influence grow. The old EU featured hard bargaining, and sometimes spectacular rows. But its core members felt united by a common purpose that now seems to be lacking. That is stoking demands for a "two-speed" Europe, probably based around membership of the Euro zone, which includes most of old Europe but excludes most of the new member states.

It would be nice to think that nothing much would change: the single market would hang together, and the baker's dozen of countries on the eastern periphery of the new core would at least remain part of a thriving free-trade area, as Norway and Switzerland do today. But the unraveling would most likely go much further. The EU already finds it hard to make Poland, for example, abide by European competition law. Without a seat at the top table in Brussels, Polish governments would find it hard to justify allowing foreigners to buy up big companies. The single market in capital would be the first to go. It would be quickly followed by restrictions on labor mobility, and soon on free trade in goods and services. The ex-communist states' wobbly finances are propped up in part by the financial markets' confidence that they will join the euro eventually. If that belief erodes, the halo effect of proximity to rich, stable Europe evaporates. Slow-lane Europe's bad government, backwardness, and weakness will stand starkly revealed. And who will pay then?

Worse, even the remnants of common policy toward Russia would go, too. The new "core Europe" would be dominated by France, Germany, and Italy (assuming Britain, as usual, dithered). These countries tend to see rows with the Kremlin as costly distractions. They will continue striking bargains with Russia on energy and anything else, over the heads of the countries in between. The Nord Stream gas pipeline is a foretaste of what Poland and the Baltics can expect if a two-speed Europe takes shape. Moreover, the already withered carrot of enlargement would look much less appealing. Today the EU can still hope to make the politicians of the western Balkans keep talking rather than fighting by dangling the distant prospect of full membership. But who is going to lift a finger to join the slow lane to nowhere in a two-speed Europe? Serbia's flirtation in late 2007 with the idea of political ties with Russia rather than the EU was an early sign of what to expect. The prospect of being second-class citizens of Europe should therefore be a terrifying scenario for the new member states: the rational response would be for them to smarten up their act, by hastening to adopt the euro and by restoring their reputation as reformers. But they aren't.

The paradox is that these ill-governed, tetchy, and outright intolerant countries are the front line that the West is trying to defend. In the year before the Georgian war, the EU's record became mildly more encouraging. At the EU–Russia summit in Samara in May 2007, the EU's leaders batted aside Putin's claim that their policy was being distorted by the "egocentrism" of the new member states. An attempt to isolate Poland on the issue of meat exports (which Russia has banned on hygiene grounds) proved utterly unsuccessful. After years in which every meeting had produced an upbeat communiqué and launched a plethora of new initiatives, this time the two sides simply agreed to disagree. By EU standards, this was a startlingly bold and tough-minded approach. Merkel, representing the EU presidency, coolly informed Putin that if he had a problem with one EU country, he had a problem with the whole EU. She publicly rebuked him for the Russian authorities' harassment of Kasparov and other opposition activists trying to lobby the summit.[62] A foreign ministers' meeting in Portugal in September 2007 brought even tougher language. But the overall picture is that solidarity is only superficial. On issues that matter, such as Georgia, the Kremlin needs only to hobble a handful of countries to paralyze the EU's decision-making.

Russia's most effective weapon—examined at length in the next chapter—is economic incentives and penalties, particularly in the energy supplies. The most striking example is the use of the pipelines inherited from the Soviet Union. In 2003, the Kremlin shut off shipments to the Latvian oil terminal at Ventspils, in the hope of forcing its sale to a Russian oil company. When in 2005 Lithuania sold its oil refinery at Mazõeikiai, the most important industrial installation in the Baltic states, to a Polish company, rather than to the Russian bidder preferred by the Kremlin, Russia shut down the ill-named *Druzhba* (Friendship) pipeline that supplied it.[63] Russia's official explanation was that the pipeline needed repairs. That was a blatantly political move. A Lithuanian offer to examine the nature of the problem, and to help with the cost of dealing with it, was abruptly declined. "Sorry, guys, you sold the refinery to the wrong people," a visiting Russian parliamentarian confided to his Lithuanian counterparts. Russia now says that the pipeline is so old that it is not worth repairing at all. Lithuania is importing oil to Mazõeikiai from its coastal terminal at Butinge._ That is profitable while oil prices are high; when they fall, Mazõeikiai risks bankruptcy. After a row with Estonia over a Soviet-era war memorial in 2007 (see above in this chapter), Russia cut oil shipments. "Business will develop where the situation is comfortable and profitable and where the moral and political climate is favorable," said the transport minister, Igor Levitin.[64]

As a study[65] by Robert Larsson of Sweden's Defense Research Institute shows, Russia uses the energy weapon with surprising frequency, while at the same time insisting that it is an ultra-reliable supplier. The secret of this apparent paradox is that supplies to West European countries are rarely interrupted, and never deliberately. The targets are invariably the former satellite states that—unlike their Western counterparts—typically have no other independent source of supply. The simplest approach is to cut supplies off, while blaming sabotage or natural disasters. Power lines to Georgia, for example, fell victim to mysterious and simultaneous bombing attacks in 2006. Russia not only refused to allow Georgian investigators to see the evidence, but also declined any offer of help to speed the repair work. The other means is sharp price rises, which often seem to bear no relation either to geography or history. In the long run, crude use of the energy weapon is inadvisable for the Kremlin, as it sharply underlines the case for diversification: Georgia, for example, managed to restore a decrepit Soviet-era pipeline to bring gas from Azerbaijan. What works rather better is to create economic dependence through friendly economic ties, creating a strong business lobby that wants good relations with Russia no matter what.[66]

And that is the hinge on which Europe's security turns. Should, say, German households pay more for gas in order to safeguard the interests of faraway Estonia? That may seem as absurd a linkage as the notion in 1938 that Chamberlain found so "horrible, fantastic and incredible": that British citizens were trying out gas masks because of disputes over the Sudetenland. In fact it is a topical and practical one. Disdain for the interests of the East European states betrays ignorance of both the defeat the free world suffered in the 1930s, and of the route to victory in the old Cold War. Division among strong countries means the destruction of their weaker allies. If Germany, America, and France cannot agree on, say, how to defend Georgia, Moldova, or any other pipsqueak state now being menaced by the Kremlin, then their chances are little better than those of Czechoslovakia in the late 1930s.

CHAPTER SEVEN

PIPELINE POLITICS

The Threat and the Reality

The Kremlin's aims in the politics of energy are no secret. They are outlined in the country's energy strategy, approved by President Vladimir Putin in the summer of 2003, which puts energy policy at the center of Russian diplomacy. It echoes a point made by Putin in what purports to be his economics dissertation,[1] written in the 1990s and presented in 1997. The title is a mouthful: "The strategic planning of the reproduction of the mineral raw materials base of the region under conditions of the formation of market relationships." But the message is clear—the management of Russia's natural resources is too important to leave to private business. The few published extracts of this thesis make no reference to globalization or market forces. They argue that the aim of the natural-resource industry is to boost the geopolitical strength of Russia. In practice, that means four things. The Kremlin wants to prevent European countries from diversifying their sources of energy supply, particularly in gas. It wants to strengthen its hold over the international gas market. It wants to acquire "downstream assets"—distribution and storage capability—in Western countries. And it wants to use those assets to exert political pressure.

As Ariel Cohen of the U.S.-based think tank, the Heritage Foundation, rightly notes, Russia's policies are usually camouflaged by stealth, gradualism, and apparent reasonableness.[2] But since 2005, all four aims have been proceeding with remarkable speed. The contest resembles a battle-hardened chess grand master playing against a bunch of inattentive and squabbling amateurs. Europe's fundamental weakness in dealing with Russia is that it is not a single energy market. It is a series of energy islands, each administered and regulated by a national government. Naturally enough, each government thinks about its own interests, trying to ensure cheap energy for its consumers and jobs for its producers. Nobody wants to tell voters they have to make sacrifices in order to help out some other country. Unsurprisingly, given the European Union's (EU) failure to create deep, liquid, and competitive energy markets at home, it has also failed to get Russia to agree to liberalize its own monopolistic practices. In Putin's words:

> The gas pipeline system is the creation of the Soviet Union. We intend to retain state control over the gas transport system and over Gazprom. We will not split Gazprom up. And the European Commission should not have any illusions. In the gas sector, they will have to deal with the state.[3]

Were those pipelines carrying vodka, or even oil, it would not matter. Europe can make its own vodka; it can import oil from anywhere in the world by tanker. But gas is different. Pipelines are not only by far the cheapest and most practical way of delivering gas, but Europe is dependent on imported gas from Russian pipelines— a dependence that is set to increase. Of Europe's gas consumption, 60 percent is imported, nearly half of that via Russia. Over the next 20 years, at least according to some projections, the imported share will rise to 80 percent as Europe's own gas production falls and demand rises. For some European countries, such as Britain, this is still not too serious: A mixture of imports of liquefied natural gas (LNG)[4] and supply from the North Sea mean that Russia is unlikely to dominate the market. Farther east, it looks different. The following table (see facing page) shows selected European countries' dependence on imported Russian gas:

European policymakers see the problem, but have so far been able to do little about it. An EU–Russia Energy Dialogue, launched in 2000,[6] was based on the idea that Russia would progressively liberalize its energy markets. Instead the reverse has happened, and Putin has repeatedly[7] made it clear that Russia will not ratify the Energy Charter, which would among other things demonopolize oil and gas export pipelines. The hope was that Russia would accept this in return for a free trade agreement. However, as Russia's exports to the EU chiefly consist of raw materials, this proved an unattractive offer. Instead Russia demands "reciprocity" in energy dealings with the EU. This does not mean a legal framework

Table 7.1   Europe's Gas Dependency

Switzerland	13%
Netherlands	17%
France	23%
Italy	32%
Germany	40%
Slovenia	51%
Romania	63%
Poland	63%
Czech Republic	75%
Hungary	77%
Austria	78%
Greece	84%
Bulgaria	100%
Slovakia	100%
Finland	100%
Estonia	100%
Latvia	100%
Lithuania	100%

Source: Eni S.p.A, *World Oil and Gas Review 2006*[5]

that applies equally to both sides; instead, it means allowing European countries to invest in oil and gas fields in Russia only if they sell to their Russian partners distribution networks and other assets of equal value in Europe. That sets the stage for a fundamental clash between the EU's liberal, market-based system and the dirigiste and monopolistic approach of the Kremlin in which, so far, Russia is winning hands down. The EU may bleat, but nothing stops British, German, Dutch, and Italian companies (to name only a few countries) from doing their own deals with Gazprom and Rosneft. Gazprom, for example, now has investments in at least 16 out of 27 EU countries; in Britain, Italy, Germany, and France, among others, it has won direct access to at least some consumers, with all that implies.[8]

This would not matter if Gazprom were just another publicly traded, law-governed energy company. But it is not. Western companies who deal with it insist that they do not wish to condone theft, censorship, and say they see no sign of such things in Russia. But the fact is that Gazprom is the gas division of Kremlin, Inc. and is, for example, directly linked to the end of press freedom in Russia: It has bought up troublesome media outlets such as NTV and bent them to the Kremlin's will. Deals with Gazprom also raise a question about Europe's own rules: If the Kremlin does not allow any competition in its core business (such as export pipelines) at home, why would it respect the rules of the European market? It is more likely that it will try to change them. Gazprom certainly does not like the slightest scent of EU scrutiny of its activities. In October 2006, Europe's leaders asked the EU's competition directorate, which polices the internal market against cartels and monopolies, to investigate Gazprom's growing role in the EU.[9] Putin complained sharply. German diplomats say that Chancellor Angela Merkel told him that Gazprom should find it "an honour to be treated like Microsoft."[10] If the EU is able to start serious liberalization of the energy market, unbundling distribution, sales, and imports, Gazprom will have more than that to worry about. The 30-year contracts it has with ENI in Italy, BASF in Germany, and Gaz de France may need to be redrafted, at least to exclude its direct access to end users. The EU is also considering new rules that would prevent Russian and other state-backed buyers taking control of downstream energy assets such as distribution networks and refineries. That could include giving the EU power to block outside investments that damage common strategic interests.

Such moves would be welcome, but they are a long way off and subject to sabotage by Russia's allies in Europe. So far, the stage has been set perfectly for the Kremlin's favourite tactic: divide and rule. Its success can be seen most clearly in the tale of two pipelines. Nord Stream—backed by Russia—aims to take gas under the Baltic Sea to Germany.[11] Nabucco—backed by the EU—aims to take gas from Central Asia and the Caspian to Europe.[12] In reality, neither pipeline is likely to be built. Russia and Iran can veto any pipeline laid on the seabed of the Caspian, because this body of water–once an internal lake of the Soviet Union, regulated by treaty with Iran–has not been re-regulated by a definitive agreement of all the littoral states. Each has taken a disputable body of water and seabed for a national economic zone–that means, for oil and gas drilling. But the political wrangling around each highlights the West's weakness, and Russia's strength.

Nord Stream is the child of the most notorious diplomatic alliance in Europe's modern history, between the previous German government headed by former Chancellor Gerhard Schröder and Putin's Kremlin. It was blessed with a secret €1 billion loan guarantee issued just days before the German leader left office—shortly to become chairman of the pipeline consortium. Schröder is prickly and litigious, making it hard to discuss his activities in public. In

2006 he successfully sued Guido Westerwelle, the leader of Germany's FDP (Freie Demokratische Partei), who drew a connection between Schröder's behaviour in office and the benefits he has reaped once out of it. Though Westerwelle was forbidden by the court from repeating a particular formulation of his criticism of the former chancellor, he continues to do so in other terms. After losing the case Mr Westerwelle said he continued to believe that Mr Schröder's behaviour was distasteful and questionable. Tom Lantos, the American congressman and Holocaust survivor, went further, saying that he wanted to call Schröder a "political prostitute" but that the sex workers in his congressional district objected[13]. The biggest shareholder in Nord Stream is Gazprom—in effect, the gas department of the Kremlin. The other shareholders, with 24.5 percent each, are Germany's biggest energy companies, E.ON Ruhrgas and Wintershall, part of BASF. The pipeline, 750 miles (1,200 km) long, will be the most expensive ever built. Originally to cost €4 billion when announced in 2005, Gazprom raised the estimate to €5 billion in 2006 and €6 billion in 2007. Outside estimates are that the real cost will be nearly double that by the time it is completed. The supposed completion date of 2010 looks unrealistic too: The deadline for bidding to supply pipes was postponed by several months in 2007.[14] The drawbacks are formidable. Underwater pipelines are far more expensive than their land-based counterparts. The Baltic seabed is littered with munitions from two world wars. Every other country on the Baltic littoral dislikes the plan and has raised a plethora of environmental objections: Finland wants the route shifted away from its coast, strengthening Estonia's bargaining position; Poland wants it moved closer to the Danish coast; Sweden objected to a planned compressor station to be built on a sea platform near its island of Gotland, which had worried security-conscious Swedes who thought it might be used for electronic espionage[15] or allow the Kremlin to intervene on the pretence of an "anti-terrorist" operation to protect the platform. In mid-2007 the pipeline consortium said it might not build the platform after all, though this would increase still further the project's technical difficulties and cost. Despite all of these difficulties, Nord Stream's advantage for the Kremlin is clear. Russia's two existing gas export pipelines to Germany go across other countries—Belarus and Poland in the north, and Ukraine, Slovakia, and the Czech Republic to the south. That means that deliveries to Germany are hostage to those transit countries' goodwill; put another way, if the Kremlin tries to punish those countries, its more important customers further west may suffer.

The most striking example of this came at the end of 2005, when Russia tried to raise the price of natural gas deliveries to Ukraine.[16] Ukraine certainly had had its gas cheap in the past, at a mere $50 per thousand m³. In one sense, Gazprom has the right to charge what it likes; moreover, higher gas prices would be a good thing everywhere in the former Soviet Union, where energy is still used astonishingly wastefully. Indeed, Western countries had been urging Russia to stop subsidising domestic gas prices as a condition for its membership of the World Trade Organization (WTO). Still, given Russia's monopoly hold on Ukrainian gas supplies, a responsible country would have used its pricing power carefully, avoiding unpredictable moves and any suspicion of politicization. Russia did exactly the opposite, doubling the price at short notice. The strong suspicion in Ukraine and in the West was that Russia was punishing its southern neighbor for the Orange Revolution: essentially saying, if you won't vote for our candidates (and allow them to rig elections) then don't expect us to sell you cheap gas. When Ukraine refused to pay, Russia cut the supply, with the result that Ukraine then diverted for its own needs deliveries meant for Germany. That was not wholly Russia's fault; but its credibility in Western Europe as a reliable partner was badly dented.

Nord Stream offers the Kremlin a chance to sidestep such problems by delivering gas independently. It can raise prices for deliveries to Ukraine, Belarus, or Poland; if they do not pay, it can cut them off without worrying about supplies to its customers farther west. The advantage of gas-based diplomacy is that Russia does not need to actually do anything practical. The mere knowledge that it could do so increases its political and economic leverage. In fact, the Kremlin has already strongly increased its hold over both Ukraine's and Belarus's gas access by use of this approach. Even before a drop of gas flows through Nord Stream, the effect of its construction on the politics of land-based gas transit may have rendered it unnecessary. Nord Stream is also of symbolic importance, highlighting the German–Russian axis and thus intimidating the smaller countries in between, which find the idea of the continent's future being stitched up between Berlin and Moscow distasteful or outright scary. Radek Sikorski, then Poland's defense minister, described it in 2006 as the energy version of the Molotov–Ribbentrop Pact.[17] That prompted claims that he was exaggerating, but the parallels were striking: Both were German–Russian deals drafted in secret for the mutual benefit of the two continental superpowers, against the interests of the countries in between. Though Nord Stream's backers insist that the project is business pure and simple, this would be easier to believe if it were more transparent. The company is based in Zug, a tax haven in Switzerland—a country noted for its banking secrecy laws. Despite this respectable Western front end, the pipeline itself will be designed, built, and operated by Gazprom. Nord Stream boosters also claim, misleadingly, that the EU supports the project. It is true that the EU gives its blessing to many projects that diversify its gas supplies, but the EU energy commissioner, Andris Piebalgs, has said firmly that the European commission does not support Nord Stream "over other options."[18]

The Nord Stream project highlights many of the most troubling aspects of German–Russian relations in the Schröder era. The German chancellor developed a close friendship with his Russian counterpart, spending Christmas and other holidays together, at a time when Putin was systematically reducing political freedoms in Russia.[19] Putin enabled his German friend to adopt two Russian orphans—in seeming contradiction of Russia's ban on foreign adoptions. Suspicion was also stoked by the project's choice of chief executive officer (CEO), the head of Dresdner Bank in Russia, Matthias Warnig. He had been a senior officer in the *Stasi* in the Soviet-occupied zone of Germany and is believed to have met Putin during his service with the KGB in the East German city of Dresden. Warnig now claims that he met his Russian friend only in St. Petersburg in the 1990s.[20] Dresdner's record in Russia has already attracted controversy since the bank took part in the dismemberment of Yukos.

Gazprom itself is even more dubious. Its standard mode of operation is to export via intermediary companies with murky ownership structures, meaning that the profits can be diverted to unknown beneficiaries. The most conspicuous of these used to be Itera, a company whose role seemed to consist solely of buying Russian gas cheaply and selling it to export customers at a hefty mark-up. Itera's shareholders, as far as could be discovered, were relatives of the senior management of Gazprom. Itera was swept aside during Putin's first term, to the delight of Gazprom's Western shareholders. But similar structures soon returned. In the case of export to Ukraine, the first lucky beneficiary company of a gas export business via Russia (in fact, largely Turkmen gas) was called EuralTransGas (ETG). Like Itera, it had no pipelines, compressors, storage facilities, or indeed any other assets. It employed only 30 people. Yet in 2003, its only full year of operation, ETG had revenues of $2 billion, though it declared a profit of a mere $220 million. Aside from $425 million paid to Gazprom (for the gas) it was unclear where the rest of the money went; presumably its senior staff were adequately rewarded for their demanding jobs.[21]

EuralTransGas then gave way to RosUkrEnergo. This is registered in (no surprises here) Zug in Switzerland. Half its shares are owned by Gazprom; the rest is held in a trust by Austria's Raiffeisen Bank on behalf of two controversial businessmen, Dmitriy Firtash (who has 90 percent) and Ivan Fursin (10 percent). Both the chairman and deputy chairman of Ukraine's national gas company, Naftohaz Ukrainy, have served on Rosukrenergo's board. Raiffeisen—set up by one of Austria's greatest philanthropists—seems to feel no need to clarify matters. Raiffeisen's association with RosUkrEnergo has given rise to lurid speculation. The bank, along with all others concerned, vehemently denies any wrongdoing. But it is hard to argue that the interests of gas customers, or for that matter those of shareholders in Gazprom and of taxpayers in Russia, are best served by secrecy about the company's activities and business model. A further issue is the ultimate beneficial ownership of RosUkrEnergo. The company's shareholders strenuously deny ties with Semion Mogilevich, a Ukrainian-born businessman with Israeli citizenship, believed to be living in Russia, who is on the FBI's wanted list for racketeering. He denies these charges as well as any links with RosUkrEnergo. But the connection between Mogilevich and the company was suggested in 2005 by the then head of Ukraine's security service, Oleksandr Turchynov. An investigation into this issue in Ukraine has stalled, amid claims of Kremlin pressure. Gazprom's own shareholding structure is, of course, unclear; so is its contribution to the Nord Stream project. As a privately held company, Nord Stream publishes no financial data. It gives only the scantiest details of the project: $7.5 billion will be invested, and the project is to be profitable.[22] More than that, nobody is saying. But even on the data available, the case for Nord Stream looks flimsy. The cited cost of €5 billion is between a third and a half of the likely real total. Costs for operation, maintenance, and decommissioning are not included. It would be possible instead to double up the existing land-based pipelines for less than half the stated €5 billion. Furthermore, it is unclear if Nord Stream's gas will really be needed. Nord Stream cites projections from the International Energy Agency (IEA) that show Europe's demand for imported gas soaring; however, it does not take into account energy conservation or a

switch to imported LNG or to another source of fuel, such as nuclear power. It is unclear both where the 55 billion m^3 planned for
the pipeline's annual throughput is coming from (Russia is facing a
gas shortage) and where it is going to (the destination countries are
still to be decided). Even the route is unclear. Nord Stream may go
in Sweden's economic zone; but—if Estonia, Finland, Latvia, and
other countries agree—it may also take a different (and somewhat
less expensive) route on the eastern side of the Baltic Sea. The eco-
logical difficulties are great but also surmountable. Other branch
pipelines may go to Denmark, Poland, the Netherlands, and Britain.

It is even less clear how Nord Stream's gas will be saleable in
what may well by then be a liberalized European energy market. If
Nord Stream's shareholders try to force-feed expensive gas from
their pipeline to Germany's power stations, rather than—for example—cheaper LNG from Britain or even Norwegian North Sea gas,
it will be completely illegal. Such worries are mainly for energy specialists. But even those utterly uninterested in the intricacies of energy economics are alarmed by something else: the military
dimension. The Kremlin has given Gazprom—a private company—
the unusual right to recruit and operate its own military forces to
protect its overseas pipelines.[23] Russia is also beefing up its Baltic
fleet in order to help prospect the seabed, and to protect the pipeline
once it is built.

So far, the picture is clear. The Nord Stream project, with all its
associated controversy and uncertainty, suits the Kremlin and worries its former satellites. The big question is why it suits Germany,
which has on other fronts been a strong supporter of the ex-communist countries freedom and security.[24] A strong personal relationship in the past between two top politicians is hardly enough to
explain the strong support it has gained across a wide section of
that country's politics and business. The partial answer is that Germany's special relationship with Russia goes back centuries.
Catherine the Great invited German farmers to come and settle in
the Volga basin. German nobles ran the then Baltic provinces of the
Tsarist-era Russian empire. The royal families intermarried. Germany was one of the biggest investors in prerevolutionary Russia;
some machinery from that era can still be found in good working
order, nearly a century later. In both world wars, the casualties on
Germany's eastern front dwarfed those in the better-known battles
in Western Europe. A mixture of guilt, resentment, and fear makes
Germans flinch at any kind of public confrontation with Russia.
Restoring diplomatic ties with the Soviet Union was a prized

achievement of Konrad Adenauer's Christian Democratic Union (CDU) government in 1956, and every government since then has tried to improve relations further. During the old Cold War, many Germans felt they were paying a heavy price to be in the front line of someone else's conflict. Although the foreign-policy elite in the Federal Republic of Germany consistently supported the Atlantic alliance, the public's viewpoint was more anti-American. In many eyes, the Soviet Union and United States were seen as equal partners in the division of Europe—and of Germany.

At a time when German–American relations were strained by the issue of medium-range nuclear weapons,[25] Gorbachev's arrival in the Kremlin in 1985 fuelled that sentiment further. To many Germans, he was a far more attractive figure than U.S. President Ronald Reagan. That era of "Gorbymania" was entrenched by the Kremlin's relaxed attitude to the collapse of its puppet regime in eastern Germany. Under Chancellor Helmut Kohl, West Germany was able to negotiate reunification with astonishingly little resistance. Gorbachev agreed to withdraw Soviet forces and to allow the united German state to be a member of NATO; Yeltsin honored the bargain, withdrawing the remaining troops to Russia. Kohl's ties with Yeltsin were closer than those enjoyed by any other Western leader. Germany provided billions of deutschmarks in financial support for Russia. German companies were early investors; by 1998 they had invested DM2 billion, behind only the United States and Cyprus (the latter being mostly recycled money from Russia).[26] In 1997, Germany and France suggested starting regular trilateral summits with Russia.[27] The aim was to make Russia feel that it was not excluded from European decision making. But east European countries, at that stage not yet in either the EU or NATO, regarded that with concern.

When Schröder came to power in 1998 he denounced his predecessor's "Sauna-diplomacy." But in his friendship with Putin, the new German leader, he soon exceeded even the sweatiest personal ties of the Kohl–Yeltsin era, visiting Russia dozens of times on both personal and political business. He proved a staunch defender of Putin's human-rights record, and gave Germany's strong support for grand schemes of integration, especially in energy. From 1998 to 2006, trade rose threefold, from €15 billion to €50 billion. Russia sells mostly energy to Germany. German exports to Russia, once mainly food and consumer goods, now include industrial machinery and chemicals. The number of German companies active in Russia has doubled in five years, to 4,500. At the heights of the German economy, ties with Russia are particularly close. Oleg Deripaska, the Kremlin's favorite oligarch, has bought a stake of nearly 10 percent in Hochtief, Germany's biggest construction company, and is trying to buy more. His holding company Basic Element has bought 30 percent of Strabag, Europe's largest tunnel and bridge builder.[28] Germany's biggest energy firm, E.ON Ruhrgas, owns 6.5 percent of Gazprom; the two chief executives sit on each others' boards. It is perhaps the only outside shareholder that the Russian gas behemoth treats with respect. The connection is highly profitable for both companies. E.ON provides extensive technical assistance to Gazprom in modernizing that company's rickety compressors and leaky pipelines. Gazprom provides cheap and reliable gas supplies.

That exemplifies the problem. It is hard to fault German companies for acting in the interests of their shareholders. And it is hard to fault their combined lobbying of the government. The *Ostauschuss der deutschen Wirtschaft* (Eastern Committee of German Industry) promotes and protects trade and investment in a highly promising market. Its chairman, Klaus Mangold, is an eloquent critic in private of Russia's political shortcomings while striking a publicly optimistic note about the country's development.[29] As Russia hurries to modernize its dilapidated infrastructure and worn-out industrial plant, Mangold rightly sees great opportunities for German companies, which are world beaters in both machine-building and construction. But this ignores the wider picture—one that is in sharp focus for Schröder's successor as federal chancellor since 2005, Merkel.

Brought up under communist rule in the GDR, Merkel is the first—and probably last—leader of a big industrialized European country in this century to have firsthand experience of adult life under totalitarianism. Unlike Schröder she speaks Russian and has friends not in that country's power elite, but in the liberal intelligentsia. Privately, she regards Putin with the deepest suspicion. Since taking office, she has presided over a sea-change in Germany's stance toward its eastern neighbors. Whereas Schröder described Putin as a *"lupenreiner Demokrat"* [flawless democrat], Merkel repeatedly and publicly raises embarrassing questions about political repression in Russia. Schröder shunned Russian human-rights activists; Merkel makes a point of seeing them when she visits there. In October 2006, Putin offered Germany a one-off deal on access to one of its most tempting unexplored gas reserves, the offshore Shtokman field. Russia had just broken off negotiations with other big world energy companies, saying it would develop the field alone. But Merkel declined to discuss this, citing the common EU energy policy. She also criticized the Kremlin's treatment of investors at the Sakhalin project in Russia's far east, saying: "If Russia creates obstacles to European investment, it shouldn't object to reciprocal measures."[30]

Merkel has also made a point of meeting senior politicians from Poland and other former Soviet satellites both before and after her meetings with Putin (which number more than ten since taking office). The aim is both to put forward their views, and to report back to them afterward. That has already gone a long way to dispel suspicions about a Germany's real intentions. The same goes for her officials. In the Schröder era, calls from Baltic officials in particular went either unreturned or got only a cursory answer; now the response is speedy and helpful. This, at least, is the change of tone in the federal chancellery. But the acid test is how far Germany's policy actually changes. German–Russian relations are still marked by pragmatism and by what seems to many outsiders as rather too much mutual goodwill. The key concept is still "*Annäherung durch Verflechtung*" [rapprochement through interdependence]. Merkel heads a coalition government in which views on policy toward Russia differ widely. Her own foreign minister, Frank-Walter Steinmeier, was one of Schröder's closest ministerial colleagues and continues to push his policy hard. He and other members of the junior coalition partner, the Social Democrats (SPD), have echoed Russia's complaints about Polish and Czech willingness to host bases for a planned American missile-defence system. Many in the SPD are so viscerally opposed to the current American administration that they regard Putin as a more congenial ally. That view is shared by German public opinion, which shows a surprising tendency to sympathize more with the Kremlin than the current American administration.

So Merkel is fighting on two fronts: against the anti-American left, and against the pro-business right, both of which are willing to overlook the Kremlin's shortcomings for reasons of their own. Even her own party allies seem open to the blandishments of a special friendship with Russia. For all Merkel's efforts, the fact remains that Russia has unparalleled influence in Germany, which seems to survive even a sharp change of political tone at the top. That Germany after 2012 will be importing two-thirds of its gas from Russia has rung not an alarm bell but a dinner bell. Gas companies in other countries are scrambling not to be left behind. Gasunie of the Netherlands, for example, has bought a 9 percent stake in Nord

Stream. In return it is offering Gazprom a share in an undersea pipeline to Britain.[32] In 2006 Gazprom has gained a 50 percent share in Wingas, the energy trading unit of the BASF subsidiary Wintershall, positioning it well for any future energy liberalization in Europe. The two companies have set up a fifty-fifty joint venture, Wingas Europe, to market Russian gas in Germany and other European countries. Gazprom also wants a share in Wintershall fields in the North Sea and Libya.[33] In exchange Wintershall gained a 25 percent stake, worth roughly $500 million, in the largely undeveloped Yuzhno-Russkoye gas field, plus an extra 10 percent in nonvoting shares in a company that will develop the field.[34] Yuzhno-Russkoye's reserves are equivalent to 15 years of Russian gas exports to Germany at current rates. As this becomes more valuable, Gazprom is asking E.ON to hand over stakes in its businesses elsewhere in Europe. E.ON offered its businesses in Hungary, but Gazprom dismissed that as not big enough. It wants a stake in Ruhrgas's vast electricity and gas distribution businesses in Germany. In August 2007 it asked E.ON to hand over its electricity generating business in Britain.[35]

In Latvia and Estonia (where Gazprom is well entrenched thanks to its stake in the local gas companies), governments have eyed participation in the Baltic pipeline too. Latvia hopes that Russian investment will make a profitable concern of its large and unexploited underground gas storage capabilities. Estonia's government originally hoped to make some money from allowing the pipeline to cross its territorial waters or seabed economic zone. Schröder, indeed, was heading to Tallinn to discuss this when the row over the "bronze soldier" war memorial broke, only his remarkably unwise comment that the Estonian decision to move the statue "offended every form of civilised behaviour" forced his hosts to cancel the trip. Estonia now says that the pipeline may not cross its maritime economic zone. Gazprom also hopes to extend the pipeline into the North Sea and to use Belgium as a "regional hub" for gas transmission to nearby countries, including Britain. It has signed a 25-year deal with Fluxys, a Belgian gas firm, to build a storage site at Poederlee and plans a seabed pipeline from Zeebrugge to the English coast. However, in August 2007, a Belgian anti-monopoly regulator, CREG[36], has blocked this, saying that it gave Gazprom an unfairly exclusive deal over too long a period.

If Nord Stream demonstrates Russia's ability to push its pet pipeline forward, the story of the other important pipeline, Nabucco, demonstrates Europe's inability to do the same. A glance at the map shows why Nabucco is necessary.

The pipeline, supposedly to be completed in 2012, would bring a planned 30 billion m³ of gas to Europe from four possible sources: Iraq, Iran, Azerbaijan, and Central Asia. Crucially, it would do this by running across Turkey and the Balkans, not Russia. It is hard to overstate the importance of this. Although Nabucco would not carry large quantities of gas—only around a tenth of Europe's needs—it would have huge effects. First, it would free countries such as Turkmenistan and Kazakhstan from total dependence on the Soviet-era pipelines that allow the Kremlin to dictate the price and quantity of their exports. Second, it would allow European gas companies to bargain with Gazprom from a position of greater strength. Perhaps most importantly of all, it would signal to the Kremlin that Europe is able to deal jointly with energy security in a serious way. That is entirely the right approach—in theory. But Russia's victory has been near-total and deeply humiliating, and by late 2008 it seemed not to have just checkmated Nabucco's backers, but to have swept the pieces from the board and gone home.

Problems have arisen at every point. For a start, the vital linchpin in the plan, Turkey, is increasingly estranged from both the United States and the EU, and snuggling closely up to Russia, with which it built the $3.7 billion Blue Stream pipeline across the Black Sea. To this day it is not clear what, whom, or how much Gazprom paid in Turkey to get the pipeline built. Although Turkey is a member of NATO, its military and security services—with their commercial allies—are a law unto themselves. But this astonishing feat of deepwater seabed engineering is used only to less than a third of its capacity; it would therefore make sense from a purely commercial point of view for Turkey to exploit Blue Stream fully, rather than to build new pipelines. That sentiment is not counterbalanced by any political support in Turkey to help out its traditional allies. The refusal to support the war in Iraq, plus the creation of an American-backed semi-independent Kurdish state in that country's north, have severely strained both ends of the American–Turkish strategic partnership. Turkey thinks America is soft on Kurdish separatism and terrorism. The United States thinks that on a crucial issue of international security Turkey failed to show solidarity. But those difficulties are minor compared to the strain on Turkish relations with the EU. Talks on Turkish membership risk being postponed indefinitely, with both the president of France, Nicolas Sarkozy, and Merkel publicly opposed to it in principle.

Even worse is that none of the potential sources of gas are easily available. Relations with Iran are in the deep freeze, thanks to the Tehran regime's determination to pursue (with Russian help) advanced nuclear technology. Gazprom has effortlessly check-mated Iran's only attempt to export large amounts of gas so far, by way of Armenia, by investing a wholly unnecessary $2 billion in a refinery and power plant there. The deal came with one condition: Armenia could build a small gas import pipeline from Iran, free-ing itself from any potential blockade by Georgia and Azerbaijan, its northern neighbors, but it was to abandon any plans to export gas for Nabucco northward. Most other sources look fanciful too. The failure to bring peace and security to Iraq means that that country's potential as a gas exporter is still purely theoretical. The failure to reach a Middle East peace settlement, instability in Lebanon, and Syria's continuing pariah status means that nobody is going to invest money in Arab transit pipelines to Turkey in the foreseeable future.

That leaves the Caspian, where the West's hopes rest on the flimsy chances of persuading two dictatorships, ultra-cautious Kazakhstan and impenetrable Turkmenistan, to take the risk of snubbing Moscow and selling their gas westward. Unsurprisingly, in the battle for the Caspian, Russia has so far outwitted the West at every turn. The chances never looked good. Russia regards the Caspian Sea as a lake. Under international law, the countries around a lake have a power of veto over the economic exploitation of the land under it; Russia can therefore block any attempt to build a pipeline on the Caspian seabed linking Turkmen and Kazakh gas fields to Azerbaijan's existing pipeline westward. To underline its legal case, it has also been building up its naval forces in the Caspian. But in fact, Russia used an even more powerful weapon than either gunboats or international lawyers: simple diplomatic clout. In May 2007 Putin signed a deal with the leaders of Kaza-khstan and Turkmenistan to build a new gas export pipeline skirt-ing the northern shore of the Caspian and taking the region's gas riches to Europe by way of Russia.

Nabucco was thus kyboshed on two fronts. But Russia has added two more. First, it has suggested building South Stream, a $5.5 billion westward extension of Blue Stream, landing in Bulgaria and bringing 30 billion m^3 annually of Russian gas to Europe through the Balkans.[38] That would mimic Nabucco's route—but with the crucial difference that the pipeline would be built, filled, maintained, and operated by the Kremlin. Like Blue Stream, it would be jointly built with Italy's giant energy firm ENI. One spur will go to southern Italy via Greece, the other to northern Italy by

178 THE NEW COLD WAR

way of Romania, Hungary, and Slovenia. It may also reach as far as Austria. This proposed pipeline was potentially devastating news for policymakers in both the EU and the United States. The economics of gas pipelines are simple: whoever builds the first one has a big advantage. It can offer the cheapest gas, making it impossible for a newcomer to attract investors. Russia's final move has been to stitch up the European countries that are shareholders in Nabucco, and would in theory be its biggest beneficiaries. It starts with Bulgaria, where the ex-communist government is deeply influenced by Russian business interests. The Russian-owned refinery at Bourgas is Bulgaria's single biggest private-sector taxpayer. Russian economic—and some say criminal—circles are deeply connected with Bulgarian decision making. Although Bulgaria is militarily a loyal American and NATO ally, on the energy front it is in Russia's pocket.

Much the same is true of neighboring Romania, where the Atlanticist President Traian Basescu has lost control of the country's foreign policy to a business-friendly government that is keen to make the country the energy hub of the Balkan region. In August 2007, the country's biggest oil company, Rompetrol, sold a 75 percent stake to Kazakhstan's KazMunayGaz. On the surface, this move could strengthen Romania's energy independence. But at any time in the future the new Kazakh owner may find it convenient, or necessary, to sell Rompetrol on to Russia. Russia is also back in business in ex-Yugoslavia—a region that is a prime candidate for integration into the rest of Europe, and where Western influence has long been predominant. It was American arms, air power, and diplomatic pressure that allowed Croatia to break away successfully from Yugoslavia. Bosnia owes its precarious unity and independence to the intense and energetic involvement of both the EU and the United States. Yet the mere sniff of Russian money seems to have turned the geopolitics of ex-Yugoslavia upside down. At an energy summit held in the Croatian capital Zagreb in mid-2007, all six former Yugoslav republics, plus Greece, Bulgaria, Romania, and Albania, gave a servile welcome to Putin, who announced a series of new oil and gas initiatives that leave the Western efforts in tatters. Putin pointed out that in 2006, 73 billion m^3 of gas—half of Russia's gas exports to Europe—went to countries in the southern and southeastern parts of the continent.[39] He offered not only Russian investment in infrastructure (transit, storage, and distribution) but also in modernization of energy generation. That was a powerful message in an energy-starved region of Europe, where countries such as Macedonia and Albania experience infuriating power cuts and where the EU-forced closure of Bulgaria's ancient nuclear power station at Kozluduy is regarded as almost insanely insensitive and damaging. Russia's investment, said Putin, would form an electricity "ring" around the region. If it creates over-whelming energy dependence on a monopoly supplier, that ring may turn out to look more like a chain.

The coup de grâce for Nabucco may be a lack of commitment to it in Austria and Hungary, the countries that should be the pipeline's destination, and thus its greatest beneficiaries. At the commemorations in Budapest marking the 50th anniversary of the 1956 Hungarian uprising, Putin delivered some words of guarded apology. This was a coup for the Hungarian prime minister, Ferenc Gyurcsány, who is engaged in a vigorous internal political battle with opponents who regard him and his party as little better than the heirs of the Soviet murder squads that put down the revolt. Gyurcsány's government seemed to have shifted against Nabucco. "We don't need dreams. We need projects," he said in early 2007. That was understandable: the effect of Europe's weak energy policy has been to leave all those concerned with the firm belief that Brus-sels merely talks about plans whereas the Kremlin actually talks business. But in September 2007, Gyurcsány wobbled again, insist-ing that his country was still a strong supporter of Nabucco.[40]

This change may reflect Hungarian crossness about the Krem-lin's increasing influence in neighboring Austria, where the main oil and natural gas company, ÖMV, is meant to be coordinating the Nabucco project. When Putin visited Vienna on May 23 and 24, 2007, he promised to make Austria a "hub" for Russian exports of natural gas—including, ironically, much of the central Asian gas that was supposed to flow through Nabucco. In 2006 Austria had signed a long-term contract under which Gazprom would supply 80 percent of Austria's gas requirements over the next 20 years.[41] Dur-ing Putin's visit, he celebrated the start of work on a big under-ground gas storage installation near Salzburg. With a 2.4 billion m^3 capacity, the €260 million facility will be the second-largest of its kind in the region. In return for the long-term supply contract, Aus-tria has allowed Gazprom to buy a share in gas distribution busi-nesses in some of Austria's biggest federal states. Gazprom is also to acquire a stake in Austria's gas transit business and will build a joint gas transit management center with ÖMV, the largest in Europe.[42]

Gazprom appears to have been trying to create competition be-tween the Hungarian and Austrian energy industries over which it will have the closest ties with Russia. In the summer of 2007 ÖMV, in what was believed to be a joint move with Gazprom, launched a surprise hostile bid for its Hungarian counterpart, MOL, raising its stake from 10 percent to over 18 percent: That included the €1 billion it paid for a 6 percent stake in MOL originally acquired by a controversial Russian tycoon, Megdet Rakimkulov.[43] The takeover looks odd for several reasons. It makes little business sense other than in sheer scale. First, MOL is in many ways the stronger company, having done better than ÖMV in acquisitions in the former Yugoslavia and Italy. In addition, ÖMV is only slightly larger than its target and is having to borrow €13.5 billion from Barclays and JP Morgan Chase to pay for the takeover of MOL. The aim is to lever open Austria, Hungary, and Slovakia to Russian acquisitions. This would most likely happen once EU competition laws make ÖMV sell one of MOL's top refineries, most likely Slovnaft, near the Slovak capital Bratislava. This would be almost certain to fall into Rossneft's hands, as it can operate only on Russian oil, flowing along a Russian-owned pipeline. As its part of the deal, ÖMV is likely to get shares in upstream assets in Russia in return for downstream assets in central Europe.

Unsurprisingly, this maneuvering seems to have alarmed Hungary, and outweighed the influence of the lobby there that concentrates only on cheap gas and high profits. In the 1990s, Hungary had already fought off an attempt by a shady Russian-backed company to build up a stake in MOL—the country's largest company. The question, however, is how far Hungary will be able to resist. In April 2007, the EU forced the Hungarian state to sell its "golden share" in MOL, meaning it no longer has a veto over the future of MOL. Not for the first time, the EU's liberal and market-based principles are proving an ideal framework for the illiberal, anti-competitive polices of the Kremlin's gas business: so is the desire of individual managers, officials, and politicians in the West to further their own careers.[44]

For all that, Nabucco is not, yet, quite dead. Russia may have had a triumphant year in the gas wars but European and American diplomats insist that they still have some cards to play. Turkey, they argue, does not want to be dependent solely on Russian gas. Many outsiders said that the Baku-Tbilisi-Ceyhan oil pipeline, which brings Azeri crude to Turkey's deepwater Mediterranean port, would never be built. Thanks to strong American pressure, it was not only built, but turned into a big success. Last year it pumped 143 million barrels of crude oil. It may be possible to bring Turkmen gas to Turkey by way of Iran, instead of across the Caspian, or indeed buy Iranian gas; but that would require the West to turn a blind eye to a deal that would be highly beneficial to the regime in Teheran, at a time when international pressure is supposed to be weakening it. It would also depend on Russia being unable to block it, either through its own links with the Iranian regime, or through pressure on Turkey. A gas pipeline from Turkey to Greece and Italy is still possible, whatever the other reverses in the Balkans. Brave talk and ingenious schemes are plentiful. But the champions of Western interests look outgunned. Europe is disunited, and America far away. European Union energy commissioner Piebalgs conspicuously lacks the backing of big EU member countries such as Germany, Italy, and the Netherlands, all of which prefer bilateral deals with Russia. The impressive figure of Matt Bryza, an up-and-coming diplomat who is the U.S. Deputy Assistant Secretary of State for European and Eurasian Affairs, can hardly expect to counter a policy that has the explicit backing and concentrated attention of Putin and his senior officials, as well as the world's largest gas company.

These pipeline wars may prove the first act of the drama. The plot of the second act concerns the Kremlin's attempt to stitch up the world gas market, rather than just the European one. The main vehicle for this plan is a body, founded in 2001, called the Gas-Exporting Countries' Forum (GECF). It has no staff, headquarters, fixed membership, budget, charter, legal basis, or even—at the time of writing—Web site: in effect, it is a meeting with a label. Some countries who turn up are not exporters, and important exporters (including the main Western producers: Australia, Canada, the Netherlands, and Norway) are not members. However, the 15 countries that regularly attend its meetings account for 73 percent of the world's gas reserves and 41 percent of production. At its meeting in Doha, Qatar in April 2007, the GECF decided to set up a high-level group, coordinated by Russia, to research markets and discuss how gas prices should be determined. This group will report back to the GECF meeting in Moscow in 2008. The meeting did not endorse demands by Venezuela, Bolivia, and Iran to set up a cartel immediately. But it may have a powerful effect nonetheless. The key Kremlin aim is first to prevent the development of a liquid international market for gas, such as already exists in oil, and second to stop countries from diversifying their gas supplies. Instead, Russia wants to carve up the world markets by area, so that gas suppliers do not undercut one another. It wants a common approach by GECF participants on new pipelines (thus further weakening customers' attempts to diversify), and "joint" exploration, development, and liquefaction plants: "Joint" in this case is code for "Russian-backed."

It may sound ambitious, but it will be quite straightforward for GECF members to stop LNG—the best hope for energy independence in both Europe and America—being traded on the spot market. In other words, the GECF will become an umbrella organization for regional cartels, such as the one that already exists in South America. In Europe, that will mean Russia strengthening its commercial and political ties with other gas exporters, and making sure that any independent-minded customers' room for maneuver is as constrained as possible. An early example of what this might mean is found in Gazprom's growing relationship with Algeria's state company Sonatrach, which is the second-largest gas exporter to Europe, providing 10 percent of the continent's consumption compared to Russia's 25 percent. A debt swap in 2006, coupled with a big arms purchase from Russia, prompted Piebalgs to give warning of a growing regional gas cartel. The deal in effect put 69 percent of Italy's gas supply, under Gazprom control and gave the Russian side access to Algeria's LNG technology—something that it is has so far lacked. Italy's main energy company, ENI, already a close Gazprom ally, helped bid for Yukos assets, which it promptly sold on to its Russian friends.

Russia's energy policy means that insiders gain and outsiders lose. That is a potent weapon. But is it loaded? Few worry as much as they should about whether Russia will have enough gas to meet the demands of the next decades, and what that means for counterparts and customers. At first sight it seems preposterous that a country with 47 trillion m^3, the world's largest proven gas reserves, could be running short. But it is. Vladimir Milov, an outspoken former deputy energy minister who now runs an independent think tank in Moscow, says that both oil and gas extraction are facing a "crisis," with gas in a worse state than oil. The figures are stark and simple. Gas production has stalled and is likely to decline. Demand is going up—by roughly 50 billion m^3 a year in Europe. According to Milov,[45] the gas deficit between Gazprom's own production and what it can import from Central Asia, and what it needs to supply to domestic and foreign customers, will be 132 billion m^3 in 2010. The IEA reckons that the deficit by 2015 will be 200 billion m^3. By 2020, all Gazprom's production would be needed for the Russian market, leaving none for export. And these are the conservative, optimistic projections.

There are two reasons: waste and theft. Russia uses gas (like all other forms of energy) with colossal inefficiency, consuming more than twice as much energy per unit of output than other big industrialized countries such as Canada or Germany. This is not surprising, given how little industry pays for gas: around $50 per thousand m³, compared to four or five times that paid in the West. Ex-communist countries that pay world prices have sharply increased their energy efficiency; Poland, for example, has doubled the amount of output it gets from a unit of energy. Russia's efficiency has hardly budged from the dismally wasteful levels of the Soviet Union. That may change if the Kremlin will stick to the price hikes agreed last year that double the domestic gas price by 2011. Russian consumers will have seen nothing like this before; subsidized gas is one of the last remaining elements of the Soviet planned economy. Given the Kremlin's timid reaction to the public protests about the limited welfare reforms in 2004, it is questionable whether it will back these much more painful price rises to the end. The problem is not raising prices, but cutting off those who will not or cannot pay them. In a country where the temperature drops below −30° Celsius in winter, that is a matter of life and death. Faced with a choice of whether to freeze voters or hurt its export customers, the Kremlin is likely to choose the latter.

Even if gas becomes more expensive and is used more thriftily, problems are looming elsewhere. Russia's strong economic growth means more demand for electricity, which in turn creates more demand for gas. Russia's creaking power sector urgently needs to build more gas-fired capacity: it will face a deficit of 20,000 megawatts by 2012 if it does not. Worse, Russia is pressing ahead with "gasification"—the supply of gas to domestic homes for heating and cooking. This is as politically popular as it is economically insane. It involves building 12,000 km of new pipelines at a cost of $1.3 billion—and creates another 9 billion m³ of demand at a time when Gazprom is already struggling to supply both its domestic and export customers.[46]

Gazprom is one of the most inefficient energy companies in the world, rivaled only by Petrobras in Brazil. Its return on total assets—at a time of sky-high energy prices—is a measly 8.9 percent. In the last year before it was attacked, Yukos, by contrast, returned 30 percent. Novatek, an independent gas producer now taken over by Gazprom, returned 21.4 percent. Hundreds of billions of dollars flow into Gazprom's coffers, but they are plundered for other purposes: colossal perks for the top management, overstaffing, ludicrously grand buildings, holiday resorts, yachts, and other gimmicks. Although high energy prices have raised revenues, most is frittered away in higher costs. Little is left for the important business of finding new gas supplies. In the period of 2000 to 2006, it spent only $12.5 billion on developing new fields, compared to $17.9 billion on buying companies outside the gas industry (such as a big stake in Russia's coal and electric power industries). It spent a staggering $30 billion on capital investments in non-gas areas. Gazprom flatters its production figures by buying other gas companies—which are much more efficiently run, at least until they are acquired. But it is unimpressive in the vital work of developing new ones of its own. Indeed, Gazprom has not brought a big new gas field onstream from scratch in its history. Its wealth rests on its political connections, the export monopoly that they bring, and the work of others: chiefly, long-forgotten Soviet-era engineers and geologists.

Their legacy has been sadly neglected. Over 70 percent of Russia's high-pressure gas pipelines were built before 1985; the average age of main pipelines is 22 years; 14 percent are older than their design life. According to the IEA, at least 30 billion m^3 of natural gas, or a fifth of Russian exports to Europe, are wasted, mostly because of leaky pipes and worn-out compressors. Vast quantities of gas are "flared" (simply burnt) because oil companies do not have access to the pipelines (thanks to Gazprom's ill-managed monopoly) needed to sell it. According to Gazprom, flaring accounts supposedly for a "mere" 15 billion m^3 but is estimated by other experts as being as much as 60 billion m^3. To deal with that, Gazprom needs not only to modernize, but also to develop new fields. The problem is that these fields are in some of the most inhospitable places on the planet: the far north and east of Russia. Getting the gas out is technically difficult and expensive; so is building thousands of miles of new pipelines to get it to new markets. Developing the supergiant new Yamal field in western Siberia, for example, will cost $70 billion. Gazprom itself, laden with costs and debts, cannot provide that money itself. Nor can the company raise it through Russia's underdeveloped financial system. After the way in which Western energy companies have been treated in Russia (described in Chapter Four), their shareholders may be unwilling to put up cash for an investment whose profits seem destined to be kept within Russia.

The problems are even greater in offshore development. Under the icy waters of the Barents sea, some 300 miles (550 km) from the northern Russian coastline, lies one of the world's largest gas fields, named after a Soviet-era geophysicist, Vladimir Shtokman. With up to 3.7 trillion m^3 of untouched gas, it could supply the EU's total needs for seven years. Discovered in 1988, it is one of the jewels in the crown of Russia's natural resource riches. The problem is turning the gas into cash. Norway's Statoil, one of the world's most technologically advanced companies in energy extraction, started development of its similarly challenging Snohvit field (which is less than a tenth the size of Shtokman) in 2002. It was due to ship the first cargo of LNG only on December 1, 2007. Gazprom insists that it is now getting ready to invest heavily in development and that it will raise its output to 570 billion m^3 in 2010 and 670 billion m^3 in 2020 Maybe it will. But the company is so secretive, and its history so poor, that outsiders have little basis to trust it. The lesson from Russia in the past 15 years is that Kremlin interference plus corruption make a lethal mixture when long-term investment planning is concerned.

So the biggest question for Europe in the coming decade is likely to be how to deal with a Russia that is short of gas, and that has an increasing number of outside customers to sell it to. The effect of raising gas prices in Russia, and those paid by the ex-Soviet countries such as Ukraine and Belarus that have previously received it cheaply, is that Gazprom's loss-making sales in the home and ex-Soviet markets will shortly become profitable and therefore more attractive. Moreover, the closer to the source gas field a country is, the better a customer it becomes: the supplier does not need to worry about transit fees, or being held hostage to political rows. Furthermore, Gazprom is also hoping to sell gas from eastern Siberia to China, Japan and South Korea, and a big planned move into LNG will also allow it to sell to America.

That will change the balance of power in Europe. For now at least, the EU countries have a strong potential hold on Russia. They need it as a supplier, but it needs them as customers. The success of the Kremlin divide-and-rule policy has prevented the latter factor having much importance, but it is certainly there if the EU chooses to act on it. In future, though, that will change. Europe will still need gas, but Gazprom will have lots of places to sell it to. A sign of those coming times, and the likely profound political effects they will bring, comes from the behavior of the companies that know Gazprom best: its German partners. Both E.ON and BASF have nailed down supply contracts with Gazprom up to 2036. Other European contracts run out much sooner—mostly in the course of the next ten years. That will give the Kremlin an unrivalled opportunity to drive a hard bargain, both commercially and politically, with those companies and countries that find themselves at the back of the queue.

Such worries still lie in the future. The immediate question is Gazprom's choice of partner in the development of Shtokman. The company initially short-listed five Western partners: Total, Chevron, ConocoPhillips, Statoil, and Norsk Hydro. All of these have the expertise in deep-water offshore gas development that Gazprom lacks. But in 2006 the Russian side announced that the foreign partners would not have equity stakes in the project and could take part only as contractors. In July 2007, Gazprom announced that France's biggest oil and gas company, Total, would gain a 25 percent share in a new company (51 percent owned by Gazprom) to design, finance, and build the first phase of the project. The remaining stake would go to other foreign partners. This was probably the worst deal a big Western energy company has ever had to accept from a resource-rich country. It separated for the first time access from ownership: Total has no rights to the gas itself, only a share in the company that extracts it. In effect, Gazprom auctioned the right to be involved in Shtokman among foreign oil companies desperate to be able to claim at least some share in Russia's hydrocarbons. Total expects to invest $15 billion in the field, in return for—supposedly—a 25 percent share of the gas produced after it comes on stream in 2013.

The growing importance of offshore natural resources (and the scarcity of onshore ones) was highlighted by an audacious geopolitical adventure in and under the Arctic Sea in the summer of 2007, as popular inside Russia as it was troubling for outsiders. A Russian expedition made the first manned trip to the seabed at the North Pole, symbolically claiming it for Russia. The natural resources of the Arctic have been frozen both in law and in nature for decades. But global warming is making the Arctic look more accessible. Below the seabed lie not only perhaps 10 billion tons of oil and gas deposits, but also tin, manganese, gold, nickel, lead, platinum, and diamonds. It may have some of the last untouched fish stocks in the northern hemisphere and—if the ice really thins or melts outright all year round—it could be an important route for maritime freight. The five countries around the Arctic Circle—the United States, Canada, Denmark (which looks after Greenland's interests), Norway, and Russia each have the 200 nautical mile (370 km) "economic zone" allowed by the United Nations Law of the Sea Convention. Russia argued in 2001 that its continental shelf stretched out into the Arctic, entitling it to a larger chunk. A UN tribunal said it needed to provide more evidence.

That is what the 2007 expedition, led by Russia's most glamorous explorer, Artur Chilingarov, aimed to supply. By taking samples from the seabed, it hopes to show that the Lomonosov Ridge, an underwater mountain chain, is indeed a continuation of Russia's landmass. If accepted, that would allow the Kremlin to annex a 460,000 square mile wedge of territory, roughly the size of western Europe, between Russia's northern coastline and the North Pole. Such wrangles about international maritime borders normally go at a snail's pace, and are stupefyingly boring. When Denmark allocated the equivalent of $25 million in 2004 to try to prove that the Lomonosov Ridge was connected to Greenland, few noticed or cared. The 2007 Russian expedition did not just collect symbolic rocks (real geological evidence would have come only from drilling deep below the seabed). It placed a titanium canister bearing the Russian flag on the yellow gravel 4,200 meters below the surface, at the site of the North Pole. That was the first manned mission to the polar seabed and one mounted by a flotilla that no other country could match. A mighty nuclear-powered icebreaker shepherded a research vessel that launched sophisticated submarines capable of pinpoint navigation under the Arctic ice. Adding an extra touch of technological wizardry, the submarines established a direct link from the seabed to the Mir space station. For outsiders used to stories of Russian bungling and backwardness, the stunt was a salutary reminder of the world-class technical clout and human talent the Kremlin can still command. Even more startling, though, was Russia's rhetoric. "The Arctic is ours and we should manifest our presence,"[47] said Chilingarov, a charismatic figure whom Putin has named as "presidential envoy" to the Arctic. "This is like placing a flag on the moon,"[48] said a spokesman for Russia's Arctic and Antarctic Institute. Planting a Russian flag on the seabed has symbolic, not legal, force, but it still scandalized Canada's foreign minister Peter MacKay. "This isn't the 15th century," he complained. "You can't go around the world and just plant flags and say 'We're claiming this territory.'" Russia's foreign minister, Sergei Lavrov, insisted that his country was doing nothing of the kind. But Andrei Kokoshin, chair of a Russian parliamentary committee dealing with the ex-Soviet region, said Russia "will have to actively defend its interests in the Arctic," adding "There is something to think about on the military side as well. We need to reinforce our Northern Fleet and our border guards and build airfields so that we can ensure full control over the situation."[49]

The next day, Russia's top admiral said it was time to restore the navy's permanent presence in the Mediterranean. How seriously to take Russia's new military posture is the subject of the next chapter.

CHAPTER EIGHT

SABER-RATTLING, OR SELLING SABERS

Russia's Foreign Policy Unpicked

O n the face of it, Russia is still an intimidating military power. It has one of the world's largest armies, excellent special forces, and some remarkable modern weapons. The *Shkval* [Squall] torpedo, for example, is an underwater rocket that travels in a capsule of gas created by its specially designed cone. Fired from a super-silent submarine, it is one of the few weapons that could endanger an American aircraft carrier. So is the *Moskit* supersonic ship-launched missile. Russia's new S–400 air defense system has twice the range of American-made Patriot missiles. The Topol-M is an intercontinental ballistic missile (ICBM) with a multiple warhead. Unlike its liquid-fuelled counterparts that usually launch from vulnerable silos, it has a propulsion system based on much more stable solid fuel. Its can be kept in constant readiness, and launched from anywhere. Russia has hugely increased its military procurement budget: the latest published figures are for nearly five trillion rubles (roughly $190 billion) to be spent in the period up to 2015.[1] The aim is to replace 45 percent of Russia's arsenal with new equipment, with an emphasis on long-range nuclear weapons. Pride of place goes to a new submarine-launched ballistic missile, the Bulava, and to at least 50 new Topol-M land-based missiles.

Russia is certainly flexing its military muscles as never before: In the summer of 2007 it restarted the old Cold War practice of regularly buzzing Western countries' airspace to test their reactions. Initially this was in the North Atlantic and the North Sea, where British and Norwegian pilots used to sometimes fly so close to their Soviet adversaries that they could taunt them by waving *Playboy* center-folds (even the softest porn was banned in the puritanical Soviet system). In August 2007, Russia made the practice explicit, flying two lumbering Tupolev–95 bombers from their base on the Russian–Chinese border to the American military base at Guam in the middle of the Pacific Ocean. That, again, was a familiar sight in the old Cold War, when these bombers, the workhorses of the Soviet Union's airborne nuclear deterrent, would cruise down America's east coast. President Vladimir Putin proudly announced that Russia could now afford to keep nuclear bombers in the air at all times.

But even thriller writers find it hard to imagine the Kremlin posing a direct military threat to NATO. In overall defence budgets, the United States outspends Russia by around 25 to one. Since the end of the old Cold War, Russia's nuclear arsenal has slipped far behind that of America's, once its main strategic adversary. Most Russian nuclear weapons are old; many have exceeded their design life. Russia has the world's largest stockpile of nuclear weapons, with an estimated total of 16,000 warheads, half the Soviet Union's estimated total of 35,000 in the mid-1980s.[2] The Americans have a smaller stockpile, of 10,640. However, more of America's weapons—around 6,390—are actually usable. As well as tactical nuclear weapons, Russia has 3,300 to 3,400 strategic nuclear warheads. But Russia also lacks modern means of delivering them from land, sea, and air. Russia has built only one of a planned eight Borei submarines, the *Yuri Dolgoruky,* which after ten years of intermittent work was launched in 2007 and will be handed over to the Russian navy in 2008. But, like Russia's remaining three huge Typhoon-class nuclear subs, the *Yuri Dolgoruky* has no ICBMs until the Bulava missile is working properly. So far it has failed four out of its five tests. And it is far from clear if Russia's rundown nuclear factories can manufacture it in the quantity or quality required.

The Topol-M launchers rarely venture out of their bases, just as the nuclear-armed submarines mostly stay in harbor. The early warning system is technologically backward and patchy. Conventional forces are in even worse state. The Russian navy, for example, has barely 20 seaworthy major surface ships, divided between the Black Sea, the Northern Fleet, the Baltic Sea, and the Pacific. Russia has only a single aircraft carrier, the unreliable *Admiral Kuznetsov;* though it plans to build more, it lacks even a shipyard capable of such a task. Russia has found it hard to refurbish the Soviet-era carrier, the *Admiral Gorshkov,* which it sold to India in 2004 with a promised delivery date of 2008. It is now unlikely to be ready before 2011. If Russia does return to the Mediterranean, it will be with a token naval force that lacks air cover.

Once the fear was that Russia, with a surprise attack, could win a war against NATO. Now the question is whether the United States—at least in theory—could knock out Russia's entire nuclear arsenal in a first strike. Nobody in Washington is planning that, of course. Though Russia's increasing nuclear weakness may make the Kremlin dangerously jittery. Russia's remaining military might does two things. It can tip the balance in other conflicts, hot or cold, either by projecting a mainly symbolic presence, or by selling weapons. Second, it allows the Kremlin to posture: in talks about arms control agreements already concluded, in agreements that NATO wants to update, and in talks about weapons systems that have yet to be deployed.

The arms sales are growing fast. One of Putin's first acts in power was to create a strong state arms-export company, Rosoboroneks–port.[3] Since then, Russian arms sales have risen by more than 70 percent, making the country the world's second-largest arms exporter after the United States. The trend is accelerating: in 2006, the order book more than doubled to $30 billion. The main beneficiaries so far have been China, followed by India. In 2006, for example, China received half of Russia's $6 billion arms sales. But the new trend is sales to countries that detest the West. Oil-rich Venezuela has bought $3 billion-worth of Russian weapons, including 53 military helicopters and 24 advanced Sukhoi SU–30 fighter jets. It is now planning to buy five Project 636 Kilo-class diesel submarines, with an option on four more modern ones later. Russia has sold advanced anti-tank and anti-aircraft missiles to Syria, and has matching strong military intelligence cooperation with the regime there. It has sold 29 short-range Tor missiles to Iran to protect the Russian-built Bushehr nuclear reactor. It is discussing sales of the more advanced S–300 air defense system and the *Moskit* missile; it may have helped Iran develop its own version of the *Shkval*—something that could be crucial in a naval confrontation with the United States in the Gulf. Russia has sold small arms and other equipment to Sudan, some of which has been used in Darfur. Before the war in Iraq it used Belarus as a back-door means of selling air defence systems to Saddam Hussein, training Iraqi technicians to operate them. Along with other Russian defence contractors, Rosoboroneksport is as a result banned from doing business in America.

The rhetoric that accompanies such sales seems straight out of the Soviet playbook. Just days before he visited U.S. President George W. Bush in Maine in the summer of 2007, Putin played host to Venezuela's President Hugo Chávez, who called for a "worldwide revolution" against American "tyranny": His adoring remarks to Putin were redolent of the tributes paid by leaders of Soviet allies visiting Moscow during the old Cold War.[4] He then went on to visit Belarus and Iran. Such moves are an irritant to NATO and its allies, and are an ominous sign of the Kremlin's preferences. But they do not yet come close to changing the strategic balance. America's military planners worry about lots of things; Russian rockets are just one of them, and a long way from the top of the list. Even a huge increase in defence spending over many years would not restore Russia's military-industrial complex to the heights reached during the Soviet era. Brilliant design is one thing: turning it into mass production is another. Nearly two decades of neglect and mismanagement mean that Russia's arms factories lack the people and tools necessary for a world-class weapons industry, either for export or for domestic consumption. The workforce is ageing; the necessary base of subcontractors is missing, and the skills base has eroded sharply since the Soviet era. Russia's latest prototype fighter, the supposedly "fifth generation" SU–47 Berkut [Golden Eagle], wows observers at foreign air shows—but it is just that: a single prototype. As with so many things, Russia is still living off the conscripted brilliance and perverse sacrifices of the past. Much of what counts as arms sales still involve flogging off mothballed Soviet-era equipment relabelled as new. Russia's main selling proposition is that its weapons are rugged, reliable, and cheap, not that they are the height of technological sophistication. Customers for sophisticated weapons want reliable after-sales service, something that Russia has so far not been able to provide.

Sales of nuclear technology are another matter. Rumors persist that Russia not only supplied Iraq with weapons of mass destruction but also moved them out via Syria before the American attack. Similar rumors now say that Russia is helping Iran not just with publicly acknowledged civilian nuclear technology, but also with enrichment and other capabilities necessary to build nuclear warheads. But it is hard to see what Russia would gain from selling weapons of mass destruction to unpredictable dictators. It is more likely that the Kremlin enjoys hinting that it might sell terrifying weapons to America's adversaries, rather than actually doing so. While not insisting that Iran gives up its plans to enrich uranium,

Russia has stopped deliveries of nuclear fuel to Iran until that country makes peace with the International Atomic Energy Agency.

It is the same story—of sulks and threats, and ominous trends rather than immediate menace—with America's planned missile defence bases in Europe, and the Conventional Forces in Europe (CFE) Treaty. Russia objects strongly to the first, saying that it will if necessary target its nuclear weapons on European countries involved in the project. And it has given notice that it wants to withdraw from the latter—a landmark agreement signed in November 1990, at a time when the Warsaw Pact was already disintegrating. Neither row is what it seems. As a glance at the globe shows, the American bases (interceptors in Poland and a radar base in the Czech Republic) are aimed at Iran's missiles not Russia's. If Russia wanted to hit America with nuclear weapons, the least likely trajectory would be over central Europe (a route over the Arctic and North Atlantic would be much more plausible). The ten interceptor rockets, once installed, might give an Iranian regime with only one or two missiles pause for thought. They would not affect the credibility of Russia's much larger nuclear deterrent.

American military scientists have explained this repeatedly to their Russian counterparts, with at least ten detailed technical presentations, including a full briefing at the NATO–Russian council, but have not succeeded in denting the Kremlin's furious opposition to the plan. As Stephen Blank, an American academic notes, "abundant ironies exist in Russia's position."[5] For a start, the Kremlin does have a good case on other arms-control issues that the American administration has refused to discuss seriously. In particular, it has rebuffed Kremlin proposals for a third Strategic Arms Reduction Treaty (START–3) to replace START–1, which expires in 2009. Strategic unilateralism in nuclear matters is not just unwise, it is dangerous. Simply trying to maximize the credibility of America's nuclear deterrence stimulates insecurity elsewhere, and encourages other countries to think nuclear weapons are the best means of fighting wars. But Russia's arguments on missile defence are much weaker. The Kremlin both complains that the new system threatens its security, while boasting that its missiles are so technologically advanced that it poses no threat. Second, the only powers that could actually hit Russia with intermediate range missiles are the Kremlin's so-called friends, Iran and China. Third, these countries have this capability thanks only to Russian technology and assistance. If Russia does take what it calls "adequate" measures against America's new defensive installations, by targeting them with its own missiles, surely it should also do so against the far more dangerous potential threat from rogues and rivals in Iran, North Korea, Pakistan, and China?

Even odder, Russians and others doubt very much whether this missile defence system, or indeed any foreseeable one, will work. The technical difficulty is akin to hitting a bullet with a bullet. It is conceptually flawed: Would a rogue state mad enough to use nuclear weapons at all be deterred by the slight chance that they might be intercepted? Would not such a state try to smuggle a nuclear device into its target country, and detonate it terrorist-style, rather than go to all the trouble of delivering it via an ICBM? These are strong arguments. It may be that a future generation of missile defence systems will be cheap and effective. But for now, the only certain winners from the development of the planned system are the companies of America's own military-industrial complex. If the American politicians whose campaigns they finance are gullible, paranoid, or corrupt enough to shower billions of tax dollars into these firms' pockets, why should Russia mind? Nor does the supposed Kremlin countermeasure, of retargeting missiles on European countries, make much sense. It is the number of missiles, the size of their warheads, their range, and their detectability that affect the strategic balance, not their targets. To change the targets is a matter of a few minutes' work on the computer. It has a powerful symbolic effect, but almost no practical one. In fact, the argument is heated because it has everything to do with politics, and almost nothing to do with serious questions of nuclear strategy.

On the face of it, Russia is annoyed that the United Sates is basing anything important in former Soviet satellite countries. That breaks an promise made by the West, the Kremlin claims, made when the Russian forces pulled out of Eastern Europe in the early 1990s. The Kremlin's real argument, however, is a different and more subtle one, which becomes alarmingly effective on issues such as this. The missile defence plan is highly unpopular in Europe. West Europeans see it as a characteristically ill-thought-out bit of hi-tech swaggering by the global superpower. Even the Czechs and the Poles do not welcome the new bases. The practical effect so far is that America's peremptory request, and lack of any obvious carrot to reward its allies for the risk involved, has alienated public opinion in even these, which are among the two most Atlanticist, countries in the region. By kicking up a fuss, even with empty threats based on the shakiest logic, Russia moves closer to a strategic prize that has been the Kremlin's aim ever since the start of the last cold war: to split the once formidable Atlantic alliance.

The means for that are now in place. The glue that held Europe and American interests together for four decades was composed of two ingredients: European fear of the Soviet Union, and the American belief that Europe's fate mattered across the Atlantic too. Twice in the last century, America stood by at the start of a European fight, only to have to intervene, belatedly and expensively, towards the end. Postwar strategic thinking was based on the assumption that it was better not to make the same mistake again. After the collapse of communism both components weakened. European countries no longer felt a military threat from Russia, while America saw more pressing threats elsewhere: chiefly China and—after 9/11—the "war on terror." In neither regard did Europe look like a particularly useful ally. Indeed, it often looked like an ungrateful one. From this point of view, the main value of the missile defence system is symbolic: It shows that America's European allies are still valued and useful. But conversely, opposition to the plan has been a propaganda gift to anti-American politicians across the whole continent of Europe. "Here are the Americans clumsily provoking Russia and endangering our security," they argue. It isolates the pro-American politicians that agreed to host it.

America's allies are already exposed by the catastrophic failure of the Bush administration's war in Iraq. For reasons of both principle and pragmatism the ex-communist countries were among America's staunchest allies in Afghanistan and Iraq after 2001. Toppling a brutal dictator and the one-party state he had imposed was a resonant cause. Joining the "coalition of the willing" was not only a good way of showing gratitude to America for its support of NATO enlargement, but also underlining that the ex-communist countries were not just consumers of security, but contributors to it. That goodwill and loyalty has been drained and strained, in most countries to the point of almost complete exhaustion, for lamentably little result. Politicians who backed the war now look stupid. Those who supported Russia's criticism of it have been vindicated. An extra, and especially damaging, issue is the alleged cooperation of Poland and Romania, and possibly others, in the CIA's "rendition" of terrorist suspects for interrogation under torture. If the Kremlin had been writing the script itself it could hardly have found a better storyline: after fighting a greedy, brutal, and incompetent war, the United States is now trying to put an unpopular, scary, hi-tech defense system in Europe, despite the objections of almost all concerned. What better illustration could there be of the deep-seated unfairness of the transatlantic relationship? When Putin said in September 2007 that Europe should drop its "silly" Atlantic solidarity and concentrate on improving ties with Russia,[6] it was striking that almost no voice was raised in criticism.

Russia's behavior on arms control issues may lack military logic, but it has profound if concealed political effects. The CFE Treaty, the cornerstone of conventional weapons reduction talks at the end of the old Cold War, had a practical effect when both superpowers had large, capable conventional forces in Europe. Now it is of mainly symbolic value; America's forces, once 600,000 strong, are down to 60,000. The Kremlin has withdrawn completely from European countries to its west and south. The treaty brings no meaningful restriction on Russia's own military capabilities. Russia is allowed to have 6,400 tanks, 11,480 armored vehicles, 6,415 artillery pieces, 3,450 combat aircraft, and 890 armed helicopters in European Russia (i.e., the region west of the Ural Mountains).[7] In every case, Russia has less than these ceilings—usually by some way. When Russia did need more forces, during its wars in Chechnya, it hugely breached its regional "flank" ceilings, prompting only murmurs of protest. In 1999, the flank ceilings were revised, on condition (the West says) that Russia withdraw its remaining forces from Moldova and Georgia. It didn't. Then in 2005, after years of prevarication, Russia suddenly agreed to withdraw its forces from Georgia, except for the "peacekeeping" base in Abkhazia. It continues to keep a base in Transdniestria, partly to protect the separatist regime there, and partly as a backstop to ensure Russian influence over it.

For all its irrelevance, the CFE Treaty has been the subject of lengthy political wrangles. Because of Russian foot-dragging in Georgia and Moldova, Western countries that had signed the CFE Treaty refused to ratify it. Russia claims to find that infuriating. Putin also complained, in an address to the Russian parliament in 2007, that the West is "building up armed forces in direct proximity to Russia's borders."[8] It is true that under the treaty armed forces of the new NATO members like Estonia count, oddly, as Russian, but these militaries are so small that they have no significant effect on the total numbers.

The only new factors are logistics and training bases the United States is developing in Bulgaria and Romania, plus the (planned) missile defence installations. Neither is directed against Russia; indeed, conventional capabilities in Europe are so rundown and overstretched that it is doubtful if NATO could mount even a defensive operation in Eastern Europe, let alone an offensive one against Russia. In short, none of Russia's arguments stands scrutiny. The CFE's nonratification remains a minor diplomatic inconvenience for the Kremlin, but only because it highlights the mildly embarrassing fact that Russia props up two illegal regimes. Moreover, the practical steps Russia is threatening in response are as ill-grounded as the arguments. No provision for the planned "moratorium" announced by Putin in April 2007 actually exists in the treaty.[9] It is indeed possible to withdraw from it, with a 150 day notice period. That notice should be based on a statement of "extraordinary events" that have prompted the move; until the 150 days expire, the departing party must stick to the CFE.[10] It is questionable whether Putin appreciated this, or whether he had the proper advice from international lawyers. At an emergency conference of the CFE members in Vienna in June, Russia repeated its demand that all the parties to the treaty ratify it by July 1, 2008. As expected, the Western signatories simply repeated their demand that Russia first complete its withdrawal from Moldova and Georgia. The "split in NATO" promised by the Kremlin-controlled press never materialized. Nor did the promised presidential decree on the moratorium. Military inspections by NATO countries within the CFE framework that had initially been denied, citing "insurmountable circumstances," were then granted.

So why is Putin now making such a fuss? It is partly because the CFE was so unpopular with Soviet (and then Russian) generals, who saw it as codifying a retreat from their hard-won bridgehead in central Europe. So talking about tearing it up is a symbolic gesture to them. More importantly, if Russia does eventually withdraw, it will no longer be bound by the treaty's notification, control, and inspection regime. That will mean that, if it wants, it can concentrate forces on, for example, the border with Georgia or Estonia, without being obliged to explain what it is doing or why. In the worst case, that could be the first stage in a military intervention in either country. That is unlikely in the case of Estonia, a NATO member, but conceivable in an artificially stoked conflict between Georgia and South Ossetia or Abkhazia, or both. As Pavel Felgenhauer, Russia's best-known independent military analyst, points out wryly: "This will create less transparency and more mutual suspicion in Europe—much like the atmosphere inside Putin's Kremlin."[11]

Withdrawal from the CFE also paves the way for a Russian pullout from another cornerstone arms-control agreement from the old Cold War, the Intermediate-Range Nuclear Forces (INF) Treaty. In

February 2007, Putin said that this "no longer serves Russia's interests" and the chief of the Russian general staff, General Yuri Baluyevsky, said that if America pressed ahead with missile defence plans, Russia could pull out of the INF.[12] That would allow Russia to develop shorter-range nuclear missiles and target them on Europe. The scene would be set for another downward spiral in the transatlantic relationship. America could offer to put its own nuclear missiles in Europe, but, as in the 1980s, that would prompt frenzied protests from "peace" campaigners. Yet without American nuclear protection, Europe's security would look even more precarious. Without nuclear forces based in Europe, a future U.S. administration would find it hard to argue that it needed to keep any troops at all in Europe. That would suit the Kremlin just fine.

As well as missile defence and the CFE treaty, the third big European security issue for Russia is Kosovo, scene of the only military confrontation between NATO and Russian forces since the end of the old Cold War. That was in 1999, after Serbian forces were retreating from Kosovo following the NATO bombing campaign to force Serbian strongman Slobodan Milošević to stop persecuting the Albanian-speaking population of the province. Two hundred Russian soldiers from the international peace-keeping forces in neighboring Bosnia rushed to seize the airport at the Kosovar capital, Priština. The event is still shrouded in mystery. Russia was evidently planning to use the airfield to fly in more troops, but Ukraine and Hungary, reacting promptly to Western requests, denied overflight rights to Russian planes. It is still unclear whether the move was authorized by former President Boris Yeltsin and his defence minister or was an act of rebellion against them—and perhaps part of a broader plan.

At any rate, Russia since then has been content to let the West stew in a mess of its own making. Kosovo, nominally an international protectorate, is badly governed, a haven for organized crime, and unable or unwilling to protect the rights of its remaining Serbian minority. Independence might be a way of forcing the Kosovar leaders to face up to their responsibilities. Serbia says it will not recognize or accept independence of a province which it regards as historically Serbian, and where the rights of Serbs are endangered. Partition might offer a solution, but this has been rejected by the international community as likely to spark even more fighting. The United States wants to hurry up. It fears that, if the outside world does not recognize Kosovo, it will lose its remaining ability to influence events there. The EU broadly supports this, although some countries have broken ranks and taken a strongly pro-Serbian stance. The United Nations (UN) envoy, Martti Ahtisaari, has come up with an ingenious plan that offers Kosovo conditional statehood under international supervision. This has been modified to try to take account of Russian objections, by giving a longer period for Serbs and the Kosovar leadership to try to reach agreement. But what if they don't? Russia says blandly that it will only support an agreement acceptable to both sides.[13] That, in effect, gives the Serbs a veto. If the West ignores Russian objections, and tries to force the Ahtisaari plan through the UN Security Council, Russia will veto it. The result is a stalemate: damaging for Europe, but convenient for both the Kremlin and its Serbian allies. Attention inevitably turns to what Russia might want in return: Perhaps that the West turns a blind eye to a one-off deal on Moldova? Or does Russia want Georgia's allies to tell it to forget about recovering South Ossetia and Abkhazia?

The main aim may be simply to look tough. In the Yeltsin years, Russia tried hard to persuade Milošević to back down. Many Russians now regard that as a mistake. Nobody should take Russia's goodwill for granted any longer. Second, Russian intransigence usually has the paradoxical result of making fair-minded Europeans cast around for a "compromise." That then puts pressure on those who still advocate the original policy of Kosovar independence— chiefly the United States and its closest allies. In short, the longer the impasse goes on, the better for the Kremlin. But the common factor in all three disputes, over missile defence, over the CFE Treaty, and over Kosovo, is that they give the Kremlin a pretext to sound cross, to behave badly, and to try to divide Europe and America. The most interesting question is why this policy is needed at all.

Russia has dropped three Soviet attributes from its foreign policy: a messianic ideology, raw military power, and the imperative of territorial expansion. Instead comes the idea that, as Dmitri Trenin, a well-connected foreign-policy expert, puts it: "Russia's business is business."[14] That has special weight, he argues, because the people who rule Russia also own it. Stitching up world energy markets with other big producers, or finding customers for Russian weapons and raw materials, are much more interesting than the nuances of the Middle East peace process or the endless woes of the Balkans. In short, bad politics is bad for business. Capitalism is integrating Russia ever more deeply into the outside world and surely making political conflicts less likely, not more. So what is going on? The Kremlin's explanation goes like this. The West takes Russia for granted, swallows concessions, and offers only snubs in return. Russia abandoned the Soviet empire in eastern Europe on the strict understanding that NATO would not expand to the former Warsaw Pact countries. Yet that is exactly what happened. Far from winding up, or staying as a backstop security organization, NATO started offensive operations for the first time in its history, intervening in ex-Yugoslavia to bomb Serbia, a traditional Russian ally. That cold shoulder during the 1990s demoralized the pro-Westerners in the Yeltsin Kremlin. Now, at least in some Russian eyes, the West has treated Putin equally shabbily. In 2006, a former top Kremlin aide, Aleksandr Voloshin, went on a semi-official mission to explain Russia's frustration to American decision-makers, outlining what Putin had done for the United States since 9/11. This included offering unprecedented intelligence and security cooperation against militant Islamism, closing the two main overseas bases inherited from the Soviet Union,[15] and allowing the United States to use air bases in central Asia to support the attack on the Taliban in Afghanistan. All that, Voloshin argued, had exposed Putin to sharp criticism from hawks in the Kremlin. He had assured them that a bold gesture to America would pay dividends. But instead, the United States continued to interfere in Russia's backyard, stoking popular revolutions in Ukraine and Georgia, bringing the Baltic states into NATO, and talking about new bases in eastern Europe.

The arguments got nowhere. Though the Kremlin insists that NATO expansion is encirclement, a better way of looking at it is that Russia has willfully cut itself off from the European mainstream. Switzerland and Austria are entirely surrounded by NATO members, but do not worry that they are encircled. NATO has in fact done rather little—too little in the view of some of its new members—to counter Russian muscle-flexing. Most of the new members are militarily weak and struggle to meet their NATO commitments. The alliance's work in eastern Europe is mainly based on strengthening its members' ability to work with each other in joint training and peacekeeping. The truth is that, so long as the Kremlin insists on seeing NATO as an enemy, it strengthens the case for bringing vulnerable ex-communist countries into the alliance. In the early 1990s, that was off the agenda. Joining NATO was seen as too expensive by the potential applicants, and too destabilizing by the alliance's policy-makers. But Russia never seemed to understand why its former satellite countries might be worried about their security. By protesting loudly that NATO enlargement was provocative and "impermissible" (a favorite word in the Russian diplomatic lexicon),[16] the Kremlin ensured both that the applicants' desire grew and became more urgent; it also became morally all but impossible for existing NATO members to turn them away. The Kremlin may dislike this development. But it has only itself to blame for it.

Some Westerners may find it mildly offensive that their support for security, freedom, and justice in ex-communist countries, and attempts to prevent genocide in Bosnia and Kosovo, are dismissed as nothing more than self-interested geopolitics. Such arguments seem to make no impact, however: In 2006 Putin apparently decided that it was pointless trying to maintain a warm friendship with the West: Instead, Russia would have to gain respect by talking, and acting, toughly. That has some risks. Russia is now increasingly seen in the rich, industrialized world as an authoritarian state that hangs out with international pariahs. Second, fear of Russia may make the Euroatlantic glue stickier. For the first time since the end of the old Cold War, it is now possible to argue that America and Europe need each other in the face of a Russian threat. But Kremlin cheerleaders do not see it that way. They argue that the world is changing: The United States and Europe may have put Russia in the deep freeze, but much larger countries such as India, Brazil, Mexico, and Indonesia, all respectably free and law-governed, have not. The United States may be rich now, but developing countries, where Russia is much more popular, have brighter prospects. American hegemony, in short, is history.

Similarly, just because the United States is still the world's most powerful country does not make it synonymous with world opinion. The fire-breathing Chávez[17] may be demonized in Washington, D.C., but he is lionized elsewhere. As Aleksei Pushkov, a pro-Kremlin journalist, notes, there are no anti-Chávez demonstrations in Western capitals, and plenty of anti-Bush ones; he asks if Bush is not more of a pariah than Chávez. Indeed, Russian anti-Americanism is mild compared to the depth of sentiment in supposed American allies such as Turkey, Pakistan, France, Germany, or Britain. Not only that, a brusque approach to the self-appointed guardians of Euroatlantic virtue hardly seems to be hurting business. Since Putin started criticizing America publicly in 2003, foreign investment has soared. Former Prime Minister Tony Blair's warning that foreign businesses should take more account of the political risks in Russia came just days before an investment summit in St. Petersburg attended by a record number of corporate chiefs.

The tactics are increasingly clear and effective. But the goal is still puzzling. The short-term wish list is clear: just recognition of

Russia's primacy in the former Soviet empire and the energy "Finlandization" of Europe coupled with international parity of esteem: a seat, de facto or de jure, at the Western top tables. But these wishes are incompatible: Bullying the Balts pretty much precludes a friendly reception in Brussels or Washington, D.C. If anything, it guarantees a series of embarrassing public snubs. The Kremlin may be assuming that the West will eventually abandon its new allies, or that they will become indefensible by their own efforts. But pending a split in the West, or its surrender, Russia's choice is a stark one. It can drop its pretensions to empire and its peculiar version of history, in which case it can move sharply closer to the EU and NATO. Or it can go down the route of independent foreign policy, either in alliance with the Muslim world or with China.

The Kremlin is certainly making an effort to restore at least some of its Soviet-era clout in the Muslim world, to some extent on the basis of "my enemy's enemy is my friend." When America identified Iran as part of the "axis of evil" it kickstarted Russian goodwill. Russia joined the Islamic Conference Organisation as an observer in 2005 and Putin attended its 2003 conference in Kuala Lumpur, Malaysia, where, amid anti-Semitic tirades from some of the other participants, he described Russia as Islam's "historical defender."[18] Unlike almost all Western countries, Russia is prepared to talk to radical Islamist movements such as Hamas and Hizbollah. As Aleksei Malashenko of the Moscow Carnegie Centre argues,[19] the Kremlin approach seems to be to draw a rather arbitrary (indeed probably fictional) line between "good" and "bad" Islamic militants: The "bad" are the Chechen separatists and their allies in the North Caucasus and Tatarstan and the "good" are the ones who tweak America's nose. This echoes faintly the Soviet Union's attitude from 25 years earlier: "Good" Muslims attacked Israel and America; "bad" ones attacked the Soviet boys in Afghanistan.

Perhaps aware of the contradiction, the Kremlin tries to keep a little distance from Hamas and the like: They are welcomed warmly in Moscow by pro-Kremlin ideologues and propagandists, but not by senior Kremlin figures themselves. Aleksandr Prokhanov, editor of the "red-brown" (i.e., Soviet-fascist) newspaper *Zavtra* [Tomorrow], congratulated the Hamas leader Khaled Mashal "with all his heart" on the movement's victory in the Palestinian territory elections.[20] Yet the same paper is an ardent supporter of the most ruthless tactics against Chechen rebels. Russia's engagement, such as it is, does not seem to have nudged either Hamas or Iran into a more moderate position. The latter's nuclear-weapons ambitions are proceeding unchecked; Hamas shows no sign of wanting to recognize Israel, even tacitly. Russia seemed to have no leverage in the war in Lebanon in the summer of 2006, despite its supposedly close links to Syria and Hezbollah. Its influence in Iraq is close to zero—and when Russian embassy officials were seized, and eventually murdered, in Iraq in 2006, none of the Kremlin's Muslim allies seemed to do anything to help.

The main reason is simple: Russia's flirtation with the Muslim cause is seen, rightly, as opportunist. The Soviet invasion of Afghanistan (plus support for the American attack on the Taliban in 2001), two wars in Chechnya, and strong support for the Milošević regime's harsh stance toward Muslim populations in Kosovo and Bosnia make it hard to regard Russia as a serious ally for the Islamic world. Muslims appreciate Russia as a counterweight to American influence, and as a possible source of useful weapons (officially or unofficially). But it goes no further. Russia's relations with the Muslim world are complicated by another factor: Israel. During the old Cold War, relations with Israel were icy; the Soviet Union was profoundly anti-Semitic and strongly supported Arab countries trying to destroy the Jewish state. Full diplomatic relations were restored only as the Soviet Union was already in its death throes. A million Russian-speaking immigrants in Israel make the country now one of Russia's most important foreign cultural partners. More Russian books, newspapers, and television programs are produced in Israel than in any other country outside the former Soviet Union and Israel is a popular tourist destination (being one of the few places where monoglot Russians can feel at home in a "real" foreign country). The majority of Russia's Jewish population has now emigrated; anti-Semitism has not disappeared, but it is dormant—and eclipsed by prejudice against other minorities. Few Russians objected to the fact that the prime minister from 2004 to 2007, the low-key Mikhail Fradkov, is Jewish.[21] Many Russians feel instinctive sympathy for Israel's predicament: Russia has suffered ruthless Islamist terrorism too, they feel. The presence (perhaps exaggerated) of "Arab" fighters in Chechnya adds to the feeling of linkage. That is not enough to change Kremlin policy very much. Israel objects strenuously to Iran's nuclear ambitions, which depend almost wholly on Russian know-how and technology. Russian arms sales to Syria could shift the military balance significantly against Israel (though Russia did block a planned sale of Iskander surface-to-surface missiles in 2005). After the Kremlin opened contacts with Hamas, Israel crisply snubbed the idea of a peace conference in Moscow.

The Chinese option, at least in comparison, looks more attractive. The "strategic partnership" between Russia and China is one of the big achievements of the Putin years in foreign policy. A longstanding squabble over the border has been settled. Worries about illegal migration (overblown in the Yeltsin years, but widely believed) have calmed down. Trade with China has more than tripled since Putin came into the Kremlin. China has invested $500 million in Rosneft, the Kremlin's oil subsidiary, and Russia has agreed to build an ambitious gas pipeline to China.[22] Both countries share a strong dislike of Western universalist values and a belief that economic growth and stability are preferable to imported notions of freedom. The Kremlin's homegrown ideology of "sovereign democracy" and China's nominal "communism" have a lot in common: a horror of instability, a strong nationalism, and a belief that the proof of the authoritarian pudding is in the eating. The message, crudely, is "who needs your kind of democracy when we have our kind of growth."

Based on such similarities in worldview, it is possible to see Russia and China as two pillars of what some have called the "World without the West," or the WWW.[23] The WWW is strictly pragmatic, shuns idealistic political approaches (which it sees as hypocritical), and detests outside interference in other countries' affairs. It is the antithesis of the American idea of liberal internationalism, which believes that intervening to prevent genocide, say, is not just the right but the duty of a civilized country. The WWW favors state-dominated market economies in which the heights of political and economic power converge. Yet it is not the embodiment of a comprehensive rejection of the West, an "anti-West" so to speak: It wants economic cooperation with the advanced industrialized world, particularly in order to catch it up in technology and education.

The most practical expression of the WWW is the Shanghai Cooperation Organization (SCO), an outfit that creates a potentially formidable new security axis between Russia, China, and central Asia. In 2007 this started to develop a strong military component in the organization: Its summit in the Kyrgyz capital, Bishkek, in August 2007 was marked by ten days of joint military exercises[24] in Chelyabinsk in the Urals and Urumqi in Chinese Turkestan. These were the SCO's biggest military exercises; the first time that Chinese airborne forces have taken part in such military drills abroad; and the first time that Russian forces have exercised in China. The end was observed by the six defence ministers of the SCO core members: China, Russia, Kazakhstan, Kyrgyzstan, Uzbekistan, and Tajikistan.

The SCO is linked to Russia's answer to NATO, the Collective Security Treaty Organization (CSTO). It has the same five ex-Soviet members, plus Armenia and Belarus, creating an embryonic security sphere that stretches from the Arctic to the South China Sea, and from the Bering Straits to the Polish border. Putin says any comparison between the SCO and the old Warsaw Pact is "idle talk" and "improper either in content or form."[25] But the fact remains that a big anti-Western alliance, however loose, is taking shape.

The immediate aim is to force NATO to recognize the CSTO as a counterpart, chiefly on issues such as narcotics, Afghanistan, and counterterrorism (issues which often overlap widely). That is something that NATO has always resisted. It prefers to deal with CSTO members bilaterally—a policy that interestingly echoes Russia's attitude to Western collective security organizations. The SCO and CSTO have done well in signaling to America that no security vacuum exists in central Asia—and that kyboshes grand designs from previous years about bringing countries like Uzbekistan or Kazakhstan into close strategic relationships with the West. China strongly backs Russia's position in keeping NATO out of central Asia, and in the row over missile defence (not least because its own smaller nuclear arsenal would be more directly affected if America's system ever became workable). The next big question will be whether to promote Iran from observer status to full membership of the SCO. The Iranian leadership has been strongly pushing for this, hoping that it will give it useful diplomatic support against America's increasingly alarming demands. China, which does not want to aggravate relations with the United States, has resisted so far. If the SCO agrees, it will crystallize the organization's role as the core of a global anti-American alliance, however opportunistic.

It is one thing to agree on anti-American positions; another to agree on who is the top dog in a shared backyard. Russia may have invented the SCO, but China clearly thinks of itself as the natural leader by virtue of its size and economic weight. Russia and China may be partners in keeping the United States out of central Asia, but they are also rivals there. Within the region, Kazakhstan and Uzbekistan each want to be the leader. China has been strenuously trying to do its own bilateral gas deals with Turkmenistan (not an SCO member) and with Kazakhstan (which is). These deals threaten Russian interests. The biggest problem is that Russians' old-fashioned zero-sum geopolitical thinking makes it hard to conceive of a deep strategic alliance with anyone. China's huge population and shortage of natural resources (coal aside) are a painful contrast to

Russia's demographic collapse and mineral-rich eastern regions. As a result, the two countries may make common cause, but they are not natural allies. Andrei Piontkovsky, one of Russia's sharpest foreign-policy analysts, calls the notion "an alliance between a rabbit and a boa constrictor."[26]

This leaves Russia stuck. It is too weak to have a truly effective independent foreign policy, but it is too disgruntled and neurotic to have a sensible and constructive one. It wants to be respected, trusted, and liked, but will not act in a way that gains respect, nurtures trust, or wins affection. It settles for being noticed—even when that comes as a result of behavior that alienates and intimidates other countries. It compensates for real weakness by showing pretend strength. Little of that—advanced weapons sales to rogue regimes aside—immediately threatens global peace and security. In that sense, the New Cold War is less scary than the old one. But Russia's behavior is alarming, uncomfortable, and damaging—both to its own interests and to those of other countries. And the trajectory is worrying. If Russia becomes still richer and still more authoritarian, all the problems described in previous chapters will be harder to deal with, not easier. Russia's influence in the West will be stronger; the willingness to confront it less. The former satellite countries will be even more vulnerable; the economic levers even better positioned. In other words, if the West does not start winning the New Cold War while it can, it will find it much harder in the future. The price of a confrontation now may be economic pain and political uncertainty. But it still offers the chance of a new relationship with Russia based on realism rather sentiment, and tough-mindedness rather than wishful thinking. The price later will be higher—perhaps so high that the West will no longer be able to pay it.

CHAPTER NINE

HOW TO WIN THE
NEW COLD WAR

Why the West Must Believe in Itself

First a medieval fortress and then the citadel of Soviet totalitarianism, the Kremlin's rose-red walls have rarely made lovers of liberty and justice feel at home. It is as if Britain's government were based in the Tower of London, or France's in the Bastille. Certainly the ideas now bubbling under its onion domes would have been all too familiar to its past occupants. Put bleakly, Russia is reverting to behavior last seen during the Soviet era. So the first step towards winning the New Cold War is to accept what is happening. History is not delivering the inexorable victory that it seemed to promise in the 1980s. The collapse of communism has spread freedom and justice only to a minority of the ex-captive nations. In the rest, authoritarian bureaucratic capitalism, bolstered by natural resources, effective secret police, and stifled media, has taken root. The dominant value is not freedom but economic stability, protected not by the rule of law but by strong government. Consensus replaces the electoral mandate. The powers-that-be are accountable to history, not to the citizenry. Opposition is disloyalty at best, and outright treason if it is supported from abroad. The individual is a means to an end, not a bearer of inalienable rights; justice is a tool, not an ideal. The mass media are an instrument of state, not a constraint on its power. Civil society is an instrument for social consolidation, not diversity. Property rights and contracts are conditional; foreign policy is solely about the promotion of national interest. Intervention to protect human rights is hypocrisy.

The raison d'état rules. "Sovereign democracy" is just the latest label for this; anyone who has studied Russian history will see that many of these ideas go back centuries. Revisionist, nationalistic, and jingoistic, Russia has hauled its old ideas out of the dustbin of history, burnished them and—for now—made them work.

Having accepted the magnitude of the problem, the next step is to give up the naïve idea that the West can influence Russia's domestic politics. That was possible in the Yeltsin era, when the people running Russia—or at least some of them—truly wanted to join the West and were willing to take advice on how to achieve this goal. That era may have been illusory. It may have been wasted. It may not return for decades. It is pointless to seek friends among the feuding clans of the Kremlin. Their hatred for each other may lead to change, but not necessarily change in the West's interests. Instead, we are back in an era of "great power" politics. If we want to defend our interests, we will have to think clearly and pay dearly. The difficulties facing us are not mere bumps in the road. We are facing people who want to harm us, frustrate us, and weaken us. Their main weapon is our greatest weakness: money. Just as we worried about the firepower of the Soviet war machine, now we should fear the tens of billions of dollars in its coffers, and the weakness of mind and morals on which it is applied. The 1990s are over: It is high time now to treat Russia as the authoritarian regime that it is—like China or Kazakhstan—rather than a member of the European family experiencing an unfortunate but temporary aberration.

A developed Western consensus on how to deal with Russia took shape only slowly in the last Cold War, and a new one will not be arrived at overnight now. But the elements are clear. First, Europe and the United States must realize that the Kremlin's aim is to split them. The United States must not accept divisive deals from Russia on security (trading help in Iran for the abandonment of Georgia, for example). Similarly, the European Union (EU) must drop its lingering disdain for the United States. Certainly the current U.S. administration's foreign policy has been open to criticism. But the common transatlantic interests are far deeper and more important than the temporary disagreements over Iraq, the Middle East, or climate change. Europeans may sometimes privately agree with Russian complaints about American arrogance or incompetence, but they should be careful about echoing them publicly. Faced with a resurgent Russia, Europe needs the United States more than it needs Europe. United, they are easily capable of standing up to a resurgent Russia. Divided, each is vulnerable, Europe most of all. The Atlantic alliance may never regain the unity and importance of the last Cold War, but it is still the basis for victory in this one.

Second, it would be neither possible nor desirable to block trade with Russia or investment in it outright. The lesson of sanctions is that they create wonderful opportunities for corruption, stoke the paranoia and isolation of the targeted regime, and do little or nothing to dislodge it. But Russia cannot expect to take advantage of the liberal and open economic system of Europe and America if it does not play by the same rules at home. The EU is already rightly alarmed by the investments made and planned by state-run "wealth funds" from Russia and China. That alarm needs urgently to turn into firmly enforced rules. Countries that do not respect outsiders' property rights cannot expect to buy whatever assets they like in countries that do; those who defraud shareholders in Yukos should not then be able to use that loot to buy up more companies abroad. It is time to stop the Kremlin having the best of both worlds. Most of the time it claims its companies are normal economic actors maximizing profits like everyone else—until suddenly it claims national interest and, for example, cuts off oil deliveries to Lithuania and Latvia, or electricity to Georgia, because of pressing political reasons. That is entirely rational in current conditions from a Russian point of view—but intolerable from a European one. In future, the Kremlin cannot have it both ways. If it depoliticized and demonopolized its own energy industry—chiefly by allowing third-party access to its gas pipeline monopoly—it could defuse the controversy over energy security. Until that happens, the outside world must regard every investment Russia makes abroad as a politically loaded expression of foreign policy, and not a neutral business transaction. In other words, energy security is national security, and cheap energy from ill-wishers is a bad bargain.

The EU must focus sharply on gas, which is now the continent's greatest vulnerability. Securing supplies and breaking Russia's growing monopoly may be painful and costly. The Kremlin has already said that if the United States or the EU start blocking its investments on national-security grounds it will retaliate against Western companies in Russia. That may be a bluff: Russia needs Western technology and would be foolish to scare them away. If it is not bluff: too bad—the price is worth paying. It is better to shave pennies off these companies' dividends than to let the Kremlin into the heart of our economic and political system. Putting security of supply above cost means both bargaining collectively with Russia and making Europe's own energy infrastructure more robust, and therefore less vulnerable to outside pressure. That means, for example, enforcing competition laws so that Nord Stream is not built, while providing taxpayers' money and political backing to make sure that Nabucco is. Similarly, liquefied natural gas (LNG) terminals are expensive and no cure-all, but still worth the money because of the diversification that they allow. Europe needs better strategic gas storage and to link its national "energy islands" with interconnecting pipelines and electricity lines. The result will be a gas supply system that is both physically and economically robust, and therefore much harder for an outside supplier to dominate. Once supply shocks are less painful, it is less likely that anyone will bother to inflict them. Such a policy will mean a change of course: Liberalization and competition, the great goals of the past decade, are desirable for many other reasons, but they have not brought these changes about so far and are unlikely to do so now. National security is a job for politicians, not those in business.

Similarly, the regulators of the world's financial centers must rethink how they deal with Russian (and for that matter Chinese) companies wanting to use them. The free market cannot be decoupled from the free society. The industrialized world has shown its capacity for collective action in dealing with money laundering. It could do the same for corporate governance and property rights. That would mean, for example, that any company wanting to list its shares or sell its bonds in London, New York, or Frankfurt would have to make it clear that it was engaged in a real business, not the collection of artificial rents[1]; that its property was not stolen; and that its ownership was clear and truly private. Gazprom and Rosneft, along with most big Russian companies, would be immediately disqualified. Only those blinded by greed can overlook Gazprom's legally entrenched export monopoly: the majority shareholding held by the state, the management's fondness for related-party transactions and relationships with dodgy intermediary companies. Similarly, Rosneft's participation in the rigged auctions and forced dismemberment of Yukos should disqualify it permanently from any access to international capital markets.[2] Just as NATO would not have arranged its defence spending solely to suit arms manufacturers during the old Cold War, the West now must make its banks' and energy companies' commercial interests take second place to the question of national defence. Capitalism thrives under freedom, security, and justice, but a good business climate is a symptom, not a goal, of a well-governed country.

Winning the New Cold War means not just rewriting the rules for business, finance, and the energy market. It means rediscovering the virtues of collective action and solidarity in traditional politics and diplomacy. The West should bargain where it needs to, cooperate where it can—but not assume that there is much in the way of common ground. Such wishful thinking is most tempting when reality is truly ghastly. The idea of building a "strategic partnership" with Russia is deeply rooted, even though the "shared values" that are meant to be the foundation for this are now almost nowhere to be seen. As Katinka Barysch of the think tank, the Centre for European Reform puts it:

> Many Europeans are still struggling to come to terms with the fact that their initial blueprint for EU-Russia relations has not materialised. The EU had hoped that by working closely with Russia, and by offering aid, advice and its own best practice, it could help the country become more open and democratic. During the decade or so that the EU has followed this approach, Russia has moved in the opposite direction. Yet many Europeans have been reluctant to question the underlying assumption of the EU's original Russia policy, namely that Russia wants to be 'like us'. Rather than conducting a cool-headed re-assessment, the EU has sometimes behaved like a sulking lover whose well-meaning advances have been rejected. For the EU, what happens inside Russia is of great importance. But it needs to stop pretending that it can somehow convert Russia to pluralism and liberalism.[3]

A powerful and immediate weapon may be simply to do nothing. The West, particularly the EU, must stop dangling carrots, individually or jointly, in front of Russia in the vain hope that concessions will build confidence, weaning Russia from bad habits and promoting good ones. Those carrots have been munched, but the habits have changed for the worse, not for the better. Russia systematically breaks the promises it makes; far from provoking outrage, the response is mere disappointment, followed by a scramble to find yet more inducements for good behavior. A simple decision by the West to sit quietly, or in the jargon of the foreign-policy world to take a "strategic pause," sends a powerful signal. When Russia is ready to cooperate, the West is ready. So long as it is not, we have plenty of other problems to worry about.

Nor should it accept the carrots dangled by the Kremlin. Bilateral bargains are not only immoral, but fruitless, meaning that we are penalize our friends while supporting our enemies. Outrageously, it is easier for Russians to get visas to visit the EU than it is for the citizens of countries that are on the verge of starting membership talks.[4] The main aim now must be that Russian neo-imperialism gains not an inch more territory. The threats, interference, and mischief directed against the ex-Soviet republics need to meet a consistent firm response, not shilly-shallying and equivocation. When Russia bombs Georgia it should prompt the same storm of protest as would be raised if it fired a missile at Finland.

Georgia is on the brink of being offered a Membership Action Plan that will bring it into NATO once its military modernization and other reforms are complete. The single most important thing the West can do now to protect both itself and its protégés is to make that offer to Georgia and stick to it. Second, both Ukraine and Georgia need as much help from the EU as possible: The more they experience the free movement of goods, capital, services, and people, the more closely integrated they are into our world, and the less leverage the Kremlin has on them. The more Russians live in freedom and prosperity outside Russia, the harder it is for the Kremlin to maintain its posture of exceptionalism. Countries like Estonia, Georgia, and Moldova may seem too obscure, faraway, or unimportant to care about. But now they are the crux of our own security. It is all too easy for Russia to think that when it bullies Estonia, for example, it is treading only on the tiny toes of a flyweight ex-colony. A central message of this book is that the world's richest and strongest free countries must stand behind these small states now under threat from Russia. It may be inconvenient, costly, or even painful to do so, but if we do not win the New Cold War on terms of our choosing, we will fight at a time and place chosen by our adversary, and the odds will be tilted against us.

The West must also hold Russia to the commitments it made when it joined international clubs based on freedom and justice, and downgrade the importance of bodies that now seem consigned to paralysis by the Kremlin. The United Nations Security Council was useless for much of the old Cold War because of Soviet vetoes. If the Kremlin tries the same tactics now, it will guarantee that the council—the only international decision-making body to which it belongs by right—becomes useless again. The same applies to the OSCE. Russia cannot be expelled, but if it continues to hamper the organization's work then it will end up with a mere talking shop. In bodies where Russia's membership is conditional the conditions should be applied strictly. The time for wishful thinking is over. Agreeing to Russia's membership of the

Council of Europe in 1996, for example, now looks a catastrophic mistake. Belarus was suspended from that body's Parliamentary Assembly in 1997, at a time when repression there was mild compared with Russia now; the Kremlin must realize that its policies at home and abroad will inevitably and speedily bring the same penalty, and one that would be much more effective than the perennial complaints that Russia's elections are not free. It is hard to see why Russia should belong to the Group of Eight (G8). Either it should become a big-economies club (in which case China, India, and Brazil should join), or it is a body for rich countries that respect the rule of law and political freedom. In that case Russia does not even belong in the waiting room.

Exclusion from Western clubs will bring tantrums, but it will also bring clarity. As with the old Cold War, the New Cold War was not started by the West and we are fighting it reluctantly. But like last time, it is up to us to limit the damage. Where we can cooperate on nuclear power, on preventing the proliferation of weapons of mass destruction, and on seeking peace in the Middle East, we should. It may be possible to do more: New talks on strategic nuclear issues are urgently needed, to keep reducing stockpiles and reduce the risks of accidental launches and misperceptions of each side's posture. Another urgent issue is Afghanistan, one of the few places where NATO–Russian cooperation has had a real effect. It is hard to think of another issue where Iran, Russia, and NATO all share at least some common interest. If Russia sincerely wants to contribute to global security and to be treated as a great power, Afghanistan is a good place to test its willingness for serious cooperation—though only an arch-optimist would believe that the Kremlin fully shares our long-term aim of a stable, prosperous, and pro-Western Afghanistan. In all dealings with Russia, we should jettison the last vestiges of wishful thinking; if we allow ourselves to hope for the best, which must not distract us from preparing for the worst.

The biggest question is how to fight the war of values. It is tempting to argue that we should save our breath. If the Kremlin spin doctors try to provoke us, we should ignore them, just as we do the bilious outpourings of North Korea or Osama bin Laden. That would be a mistake: Despite the hostile propaganda of the state-run media, millions of Russians and others in the ex-Soviet countries still look up to the open societies of the West. It is important to show them that our dislike of the Kremlin is not motivated by russophobia. Anti-Westernism in Russia may be bad now among the

country's rulers, but it is not yet either deep or solid. It is in our interest to prevent it spreading from the ex-KGB people in the Kremlin deep into the public's worldview. As in the last Cold War, soft
power is still our greatest asset.[5] It is worth recalling the effect of the
ideological challenge in the past—the differences between a free society and a closed one were central themes of international and domestic political discussion. The desire to outperform the Soviet
Union on what it said it did best was a useful stimulus to good government, thus increasing further the West's competitive advantage.
If the Soviet Union proclaimed a triumph, the West looked closely
and tried to see how it could be copied, on everything from the
space race to the treatment of chess prodigies. A renewal of both
that moral competition and moral distance is needed now. In the
old Cold War, mainstream Western politicians might differ on the
details of defence spending, *Ostpolitik,* or the emphasis to give
human-rights issues in the Soviet block. But everyone outside the
political fringes agreed that the essence of the Soviet system was
alien, repulsive, and dangerous. Moral equivalence, which matched
every Soviet misdeed with a real or imagined example of Western
one,[6] was a minority pursuit. Yet one of the most peculiar features
of the Putin years has been the number of Western commentators
who are so keen to protest about the "demonization" of Russia and
so unwilling to criticize what is happening there.

Tempting though it may be to ignore, the best course is to take it
seriously. It may well be that individualism and materialism are an
inadequate basis for a happy life; corruption and influence-peddling
in Western political systems may be an indefensible distortion of the
principles on which they are founded; freedom may conflict with
justice. If Russia's caustic criticism makes those in positions of
power in the West think more clearly and govern more cleanly and
fairly, that is all to the good. But that is not the same as taking the
Kremlin's claims about its own system at face value; such a balanced
approach would be absurd. Our system is not perfect, but it is better: cleaner, fairer, kinder, and more tolerant than Russia's authoritarian crony capitalism. It is self-critical: Where our system falls
short of our ideals, we have to burnish it. But it must not be self-
hating. The West preaches, and tries to practice, different forms of
what it loosely calls "democracy": that is, open, law-governed political pluralism. The details may vary, but the central principles are the
same: the rule of law, the separation of powers, the accountability of
the executive and the core principles of due process and the pre-
sumption of innocence in the legal system; plus the freedoms of

speech and association, crowned by freely contested and fairly counted elections. Western governments feel at least loosely obliged to offer high-quality public services, to uphold honesty in public life, and provide social protection for the weak. The West believes in international law, and in the duty of free countries to promote universal human rights everywhere. These ideas are chipped and faded now and tainted by compromises, short-cuts, and hypocrisies, particularly those stemming from the disastrous "war on terror." But they are real. Until we make it clear that we believe in our own values, we cannot defend ourselves against the subversion and corruption that are leaking into our citadels of economic and political power. And we stand not the slightest chance of persuading Russians themselves that the authoritarian, xenophobic, and distorted version of capitalism peddled by their rulers is not a new civilization but a dead end.

NOTES

Links to the URLs cited here can be found on edwardlucas.com

FOREWORD

1. Released by the Bureau of Democracy, Human Rights, and Labor, Washington, D.C., March 11, 2008. http://www.state.gov/g/drl/rls/hrrpt/2007/100581.htm
2. In August 2007, a Novosibirsk regional court ruled that Nikolai Baluyev, a member of the National Bolshevik Party, should undergo psychiatric treatment. On November 23 2007, an activist from the opposition Other Russia movement, Artem Basyrov, a resident of Mari-El, was involuntarily hospitalized just before a planned demonstration. He was released in late December. Andrei Novikov was released in December after a ten-month term in a Yaroslavl psychiatric institution; he was convicted a year previously on charges including sedition and inciting violence.
3. Mark Franchetti, "Putin Brings Back Mental Ward Torment," *Sunday Times*, August 26, 2007. http://www.timesonline.co.uk/tol/news/world/europe/article2327824.ece
4. See Paul Goble's blog entry "Three Disturbing Developments on the Russian Media Scene," August 25, 2008. http://windowoneurasia.blogspot.com/2008/08/window-on-eurasia-three-disturbing.html
5. "Morar to Be Held Accountable Under Constitution," *Kommersant*, August 25, 2008. http://www.kommersant.com/p1016161/Morar_constitution/
6. Nina L. Khrushcheva, "Lost in Byzantium: Putin May Be Endangering Russia's Future by Revisiting the Past," *Los Angeles Times*, June 1, 2008. http://www.latimes.com/news/opinion/sunday/commentary/la-op-khrushcheva1-2008jun01,0,5272935.story
7. Correlli Barnett, "World Peace? Give Me Putin Anyday!" *Daily Mail*, August 21, 2008. http://www.dailymail.co.uk/news/article-1047509/OPINION-World-peace-Give-Putin-anyday.html
8. *Putin—the Bottom Line. An Independent Expert Report.* Available at http://www.docstoc.com/docs/520723/nemtsov-bookform#centerdoc
9. "Russia's Future under Medvedev," London 2008, http://www.sigma-econ.ru/.files/2083/Bookblock.pdf
10. "Russia's Medvedev Unveils Anti-corruption Steps," March 27, 2008. http://www.reuters.com/article/GCA-Russia/idUSL2764828020080327
11. Mark Leonard and Nicu Popescu, "A Power Audit of EU-Russia Relations," European Council on Foreign Relations, November 2007. http://ecfr.eu/page/-/documents/ECFR-EU-Russia-power-audit.pdf
12.

"Trojan Horses":	Cyprus, Greece
"Strategic Partners":	France, Germany, Italy, Spain
"Friendly Pragmatists:	Austria, Belgium, Bulgaria, Finland, Hungary, Luxembourg, Malta, Portugal, Slovakia, Slovenia
"Frosty Pragmatists"	Czech Republic, Denmark, Estonia, Ireland, Latvia, the Netherlands, Romania, Sweden, UK
"New Cold Warriors"	Lithuania, Poland

13. Certainly the most hard-line of the "siloviki" (ex-KGB) clans that, led by Igor Sechin, appeared to lose ground. That seems to have started in the autumn of 2007, when behind-the-scenes squabbling broke embarrassingly into the open. The head of the anti-narcotics agency, Viktor Cherkesov, a prime foe of Sechin's, had the embarrassment of seeing his right-hand man, Aleksander Bulbov, arrested on corruption charges. Two more officers from his agency were murdered. That seems to have persuaded Putin to play safe in the choice of his successor, going for Medvedev rather than the hawkish (and ex-KGB) Sergei Ivanov.

Neither of Putin's direct deputies, or "first deputy prime ministers" as they are known in post-Soviet bureaucratese, Igor Shuvalov and Viktor Zubkov, are siloviki. Shuvalov is a seasoned "sherpa," navigating the G8 and other summits on behalf of Putin. At a meeting of the Baltic sea states in Riga in June, he attracted favorable attention by his politeness and adherence to protocol: a sharp change from the bombastic tactics favored lately by Putin. Zubkov, who served briefly as prime minister, is a close friend of Putin's with a background in settling messy financial problems in St. Petersburg. He has kept a low profile since his appointment. Zubkov's son-in-law is the defence minister, Serdyukov.

The siloviki have not disappeared, however. Sechin, once Putin's all-powerful Kremlin sidekick, is still at his side, but as a mere deputy (not "first deputy") prime minister, responsible for heavy industry; Sergei Naryshkin, the fast-rising former spy who was a deputy prime minister under the old regime, is now head of the presidential administration; some see his role as being a minder for Medvedev. Naryshkin gave up his position as chairman of the board of directors of the United Shipbuilding Corporation, making way for Sechin. Sergei Ivanov, another hawkish ex-spy, has been demoted slightly, to be deputy prime minister in charge of the defense and high technology industries. Nikolai Patrushev, another top "Sechinite," stepped down as head of the FSB and became secretary of Security Council; what this means is unclear as that body's importance has fluctuated sharply over the years. Another hardliner from the Putin era, the former prosecutor-general and justice minister, Vladimir Ustinov, moved sideways and downward to run the southern federal district of Russia. Viktor Ivanov, the former deputy presidential administration head for personnel, and the man who communicated the Kremlin's wishes to supposedly independent organs of state such as the judiciary, has moved to the Federal Anti-Narcotics Agency.

For an excellent discussion of way in which siloviki became the new oligarchs (tycoons), see Daniel Treisman, "Putin's Silovarchs," October 2006, http://www.sscnet .ucla.edu/polisci/faculty/treisman/siloct06.pdf

14. Gordon Hahn, "The Siloviki Downgraded In Russia's New Configuration of Power," July 21, 2008. http://www.russiaotherpointsofview.com/2008/07/the-siloviki-do.html

INTRODUCTION

1. Although 'enemies of the nation' is no longer on the site, it can be viewed using an internet archive tool on http://web.archive.org/web/20061121213231/http://www .russianwill.org/material/vragi.html

2. I use the "Kremlin" in this book as a shorthand term for the colossal concentration of political, bureaucratic, legal, and economic power, mainly among KGB veterans, over which Putin presides. The Kremlin is not monolithic. It includes clans whose rivalry is based on competing commercial interests (for example, the gas giant Gazprom and its oil counterpart Rossneft) and on personal allegiances (for example, the—supposedly—more liberal-minded ideology chief Vladislav Surkov and the ex-military spy Igor Sechin. Though these conflicts are fluid and fast changing, the central features of Kremlin power remain constant: opacity, wealth, and ruthlessness.

3. Her books include *A Small Corner of Hell: Dispatches from Chechnya* (2003), *Putin's Russia* (2004), and *A Russian Diary: A Journalist's Final Account of Life, Corruption, and Death in Putin's Russia* (2007).

4. In an interview in Germany's *Süddeutsche Zeitung*, Putin said:

> "First of all I would like to say that a murder is a very serious crime both with respect to society and with respect to God. The criminals must be found out and correspondingly punished.
>
> Unfortunately, this is not the only such crime in Russia. And we will do everything we can to bring the criminals to justice.
>
> And now, with respect to the political aspect of this affair. The investigation is looking at all possible variants. And of course, one of them, one of the most probable, is related to her work as a journalist. She really was a critic of the present authorities—something that is common to all media representatives—but she often adopted radical positions. And recently she mainly concentrated her attention on criticising the authorities in the Chechen Republic.
>
> I must say—and I think that experts would agree with me—that her political influence inside of Russia was negligible and that she was probably better known among human rights organisations and in the western media. In connection with this I think that one of our newspapers was correct when it stated today that Anna Politkovskaya's murder has caused much more damage to the current authorities in general, and to the Chechen authorities in particular, than her reporting did.
>
> In any case, I repeat that what has happened is absolutely inadmissible. This horrendous crime is damaging for Russia and must be solved. It causes both moral and political damage and is damaging for the political system that we are building, a system which must have places for all people, independently of their points of view. On the contrary, we must ensure that people receive the possibility to expose their points of view, including in the media.

Vladimir Putin, interview, *Süddeutsche Zeitung*, October 10, 2006, http://kremlin.ru/eng/speeches/2006/10/10/1519_type82916_112362.shtml.

In a speech at a meeting in Munich, Putin expressed himself in similar vein:

> Perhaps because Ms. Politkovskaya held very radical views she did not have a serious influence on the political mood in our country. But she was very well-known in journalistic circles and in human rights circles. And in my opinion murdering such a person certainly does much greater damage from the authorities' point of view, authorities that she strongly criticized, than her publications ever did. Moreover, we have reliable, consistent information that many people who are hiding from Russian justice have been harbouring the idea that they will use somebody as a victim to create a wave of anti-Russian sentiment in the world. I do not know who has carried out this crime. But whoever they were and whatever their motives, they are criminals. They must be found, brought to justice and punished. The Russian authorities will do everything they can to ensure that this takes place.

Vladimir Putin, Speech at the St. Petersburg Dialogue Social Forum, Munich, October 10, 2006, http://www.kremlin.ru/eng/speeches/2006/10/10/2138_type82914type84779_112411.shtml.

5. I use "Western" and the "West" as shorthand for the advanced industrialized countries of the world, chiefly in Europe, America, East Asia, and Australasia. A common feature is membership of the Paris-based Organisation for Economic Co-operation and Development (OECD).

6. Aleksander Litvinenko, "In full: Litvinenko statement," BBC News, November 24, 2006, http://news.bbc.co.uk/1/hi/uk/6180262.stm.

7. At the price charged by a Western commercial supplier for the tiny quantities used in industry, the large dose used against Litvinenko would have cost $10 million (£5 million).

8. Extradition is illegal under the Russian constitution. But what really riled British officials was the attitude on the Russian side that they were fussing about nothing. Other countries such as Israel also do not extradite their citizens—but close cooperation with foreign criminal justice systems mean that wrongdoers rarely go unpunished.

9. The manufacturing process of Polonium–210 leaves a 'fingerprint', a residue of other isotopes that can identify the precise date of manufacture and even the reactor used.

10. After its unsuccessful intervention in the Russian civil war from 1917–20, nearly three decades of communist rule in Russia proved little worry for the West, which largely ignored the terror imposed by Lenin and Stalin. Under U.S. President Herbert Hoover, the American taxpayer even helped Soviet Russia fend off starvation. Outside investment poured in. Many believed that Stalin stood for tough modernization of a backward country, not mass murder and enslavement fuelled by his personal paranoia. Not until 1946, nearly three decades after the Bolshevik revolution, did Winston Churchill coin his fateful phrase, the "Iron Curtain." The Cold War lasted for the next 30 years, until the Helsinki agreement of 1975, at the then Conference on Security and Cooperation in Europe (CSCE), which marked the beginning of the Soviet Union's ideological surrender. The West accepted the division of Europe on its current frontiers (with some countries slightly reserving their position on the Baltic states). In return, the Soviet block signed up for universal human rights. The Soviet leadership mistakenly thought this would be merely a paper concession. In fact, it allowed dissidents behind the Iron Curtain to complain that their governments were violating their international commitments—something that became a potent propaganda weapon.

11. Speech at military parade on the 62nd anniversary of victory in the Great Patriotic War. 9 May 2007. www.kremlin.ru

12. I use "Communist" when referring to a specific party, and "communist" for the general ideology and sentiment.

13. From *nomenclatura,* a Latin word meaning literally a list of names. In the Soviet Union it meant the upper reaches of the Communist Party who were entitled to an array of personal and professional privileges.

14. However the authorities have tightened control over the Internet (see Chapter Two). Even before Mr. Putin took power, service providers had to install a device that allows the authorities to track all incoming and outgoing information. During his first week as president, Mr. Putin gave seven other federal agencies access to the intelligence gathered.

15. See Lew Rockwell, "What To Think About Ukraine" (Breaking News: The LRC Blog, November 26, 2004, http://www.lewrockwell.com/blog/lewrw/archives/006682.html) for one of many such examples. Members of the ill-named British Helsinki Human Rights Group as well as the *Guardian* journalist Jonathan Steele have also made similar arguments, along with many Russian commentators. However, arguing foreign policy by analogy is usually mistaken: New England was not forcibly incorporated into the United States by a totalitarian regime that imposed an alien language and culture and deported the brightest and best to slave labor camps in Alaska.

16. On March 11, 1990, the Lithuanian parliament declared independence. The West was alarmed, and painfully timid. Few countries had formally recognized the Soviet annexation of the Baltic States. A handful of elderly exiled diplomats still staffed dusty embassies in America, Britain, and Italy. But the idea that these historical curios might suddenly mean something practical was deeply unsettling to a generation of Western diplomats and policymakers who were still whistling with relief that the Soviet leadership had suddenly become so amenable. I decided, with the help of my London-based colleague Steve Crawshaw, to offer some symbolic support. I took the only direct route to Lithuania (a weekly Aeroflot flight from East Berlin), managing to check in and board the plane without a Soviet visa. British citizens had required no visa before 1940, we reasoned, so why should I need one now?

At the airport in the Lithuanian capital Vilnius a grim-faced Soviet border guard confiscated my passport. But minutes later I was met by a delegation led by the new

Lithuanian foreign minister, Algirdas Saudargas. "What if I don't get my passport back?" I asked, as we sat nervously on the red velvet sofas of the VIP lounge. "Then we climb out of that window. You can get another passport. But we cannot get another you," said the biochemist-turned-politician, in stilted but heartfelt English. For a brief moment, I was a symbol of Lithuania's perilously fragile status. If they could get at least one foreigner into their country across a Soviet-controlled border, then it was a sign to the rest of the world that their independence was more than a brave declaration. When the border guard returned, Mr. Saudargas produced a stamp from his pocket and gave me Lithuanian visa 0001.

17. From the Greek word meaning "rule by a few." *The Oligarchs: Wealth and Power in the New Russia* by David Hoffman (New York: PublicAffairs Books, 2002) explores their origins as power, as does *Sale of the Century: Russia's Wild Ride from Communism to Capitalism* by Chrystia Freeland (New York: Crown Publishing, 2000).

18. See Peter Duncan: "Contemporary Russian Identity between East and West" *Historical Journal*, 48 (2005): 277–294.

19. After the financial crash of August 1998, when Russia seemed mired in chaos and incompetence, I wrote an article in *The Economist* entitled "The Western Man's Burden," in ironic reference to Kipling's famous (or notorious) poem "The White Man's Burden": "When a country habitually lacks people or governments capable of keeping essential services going, outsiders sooner or later begin to fill the gap. One word for this is colonization. It is early days, but something of the kind may be starting to happen in Russia." *The Economist*, December 12, 1998.

20. Literally so, given the way in which senior spooks began gaining lucrative positions in industry.

21. Lithuania's Mažeikiai refinery and Latvia's Ventspils oil terminal are both prime takeover targets for Russia's energy giants. The 2006 sale of Mažeikiai to a Polish energy company, PKN Orlen, infuriated Russia's energy companies. Shortly afterward Russia cut off supplies from the pipeline feeding the refinery, saying that it needed to be repaired. The issue has been extensively discussed in the Jamestown Foundation *Eurasia Daily Monitor* (Vladimir Socor, "Russian Oil Pipeline Shutoff to Lithuania: Wider Ramifications," *Eurasia Daily Monitor*, The Jamestown Foundation, June 6, 2007, http://www.jamestown.org/edm/article.php?article_id=2372212).

22. Covered by many Western media: see, for example, Reuters "Estonia and Russia: The Right to Be Wrong," *The Economist*, May 3, 2007, http://www.economist.com/opinion /displaystory.cfm?story_id=9116990; and "Estonia—Bronze Meddling: Russian Hypocrisy and Heavy-Handedness towards a Former Colony," May 3, 2007, http: //www.economist.com/world/europe/displaystory.cfm?story_id=9122766.

23. Their combined population of around 7 million is slightly smaller than Austria or New Jersey; Estonia has 1.3 million people, Latvia 2.4 million, and Lithuania 3.6 million.

CHAPTER 1

1. The weak but reform-friendly Sergei Kiriyenko left after the August financial crash. The Duma rejected the man Yeltsin tried for two weeks to reinstall as his successor, Viktor Chernomyrdin, who had been prime minister for much of the 1990s. Russia then had eight months under Yevgeny Primakov, a steely career spy-turned-foreign minister. But his growing alliances with powerful regional chiefs made him too powerful in Kremlin eyes, and he allowed the prosecutor-general's investigations into the Yeltsin family's financial dealings to reach a dangerous pitch. He was replaced from May 12 to August 9, 1999 by Sergei Stepashin, a former interior minister, who then gave way to Putin.

2. Often described as "fluent" and "native-level," Putin's German is grammatically correct but heavily accented and would be better described as "passable" or "comprehensible." See Vladimir Putin, "Incident at the Putin's Press conference" (video), YouTube,

http://www.youtube.com/watch?v=yMifzZehatE (accessed October 17, 2007) for an edited sequence in which he clumsily berates a protestor at a press conference. His German may have been better in his days as a spy.

3. Then still known by its Soviet-era name, Leningrad.

4. "He [Putin] is credited by his successors with having brought Coca-Cola, Dresdner Bank, and Crédit Lyonnais to St. Petersburg. He was also responsible for creating two economic-development zones on the outskirts of the city that ended up attracting firms such as Gillette and Wrigley." Samuel Charap, "The Petersburg Experience: Putin's Political Career and Russian Foreign Policy," *Problems of Post-Communism*, 51, no. 1 (2004):

5. The KGB was supposedly dissolved after the failed hard-line coup of August 1991. In fact, it was relabeled. The notorious Fifth Directorate, responsible for persecuting dissidents, became the core of the new tax police. Many other functions transferred to the Federal Counter-Intelligence Service, known by its Russian initials FSK; a law passed in April 1995 renamed this body the FSB.

6. The *Ministerium für Staatssicherheit* (Ministry for State Security, or MfS).

7. "Russia under Putin: The Making of a Neo-KGB State," *The Economist*, August 23, 2007, http://www.economist.com/world/displaystory.cfm?story_id=9682621.

8. Olga Kryshtanovskaya and Stephen White, "Putin's Militocracy," *Post-Soviet Affairs*, 19, no. 4, (2003): 289–306. Another handy term for them was "securocrat," first coined by the South African liberal politician Frederik van Zyl Slabbert to describe apartheid-era security and military chiefs.

9. For *Glavnoye Razvedyvatelnoye Upravleniye Generalnovo Shtaba* (Main Intelligence Directorate of the General Staff), created by Lenin in 1918.

10. The NKVD or *Narodny Komissariat Vnutrennikh Del* was the People's Commisariat for Internal Affairs; OGPU (1922 to 1934) was the *Obedinennoye Godarstvennoye Politicheskoye Upravleniye* (Joint State Political Directorate).

11. He repeated this in a speech on Chekists' Day in 2005.

12. *Moda na KGB? Nevedomstvennye razmyshlenia o professii* [The KGB in fashion? Non-departmental thoughts about the profession], *Komsomolskaya Pravda*, December 29, 2004.

13. Vladimir Putin, *Judo: History, Theory, Practice* (Berkeley, CA: North Atlantic Books, 2004).

14. The Chechens had been deported en masse to central Asia by Stalin in 1944 as a punishment for their presumed Nazi sympathies. Czarist imperial expeditions had found them the hardest nut to crack in the 19th century, and many Chechens hoped that the collapse of the Soviet Union would mean independence for them, just as it had for the Baltic States. But an accident of history meant that Chechnya's status was not a Soviet Socialist Republic (SSR), like its neighbor Georgia, but an "Autonomous Soviet Socialist Republic," a lesser status and one that was within the Russian federation. When the Soviet Union collapsed the 15 SSRs regained statehood whether they wanted it or not. For Chechnya to leave Russia was going to be much harder. For three years, the republic enjoyed (or rather suffered) an uneasy semi-independence. The clan-based Chechen society was even less suitable for building the institutions of good government than that of Russia. Banditry flourished, and Russians came to loathe the Chechen "mafia," whose ruthlessness and impenetrable mutual loyalties fitted them ideally for running protection rackets. In 1994, in an effort to distract attention from his political problems, Yeltsin had been persuaded to mount what was supposed to be a "short victorious war" against the pint-sized autonomous republic, in which around half of Russia's 1.36 million Chechen population lived. The war was neither short nor victorious, and turned a mess into a disaster. The Russian army's lumbering tanks and raw conscripts were beaten back by the well-led, lightly armed separatists. In 1996 Russia signed a ceasefire with Chechnya, offering roughly a return to the status quo: independence, but not quite. That was a chance for stability and freedom, but it was woefully mismanaged. Part of the blame rests with Russia, which continued to destabilize the republic, but much of it lay with the Chechens themselves. Inside Chechnya,

alarming banditry turned into atrocious warlordism. Their leaders, such as Shamil Basayev, were ruthless warriors but hopeless politicians. Kidnappings were rife, sometimes ending in gruesome beheadings. Foreigners, including those linked to Al-Qaeda, used Chechnya as a base for training camps—and, some said, as a toehold for Islamic rule in the whole of Russia's impoverished and ill-governed southern fringe. That theory was supported by the raid on Dagestan, one of many such provocations, and led by Basayev, a Kremlin ally-turned-foe whom most Russians regarded as the country's top terrorist. Russia responded by bombing some villages in Dagestan occupied by Islamist radicals. Few took notice: Low-intensity warfare in the northern Caucasus, sadly, was nothing new.

15. Another example of Putin's foul-mouthed turn of phrase came in a meeting with Prime Minister Ehud Olmert of Israel in October 2006, when he praised the Israeli president Moshe Katsav, who was facing accusations of multiple sexual assaults against employees. "Say hello to your president . . . he really surprised us," said Putin approvingly. "We did not know he could deal with 10 women. . . ." Associated Press "Kremlin tries to explain away Putin rape joke," October 20th 2006.

16. And no bombings of such scale and sophistication have been organized since.

17. "The Kremlin's housekeeper". *The Economist,* Sep 16th 1999 http://www.economist .com/business/displaystory.cfm?story_id=E1_PNQRSS. "Yeltsin linked to bribe scandal" September 8, 1999 http://news.bbc.co.uk/1/hi/business/the_economy/441916.stm gives a contemporary account of the credit card affair. "Accusations of Bribery In the Kremlin Mount Up" by John Tagliabue and Celestine Bohlen, *New York Times* September 9 1999 http://query.nytimes.com/gst/fullpage.html?res=9C01E4DE143DF93A A3575AC0A96F958260&sec=&spon=&pagewanted=print is longer and more skeptical.

18. "НОВОСЁЛОВ" can also be transcribed as "Novosyelov."

19. He cast doubt on the nature of the "bomb," saying only that FSB laboratories in Moscow would have to investigate further.

20. Broadcast on the *Vesti* evening news. Translation from Yuri Felshtinsky and Alexander Litvinenko, *Blowing Up Russia: Terror from Within* (London: Gibson Square Books, 2007).

21. Ibid.

22. A detailed investigation of the Ryazan "bombing" can be found in David Satter's book *Darkness at Dawn, the Rise of the Russian Criminal State* (New Haven, Conn: Yale University Press, 2003).

23. Furthermore, if Ryazan was truly a dummy run, it broke all the rules. In bureaucracy bound Russia, such exercises involve extensive planning and paperwork. Official observers must be nominated, every detail of the "plot" written down, and the whole thing approved by senior officers. The start and finish are minuted and the conduct of all participants assessed. In particular, the head of the local FSB must be informed.

  The Ryazan exercise breached all these, and some other rules too. Most signally, in Russia as in most other countries with serious armed forces, conducting exercises that involve "active duty" armed personnel is strictly forbidden; in other words, a military base cannot test its readiness by having one lot of soldiers "attack" a location guarded by real sentries armed with live ammunition. The reason is simple: Those taking part in the exercise risk being maimed or killed. The sentries might end up shooting fellow-soldiers. So such an exercise could not have been planned for Ryazan, which was already on high alert because of the previous bombings in Moscow: The FSB officers planting the "sugar" risked being shot if caught by a trigger-happy policeman. If it was truly an exercise, it was an almost insane risk for its planners.

24. Even odder was a story that emerged from a special-forces base near Ryazan. *Novaya Gazeta* reported that a paratrooper called Alexei Pinyaev, while guarding a warehouse, noticed some sacks labeled "sugar" and had opened one with a bayonet in the hope of using some of the contents to sweeten his tea. The result had tasted nasty. He informed his commanding officer who, remembering news reports of the sacks found in

the basement of Novosyolov Street, informed the local FSB. Experts identified the contents as hexogen.

The authorities reacted sharply. First they claimed that *Novaya Gazeta* had invented the story. Mysteriously, the paper's next issue failed to come out; someone had hacked into its computer network and deleted the files that were due to be sent to the printer. Then Pinyaev's unit commander and fellow-soldiers were dispatched to Chechnya, while he made a public retraction, and was then disciplined for breaching state secrets and stealing state property—in the form of sugar.

That might have seemed absurd enough, but in March 2000, Pinyaev's regiment sued *Novaya Gazeta*. Its commander, Colonel Oleg Churilov, said Pinyaev did not exist and no one with his supposed duties would have had access to an ammunition warehouse anyway. If that was supposed to squash the story, it certainly failed.

25. In March 2000, for example, a motion to ask the prosecutor general to answer to outstanding questions about the incident passed by 197 to 137, but failed to reach the absolute majority needed in the 450-strong body because the pro-Kremlin party (which at the time was called "Unity") voted unanimously against it.

26. Shchekochikhin died suddenly on July 3, 2003 after a sudden illness. The authorities refused to release his medical records to his relatives or to supply tissue specimens for independent analysis. His family did manage to send a skin sample to a London toxicologist, who made a tentative diagnosis of poisoning by radioactive thallium, a toxin used by the KGB during the Cold War. His family and his colleagues believe his investigative work brought him a death sentence.

Yushenkov was shot dead by an unknown assassin near his Moscow home in April 2003. Four people were convicted of his murder in a controversial verdict denounced by friends and relatives. Those convicted include a colleague from the opposition party Liberal Russia who strenuously protests his innocence.

27. Sometimes known as Latsis, which is how the Russian spelling of his (Latvian) surname would be rendered in English.

28. The 15 Soviet Socialist Republics were the constituent parts of the Soviet Union (though some outsiders regarded the three Baltic states as being occupied territories because of their contested legal status). Russia was by far the largest of the 15, and itself a federation, hence its full name, the Russian Soviet Federative Socialist Republic. Its constituent parts included ethnic Autonomous Soviet Socialist Republics (ASSRs) such as Chechnya and Tatarstan, which now, along with cities such as Moscow and regions such as Novgorod, are among the 80-plus "federal subjects" of the postcommunist Russian Federation.

29. From the West's point of view, Gorbachev had been an improvement on any of his predecessors. He saw that the Soviet system was not only unworkable but also abhorrent. Whereas Andropov had tried to fix it by toughening up, Gorbachev decided to try liberalization: freedom of speech, contested elections, modest decentralization, and some limited economic reforms. In 1987 he allowed state enterprises to trade their surplus production freely. In 1988 he permitted the establishment of cooperatives outside the planned economy. He allowed some foreign investment. Censorship slackened and disappeared. In May 1989 the first partially free election in Soviet history produced a lively legislature: the Congress of People's Deputies. In the space of a few months, the Communist Party of the Soviet Union gave up its "leading role" (i.e., monopoly of power); the media began exposing the lies and crimes of the past. Outside Europe Gorbachev briskly closed down a series of Soviet-stoked conflicts in Southern Africa, Afghanistan, and Latin America. It was welcome, but doomed. The Soviet system was so ramshackle and unstable that once the binding threads of command and control were loosened, the economy, and the whole Kremlin empire, started a rapid collapse. The satellite countries of central Europe, and the peoples of the Soviet Union, realized that the Kremlin would no longer kill to keep control. They took their chance. In quick succession Hungary, Poland, East Germany, and Czechoslovakia ripped up the Warsaw Pact rulebook and regained their sovereignty.

The Baltic states of Estonia, Latvia, and Lithuania did the same, making modest suggestions for autonomy that soon catalyzed into forthright demands for restoration of independence.

The gratitude in the West was immense. For all Gorbachev's muddle and wobbles he had done the world a great service. He had allowed Communism to collapse with astonishingly little blood being shed. By the standards of other European empires, that was a praiseworthy feat.

30. Interview with the author, Warsaw, 1994.

31. *The Economist*, "The World's Worst Central Banker" October 16, 1993,

32. Yeltsin's second volume of memoirs brought him $3 million, largely thanks to the intervention of Berezovsky and others. The monthly interest on this was deposited in cash in Yeltsin's office safe. He apparently regarded this as a solid nest egg. By the standards of the provincial Soviet Union it was indeed a fortune. But by the standards of those around him, it was chicken feed.

33. Putin also benefited from the economy's recovery from the 1998 crash. Though the boom in oil and gas prices was yet to come, a cheap ruble stoked demand for Russian-made goods. Imports had suddenly become four times more expensive and Russian manufacturers seized their chance, producing properly packaged food and consumer goods at competitive prices. Russian-made beer, soap, juice, and detergent, once shunned by all but the poor, began appearing on the shelves of the smartest supermarkets.

34. It is interesting to speculate what hold they had on him in order to be so sure that he would honor his side of the bargain.

CHAPTER 2

1. One featured the "Napoleon" cake, which contains a large dose of egg custard. A man goes into a shop and asks for a "Putin" cake. "What's that?" asks the sales assistant. "It's like a Napoleon, but without eggs," comes the reply. (*Yaitse*, "eggs" in Russian, is also the common slang term for "balls.")

2. *Larry King Live* "Russian President Vladimir Putin Discusses Domestic and Foreign Affairs". Aired September 8, 2000–9:00 p.m. ET http://transcripts.cnn.com/TRANSCRIPTS/0009/08/lkl.00.html

3. Since Estonia introduced a "flat" (nonprogressive) tax on incomes in 1994, this has become a popular and successful policy across much of the ex-communist world. Although it involves a large tax cut for high earners, it has so far always resulted in higher tax revenues, because it becomes attractive to repatriate earnings and end tax-dodging scams. It is particularly well-suited to countries with large black economies where tax might otherwise go uncollected, and where administrative weaknesses put a premium on simplicity and transparency. As well as Russia, flat-tax countries include Albania, Bosnia, Bulgaria, the three Baltic States, Georgia, Macedonia, Montenegro, Romania, Serbia, Slovakia, and Ukraine. No ex-communist country that has introduced a flat tax has yet reversed it.

4. Sergei Naryshkin's rapid ascent to power suggests he may be a contender for the presidency or other high office. He is deputy prime minister for foreign economic relations, and has been an adviser at Gazprom, head of investment at Promstroibank and on the board at several military shipbuilding companies. Although he has worked with all the important factions and clans in the Kremlin, he has so far remained neutral between them; if he maintains that, it may be a powerful recommendation in the president's eyes.

5. Some of the connections are almost comically nepotistic. Andrei Patrushev, the 26-year old son of the FSB chief, was seconded from the FSB to Rosneft where he is now advising Sechin. The lucky Patrushev Jr. received a Kremlin medal from Putin after only a few months, citing his "many years of conscientious work." *The Economist* Russia under Putin, the Making of a neo-KGB state. August 23, 2007 www.economist.com/displayStory.cfm?story_id=9682621

Even those officials without a visible KGB background enjoy close ties to the business world. Dmitri Medvedev, a first deputy prime minister, is the chairman of the board of directors of Gazprom; Victor Khristenko, the minister of industry and energy, is the chairman of the board of directors of Transneft; the science and education minister, Andrei Fursenko, has been appointed head a new state nanotechnology corporation. Alexei Gordeev, the minister of agriculture, is the chairman of the board of directors of Rosagroleasing; Anatoly Serdukov, the defense minister, is the chairman of the board of directors of Chimprom, a chemicals giant. German Gref, the minister of economic development and trade, is the chairman of the board of the Russia Venture Company; Igor Levitin, the transport minister, is the chairman of the board of directors of the company running Moscow's Sheremetyevo airport; Igor Shuvalov, a foreign-policy adviser to the president, is the chairman of the board of directors of Russian Railways; his colleague Sergei Prikhodko is the chairman of the board of directors of Tactical Missile Weapons. The issue is discussed in a Hudson Institute colloquium, "US–Russian Relations: Is Conflict Inevitable? (Washington, D.C., March 26–27, 2007), http://hudson.org/files/publications/HudsonRussianGroupJun26_2007.pdf.

6. *The Captive Mind* (New York: Vintage Books, 1953) is a classic account of the intellectual compromises forced by communist rule.

7. The most dedicated blackmarketeers were from a distinct criminal caste, known as *Vory v zakone* [Thieves-in-Law]. Set up for mutual support among criminals in the prison camps of the Stalin era, the "Law" was a mixture of rituals, solidarity, and hierarchy enforced by death or mutilation. It forbade any cooperation with the Soviet system in any way, whether in prison or outside it. Members were allowed to live solely by criminal activity and had to cut ties with existing friends and family. Marriage was forbidden. Rank was indicated by a graduated system of tattoos; communication was in *Fenya*, an impenetrable argot originally developed by prerevolutionary peddlers.

In a hotel lobby in 1991 I encountered a professor carrying a metal container filled with three kilos of bee venom; he hoped to sell it to a Western pharmaceutical company for "some thousands of dollars." My fax machine, in an office previously occupied by a fly-by-night metals trader, used to spit out offers of kilos of rare metals such as osmium and scandium. A suitcase full of that would go for many thousands of dollars in Europe.

8. Web sites run by opposition groups and Chechen separatists are sometimes blocked; how far this is on explicit official instructions is unclear. Bloggers have been running foul of extremism and other laws too. In August 2007 a 21-year-old blogger named Savva Terentyev from Syktyvkar was charged with inciting hatred toward the police after a post appeared on his blog saying that corrupt policemen should be publicly incinerated.

9. The British Broadcasting Corporation (BBC) has lost its FM frequencies, apparently for political reasons.

10. The Organisation for Economic Co-operation and Development (OECD) says of Russia's goal of reaching a standard of public administration similar to the G–7:

> Russia will find it extremely difficult to reach that goal, even over the very long term, if the reform of public administration is approached in a narrow, technocratic fashion rather than proceeding in tandem with improvements in the in the institutional environment within which the state bureaucracy operates. In this respect, the greatest dangers may arise from the apparent disjuncture between, on the one hand, a reform approach that aims to empower citizens vis-à-vis the bureaucracy and to make public bodies more transparent, responsive and accountable to them, and, on the other hand, a political system that appears to be moving in the direction of less transparency and accountability.

From *"Clientelism" to a "Client-Centred Orientation"? The Challenge of Public Administration Reform in Russia,* Organisation for Economic Co-operation and Development, Paris 2007.

11. In the form of the British 1980s series "Spitting Images," the show used grotesque but highly recognizable puppets. In the early weeks of his presidency it portrayed Putin variously as an impotent young king on his wedding night, a monarch dithering over his coronation robes, and as an ignorant literary censor. By 2003, when it was finally taken off air, Putin was appearing as a hideous and malevolent dwarf.

12. On almost my last day in Moscow in 2002, I reluctantly apologized to Khodorkovsky for the negative coverage of the past years, which included an article in 1998 called "Oily Charm" mocking his clean-up efforts. That had prompted an angry and rather scary threat of a lawsuit for defamation. But the Yukos share price had risen tenfold since my article. At least in *The Economist*'s moral universe, in which market capitalization is the purest representation of outsiders' trust, Khodorkovsky had been vindicated. I had therefore been mistaken. He accepted my rather qualified apology with surprised graciousness.

13. The demand had first been made on December 30th of the previous year, and was still being challenged by Yukos.

14. Cut to eight years on appeal.

15. A breach, incidentally, of a Russian law that says prisoners should serve their sentence close to home.

16. At the time of the Soviet Union's breakup, these numbered 89. After some mergers, there are now 85, comprising 47 *oblasts* (provinces), 21 republics, eight *krais* (broadly the same as *oblasts*), six *okrugs* (autonomous districts with slightly lesser status), two federal cities (Moscow and St. Petersburg), and the Jewish Autonomous Oblast.

17. Address by President Vladimir Putin, September 4, 2004, http://www.kremlin.ru/eng /speeches/2004/09/04/1958_type82912_76332.shtml.

18. Though ethnic Russians make up 75 percent of the population in the country as a whole, in some parts they are barely a plurality, and the birthrate among the Muslim minorities is much higher than among ethnic Russians.

19. It is interesting to imagine the furious way Russia would have reacted, by contrast, if one of the Baltic States had suggested writing Russian in the Roman alphabet.

CHAPTER 3

1. Although not fully teetotal, his abstemious habits certainly make him a "nondrinker" in a country where drinking half a liter of vodka in an evening is considered unremarkable.

2. When the Russian leader caught a 20-inch sea bass from President George Bush's boat during a fishing trip in 2007, two of the three main television news channels in fishing-mad Russia referred to it sardonically as "not too big"—though the third, NTV, inflated the modest catch to "many" fish.

3. Though plenty of jokes suggest that this will eventually change: that the first town on the moon will be called Putinsk, for example.

4. Among those who spent years wrongly incarcerated in psychiatric hospitals was Vladimir Bukovsky, who now lives in the British university city of Cambridge; at the time of writing he was planning to stand in the presidential election due on March 2, 2008.

5. The *Yezhednevniy Zhurnal* [Daily Journal] reported this case in detail on June 22, 2007. The article, in Russian, is available at http://ej.ru/?a=note&id=7182 Zoya Svetova (author) "*Zloupotrebleniye psikhiatricheskoi vlastyu*" (Abuse of Psychiatric Authority) http://ej.ru/?a=note&id=7182.

6. Email to the author., August 2007

7. Mikhail Trepashkin was held in harsh conditions and wrote me an anguished personal letter, saying that his eyesight was failing and that he feared he would die in prison, forgotten by the outside world. See also "Amnesty International's concerns and recommendations in the case of Mikhail Trepashkin," Amnesty International, AI Index: EUR 46/012/2006, http://web.amnesty.org/library/index/engeur460122006.

8. ˎ Certainly Khodorkovsky's trial was a sham; the looting of Yukos by the Kremlin's business cronies counts as one of the most scandalous abuses of property rights that Russia
has seen since the Bolsheviks expropriated industrialists after the Russian Revolution.
The truth is that almost all Russian businesses break the law, because the laws are so
vague and contradictory. Khodorkovsky's early business career makes it hard to count
him as saintly or blameless. But he was clearly singled out for prosecution because of
the political challenge that he presented to the Kremlin. His lawyer, human-rights advocate Yuri Schmidt, says: "When Khodorkovsky was arrested, I determined at once
that this is my case—a political case, a case related to the advocacy of human rights, a
law-forming case. This is a case concerning the crucial challenges of our society and
our common survival—not physical, but human and intellectual . . . The issue of the
Khodorkovsky case will determine a further development of Russia." Yury Shmidt,
SOVEST, The support group for Mikhail Khodorkovsky and other defendants in the
YUKOS case, http://www.sovest.org/gb/.

9. Known as Gorky in the Soviet era. Andrei Sakharov, Russia's greatest dissident, was exiled there under Brezhnev in 1981 and triumphantly returned at the personal invitation of Mikhail Gorbachev in December 1986. Nizhny Novgorod became known as a
cradle of economic and political reforms.

10. Some of the harassment was more bizarre than thuggish: According to Tatyana Lokshina of the Moscow Helsinki Group, one organizer found his front door glued shut
from the outside. He climbed out of his window and joined the march anyway.

11. A full account of the demonstration can be found at www.opendemocracy.net
/globalization-institutions_government/iceberg_report_4558.jsp (Oksana Chely-
sheva, "Russia's Iceberg: a Nizhny Novgorod report," Open Democracy, April 25,
2007) and (in Russian) 'Poboishche na ploshchad Gorkogo: Nizhegorodskii "Marsz Neso-
glasnykh" razognali na glazakh u soten detei' (Slaughter on Gorky Square: "Dissenters'
March" dispersed before the eyes of hundreds of children) Sergei Anisimov, Novye
Izvestia, March 26 2007 www.newizv.ru/news/2007–03–26/66305/.

12. The extremism law can cut both ways, squashing not opposition causes but discussion
that the Kremlin finds too inflammatory. In September the newspaper Izvestia received an official warning from Rossvyazokhrankultury (whose full name is the Or-
wellian "Federal Service for Supervision in Mass Communications, Communications
and Preservation of Cultural Heritage") for an article it published in May about discrimination against ethnic Russians in Sakha, a vast, thinly populated territory in the
east of the country. In a classic example of bureaucratic intimidation, Rossvyazokhrankultury said it had discovered "signs of extremism" in the article after a "commission of linguistics specialists" (unnamed) had examined the article. In a protest
against the move, Izvestia wrote: "The 'signs of extremism', in our opinion, are contained not in the words in which we described what we saw [. . .] The 'signs of extremism are contained in what actually happened there." 'Priznak ekstremisma zabrel v
"Izvestiya"'? (A sign of extremism strays into "Izvestiya") Andrei Bilzho August 29,
2007 www.izvestia.ru/opinion/article3107705/.

13. In November 2005 the management dismissed Olga Romanova, presenter of its flag-
ship program, after she told Radio Liberty that the channel had declined some important stories for political reasons. One involved an accident involving a car driven by a
son of the then defense minister, Sergei Ivanov, in which a woman died. Several fellow
journalists resigned soon thereafter.

14. The magazine appears under the English version of its title, though the publishing
house uses the Russian equivalent, Novoye Vremya. Its website is www.newtimes.ru.

15. Novaya Gazeta's independence is thanks to its proprietor, a KGB officer-turned-banker
named Aleksandr Lebedev. Originally a supporter of Putin, he has become an increasingly outspoken critic of the Kremlin, saying that the current lack of press freedom is
"completely unacceptable" and comparing it to the Brezhnev era. Matthias Schepp,
Spiegel Interview with Novaya Gazeta Co-Owner, "Russian Media Is Like 'Brezhnev-Era

Propaganda,'" interview, SpiegelOnline International, September 3, 2007, www.spiegel
.de/international/world/0,1518,503609,00.html.

16. Hoping to help, I featured *New Times* in a column. I urged everyone interested in the
future of Russian press freedom to subscribe. Mischievously, I also suggested that
businesses in countries that suffer Kremlin-imposed economic sanctions, such as
Georgia and Estonia, should take out advertisements to fill the gap left by the browbeaten Russian businesses. The result, Yevgenia Albats told me sadly, was to scare potential advertisers even more.

17. 'Delo o "Trekh Kitach": Sudye ugrozhayut, prokurora izolirovali, svidetelya ubili' (The
"Three Whales" affair: they threaten the judge, isolated the prosecutor and killed the
witness) Yuri Shchekochikhin. *Novaya Gazeta,* June 2, 2003, www.novayagazeta.ru
/data/2003/39/00.html.

18. The murder of journalists is nothing new in Russia. Even in the Yeltsin era, when the
media was considerably more pluralistic, brave reporters risked being killed. Dmitry
Kholodov, a young reporter investigating corruption in the military, died after picking up a booby-trapped briefcase at a Moscow railway station in October 1994. His
newspaper accused the military leadership of ordering the contract killing. Six men
were acquitted after an investigation denounced by his parents. The difference is
that Kholodov's murder caused a national outcry—albeit not one fully shared in the
Kremlin.

19. Bret Stephens. "For the Sake of One Man: Getting the facts straight about the old-new
Russia.," *Wall Street Journal,* July 17, 2007

20. In September 2007 Russian prosecutors arrested 11 people, including figures with alleged connections to the Chechen criminal underworld, and an FSB colonel. Senior
Russian figures said that those arrested had been working on behalf of a foreign
enemy of the Kremlin's—taken as a reference to Berezovsky, who has always denied all
involvement in the case. Politkovskaya's family and colleagues said they feared that political interference would derail the investigation, and criticized the authorities for
sidelining Pyotr Garibyan, one of Moscow's most competent prosecutors, who had
previously had charge of the case.

21. The public is unconvinced. A FOM *Fond 'Obshchestvennoye Mnenie'* (Public Opinion
Foundation) poll conducted in June 2006 showed that 31 percent of respondents
thought television was objective. The Public Opinion Foundation Database, TV Coverage of Popular Events, Population Poll, June 29, 2006, http://bd.english.fom.ru
/report/map/az/0–9/edomt0625_1/ed062521. A Levada Centre poll on Chechnya in
March 2007 showed 49 percent saying that coverage is superficial; 28 percent said it
concealed problems: Only 11 percent pronounced themselves satisfied. Levada Center,
March 2007. Quoted in "Poll finds a plurality of Russians distrust Ramzan." http:
//www.jamestown.org/publications_details.php?volume_id=421&issue_id=4037&art
icle_id=2372009 }

22. A further amendment in December 2006 enlarged the list of citizens ineligible to
participate in elections to include those convicted of "extremism."

23. Office for Democratic Institutions and Human Rights, "OSCE/ODIHR Election Observation Mission Report, Russian Federation Presidential Election 14 March 2004"
(Warsaw, Poland, June 2, 2004), http://www.osce.org/documents/odihr/2004/06/3033
_en.pdf.

24. Masha Lipman "Putin's Power Vacuum" *Washington Post,* July 14, 2007

25. By one account, Putin's fortune started with a hotel in Turku, Finland, acquired when
he was in charge of the city of St. Petersburg's foreign economic ties. Certainly St. Petersburg companies with shadowy ownership structures have flourished under his rule.
A mobile phone company linked to his wife acquired a coveted license with remarkable
ease. Western intelligence services say his personal fortune is $11 billion; a well-in-
formed Swedish source puts it at several times that. A colossal yacht is being built in
Finland for an unknown Russian customer; other shipyards have been told that no

Russian now wants anything over 590 feet (180 meters) in order not to give offence to Putin. And what of Putin's relationship with Abramovich? The multi-billionaire tycoon used to be the Yeltsin family's closest financial confidant, and now he divides his time between London (where he owns Chelsea football club) and Moscow. See "Putin Becomes the Richest Candidate," *Kommersant*, February 4, 2004, http://www.kommersant .ru/doc.aspx?docsid=446423 (in Russian).

26. Dirty tricks are not always so spectacular. But they are endemic in Russian politics. *Kompromat* [compromising material] is the main political currency. It can be real, or invented. During an election in the Siberian town of Tomsk in 2007, opponents of the small liberal-conservative Union of Right Forces (SPS in its Russian acronym), produced a leaflet purporting to offer AIDS patients lucrative work on the campaign, plus the chance to shake hands with voters: an effective smear in a country deeply prejudiced against both homosexuals and those infected with HIV. In Krasnoyarsk, slogans on SPS placards reading *Za Dostroyku* [To complete construction] were neatly replaced with ones reading *Za Dovoruyku* [To complete the looting]—an effective jibe at the party's unpopular business backers.

27. See Valery Vyzhutovich, "The Other Russia and the Others, " *Rossiiskaya Gazeta*, July 13, 2007, ". http://www.rg.ru/2007/07/13/vyzhutovitch.html (in Russian). However, foreign scholars have come to different conclusions.

28. According to Transparency International, a lobbying group, in 2006 Russia came in 121st out of 163 countries surveyed, jointly with Benin, Gambia, Guiana, Honduras, Nepal, the Philippines, Rwanda, and Swaziland. In 2007 it was 143 out of 179, jointly with Gambia, Indonesia, and Togo. Transparency International, Corruption Perceptions Index (2007) (Survey graph), http://www.transparency.org/policy_research/surveys _indices/cpi/2007; Associated Press, "Annual Bribe-Taking in Russia Almost Equal to State's Entire Revenues, Says Senior Prosecutor," *International Herald Tribune*, November 6, 2007, http://www.iht.com/articles/ap/2006/11/07/business/EU_FIN_Russia _Corruption.php; and (in Russian) 'Ni Dat, Ni Vzyat' (Neither give nor take) Andrei Sharov *Rossiskaya Gazeta*, 11 July 2006 http://www.rg.ru/2006/11/07/buksman.html

29. Though "democracy" is usually treated as being synonymous with political freedom and pluralism, representative government, the rule of law, and other good things, I have tried to avoid using it in this book. It is worth remembering that "democracy" came into common usage during the 1930s as a way of highlighting the weakness of the authoritarian regimes in Germany, Italy, and elsewhere. Before that it was more often regarded as having connotation of "mob rule." Since then it has been so debased by its use as a fig leaf for dictators who claim popular backing that it has become almost useless, as in the "German Democratic Republic" or the grotesquely authoritarian Democratic People's Republic of Korea.

30. Even using the English word "judiciary" to describe it is misleading. It would be better termed the "Office of Penal Affairs," or perhaps simply the "Inquisition." The International Bar Association's June 2005 report "Striving for Judicial Independence: A Report into Proposed Changes to the Judiciary in Russia" (International Bar Association Human Rights Institute Report, London, U.K) provides a detailed account of the shortcomings in the Russian system. It is available at http://www.ibanet.org/images /downloads/2005_06_June_Report_Russia_Striving%20for%20Judicial%20Independence_Final_English.pdf.

31. Transparency International Global Corruption Report 2004, www.transparency.org /content/download/18707/255317

32. Reuters, "Political interference Hurting Russia Business," audio from Russia Investment Summit, September 12, 2007, http://summitnotebook.reuters.com/category /summit/russian-investment-07/.

33. It is overly romantic to see Russian criminal justice as portrayed by Martin Cruz Smith, author of *Gorky Park* (1983) and its sequels, as the same world-weary but ultimately well-meaning affair as its counterparts in Western countries.

34. Yuri Kostanov, a member of the Independent Council of Legal Experts in Moscow and vice chairman of the Moscow bar, commented to the *Washington Post* on June 3, 2007: "She's a brilliant and professional lawyer, and everyone understands very well that if they can disbar her, they can disbar anyone." He added, "I believe this is all the work of the special services. They are doing it to make everyone dance to their music and tell everyone: 'We are the power.'" Peter Finn, "Russia's Champion of Hopeless Cases Is Targeted for Disbarment," *Washington Post*, June 3, 2007, www.washingtonpost .com/wp-dyn/content/article/2007/06/02/AR2007060201135.html.

35. With only 18 percent of the population covered by the court, Russia makes up 23 percent of the cases heard.

36. In 2007, Russia's top judge went further, saying that citizens should be allowed to turn to the court only after they had exhausted every legal avenue inside the country, rather than after simply losing an appeal as at present.

37. "Public-spirited" is what people call activists they approve of. "Self-appointed do-gooders" and "busybodies" are harsher but sometimes more accurate descriptions.

38. However, in remarks to editors in August 2007 he seemed to signal that Aslyamzan should not be prosecuted. "Yes, I am well familiar with this case. But it is not worth a pin. She can return to her home country without any worry. Of course, no one will release her from administrative responsibility for her mistake, but one should not confuse a mistake with a crime." He also added: "While I am president, she absolutely does not need to worry." Vera Chelischeva *'Putin priglashayet Asalamazyan "spokoino" vozvrashchatsya na rodinu'* 'Putin invites Aslamazyan to return to her home country "without worry"' *Novaya Gazeta* October 29, 2007 http://www.novayagazeta.ru/news/152916.html

39. Still known in some international English media by its Russian name, Kiev.

40. Although Ukraine has become a much freer country, it is not a better-governed one. Yushchenko proved a chronically indecisive president, and Ukraine's politics have remained in acrimonious and bewildering stalemate.

41. The British government, spinelessly, chose not to make a big fuss about this for fear of jeopardizing British investments in Russia.

42. One of the charms of life in Moscow is that you can find a "gypsy taxi" simply by standing on the street. The resulting ride may well be without insurance, brakes, or road sense, but the conversation is fascinating and the price—negotiated on the spot—almost invariably low. The drivers come from all ethnic backgrounds, in non-descript cars that escape the notice of the ubiquitous and predatory traffic police. This utterly deregulated market is one of the last relics of the anarchic life of the Russian capital in the 1990s. It is also a way in which ordinary people of all backgrounds can earn extra rubles.

43. See for example Anna Badken "A Gathering Storm of Russian Thugs" San Francisco Chronicle August 14, 2005 http://www.sfgate.com/cgi-bin/article.cgi?file=/c/a/2005 /08/14/MNGUSE7N2D1.DTL

 And (in Russian) *'Yunyi i ochen opasnii: v molodezhnykh ekstremistskikh grup-pirovkakh sostoyat okolo polumilliona rossiyan'* (Young and very dangerous: half a million Russians in extremist youth groups) Yevgenia Zubchenko and Kira Vasileva, *Novye Izvestiya* 17 July 2007 http://www.newizv.ru/news/2007-07-17/72924/ estimate that these number over 140.

44. Sarah Mendelson and Ted Gerber, "The Putin Generation: The Political Views of Russian Youth," Center for Strategic and International Studies (CSIS), presentation, July 25, 2007, http://www.csis.org/images/stories/mendelson_carnegie_moscow_cor-rected.pdf.

45. So far, the Kremlin's own phony mass movements have been remarkably docile and have stayed focused on the intended targets. Anti-Semitism, for example, which is ingrained in Russian nationalist circles, is surprisingly absent in the rhetoric of all the Kremlin-sponsored youth groups. (Putin has excellent relations with the handpicked leaders of Russia's surviving Jewish community.) But what happens, for example, if

the generals try to switch off some campaign they have launched, but the troops dis-agree? The danger of teaching people to organize demonstrations, print leaflets, and raise public awareness is that they may decide to do it on their own.

46. The two families became neighbors in north London.

47. This allegation, vehemently denied by Russian officials on Putin's behalf, was based on the flimsiest of evidence: an occasion during a walkabout in the grounds of the Krem-lin, when the Russian president was chatting to a family and kissed their small boy on the stomach. See, for example, "Putin recalls kissing boy's belly," BBC News, July 6, 2006, http://news.bbc.co.uk/2/hi/europe/5155448.stm.

48. "Yuri Felshtinsky, Alexander Litvinenko, and Geoffrey Andrews, *Blowing up Russia: Terror from Within* (Gibson Square Books, London, 2007).

49. Like many such operations, it was botched. The Qatari authorities arrested three men, who turned out to be GRU agents. After intense diplomatic pressure they were re-leased, and returned home to a hero's' welcomes. Russia argues that it is just eliminat-ing terrorists and that there is no difference between their attempts to destroy the leadership of the Chechen separatists, who have wrought mayhem in Russia for years, and the American hunt for Osama bin Laden. One difference is that most of the Chechen leadership—at least in the early years of the war—consistently denounced the killing of civilians and repeatedly called for talks with Russia on a peaceful resolu-tion to the conflict. By killing the only Chechen leaders willing to talk peace, the Kremlin has also killed the best chance of ending the war.

50. The latter did not help his public profile with an ill-advised media interview in which he said he supported the overthrow of the Russian regime "by force." British officials let it be known that they would be delighted if their unwelcome guest would move elsewhere. See "'I am plotting a new Russian revolution': London exile Berezovsky says force necessary to bring down President Putin" Ian Cobain, Matthew Taylor and Luke Harding *The Guardian,* April 13 2007 http://www.guardian.co.uk/russia/article/0,205 6321,00.html

51. Julian Borger, Luke Harding and David Gow, "Europeans Lukewarm as Britain Tries to Rally Support in Row with Russia," *The Guardian,* July 18, 2007, http://www .guardian.co.uk/russia/article/0,2128844,00.html.

52. "Bearing the Brunt of Russia's Anger," *The Daily Telegraph,* July 19, 2007, http://www .telegraph.co.uk/money/main.jhtml?xml=/money/2007/07/18/cnrussia118.xml&DCM P=ILC-traffdrv07053100.

53. Julie Anderson, "The HUMINT Offensive from Putin's Chekist State," *International Journal of Intelligence and Counter-Intelligence,* 20, no. 2 (2007):pp258–316.

CHAPTER 4

1. Such averages can be misleading; they are flattered by some very rich Russians declar-ing their income.

2. Katya Malofeeva and Tim Brenton, "Putin's Economy—Eight Years On," Russia Pro-file, August 15, 2007, http://www.russiaprofile.org/page.php?pageid=Business&article id=a1187177738.

3. The Kremlin wants to revive Russia's hi-tech fortunes. In April 2007 Putin announced a $7 billion program to promote nanotechnology; another $1.2 billion is going into a state-backed technology fund. But past experience suggests that this money will be at best be stolen, or else wasted. The Russian state has proved an extremely poor steward of the national wealth. The chief recipient of the largesse is the Kurchatov Institute in Moscow, which just happens to be run by a close colleague of Putin's, Mikhail Ko-valchuk. If the Kremlin really wanted to improve the fortunes of the IT sector, it could try modernizing the rudimentary levels of computerization in the Russian public sec-tor, and introducing and enforcing strong intellectual-property laws.

4. "Putin Aide Resigns over Policies," BBC News, December 27, 2005, http://news.bbc.co .uk/1/hi/world/europe/4562718.stm.

5. Andrei Illarionov, "Rise of Corporatist State in Russia (The 2006 Long Telegram)" (PowerPoint presentation), Cato Institute, March 7, 2006, http://www.cato.org /realaudio/illarionov–2006–03–07.ppt or www.iea.ru/article/present/pres060307.ppt,

6. It is easy to see the attraction. In 2006 a Swiss court ruled that the then communications minister, Leonid Reiman, a close personal friend of Putin's, owned telecommunications assets in Russia worth more than a billion dollars. This caused no difficulty for Reiman, who simply issued a denial and continued in his post.

7. 'My zavisili mezhdu sotsialismom i kapitalismom' (We are hanging between socialism and capitalism). Interview with Boris Titov by Andrei Reut, Finansovye Izvestia July 11th 2007. http://www.finiz.ru/articles/article1243452/?print

8. 'Rossiya ne voidet v pyaterku krupneishikh ekonomik mira k 2020, yesli sokhranitsya nyneshnii kurs' (Russia will not become one of the five most powerful economies in the world by 2020 if the current course is maintained) Andrei Illarionov, Yezhedevny Zhurnal 27 June 2007, http://ej.ru/?a=note&id=7187

9. United Nations Development Programme, "Human Development Index" (Table), Human Development Report 2006, http://hdr.undp.org/hdr2006/statistics/.

10. Galina Stolyarova, "Russians: You Don't Call, You Don't Write," Transitions Online, July 12, 2007, http://www.ceeol.com/aspx/issuedetails.aspx?issueid=a791f8d8–778c –40aa–8907–024c97095276&articleId=474a662c–7893–4d2f–8eb3–8142ccb7aa23.

11. The Russian population has been falling by 0.5 percent annually since the end of the Soviet Union, from nearly 149 million in 1992 to 142 million now. Some of that was masked by migration of ethnic Russians from other parts of the former Soviet Union, a reservoir that has largely been exhausted. Now the decline is accelerating.

    There are some slightly encouraging signs. Infant mortality has fallen by a fifth in the past two years, and maternal mortality by 8 percent. The birthrate has risen from 8.27 per 1,000 in 1999 to 9.95 per 1000 in 2006. (By comparison the American birthrate in that year was 14.14 and the UK's was 10.71.) Some of this may be to do with Putin's exhortations, falling poverty, and better state benefits for mothers. But mostly it is a statistical fluke: The birthrate in the Soviet Union in the early 1980s was high, and that cohort of women are now at prime child-bearing age.

12. Abortions number at least 1.5 million annually. Surveys suggest 10–15 percent of all abortions are not recorded. Putin defined the population crisis as Russia's biggest problem; he has asked parliament to increase to $166 per month the stipend given to families that adopt children.

13. http://www.PWC.com/extweb/ncpressrelease.nsf/docid/FB66FD4D8CBB564080257 3050019EB74

14. http://www.PWC.com/extweb/ncpressrelease.nsf/docid/7CB1C559F9811342802572 660030A670

15. http://www.PWC.com/extweb/ncpressrelease.nsf/docid/CE48734DA6D8847780257 29C0031D354

16. http://www.PWC.com/extweb/ncpressrelease.nsf/docid/7CB1C559F9811342802572 660030A670

17. I v sluzhbu, i v druzhbu: Tovarishch Vladimira Putina budet upravlyat rossiisko-germanskim gazoprovodom (Both in the service, and in friendship: Comrade Vladimir Putin will run the Russian-German gas pipeline). Kommersant, December 9, 2005. http://www.kommersant.ru/doc.aspx?DocsID=633868

CHAPTER 5

1. However much they hated Western materialism and hypocrisy, even the most naïve and idealistic foreigners soon found Soviet communism boring. If they stayed interested in left-wing ideas at all, they drifted off to Trotskyism or even mainstream socialist parties. Only in the trades unions in a handful of west European countries did orthodox communism retain a foothold, and that owed as much to secret Kremlin subsidies as to any usefulness of communist ideology.

2. This was set up by the then prime minister, Viktor Chernomyrdin, in 1995; it described itself as "liberal" and "centrist." When he left power it morphed into the equally blandly named Unity, set up by Putin's supporters, to fend off the Fatherland party of Yeltsin's main regional challengers in the run up to Duma elections in December 1999.

3. The definition was a loose one. Dark-skinned people from the Caucasus and central Asia had until recently been Soviet citizens; many of them now had Russian citizenship. They were "foreign" only in the narrowest racial sense.

4. 'Vladimir Zhirinovsky on the sexual problems of Condoleeza Rice' (in Russian), Yaroslava Krestovskaya, Pravda, January 9, 2006. http://www.pravda.ru/world/09 –01–2006/73182-zhirinovsky–0

5. Andrei Sakharov, a Soviet physicist and human rights campaigner, was the best-known champion of freedom in the Soviet Union. He won the Nobel Peace Prize in 1975, though the Soviet authorities refused to let him travel to Stockholm to accept it. After protesting against the invasion of Afghanistan, he was exiled in Gorky (now once again known by its prerevolutionary name of Nizhny Novgorod). He died on December 14, 1989, aged 68.

6. A Soviet icon, he was the first man in space on April 12, 1961.

7. Yeltsin replaced that with the (wordless) "Patriotic Song" by the Russian composer Glinka. Putin wanted the old anthem restored, but settled for the old tune and new words. These drop any Soviet allusions but keep the notion of ancient Russian "brotherhood" (which in the eyes of the non-Russian peoples of the country may sound pretty much like imperialism).

> Russia—our sacred state,
> Russia—our beloved country.
> A mighty will, a great glory
> Are yours forever for all time!
> [Chorus:]
> Be glorious, our free Fatherland,
> Ancient union of brotherly peoples,
> Ancestor-given wisdom of the people!
> Be glorious, country! We are proud of you!

8. Historians' estimates differ. Robert Service thinks it was around 300,000; Robert Conquest reckons about 500,000; Norman Lowe says 50,000 to 200,000 were executed, and 400,000 died in prison or were killed in revolts.

9. George Orwell, 1984 (New York: Penguin Classics, 1977), p. 260.

10. The money was stolen or misappropriated by the Communist rulers and mostly never reached the intended beneficiaries.

11. That would be as if Russia would elect as its leader a veteran Cold War critic of the Soviet Union such as the British-based Vladimir Bukovsky.

12. Japan, of course, is another story altogether.

13. Vladimir Putin, Annual Address to the Federal Assembly, April 25, 2005 http://kremlin.ru/eng/speeches/2005/04/25/2031_type70029type82912_87086.shtml (in English, slightly misleadingly translated). The phrase used in Russian was "Prezhde vsego sleduyet priznat, chto krusheniye Sovetskogo Soyuza bylo krupneishei geopolitich-eskoi Katastrofoi veka" (Above all it must be acknowledged that the collapse of the Soviet Union was the most powerful geopolitical catastrophe of the century). http://kremlin.ru/appears/2005/04/25/1223_type63372type63374type82634_87049.shtml

14. "Butterfly-Polka" [Polka-Babochka] is, incidentally, an unusual choice of phrase straight from the Stalinist propaganda lexicon, when it was used to indicate something utterly alien. See this explanation by Pavel Felgenhauer, a hard-hitting journalistic critic of the Kremlin ("Kremlin Rejects 'Foreign' Approach to Russian History," Eura-

sia Daily Monitor, The Jamestown Foundation, June 27, 2007), available at http://www
.jamestown.org/edm/article.php?article_id=2372256.

15. Meeting with Participants in the National Russian Conference of Humanities and Social Sciences Teachers, June 21, 2007, Novo-Ogaryovo Excerpts in English at http:
//kremlin.ru/appears/2007/06/21/1702_type63376type63381type82634_135323.shtml
And in Russian in full at http://kremlin.ru/appears/2007/06/21/1702_type63376type
63381type82634_135323.shtml

16. *A Modern History of Russia, 1945–2006: A Teachers' Manual* (Moscow:
Prosveshcheniye, 2007). Two interesting articles (in Russian) give some background to
the issue: 'Historians should write History Textbooks' *Novaya Gazeta*, July 3 2007
(blog discussion) http://www.ng.ru/ng_politics/2007–07–03/10_uchebniki.html; and
'I would not like my name associated with this outrage' Oleg Kashin, *Novaya Gazeta*,
July 5 2007 http://www.ng.ru/politics/2007–07–05/3_pozor.html.

17. All three extracted quotations taken from *A Modern History of Russia, 1945–2006: A
Teachers' Manual* (Moscow: Prosveshcheniye, 2007).

18. Joint Interview with Federal Chancellor of Germany Gerhard Schröder for Bild Newspaper, May 7, 2005 (official Kremlin translation) http://www.kremlin.ru/eng/text
/speeches/2005/05/07/0852_type82916_87605.shtml.

19. The accusation "*u vas negrov linchuyut*" ["and you are lynching Negroes"] became a
catchphrase epitomizing Soviet propaganda based on this principle.

20. On August 25, 1968 Tatiana Baeva, Konstantin Babitsky, Larisa Bogoraz, Vadim Delaunay, Vladimir Dremlyuga, Viktor Fainberg, Natalya Gorbanevskaya, and Pavel Litvinov
assembled in Red Square with a Czechoslovak flag and banners bearing slogans, including "For your freedom and ours" and "Glory to free and independent Czechoslovakia." They were almost instantly arrested. Encouraged by the others, Baeva claimed to
have been there by accident and was released. Bogoraz was sentenced to four years in
Siberia and became chairman of the Moscow Helsinki Group in 1989. She died in 2004.
Delaunay was sentenced to two years in a labor camp. He emigrated to France in 1975
and died in 1983. Litvinov was sentenced to five years' exile in China. He emigrated to
America in 1973 and still lives there. Gorbanevskaya was not tried, as she had recently
given birth. Viktor Fainberg was pronounced insane and spent five years in psychiatric
hospital. The Tom Stoppard play *Every Good Boy Deserves Favour* is dedicated to him.

21. Andrei Sabov. "Commentary" (untitled) Rossiiskaya Gazeta, 8 September 2007, This is
not available on the newspaper's website but can be accessed http://community
.livejournal.com/ru_katyn/12893.html.

22. Little mention is made of British and American help to the Soviet war effort.

23. Each side thought they were getting the better deal. Germany could mop up the countries of central Europe and then concentrate on crushing France and forcing Britain to
sue for peace. The Soviet Union, in chaos after Stalin's purges, hoped to stand back
while the "imperialist powers" fought and weakened each other. See Paul Halsall, editor, Modern History Sourcebook, "The Molotov-Ribbentrop Pact, 1939: Text of the
Nazi-Soviet Non-Aggression Pact" (Internet Modern History Sourcebook, Fordham
University, August 1997, http://www.fordham.edu/halsall/mod/1939pact.html) for the
text of the pact and the secret protocol. http://www.regnum.ru/news/411620.html (in
Russian) gives a good account of Kremlin thinking about it now. 'Putin answers Latvia
and Estonia: before you write books, learn to read them!' February 22 2005 (no byline)

24. Estonia is almost the only country to have made inroads into the post-communist
world's biggest outstanding problem: reforming public administration. Unlike almost
any other country, Estonia built its most important institutions from scratch, shunning the temptation to use "experienced" communist-era leftovers. The result is that
the country has by some way the region's most modern and effective organs of state,
ranging from a highly effective foreign ministry to security and intelligence services
deeply trusted by their western counterparts. Its heavyweight president increasingly
speaks for the whole post-communist region.

25. To be fair, some Americans thought the same of Nicaragua under the Sandinistas, and still do about communist Cuba.

26. The journal in question was described, quite wrongly, in the Soviet ultimatum as an "Organ of the Baltic Military Entente." Fired by this historical example, I revived an English language weekly in Tallinn in 1992. Intentionally provocative, it carried a column called "Troopwatch" that monitored the occupation forces' misbehavior.

27. Born in 1920, his best-known work in English is probably *The Czar's Madman*, trans. Anselm Hollo (1992; translation, London: Harvill Press).

28. Quoted in Vladimir Socor, "Kremlin Assails Baltic States" (*Eurasia Daily Monitor,* The Jamestown Foundation, May 12, 2005, www.jamestown.org/edm/article.php?article _id=2369743) (in English) and (in Russian) *Putin posovetoval Estonii I Latvii zabit svoi "duratskiye territorialialniye trebovaniya* (Putin warns Estonia and Latvia to drop their "idiotic territorial claims"), http://www.lenta.ru/news/2005/05/10/putin.

29. *The Baltic States: The Years of Dependence, 1940–90* (London: C. Hurst & Company, 1993) by Romualdas Misiunas and Rein Taagepera gives the full story. I have focused on Estonia here because this country is at the time of writing the main target of Kremlin displeasure.

30. I am indebted to Robert Gellately's *Lenin, Stalin, Hitler: The Age of Social Catastrophe* (New York: Alfred A. Knopf, 2007, p. 389) for this remarkable fact.

31. In Putin's words in October 2007: "As a result of a shock therapy of the 1990s, the 1998 financial crisis, and the tragic events in the Caucasus the country's economy and social sphere were in depression. The same can be said about the public's morale at the time. The country's territorial integrity was under threat." Opening Remarks at the VIIIth United Russia Party Congress October 1, 2007 Gostiny Dvor, Moscow. In English on http://kremlin.ru/eng/speeches/2007/10/01/1418_type82912type82913type84779_14668 2.shtml And in Russian on http://kremlin.ru/appears/2007/10/01/1900_type63374type 63376type63378type82634_146479.shtml

32. "Hang the Kaiser" was a popular postwar slogan in Britain.

33. It also stresses that Russia should not be dictated to from outside, celebrates the campaign to bankrupt Yukos, justifies Russia's disastrous intervention in the Ukrainian "Orange Revolution," and says that the exigencies of the war on terror have forced both Russia and America to limit civil liberties in a similar way.

34. Lilia Shevtsova, "Anti-Westernism Is the New National Idea," *The Moscow Times,* August 7, 2007, available on the Carnegie Endowment for International Peace Web site, www.carnegieendowment.org/publications/index.cfm?fa=view&id=19480.

35. Responses to Questions from Russian Journalists December 6, 2004 Ankara,Turkey http://www.kremlin.ru/eng/speeches/2004/12/06/1232_type82915_80868.shtml (in English) and http://www.kremlin.ru/appears/2004/12/06/1409_type63380_80827 .shtml (in Russian)

36. Annual Address to Federal Assembly, Moscow 2006 http://www.kremlin.ru/eng /speeches/2006/05/10/1823_type70029type82912_105566.shtml And (with "'comrade" wolf') in Russian http://www.kremlin.ru/appears/2006/05/10/1357_type63372 type63374type82634_105546.shtml

37. Thomas E. Ricks and Craig Whitlock, "Putin Hits U.S. Over Unilateral Approach: Rebuke Is Called Unusually Hostile," *Washington Post,* February 11, 2007, sec. A01, http: //www.washingtonpost.com/wp-dyn/content/article/2007/02/10/AR2007021000524 .html (in English); and For text (in English): Speech and the Following Discussion at the Munich Conference on Security Policy February 10, 2007 http://www.kremlin .ru/eng/speeches/2007/02/10/0138_type82912type82914type82917type84779_11812 3.shtml In Russian http://www.kremlin.ru/appears/2007/02/10/1737_type63374type 63376type63377type63381type82634_118097.shtml And for a video of the event http: //media.kremlin.ru/2007._02_10_01.wmv

38. For a useful summary in English of Putin's remarks: 'Putin's anti-West sentiment builds' Daily Telegraph June 5, 2007 http://www.telegraph.co.uk/news/main.jhtml

?xml=/news/2007/06/04/wputin304.xml Such snide and sometimes strident commentary is still mixed with an almost fawning official desire on occasion to talk up the relationship with America. Putin has invited Bush to his dacha and let him drive his prized 1956 Volga; at the Victory Day parade in Red Square marking 50 years since the end of the Second World War, Putin ostentatiously put his American counterpart in the best seat, and described him as a guest of "special importance."

39. Much as the international legal and bureaucratic order chafes, the Kremlin is determined to join every club it can, and fiercely resists any suggestion that it does not belong in the G–8 or the Council of Europe. None of the so-called patriots in the Kremlin have explained how Russia can both be an equal partner with the West while also repeatedly denouncing the principles of interdependence, multilaterally, human rights, and openness on which the civilized world operates.

40. Lilia Shevtsova, "Anti-Westernism Is the New National Idea," *The Moscow Times*, August 7, 2007, available on the Carnegie Endowment for International Peace, http://www.carnegie.ru/en/pubs/media/76677.htm.

41. Ibid.

42. A good example of the former was the ROC-sponsored "Saint Spring" mineral water, which would have been more effectively and accurately translated as "Holy Spring".

43. By contrast, 21 percent said they were superstitious; 9 percent admitted to believing in horoscopes; 8 percent in magic; and 6 percent in UFOs The Public Opinion Foundation Database, Views on Atheism and Atheists, Population Poll, July 6, 2007, http://bd.english.fom.ru/report/cat/man/valuable/ed072321 gives another view with interesting insights.

44. Masha Lipman, "A Church for Lubyanka" (Moscow Postcard), *The New Yorker*, April 1, 2002, http://www.newyorker.com/archive/2002/04/01/020401ta_talk_lipman.

45. See article by Igor Torbakov, "Russian Orthodox Church Challenges 'Western' Concept of Human Rights, " *Eurasia Daily Monitor,* The Jamestown Foundation, April 7, 2006, http://www.jamestown.org/publications_details.php?volume_id=414&issue_id=3681&article_id=2370960.

46. 'Catholic-Orthodox Tensions Resurface; A Russian backlash greets coverage of a reconciliation-minded pope. Many in ex-Soviet lands say proselytizing is a threat to their identity.' *Los Angeles Times* April 11, 2005. Coupled with the authorities' own suspicion of both foreign organizations and minority rights, the ROC's stance has led to a sad decline in religious freedom. Non-orthodox churches find it hard to register; their foreign clergy find it hard to get visas and residence permits.

47. The idea that Russia, like every country, is nothing more than a historical accident is not considered.

48. 'Russian Political Culture: Outlook on Utopia' Transcript of remarks by Vladislav Surkov to the Russian Academy of Sciences (in Russian) on http://www.viperson.ru/wind.php?ID=322805&soch=1

49. Surkov, ibid

50. Had he wanted to give a more conventional spin to his ideas about legality, Putin could have spoken of *vlast* [rule] or *verkhovenstvo* [supremacy] *zakona*. But he didn't.

51. This centralizing approach is questionable. Common sense suggests tightly controlled rule from the center may pose problems in the world's largest country by land area. Even China finds it expedient to give local rulers some flexibility. America and Brazil flourish as federations.

52. Organisation for Economic Co-operation and Development (OECD), "Economic Survey of the Russian Federation, 2006," Policy Brief, November 2006, https://www.oecd.org/dataoecd/58/49/37656835.pdf.

53. As much as Putin preaches the virtues of tight control, he and other senior figures are only too willing to shirk responsibility when they need. In the case of the Aleksander Litvinenko poisoning, for example, the Russian line was that the state could not possibly be held accountable for the theft of a large quantity of a lethal radioactive substance

from a supposedly tightly guarded nuclear research institute, or for the way in which a security-service veteran left trails of it on his journey to London and back. The line was, in effect: "It's Russia. These things happen. Get used to it."

54. What Russia really needs is a *vlastnaya gorizontal* (literally, "a power horizontal") in which the state is accountable both to its own institutions and to society. But Putin's solution, supposedly fitting Russian political culture, is not joined-up government and public accountability, but stern top-down pressure. What makes the state work is fear, not conscience.

55. *Komsomolskaya Pravda,* November 7, 2004 *Vnutrennii vrag i natsionalnya ideya* (The Internal Enemy and the National Idea) http://www.kp.ru/daily/23398/33754/ 29 November 2004

56. Michael Yuryev, (*Tretya Imperiya. Rossiya, kotoraya dolzhna byt; The third empire: Russia as it must be*) (Moscow: Limbus Press, 2006).

57. Quoted in Reuben F. Johnson, "President Putin's Third Term," *The Weekly Standard,* August 14, 2007, available at *Front Page Magazine,* http://www.frontpagemag.com /Articles/Printable.aspx?GUID=3E0AF111–0918–4A94–947F-E1E6D2E1E5D4.

58. Surkov, ibid

59. Interviewed in *Vedomosti,* July 5, 2007.

60. Vlad Sobell, "Russia Profile Weekly Experts Panel: Back to the Future," Panel introduced by Vladimir Frolov, Russia Profile.org, http://www.russiaprofile.org/page.php ?pageid=Experts%27+Panel&articleid=a11831252

CHAPTER 6

1. The unhappy echoes of the Soviet-led invasion of Czechoslovakia provide another strong historical parallel.

2. The Slovak foreign-policy expert Mário Nicolini's definition is a good one: "Euroatlanticism represents a policy that seeks a strong Europe and strengthens the multilateral reflexes of America," Mário Nicolini, "Slovakia One Year after NATO Entry: From National to Collective Interest (and Back)," EuroJournal.org, *Journal of Foreign Policy of Moldova,* no. 11 (2005), Central and Eastern European Online Library (CEEOL), http://www.ceeol.com/aspx/getdocument.aspx?logid=5&id=b6a97a38–0a1c–4df9–84 9d–9d1e608287af.

3. The Czech Republic, Estonia, Hungary, Latvia, Lithuania, Poland, Slovakia, and Slovenia joined in 2004; Romania and Bulgaria joined in 2007. The NATO summit in Bucharest in April 2008 delayed a membership application from Macedonia, but invited Croatia and Albania to join. The next candidate for membership is Croatia.

4. Igor Rodionov, "Approaches to Russian Military Doctrine," speech given at General Staff Academy conference May 27–30 1992, reprinted in *Voyennaya mysl* (Military Thinking), July 1992.

5. The Baltic states and their more pedantic friends insist that they were not "Soviet Republics" but occupied territories. Most Western countries never recognized their annexation by the Soviet Union, and refused to have formal or high-level contact with the officials of the local administrations in the "Soviet Baltic Republics."

6. A somewhat chastened Mečiar has now returned as junior partner in the coalition government formed after the June 2006 elections.

7. He died in a jail cell in the Netherlands in 2006, while on trial for war crimes.

8. In 2007 Karimov ranked eighth in the "world's worst dictators" hit parade, down from fifth place the previous year. From David Wallechinsky, "Who Is the World's Worst Dictator?," *Parade,* February 11 2007. http://www.parade.com/export/sites/default/ articles/web_exclusives/2007/02–11–2007/dictators08.html

9. Yekaterina Grigoryev, "*Izvestia* Correspondent visits US Base in Kirghizia," June 21 2002. http://www.ferghana.ru/article.php?id=521&print=1&PHPSESSID=2d1d1ca13 806e42db563aa39ccb889f8

10. Strongly supported by Turkey, Azerbaijan believes that Armenia is illegally occupying its territory of Nagorno-Karabakh (or Karabagh). Armenia says that history, demography, and conquest give it the strongest title. Peace negotiations have gone nowhere, and Armenia is the grateful host to a Russian military base, while also quietly improving ties with Iran. In the event of a peace deal with Azerbaijan and rapprochement with Turkey, few doubt that Armenia would soon be an enthusiastic member of the Euroatlantic camp.

11. As his name would be transcribed from the Belarusan language; in Russian it would be Aleksandr Lukashenko.

12. Dmitry Zavadsky, a journalist; Yury Zakharenko and Viktor Gonchar, politicians; and Anatoly Krasovsky, a businessman. From Belarusan their names would be transliterated as Viktar Hanchar, Zmitser Zavadsky, Yuri Zakharanka, and Anatol Krasousky.

13. It is run by Borodin, formerly of the Kremlin's property department, where Putin worked after his move from St. Petersburg.

14. This grew out of the original "Shanghai Five," of Russia, China, Kazakhstan, Kyrgyzstan, and Tajikistan, that was set up in the mid-1990s.

15. This started when Armenia, Kazakhstan, Kyrgyzstan, Russia, Tajikistan, and Uzbekistan signed a collective security treaty in May 1992, which came into force in April 1994, by which time Azerbaijan, Georgia, and Belarus had signed, too. In April 1999 Armenia, Belarus, Kazakhstan, Kyrgyzstan, Russia, and Tajikistan agreed to extend the treaty for a further five years, upon which Azerbaijan, Georgia, and Uzbekistan withdrew. In October 2002 the six remaining members renamed it the Collective Security Treaty Organization. In June 2006 Uzbekistan joined.

16. When I was trying to get a residence permit to live in communist-era Czechoslovakia, I timed my application to coincide with a 1988–89 CSCE session on media accreditation. If the Czechoslovak authorities adopted their usual stonewalling tactics in my case, a friendly British diplomat explained, they would immediately present an "open goal" to their Western critics. I got the necessary papers within a couple of weeks.

17. Though some Western countries, notably America, insisted that this did not affect their non-recognition policy toward the occupation of the Baltic states.

18. Latvia and Russia finalized a border treaty in December 2007, after Latvia, controversially, agreed to Russian demands that it drop all mention of pre-war statehood.

19. Even Belarus enjoyed a few months of independence in 1918. A government-in-exile descended from those few months of statehood maintains an exiguous presence to this day. See "Home thoughts from abroad," *Economist,* December 20 2001, http://www.economist.com/world/africa/displayStory.cfm?Story_ID=883955, and "The Sorrows of Belarus" (online only), *Europe View,* November 16 2006, http://www.economist.com/agenda/displayStory.cfm?story_id=8171305&fsrc=RSS

20. This would mean not only free elections, but the lifting of restrictions on independent organizations, the media, and opposition political parties; the withdrawal of Russian troops, military intelligence and weapons; and the end of illegal economic activities such as counterfeiting, trafficking, and smuggling. It is worth noting that Moldova is no paragon in these respects either.

21. By mid-2007, the outlines of that seemed to be taking shape. On July 20, Moldova's president Vladimir Voronin admitted to having worked out with Putin a secret, albeit tentative, deal. This apparently includes an eventual withdrawal of Russian troops after a political settlement involving new elections and a guaranteed (and seemingly disproportionately generous) number of seats for Transdniestrian deputies. The Transdniestrian side would also get a guaranteed deputy minister in each ministry and the region's leader would have an ex-officio position in the government. If implemented, that would cripple Moldova's already feeble efforts to reform its public institutions. Transdniestria is the epitome of Russian-style capitalism, where the security forces, politics, and business merge into an almost seamless complex of wealth and power. In return, Russia will remove the current Transdniestrian leadership—no

doubt to a luxurious retirement somewhere in Russia—and will reopen its markets to Moldovan wine. However, by the end of the year outside pressure seemed to have derailed, or at least stalled, this deal.

22. Who made up barely a fifth of the population in their nominal homeland.

23. I went to visit a new finance minister once, who was being energetically promoted by the ever-optimistic American Embassy. His office was bright, modern, and computerized. We had an enjoyable chat about e-government and zero-based budgeting. It was pretty clear that his talents were not matched by political clout. As I left, I used an old journalist's trick and asked to use the restroom, saying that I would find my own way out. Not only was the toilet worse than a midden, but my detour to some of the other offices produced a much more convincing picture: a warren of ill-lit and dingy offices, each filled with rickety wooden furniture. Dumpy little men in ill-fitting brown suits were engaged in chain-smoking conversation with thickset men in leather jackets. Not a computer was in sight, and bare light bulbs dangled from the ceilings.

24. A detailed account of Saakashvili's peace plans and other efforts can be found at "Georgia: Tbilisi Ups The Ante Over South Ossetia," Liz Fuller, March 29 2007. http://rfe.rferl.org/featuresarticle/2007/03/86b14f63-bd12–470b-a459–2fdf9a4d1183.html

25. Known as Borjomi, Georgia's pungent sulfurated mineral water is an acquired taste. It was one of the best-selling bottled drinks in the Soviet Union. The natural park in which it is extracted was vandalized by Russian troops in August 2008.

26. Putin compared the Georgian action to the policies of Stalin's KGB chief, Lavrenti Beria. See, for example, Peter Finn, "Putin and Georgia Officials Intensify Rhetoric in Dispute: President Calls Russians' Arrests 'State Terrorism,'" *Washington Post*, October 2 2006, A16, http://www.washingtonpost.com/wp-dyn/content/article/2006/10/01/AR2006 100100898_pf.html; or in Russian: http://www.rg.ru/2006/10/02/prezident .html;http://www.vsesmi.ru/news/134556/;http://www.annews.ru/news/detail.php?ID =32208&print=Y

27. Russian officials singled out Georgians as illegal immigrants; police in Moscow started carrying out spot checks of documents of people congregating near places such as the Georgian Embassy and church. At some schools in Moscow, the police demanded lists of children with ethnic Georgian surnames. This would be as absurd as trying to round up Irish citizens in Britain or America simply on the basis of their surname. Grigory Chkhartishvili, for example, is a successful author of detective stories under the pen name Boris Akunin. Seemingly for no reason other than his distinctive surname, his publisher's offices were raided by the tax police. According to a report by Human Rights Watch, some 2,380 Georgians were expelled in the next two months, while some 2,200 others left by their own means after receiving deportation orders. An unknown number of other Georgians simply decided it would be better to leave. Some Georgians were indeed in Russia illegally, but those deported included Russian citizens of Georgian ethnic background, and Georgians with valid visas and work permits. Those detained had little right of appeal or access to lawyers, and either "perfunctory" court hearings (in the report's words) or none at all. Conditions during the deportations were often harsh and sometimes abominable. According to Human Rights Watch, some detainees were deprived of food and water for extended periods of time, or told to drink from the toilet bowl. Medical care was routinely denied, leading to at least two deaths, those of Manana Jabelia and Tengiz Togonidze. Though the anti-Georgian campaign ebbed as quickly as it swelled, the way in which Kremlin-sponsored xenophobia has leached into every corner of Russian life was alarmingly clear. See "Singled Out: Russia's Detention and Expulsion of Georgians," *Human Rights Watch Report*, Volume 19, No. 5(D), October 2007, http://hrw.org/reports/2007/russia1007/russia1007web.pdf

28. The same happened with the Baltic states in the early 1990s. Russian economic sanctions and energy blockages simply accelerated the reorientation toward other markets.

29. The same twisted logic was used in the aftermath of the Litvinenko poisoning, when the Russian Embassy in London blamed Berezovsky. Marc Champion, "Georgian Incident Deepens Russia Rift," *Wall Street Journal*, July 4 2007. http://online.wsj.com/article/SB118350332439357187.html?mod=googlenews_wsj.

30. Olga Allenova and Fedor Maximov, "Georgia Identifies Russian Missile—And Destroys It on the Spot," *Kommersant*, August 9 2007. http://www.kommersant.ru/doc.aspx?DocsID=793939 and in English on http://intellibriefs.blogspot.com/2007/08/georgia-identifies-russian-missile.html

31. One of many excellent reports on Georgia by Vladimir Socor caustically describes the international reaction. Vladimir Socor, "Moscow Pleased with OSCE's Response to Missile Drop on Georgia," Tuesday, September 11 2007, Jamestown Foundation. http://www.jamestown.org/edm/article.php?volume_id=420&issue_id=4223&article_id=2372410

32. In December the prosecutor-general produced evidence that Patarkatsishvili had been planning a coup. Audio and video recordings appeared to show a senior interior ministry official being bribed to help a coup on the day after the election. Patarkatsishvili was found dead at his home in Britain, apparently from a heart attack, on February 12. Conspiracy theorists had a field day.

33. "US Says Doubts Russia Involved in Georgia Strife," Reuters, November 13 2007, http://www.reuters.com/article/worldNews/idUSL1367375720071113, and "Crossing the Line: Georgia's Violent Dispersal of Protestors and Raid on Imedi Television," http://hrw.org/reports/2007/georgia1207/

34. OSCE/ODIHR Election Observation Mission Final Report, Warsaw, March 4 2008. http://www.osce.org/documents/odihr/2008/03/29982_en.pdf

35. Vladimir Socor, "Moscow Makes Furious but Empty Threats to Georgia and Ukraine," Jamestown Foundation, April 14 2008.http://www.jamestown.org/edm/article.php?volume_id=427&issue_id=4454&article_id=2372968

36. See "Russia Shot Down Georgia Drone," April 21 2008. http://news.bbc.co.uk/1/hi/world/europe/7358761.stm

37. A shorthand reference for the issues surrounding the four unrecognized statelets of Transdniestria, Nagorno-Karabakh, South Ossetia, and Abkhazia, all of which date from the wars fought as the Soviet Union was collapsing.

38. The arguments were well outlined in an article (not by this author) in the *Economist*, "South Ossetia is not Kosovo," August 28 2008. http://www.economist.com/opinion/displaystory.cfm?story_id=12009678

39. Pavel Felgenhauer, "It Was No Spontaneous, But Planned War," *Novaya Gazeta*, August 18 2008. http://en.novayagazeta.ru/data/2008/59/01.html

40. "Neftegazovaia Diplomatia kak Ugroza Marginalizatsii," *Nezavisimaya Gazeta*, December 28 2004.

41. Although that number was probably exaggerated, and many millions have since returned to Russia or changed their ethnic self-description.

42. "Military Doctrine of the Russian Federation, confirmed by Decree of President of the Russian Federation VV Putin no. 706, 21 April 2000" (in Russian). http://www.iss.niiit.ru/doktrins/doktr02.htm

43. *Annual Address to the Federal Assembly of the Russian Federation*, April 3 2001, Moscow.

44. Nikolai Patrushev, head of the FSB, said in 2005: "NGOs must not be allowed to engage in any activity they like." He suggested a CIS-wide legal code be brought in to regulate their activity "before the wave of Orange Revolutions spreads." "Patrushev: Foreign secret services are preparing new 'Colored Revolutions'" (in Russian), May 12 2005. http://www.novopol.ru/print2355.html

45. Sometimes these are so preposterous that it is hard to imagine anyone believing them. In 2005, for example, the now defunct www.news24.ru reported that the riots in suburban Paris had been incited by "Estonian nationalists." When Estonia's justice minister, Rein Lang, marked his birthday with a private performance of a satirical play

about Hitler, *Adolf*, by Pip Utton, Russian websites reported this as if the minister had celebrated his birthday by staging a Nazi rally: Aleksander Mikhailov, "Estonian Minister on [his] Birthday 'invites' Hitler," *Komsomolskaya Pravda*, July 6 2006. http://www.kp.ru/daily/23929.4/69696/. Lang responded here: "Estonian Minister Accuses Russia of Cultivating Nazism," *Rosbalt*, Tallinn, July 9 2007 (no byline). http://www.rosbalt.ru/2007/7/27/400684.html

46. The *Tiraspol Times*, for example, pumps out propaganda on behalf of the separatist regime in Transdniestria. It purports to be a normal newspaper, with an online edition that carries pictures of a printed version and a glossy weekly review. Anyone looking at it would think it was another one of the many English-language papers to be found throughout Eastern Europe, where eager-beaver tyros straight out of journalism school scratch a living under the direction of hard-bitten locals. The truth is rather stranger. None of the journalists who purportedly work in the "newsroom" seem to have any verifiable existence outside the paper's web pages. The paper publishes no address or phone number. No real-world journalist in either Transdniestria or Moldova has ever seen a representative from the *Tiraspol Times* at any public event – even those that are reported, seemingly first-hand, in its pages. Nor, indeed, has any Western embassy or other official source I contacted in the region ever seen a physical copy of the paper: it appears to exist only in online form. The paper's finances are mysterious: it carries very little advertising, and does not appear to take any subscriptions. Its publisher is an elusive Irishman called Des Grant with his own (real-world) media business in that country and a romantic connection to Transdniestria. He says the paper gets money from "sponsors" but declines to provide any further details. A bit of internet detective work shows that the website is registered at a real address in the Transdniestrian capital, Tiraspol – but on inspection this proves to be shared by a hotel and the headquarters of one of the main local political parties. At neither place does anyone know anything of the *Tiraspol Times*. Still stranger was the "International Council for Democratic Institutions and State Sovereignty" (ICDISS), which claimed to be a heavyweight think tank based in Washington, D.C. It had an impressive website, and had produced a heavily footnoted report, seemingly authored by distinguished international lawyers, that backed the Transdniestrian regime's case for international recognition. It even had a Wikipedia entry, cross-referenced to other real-world organizations. Russian-language media in the region gleefully took up the report, arguing that it showed that international opinion was shifting in the Kremlin's direction. On closer examination, this proved little more substantial than the *Tiraspol Times*. The ICDISS's "officers" proved to be just as elusive as the inhabitants of that paper's "newsroom." Nobody was willing to talk on the phone; e-mails provided only a series of ever more evasive excuses. The published report – which seemed to be the only one ever produced by the organization – had lifted large chunks of a quite different document, dealing with a different international legal issue. The international lawyers cited in the report angrily denied having had anything to do with it; shortly afterward, the document disappeared from the ICDISS website. It was hard to avoid the conclusion that a sophisticated disinformation exercise had been tripped up by its own overconfidence. http://www.economist.com/world/europe/displaystory.cfm?story_id=E1_SNVNJSQ and "Covering tracks" (web only), in the *Economist*, August 3 2006. http://www.economist.com/world/europe/displaystory.cfm?story_id=E1_SNV RVPQ

47. Under international law, it is prohibited for the occupying power to settle its population in the territories concerned. The Soviet Union, of course, did not regard the Baltic republics as occupied.

48. In the borders of the current Estonia the figure was still higher, around 96 percent. The 8 percent pre-war Russian minority lived largely in the areas transferred to the Russian Federation in 1945.

49. Trying to buy some stamps in the main post office in Tallinn in early 1990, a clerk told me to "talk like a human being" when I spoke Estonian – in theory an official language.

50. Certainly more could be done to speed integration. The big efforts made in the 1990s have tailed off. The current Estonian government is so focused on economic growth that it tends to ignore social issues. But Russia is not interested in the practicalities of integration. It does nothing to encourage non-citizens in Estonia to learn the language. In fact it barely supports them at all. What the Kremlin does do is stoke ethnic disharmony, in the hope of undermining the Estonian government.

51. See (the punningly headlined) "Our [Nashi] Facts to Their Arguments," *Rossiskaya Gazeta,* May 3 2007. http://www.rg.ru/2007/05/03/nashi.html

52. Ibid., and "The Ambassador of Estonia Slinks out of Moscow. Nashi Lifts Siege of Embassy" (not bylined). http://www.newsru.com/russia/03may2007/marina.html

53. Also "Russia Blasts Exhumation of Soviet Soldiers in Tallinn," *RIA Novosti,* April 26 2006. http://en.rian.ru/russia/20070426/64459134.html, and Vladimir Socor, "Russian Authorities, Media Inflame Situation in Estonia," Jamestown Foundation, *Eurasia Daily Monitor,* May 2 2007. http://www.jamestown.org/edm/article.php?article_id=23 72137

54. "Pobedy snova nastupayet data. Vpered! Na Tallin Zashchitim Soldata" (The Date of Victory Begins Again. Forward! To Tallinn! Let Us Defend the Soldier) by Ksenophont Prirodny, *Komsomolskaya Pravda,* May 3 2007. http://www.kp.ru/daily/23896.3/66766. Author's translation.

55. The *Sluzhba Vneshnei Razvedki* is the renamed First Chief Directorate of the KGB, Putin's old employer.

56. "Speech at Meeting with Senior Officers from the Armed Forces and Security Service," July 25 2007. http://kremlin.ru/appears/2007/07/25/1845_type63376_138512.shtml (in Russian only).

57. The main idea to remember is "botnets." These are remotely controlled networks of computers that have been hijacked, usually by means of virus-infected e-mails, and then used to swamp the target by deluging it with internet traffic: imagine a website that normally handles a few hundred visitors a minute, which then experiences thousands every second. Luckily, Estonia's internet capabilities are excellent. The only point at which lives could have been endangered was when, for a brief period, the cyberattacks managed to knock out the telephone number for the emergency services. But they did not succeed in disrupting electric power, or making sewage pumping stations run backwards, or any of the other nightmarish scenarios that preoccupy cyberwarfare experts.

58. http://www.wired.com/politics/security/magazine/15-09/ff_estonia has an extensive account of the incident.

59. This results from an arbitrary decision by Nikita Khrushchev in 1954 to transfer Crimea from the largely notional Russian Federation to the Ukrainian Soviet Socialist Republic. See "The Transfer of the Crimea to Ukraine," http://www.iccrimea.org/historical/crimeatransfer.html

60. Communist and pro-Moscow groups won an overwhelming victory in regional elections in March 2006. Aided by FSB and GRU officials, and family members linked to the Russian naval base at Sevastopol, pro-Kremlin Crimean politicians organized highly successful mass demonstrations against NATO exercises planned for June of that year. These exercises, involving drills for peacekeeping and emergency relief, had taken place in Ukraine since 1997 without attracting significant opposition. The protests spread to other Russian-speaking regions of eastern Ukraine, which declared themselves to be "NATO-free zones." Supporters of the defeated candidate in the 2004 presidential elections, Viktor Yanukovych, began to copy the tactics of their "Orange" adversaries, adopting the color blue and organizing rallies featuring pop music, celebrity endorsements, and other razzmatazz. Their most powerful weapon was defending the status of the Russian language, which under Soviet rule had driven Ukrainian out of public life, to the point that even speaking it in Kyiv was a strong political statement. Since independence, Ukrainian has made a comeback in central Ukraine, but remains a minority language in the Russified east of the country. Although the two languages are closely related (more so than Spanish and Portuguese, for example) older

and less educated Russian speakers fear that a "nationalist" government may some-how penalize them for a failure to speak Ukrainian. After all, say pro-Russian propa-gandists, that is exactly what happened in the Baltic states. The Crimea protests added an extra political burden to the already flimsy chances of forming a pro-West-ern governing coalition at national level in Kyiv. As soon as that coalition's chances collapsed, paving the way for a different, more pro-Russian administration, the protests abruptly stopped. Another possible flashpoint is eastern Ukraine. Russian speakers there have so far proved hard to ignite. But with a really serious political cri-sis in Kyiv, that might change: for example, Russia might covertly back an ultra-nationalist party in order to stoke separatist sentiment in the eastern part of the country.

61. Another ingredient is in some countries a sharp disregard for what Western Europe sees as the elementary values of a liberal society at home and abroad. Poland in partic-ular has attracted criticism for its clumsy and abrasive diplomacy. The country's pres-ident Lech Kaczynski, for example, scandalized Western opinion at an EU summit in 2007 by arguing for greater voting weights for Poland, on the grounds that, had it not been for Germany's actions in the Second World War, his country's population would now be 50 percent larger. That may be true, but it is a world away from the polite and tactful tones in which EU meetings are normally conducted. Such behavior confirms the world-weary West European stereotype that the new members of the EU are prickly and unpredictable – in short, perhaps not quite as civilized as the "old" mem-bers. Or, more fairly, less used to the rules.

62. Mark Landler, "Putin Prompts Split in German Coalition," *New York Times*, May 22 2007. http://www.nytimes.com/2007/05/22/world/europe/22europe.html?_r=1&n =Top/News/World/Countries%20and%20 Territories/Russia&oref=slogin

63. See Robert Amsterdam, "Druzhba Shut Down – Europe Cut Off from Russian Oil" (blog), January 8 2007, http://www.robertamsterdam.com/2007/01/druzhba_shut _down_europe_cut_o.htm; "Russia Halts Oil Deliveries to Germany," Energy Wars, *Der Spiegel*, January 8 2007, http://www.spiegel.de/international/0,1518,458401,00 .html; and "Merkel, EU's Barolo Condemn Russian Pipeline Shut-Off," Europe's En-ergy Worries, *Der Spiegel*, January 9 2007, http://www.spiegel.de/international/0,1518 ,458573,00.html; and in Russian, "Veto na Druzhbu" (Veto on Druzhba), by Andrei Lavrov, 14 May 2005, http://portnews.ru/digest/2637/

64. Quote taken from Baltic Business News (BBN Newsletter), July 24 2007, http://www .balticbusinessnews.com/newsletter/070724_bbn_news letter.pdf. Last accessed July 2007, this link now appears to be dead.

65. Robert L. Larsson, *Russia's Energy Policy: Security Dimensions and Russia's Reliability as an Energy Supplier*, FOI, Stockholm, 2006), www.foi.se

66. When the Estonian government convened a high-level seminar to discuss energy secu-rity, it invited as a matter of course a representative from the national gas company, Eesti Gaas. The invitation was accepted – but then an embarrassed company official phoned back so say that it would not be taking part on instructions from a share-holder: Gazprom.

CHAPTER 7

1. Vladimir Putin, *Strategicheskoye planirovaniye vosproizvodstva mineralno-syryevoy bazy regiona v usloviyakh formirovaniya rynochnykh otnosheniy* (The strategic plan-ning of the reproduction of the mineral raw materials base of the region under condi-tions of the formation of market relationships) (St. Petersburg, Russia: State Mining Institute, 1997). The American scholar Clifford Gaddy has produced interesting evi-dence that suggests the book is in fact heavily plagiarized. David Johnson, "'It All Boils Down to Plagiarism' [re: Putin dissertation]," interview with Brookings Senior Fellow Clifford Gaddy, Washington Profile, Johnson's Russia List, March 31, http://www.cdi .org/russia/johnson/2006–78–3a.cfm.

2. Ariel Cohen, "How to Confront Russia's Anti-American Foreign Policy," Issue Paper, Heritage Foundation (Washington, D.C.), June 27, 2007, http://www.heritage.org /Research/RussiaandEurasia/bg2048.cfm.

3. Quoted in Michael Fredholm, *Gazprom in Crisis: Putin's Quest for State Planning and Russia's Growing National Gas Deficit* (Swindon, UK: Conflict Studies Research Centre, 2006).

4. Liquefied natural gas (LNG) is compressed gas that can be carried by tanker. Though the compression and decompression are expensive, it can be traded freely, unlike pipeline gas, which is almost always delivered under a long-term contract.

5. *World Oil and Gas Review 2006*, "Natural Gas: International Trade—Imports by country of origin—Europe" (table), Eni S.p.A, http://www.eni.it/wogr_2006/gas-international_trade-81.htm.

6. See, for example, European Union–Russia Energy Dialogue Overview, European Commission, http://ec.europa.eu/energy/russia/overview/index_en.htm; and Christian Cleutinx, "The EU-Russia Energy Dialogue" (PDF presentation), European Commission, 2004, http://ec.europa.eu/energy/russia/presentations/doc/2004_berlin _en.pdf.

7. RIA Novosti (in Russian) June 7, 2007, Rossiya ne budet _____ ratifitsirovat Energeticheskuyu khartiyu v nyneshnem vide (Russia will not ratify energy charter in forseeable future). http://www.rian.ru/world/world_community/20070607/66873834 .html See also Putin's remarks in this Prime-Tass report (in Russian) December 7 2006, "V Putin says Russia will not ratify treaty on energy charter until EU settles disputed questions" http://www.prime-tass.ru/news/show.asp?id=646546&ct=news http: //www.prime-tass.ru/news/show.asp?id=646546&ct=news RIA Novosti report in the Vedomosti newspaper, June 20, 2006. "Russia is not ready thus far to ratify the Energy Charter" http://www.vedomosti.ru/newsline/index.shtml?2006/06/20/279956

8. See Agata Loskot-Strachota, *Russian Gas for Europe* (Warsaw, Poland: Centre for Eastern Studies, 2006); and Katinka Barysch, "Russia, Realism, and EU Unity," policy brief, Centre for European Reform, July 2004, http://www.cer.org.uk/pdf/policybrief_russia _FINAL_20july07.pdf.

9. See Barysch, "Russia, Realism, and EU Unity," and also Paul Belkin, "The European Union's Energy Security Challenges," The European Union Energy Security Challenges, CRS Report for Congress, Congress Research Service, May 7, 2007, http://fas .org/sgp/crs/row/RL33636.pdf.

10. Quoted in Barysch, "Russia, Realism, and EU Unity." The American software giant has been engaged in a lengthy wrangle with the EU over allegedly monopolistic features of its Windows software.

11. See Nord Stream's home page at: http://www.nord-stream.com. http://www.ewi.uni-koeln.de/fileadmin/user/WPs/ewiwp0702.pdf

12. See the Nabucco gas pipeline project at: http://www.nabucco-pipeline.com/.

13. The speech can be viewed on 'Victims of Communism: Rep Lantos—part 2' http: //youtube.com/watch?v=2EZ4QMjh2zo

14. Ariel Cohen, "The North European Gas Pipeline Threatens Europe's Energy Security," *Backgrounder,* The Heritage Foundation, October 26, 2006, no. 1980, http://www .heritage.org/Research/Europe/upload/bg_1980.pdf (p.4).

15. Though Russia's embassy in the heart of Stockholm is probably a more effective listening station than anything that could be built at sea.

16. Roman Kupchinsky, "Russia/Belarus: Is a Gas War Brewing?," RadioFreeEurope RadioLiberty, April 3, 2006, http://www.rferl.org/featuresarticle/2006/04/04805ae4-dc2a –401c–83e2-d85524b4d90d.html; and (in Russian) Putin: Ukraine can buy gas at market prices. (unbylined) Newsru.com December 9, 2005 http://www.newsru.com /finance/08dec2005/putingas.html

17. Cha "Polish DM Likens Pipeline Deal To Nazi-Soviet Pact," Reuters, April 30, 2006, via http://www.rferl.org/featuresarticle/2006/04/eb61f3cc–87b2–4bf2-a572–4175d1663f 7e.html

18. Robert L. Larsson, "Nord Stream, Sweden, and Baltic Sea Security" (Base data report), March 2007, FOI, http://www.ffa.se/upload/english/reports/foir2251.pdf (p. 27).

19. Andrea Mrozek, "Playmates or Politicians? The German Media Is Put Out by the Chancellor's Conduct in Moscow," *Central Europe Review*, 3, no. 2 (2001), http://www.ce-review.org/01/2/germanypress2.html; and http://fazarchiv.faz.net/web cgi?WID=59433–2780937–22101_1.

20. 'I v sluzhbu, i v druzhbu: Tovarishch Vladimira Putina budet upravlyat rossiisko-germanskim gazoprovodom' (Both in the service, and in friendship: Comrade Vladimir Putin will run the Russian-German gas pipeline). Kommersant, December 9, 2005. http://www.kommersant.ru/doc.aspx?DocsID=633868

21. Vladimir Socor, "New Gas Trader to Boost Turkmenistan-Ukraine Transit," *Eurasia Daily Monitor*, The Jamestown Foundation, 1, no 64 (2004), http://jamestown.org /edm/article.php?article_id=2368342. Zeyno Baran Senior Fellow and Director of the Center for Eurasian Policy, Hudson Institute, testimony to United States House of Representatives Committee on Foreign Affairs "Central and Eastern Europe: Assessing the Democratic Transition" July 25, 200

22. Robert L. Larsson, "Nord Stream, Sweden, and Baltic Sea Security," (Base data report), March 2007, FOI, http://www.ffa.se/upload/english/reports/foir2251.pdf (p. 33).

23. See, for example, Carl Mortished's article, "Gazprom to Raise its Own Private Army to Protect Oil Installations," *The Times* (UK), July 5, 2007, http://business.timesonline .co.uk/tol/business/industry_sectors/natural_resources/article2029023.ece; >>> Edward Lucas 29/10/07 14:55 >>>

24. Germany lobbied hard to ensure that Poland, despite its evident unreadiness in some respects, was included in the first wave of EU enlargement in 2004.

25. At the request of the previous German chancellor, Helmut Schmidt, America was planning to base Cruise and Pershing nuclear missiles in Europe. By putting part of America's nuclear arsenal in Europe, the idea was to make the NATO nuclear deterrent more credible, and the Warsaw Pact's overwhelming superiority in conventional forces less threatening. But by the time the missiles were actually deployed in the early 1980s, German public opinion was far more worried about the dangers of nuclear weapons than the threat from the east.

26. Klaus Margold, "Russia and German Investors," International Politik, DGAP, http://en .internationalepolitik.de/archiv/200/fall2000/russia-and-german—investors.html.

27. As opposed to the "Weimar Triangle." See http://www.diplomatie.gouv.fr/en/ country-files_156/germany_335/the-weimar-triangle_3451/the-weimar-meetings _4339.html.

28. Deripaska pokupayet 30% aktsii avstriiskoi stroitelnoi kompanii Strabag za 1.2 mldr evro (Deripaska buys 30% of the shares of the Austrian construction company Strabag for 1.2 billion euro) 25 April 2007, Newsu.com (unbylined) http://palm.newsru.com/finance/25apr2007/strabag.html In May 2007, Deripaska acquired a $1.5 billion stake in Magna, a Canadian car parts manufacturer, and is reported to have a 5 percent stake in America's General Motors. See (in Russian) this report from Vedomosti, Oleg Deripaska buys chunk of General Motors August 7, 2007, via http://auto.lenta.ru/news/2007/08/07/deripaska/.

29. http://www.aktuell.ru/russland/wirtschaft/putin_schroeder_und_russland_auf_der _hannover_messe_1096.html.

30. Quoted in Yulia Latynina's column "Sochi Doesn't Mean Retreat for Merkel" in the Moscow Times, Wednesday, January 24, 2007. Page 8.

31. http://www.moscowtimes.ru/stories/2007/01/24/007.html

32. See Ariel Cohen, "The North European Gas Pipeline Threatens Europe's Energy Security," *Backgrounder*, The Heritage Foundation, October 26, 2006, no. 1980, http://www .heritage.org/Research/Europe/bg1980.cfm.

33. See, for example, Vladimir Socor, "More Problems For Russo-German Gas Pipeline Project" (*Eurasia Daily Monitor*, The Jamestown Foundation, August 16, 2007, http: //www.jamestown.org/edm/article.php?article_id=2372380); and "Looking for oil

and gas around the globe," Wintershall prospectus (PI–07–04, March 23, 2007, http://www.wintershall.com/pi–07–04.98.html).

34. Andrew E. Kramer, "Gazprom Grows in Europe: New Gas Deal with BASF Extends its Reach," International Herald Tribune, April 28, 2006, http://www.iht.com/articles/2006/04/27/business/rusgas.php.

35. Weeks later Rosneft tried a similar deal, offering Royal Dutch Shell access to the Severo–Komsomolsk onshore oil field in return for the Western company's stake in Germany's largest oil-industry complex, MIRO, to Russia's Rosneft. If that goes ahead, it will mark the first big investment by a Kremlin firm in Europe's private-sector oil industry.

36. Commission de Régulation de l'Electricité et du Gaz

37. "Purvanov: Bulgaria will join South Stream" RIA Novosti June 24, 2007 (in Russian) http://www.rian.ru/economy/20070624/67725613.html

38. Vsem stranam Yugo-Vostochnoi Evropy dolzhen byt obespechen garantirovannyi dostup k energoresursam—Putin (All countries of south-eastern Europe should be guaranteed access to energy resources—Putin) Interfax (in Russian) June 24, 2007 http://interfax.ru/r/B/politics/2.html?menu=21&id_issue=11774951

39. "Hungary Fully Behind Nabucco Pipeline" (blog), CafeBabel.com, September 17, 2007, http://budapest.cafebabel.com/en/post/2007/09/17/Hungary-fully-behind-Nabucco-pipeline

40. Gazprom in Austria: new perspectives (in Russian) RIA Novosti May 24, 2007 http://www.rian.ru/analytics/20070524/66054411.html

41. The move was little surprise to those who remember Austria's chummy relations with the Soviet Union during the old Cold War, when Vienna was a playground for eastern bloc intelligence agents. After the collapse of communism, the Austrian capital offered a warm welcome to Russians wanting to polish their legitimate credentials—Austria, almost alone in Europe, offered anonymous bank accounts. The Austrian state, which still owns a 31 percent stake in OMV, was the first capitalist country to buy gas from the Soviet Union.

42. Judy Dempsey, "In Hungary, an Energy Battle with Russian Overtones," International Herald Tribune, August 9, 2007, http://www.iht.com/articles/2007/08/09/bloomberg/energy.php.

43. Some senior foreign business executives' behavior toward Russia is barely explicable except in terms of the expectation of future rewards. For a Western oil company boss, a decision has only to be defensible, rather than correct, in order to get past shareholders' scrutiny now and open the way to a lucrative consulting contract with a Russian company once the brief stint at the top is over.

44. Vladimir Milov, "Russian Oil & Gas Industries in the Greenfield Challenge Limbo," (PowerPoint presentation), Institute of Energy Policy, Moscow, June 26, 2007, www.energypolicy.ru/files/milov%20June26–2007.ppt.

45. Alan Riley, "The Coming of the Russian Gas Deficit: Consequences and Solutions," Centre for European Policy Studies, CEPS Policy Brief, no. 116, October 2006, http://www.city.ac.uk/law/dps/Dept_dps/riley_papers/CEPSGasDeficitPaperFinal.pdf.

46. Scott G. Borgerson, "An Ice-Cold War," August 8, 2007 New York Times www.nytimes.com/2007/08/08/opinion/08borgerson.html

47. Russia plants flag under N Pole BBC News August 2, 2007. http://news.bbc.co.uk/1/hi/world/europe/6927395.stm

48. Douglas Birch, The Associated Press, Wednesday, August 1, 2007

CHAPTER 8

1. For extensive information about Russia's military forces, the site www.warfare.ru (in English and Russian) is strongly recommended.

2. The Center for Defense Information ("Nuclear Proliferation: Russian Nuclear Arsenal" [table], April 30, 2007, http://www.cdi.org/friendlyversion/printversion.cfm?documentID=2967) gives an up-to-date summary.

3. http://www.roe.ru/ is the home page.

4. http://www.prime-tass.ru/news/show.asp?id=611581&ct=news. *U. Chaves priznalsya V.Putinu v lyubi k Rossiyu* (Chavez professes his love of Russia to Putin), unbylined, Prime-Tass July 27, 2006

5. Russia Targets Missile Defense, Stephen Blank *Perspective,* 17, no. 4, Institute for the Study of Conflict, Ideology and Policy, Boston University, July-August 2007. http://www.bu.edu/iscip/vol17/Blank2.html

6. "Drop your silly Atlantic solidarity and support us, Putin tells West" Michael Binyon. The Times (London) September 15, 2007 http://www.timesonline.co.uk/tol/news/world/europe/article2436902.ece

7. *Davno Nazrevshaya Neobkhodimost* (The Long Overdue Necessity) Yuri Fyoderov, PIR (Center for Policy Studies) Moscow, http://www.pircenter.org/data/news/fedorov_u200804.pdf

8. Poslanie Polupreyemnikam (Message to Semi-Successors) April 26, 2007, by Aleksei Lebchenko and Alya Samigulina http://www.gazeta.ru/2007/04/26/oa_237723.shtml.

9. "Russia: CFE 'Moratorium' Causes Consternation in Europe," RadioFreeEurope RadioLiberty, April 27, 2007, http://www.rferl.org/featuresarticle/2007/4/F33954AF-D1B2-491E-823E-40D8197C7E22.html.

10. The treaty text is on http://www.fas.org/nuke/control/cfe/text/cfe_t.htm

11. Pavel Felgenhauer, "Putin Cancels CFE until NATO Countries Properly 'Adhere' to its Provisions," *Eurasia Daily Monitor,* The Jamestown Foundation, 4, no 86 (2007), http://www.jamestown.org/edm/article.php?article_id=2372138.

12. *Putanitsa malogo I srednego radius* (Confusion of the small and mean radius) by Rose Gottemoeller, Nezavisimaya Gazeta May 3, 2005 http://www.ng.ru/courier/2007-03-05/13_munhen.html.

13. Victor Yasmann, "Russia: Moscow Content to Block Kosovo Resolution," RadioFreeEurope RadioLiberty, July 13, 2007, http://www.rferl.org/featuresarticle/2007/07/27947831-dfcd-4d49-afec-77455719385e.html; (in Russian) MID *Rossii ne soglasen s novoi rezolyutsei po Kosovo* (Russia's MFA does not agree with new resolution on Kosovo)

14. Dmitri Trenin's arguments are well-expressed in his book *Getting Russia Right* (Washington, D.C.: Carnegie Endowment for International Peace, 2007).

15. The two bases were the Lourdes eavesdropping post in Cuba and the Cam Ranh naval base in Vietnam. Russia retains bases in the CIS Commonwealth of Independent States including two in Belarus (a radio station for communicating with its submarine fleet and an anti-missile radar). It is now restoring a semi-derelict naval base in Syria.

16. *Kolenopreklonennoye Gosudarstvo* (Genuflection state) by Vladimir Osipov, on both http://www.rv.ru/content.php3?id=806 and http://www.rus-imperia.com/2_2002/politic3.htm.

17. See, for example, *Vchera v OON prikhodil dyavol. Do sikh por pakhnyot seroi* (Yesterday the devil arrived at the United Nations) Izvestia, Georgi Stepanov, September 21 2006 http://www.izvestia.ru/world/article3096827/.

18. Dmitri Trenin Russia and Israel: A Snapshot of the Relationship against the Regional Backdrop July 16, 2007. http://www.carnegie.ru/en/pubs/media/76545.htm.

19. The Tango with Islam, Aleksei Malashenko, published originally in *Nezavisimaya Gazeta,* and available at Moscow Carnegie Center http://www.carnegie.ru/en/pubs/media/76059.htm.

20. http://www.zavtra.ru/cgi/veil/data/zavtra/07/694/11.html. Zavtra, March 7, 2007. *Israil ne vygral ni odnoi voiny* (Israel never won a single war) Hamas leader Khaled Mashal interviewed by editor-in-chief Aleksander Prokhanov

21. Mikhail Fradkov now heads the SVR.

22. "Russia-China trade to hit $32–34 bln in 2006 – ambassador" on RIA Novosti October 25, 2006, http://en.rian.ru/russia/20061025/55110192.html

23. Naazneen Barma, Ely Ratner, and Steven Weber, "Report and Retort: A World Without the West," National Interest Online, July 1, 2007, http://www.nationalinterest.org/General.aspx?id=92&id2=14798.
24. "Peace Mission 2007 and the S.C.O. Summit," Power and Interest News Report, August 10, 2007, http://www.pinr.com/report.php?ac=view_report&report_id=672&language_id=1.
25. Putin: *sravnenie SHOS c Organizatsei Varshavskogo dogovora eto boltovna* (Putin: comparing the SCO to the Warsaw Pact is [idle] chatter. RIA Novosto June 16, 2006 (unbylined) http://www.rian.ru/world/20060616/49576897.html.
26. http://www.moscowtimes.ru/stories/2005/08/15/007.html. At the Edge of the Middle Kingdom, Andrei Piontkovsky, *Moscow Times,* August 15, 2005.

CHAPTER 9

1. That would automatically exclude companies such as Itera and Rosukrenergo.
2. The natural organization to deal with this is the Paris-based Organisation for Economic Co-operation and Development (OECD). This has already developed from being a think tank that mainly produces statistics to becoming a global guardian of good economic policy in the widest sense. It includes all the world's advanced economies and, crucially, Russia is not a member. The OECD is therefore in a perfect position to set new tough rules on corporate governance and access to global financial markets, and then monitor their observance. Just as gangsters cannot expect to use the global financial system to launder cash, the kleptocrats of the Kremlin should not be able to use it to launder assets.
3. Katinka Barysch, "Three Questions that Europe Must Ask about Russia," Centre for European Reform Briefing Note, www.cer.org.uk/pdf/briefing_russia_16may07_kb.pdf.
4. That does not mean making visa applications harder for ordinary Russians. But it should be harder for those connected with the Kremlin and other branches of law-breaking Russian officialdom and business. Gazprom and Rosneft would find their access to international capital markets much harder if their senior executives were unable to visit the United States, Britain, or Germany.
5. It is important not to be too sentimental. The old Cold War may have been the struggle of good against evil at a global level, but the West had plenty to be ashamed of in the details: the support for corrupt and authoritarian dictators in the third world; bully-boy tactics against left-wingers in Europe and America; and the cynical conflation of Western economic interests with the wider cause of freedom were among the most salient shortcomings.
6. Left-wingers protesting against martial law in Poland in 1981 used the slogan "Russian tanks, Western banks, Hands off Poland!" which equated the Western bankers—admittedly greedy and naïve—who were trying to recover the $20 billion they had ill-advisedly lent the regime with a communist dictatorship responsible for the deaths of many tens of thousands of people. A more recent example is the way that such commentators treat Vladimir Putin's career in the KGB. It would be unthinkable for a postwar German politician, let alone a head of state, to have had a career in the SS or the Gestapo. Instead Putin's career is commonly equated with George Bush Sr.'s stint as head of the Central Intelligence Agency (CIA) from 1976 to 1977. One of many such commentators is Eric Margolis ("Son of CIA Meets the KGB," blog, June 24, 2001, http://www.ericmargolis.com/archives/2001/06/son_of_cia_meet.php). Yet the two are not comparable. Bush was a political appointee, just as he was in his previous job as America's top diplomat to China. A possible comparison might be Putin's year as head of the FSB from 1998 to 1999. But even that is stretching the facts. The FSB is an unreformed part of the old KGB, which was the terrifying and bloody weapon of a totalitarian secret-police state. For all its faults and blunders, than cannot be said of the CIA.

INDEX

September 11 2001 attacks, 3, 28

Abashidze, Aslan, 140
Abkhazia, 85, 110, 146, 196, 197, 199, 241
abortions, 93, 238
Abramovich, Roman, 67, 230
Abros bank, 63
Abu Ghraib, 3
Adenauer, Konrad, 172
adoption, 71, 169
advertising, 88
Aeroflot, 24, 39, 47
Afghanistan, 126, 195, 200, 205, 213; Soviet
    invasion of, 11, 104, 109–10, 202–3
Africa, 39, 226
Afrikanisatsiya, 7
Ahtisaari, Martti, 199
aircraft carriers, 190–1
airspace violations, 10, 143, 189
Ajaria, 140
Akayev, Askar, 133
Albania, 178–9, 198
Albats, Yevgenia, 1, 63–4, 229
alcohol, 32, 118; *see also* vodka
Aleksei, Patriarch, 119
Algeria, 182
Almaz-Antei, 39
alphabets, 54, 115, 227
Al-Qaeda, 223
Amnesty International, 27, 60–1, 75
anarchy, rise of, 55
Anderson, Julie, 85, 232
Andropov, Yuri, 16, 21, 224
Angarsk, 81
anti-monopoly laws, 130
anti-Semitism, 118, 203, 231
apparatchiks, 39
Arabian Gulf, 99, 191
arabs, 203
Arap, Larisa, 59, 70
Arctic and Antarctic Institute, 187
Arctic region, 12, 186–7, 193, 205
Arctic Sea, 186–7
Argentina, 90

Armenia, 104, 133, 177, 205, 239
arms control, 10, 191, 193, 196–7
arms sales, 18, 65, 138, 191–2, 203
army, Russian, 6, 75, 222
Aslamazyan, Marina, xiv–xv, 77, 230
Associated Press, 65
atom bomb, dropping of, 109
Australia, 106, 181
Austria, xix, 15, 106, 170, 221, 246; and gas
    supplies, 165, 178–80
aviation, 91, 93
Avtovaz, 88
Azerbaijan, 104, 134, 239; and energy
    supplies, 176–7

Bagrov, Yuri, 65
Baikalfinansgrup, 50
Bakhmina, Svetlana, 61
Baku–Tbilisi–Ceyhan oil pipeline, 180
Balkans, xvii, 11–12, 159, 176–7, 181, 199
Baltic Fleet, 171, 190
Baltic Sea, 76, 98, 129; and gas pipeline, 99,
    166–7, 171, 175; seaports, 131
Baltic states, xvii, 6, 12, 15, 30, 53, 102, 239;
    CIS and, 135; citizenship and language
    rights, 136, 150, 234; Germany and, 20,
    171, 174; and history, 114, 150, 151, 196;
    and military incursions, 143;
    nationalism, 69; and NATO, 143, 185,
    200; period of independence, 137; and
    Russian foreign policy, 150–4, 238;
    Soviet annexation, 12, 114–15, 137, 150,
    151, 237, 239; Stalinist terror, 139; and
    'two-speed' Europe, 159
Baluyevsky, General Yuri, 198
banking, 7, 31, 33, 91, 98, 142, 169
Barclays, 180
Barents Sea, 184
Barysch, Katinka, 211
Basayev, Shamil, 223
Basescu, Traian, 178
BASF, 166–7, 175, 185
Basic Element, 173
Bavaria, 52

BBC, 6, 225
Belarus, 191, 192, 239; closeness to Russia, 11, 133–4, 205; and gas supplies, 167–8, 185; period of independence, 239; suspended from Council of Europe, 213
Belgium, 175
Beltransgas, 134
Benefit, 50
Berdimuhammedow, Gurbanguly, 133
Berezovsky, Boris, 23, 28, 41, 47–8, 63; and Litvinenko affair, 81–3, 241; and presidential election, 67–8
Bering Strait, 205
Berlin, 5, 12
Berlin Wall, fall of, 156
Berlusconi, Silvio, xvii, 14
Beslan school siege, 52, 64
bin Laden, Osama, 213, 232
Bishkek, 204
Bismarck, Otto von, 108
Black Sea, 32, 129, 140, 158, 176
Black Sea Fleet, 190
Blair, Tony, 94, 201
Blank, Stephen, 193
Blok, Aleksandr, 118
Blue Stream gas pipeline, 176–7
Bolivia, 181
Bolshevik Revolution, see October Revolution
Bolsheviks, 70, 104, 139
books, 43, 203
Borodin, Pavel, 24
Bortnikov, Alexander, xxii
Bosnia, 131, 178, 198, 201, 203
"botnets," 155
Bourgas, 178
BP, 13, 84, 97–8
Brandt, Willy, 105
Bratislava, 180
Brazil, 87, 88, 93, 183, 201, 213, 237
Brenton, Sir Anthony, 80
Brezhnev, Leonid, xvi, 16, 20, 21, 32, 125
Britain, xvii, xxiv, 81; anti-Americanism, 201; demographics, 121; and electricity generation, 175; and former Soviet states, 132; and gas supplies, 164–5, 171, 175; and history, 106, 111, 129, 169; and Litvinenko affair, 82–3; and migration, 157–9; money-laundering, 84; Russian influence in, 92, 98–9; and 'two-speed' Europe, 209
British Council, 77
British Helsinki Human Rights Group, 220
Browder, William, 97–8
Brussels, 64, 69, 149, 158, 179, 202
Budapest, 179
Buinaksk, 23
Bukovsky, Vladimir, 227, 234
Bulgaria, xix, 15, 32, 158; American bases in, 196; demographics, 93; and gas supplies, 165, 177–9; and history, 115; NATO membership, 131
Bush, George, Sr., 249
Bush, George W., 3, 12, 63, 117, 192, 195, 201, 247; meets Putin, 192, 227, 236; supports Estonia, 12
businesses, Russian, 13, 19, 29, 38, 41, 46, 64, 72–3, 90–3; small, 32, 33, 38, 40, 45, 115; IT sector, 89–90, 232
business interests, pro-Russian, 9, 10–15, 19, 45, 84, 94–100, 131, 132, 138, 171, 174–5, 178, 201
Butinge oil terminal, 160

cab drivers, 80, 230
Canada, 52, 181, 183, 186–7
capitalism, in Russia, xvi, 21, 44, 51, 103, 140, 199, 207; ethical basis, 92, 100, 210; memories of, 30; municipal, 46; and New Cold War victory, 214; state, 125; welfare, 13, 101; under Yeltsin, 32–3, 41
career choices, 90
car plants, 88
cars, 38, 40, 42, 84, 118
Carter, Jimmy, 15
Caspian Sea, 166, 177, 181
Catherine II (the Great), Empress, 108, 171
Cato Institute, 90
Caucasus, ix, 11, 12, 65, 104, 106, 139–41, 148; people from, 81, 234
censorship, 126, 165
Central Asia, 54, 69, 106, 132–3, 135; air bases, 200; and gas supplies, 166, 176, 179, 182, 222, 234, 237; and SCO and CSTO, 204–5
Central Europe, 11–12, 30, 129, 180, 193, 197
Centre for European Reform, 211
Centre for International Legal Defence, 75
Centrica, 98
Centre for European Reform, 211
Chamberlain, Neville, 129
Chaplin, Vsevolod, 120
Charter 77, 136
Chávez, Hugo, 90, 192, 201
Cheboksary, 58
Chechenpress website, 82
Chechens and Chechnya, ix, 22–3, 38, 75, 104, 123, 140, 223; American policy on, 117; "Arab" fighters in, 203; exiled leaders, 82–3; human rights cases, 73; Russian wars in, 1, 7, 46, 48, 59, 69, 87–8, 196, 203; separatists, 5, 7, 23, 25, 68, 76, 123, 147, 202, 226, 232
Cheka, 21, 22, 24, 85, 222
Chelyabinsk, 204
Cheney, Dick, 88
Cherepovets, 73
Cherkesov, Viktor, 22
Chernenko, Konstantin, 21
Chernomyrdin, Viktor, 47–8, 234, 221

chess, 214
Chevron, 186
children, 40, 42, 70, 71, 93, 113, 117
children's homes, 157
Chilingarov, Artur, 187
China, 94, 99, 126, 133, 208, 209; arms
    purchases, 191; and gas sales, 97, 185;
    military, 193–4, 195; relations with
    Russia, xix, xx, 11, 18, 202, 204–5; and
    SCO, 11, 135; and world economy, 87,
    93, 133, 166
Chuichenko, Konstantin, xxii
church and state, 118–19
Churchill, Winston, 218
Churilov, Colonel Oleg, 224
CIA, 81, 249; "rendition," 3, 195
City of London, 11, 13, 99
civil service, 125, 139
civil society, 70, 74, 207
Cohen, Ariel, 163, 245
Cold War, 3–6, 10–12, 14–15, 17, 195, 198,
    201, 208–10, 214; airspace violations,
    189–90; allies visit Moscow, 192; arms
    control agreements, 190, 196–7; bases
    closed, 45, 246; and blackmail, 68; and
    business interests, 99; Germany and,
    172; harassment of cultural
    organizations, 77; and human rights, 75;
    and ideology, 101, 112; and Israel, 203;
    negotiations, 127; rhetoric, 83; role of
    CSCE, 136; vetoes, 212; victory in,
    129–30; Western shortcomings, 215
Collective Security Treaty Organization
    (CSTO), 135, 205
collectivization, 104, 109
Committee to Protect Journalists, 64
Common Economic Space, 135
Commonwealth of Independent States
    (CIS), establishment of, 135, 240, 248
Communist Party, 3, 6, 16, 19, 20, 21,
    29–30, 42, 66, 125; dissolved under
    Yeltsin, 39; and Just Russia, 69; mass
    membership, 69; under Stalin, 107; and
    United Russia, 66; under Zyuganov, 29,
    46
computers, 43, 155
Conan Doyle, Arthur, 40
Conference on Security and Cooperation in
    Europe (CSCE), 136, 218
Congress of People's Deputies, 71, 224
ConocoPhillips, 186
Conquest, Robert, 234
conscription, 68, 74
Constantinople, 120
constitution, Russian, 4, 7, 55, 58, 121, 123,
    124
Constitutional Court, 72–3
construction, 41, 173
Conventional Forces in Europe (CFE) treaty,
    193, 196–7, 246

corruption, xvii, 6, 14, 17, 24, 43, 44, 65, 72,
    185, 209; in Eastern Europe, 78, 132,
    133, 157–8; in Western countries, 14,
    214–15; under Yeltsin, 33, 46, 60
Council of Europe, xxiv, 4, 136, 212–13,
    235
Crawshaw, Steve, 219
Crimea, 104, 110, 150; Ukraine and, 110,
    155
Croatia, 131, 178
Cuba, 234; Russian bases in, 45, 244
customs agency, 85, 134–5
cyber warfare, 17, 155
Cyprus, 14, 84, 172
Czechoslovakia, 5, 6, 238, 239; and history,
    104, 111, 129, 136, 228; protests against
    Soviet invasion, 110, 235
Czech Republic, xviii, xxiv, 131, 213, 237;
    and gas supplies, 165, 167; and missile
    defense, 174, 193, 194; Prague Spring in,
    xvi

Dagestan, 22–3, 221
Daiwa, 125
Danilov, Valentin, 60–1
Darfur, 191
democracy, 30, 33, 72, 204, 214
demographics, 57, 93, 206, 238
Denmark, 171, 186–7
Deripaska, Oleg, 46, 51, 173
Der Spiegel, 227
derzhavnichestvo, 120
dezinformatsiya, 17
Dickens, Charles, 40
dictatorship, 29, 48, 109, 130, 131, 177
diet, 40
diktatura zakona, 120–1
disinformation, 17, 150, 154
Dmitriyeva, Tatyana, 59
Dmitriyevsky, Stanislav, 75
Dniestr River, 137
Doha, 181
Dostoyevsky, Fyodor, 126
Dovgiy, Dmitriy, xv
Dresden, 20, 169
Dresdner Bank, 169
drug abuse, 93
Duma, 7, 24, 62, 67, 71–2, 87, 91–3, 221;
    deputies, 27, 58, 91–2; elections, 66, 102,
    233; foreign affairs committee, 149

Eastern Europe, 110, 148, 194; English-
    language newspapers in, 150; and
    Euroatlanticism, 130, 149; and history,
    104–5, 111–12; integration into EU, 139,
    156; and NATO, 200–1
East Germany, 6, 19, 20, 104, 106, 111, 169,
    172; Stasi, 20, 169
East Prussia, 106
Economist Intelligence Unit, 88

economy, Russian, 90–4, 101, 102, 106, 112, 113; black market, 41; contrasted with Estonia, 112; debt, 7, 84; domestic investment, 51, 85, 184–5; foreign exchange reserves, 88; foreign investment, 4, 13, 51, 84, 88, 91, 92, 99; GDP, 87–92; Soviet, 93, 108; and WTO membership, 14, 84–5, 168; under Yeltsin, 32–3
Educated Media Foundation, 77
education, 32, 42–3, 74, 108, 130, 133, 204; in Eastern Europe, 157–8; in Mari, 76; and religion, 156
efesbefikatsiya, 8
Egypt, 43
Ekho Moskvy, 43, 63–4
election monitoring, 135–7
elections, 16, 17, 46, 57, 66–9, 102, 115, 122, 126, 213, 215; *Nashi* involvement in, 79; parliamentary elections, 72, 83; presidential election (2000), 24, 29, 34; presidential election (2004), 7, 67; presidential election (2008), 4, 55, 103; regional elections, 66, 69
energy, xix, 92–3, 166, 171, 172, 174, 176; control of energy supplies 11–13, 178–9, 182, 199, 202, 209–11; energy policy, 164; foreign investment in, 49–50, 97, 100; inefficiency and conservation, 168, 183–4
Energy Charter, 164
English language, 40, 48, 82, 120, 138, 150
ENI, 166, 177, 182
Enlightenment, 70
Enron, 95
entertainment, 42, 66
environmental standards, 130
E.ON Ruhrgas, 98, 167, 173, 175, 185
espionage, 10, 11, 20, 60, 61, 73, 76, 78, 125, 155, 167
Estonia, xxv, 10, 12, 45, 63, 112–14, 137, 150, 155, 212; armed forces, 196; borders, 137; citizenship and language policies, 150–1; cyber warfare attack, 17, 155; defamation of, 79; economy, 92, 182, 188; and Finland, 156; and gas supplies, 144, 165, 167, 171, 175; and history, 112–14; intelligence services, 157; introduces flat tax, 224; Mari links with, 45, 76; and military threat, 145, 197; modernization, 139, 140; Russian separatists in, 147; Russians' hostility to, 45, 71, 112; Soviet annexation, 110, 149–50, 179; war memorial row, 152–3
ethnic minorities, 23, 54, 75–6, 139, 142, 150
ethnic Russians, 44, 80, 133, 143, 150–1, 155, 230, 227, 239
Eton College, 42
EuralTransGas (ETG), 169–70
Eurasian Economic Community, 135

euro, 130, 158, 159
Euroatlanticism, 130–3, 138–9, 149, 201, 238
Europe, 3, 7, 10, 12; alliance with America, 3, 15, 195, 208; energy "Finlandization," 202; energy security, 176, 209; European mainstream, 5, 74, 200; frontiers, 136; gas supplies, 11, 98, 159, 163; and history, 105–7, 112; migration, 157; Russia's pincer movement on, xix; Russian visitors, 43; think tanks, 78, 131; "two-speed," 158
European Bank for Reconstruction and Development, 11, 90, 97, 137
European Council on Foreign Relations: "Power Audit of EU–Russian Relations," xx–xxi
European Court of Human Rights, 73, 136
European Union, xvii, 16, 18–19; disdain for America, 208; energy liberalization, 100, 166, 175, 210; and Estonia, 151; expansion, 4, 5, 130, 156, 159; and former Yugoslavia, 178; and Georgia, 143, 212; and Russian opinion, 181; rivals to, 135; Samara summit, 62, 159; and Turkey, 176; and Ukraine, 212; visas, 212
evolution, 119
extremism law, 9, 62–3, 69, 226, 228
Exxon, 97

Fainberg, Viktor, 234
famines, 104, 108
Fatherland party, 232
FBI, 81, 170
federalism, 52, 236
Federation Council, 71, 149
Felgenhauer, Pavel, 197, 233, 244
Fenya, 225
feudalism, 70, 94, 119
Finland, xi, xxiv, 54, 76, 113, 212; and Estonia, 156; and gas supplies, 165, 167, 171
Finno-Ugric languages, 54, 76
First World War, 116, 118
Firtash, Dmitriy, 170
flag, Russian, 187
Fluxys, 175
Forbes magazine, 65
Ford, 88
Ford, Henry, 110
foreign policy: European, 156; German, 14, 172; Kazakh, 132; Romanian, 178; Russian, 45, 55, 189–206, United States, 208
Fradkov, Mikhail, 203
France, 15, 115, 172; anti-Americanism, 201; and business, 161; and gas supplies, 165–6, 186; and history, 106, 113; and Turkey, 176; and 'two-speed' Europe, 158–9

Frankfurt, 95, 210
FSB, xxii, 8, 19–22, 39, 52, 102, 224, 246;
    arrests Khodorkovsky, 49; assassinations,
    62; formation of, 10, 222; illegal bugging
    operations, 73; interrogations, 60, 65;
    licensed to operate abroad, 154; and
    Litvinenko, 2, 77, 81–3; museum, 103;
    and NGOs, 149–50; and Orthodox
    Church, 119; and Politkovskaya 228;
    Putin heads, 25, 28; and Ryazan bomb
    incident, 24–6, 222
Fursenko, Andrei, 224
Fursin, Ivan, 170

G8, xxiv, 4, 213, 235
Gabriyan, Pyotr, 228
Gaddy, Clifford, 241
Gagarin, Yuri, 103
Gamsakhurdia, Zviad, 139
Gandhi, Mahatma, 57
gas, 11, 15, 163, 174; and Belarus, 134; in
    Central Asia, 174; and Georgia, 142, 144;
    inefficiency and conservation, 183–5,
    242; LNG, 164, 170, 171, 182, 185, 210;
    pipelines, 16, 97–9, 159, 164, 166–9,
    170–1, 176–81, 242; revenues, 9, 87, 88,
    90, 226; shortages, 85, 182, 242, 243, 244;
    state ownership, 90–1, 96; and
    Transdniestria 139
Gas-Exporting Countries' Forum (GECF),
    181–2
Gasunie, 174
Gaz de France, 166
Gazprom, 11, 39, 166, 175–80, 243–4;
    accounting, 95, 169; acquisitions, 91;
    and Algeria, 180; buys media outlets, 47,
    165; and capital markets, xvi, 210;
    developments and contracts, 185–6;
    inefficiency, 183–5; as Kremlin, Inc., 165,
    217; military forces, 171; of pipelines,
    166–9; shortages, 182–4; sponsorship of
    Nashi, 79; visas, 246; and Yukos affair,
    50–1
General Motors, 88
Georgia, 92, 104, 129, 137, 139, 200, 208,
    209; and Abkhazia, 85, 110, 146, 196,
    197, 199, 238; and Ajaria, 140;
    demographics, 93; economy, 120, 140–3;
    and energy supplies, 177; EU and, 212;
    introduces flat tax, 224; and military
    incursions, 146; and NATO
    membership, xxiv, 131, 185, 212; Rose
    Revolution, 132, 200; Russian
    withdrawal, 196–7; and South Ossetia, x,
    141, 197, 199, 238; withdrawal from CIS,
    135
Gerashchenko, Viktor, 33
Gerasimenko, Yevgeny, 65
Germany, 6, 11, 77, 117, 158; anti-
    Americanism, 201; and gas supplies, 98,
165; and history, 104, 106, 114, 116, 126;
    and Litvinenko affair, 108; Nazi (Third
    Reich), 79, 105, 107, 108, 129, 157; and
    Polish exports, 158; reunification, 172;
    Russian influence in, 14, 15, 99–100,
    165–75; and 'two-speed' Europe, 158
Geroi Dnya, 25
glasnost, 6
Glazyev, Sergei, 67
globalization, 163
global warming, 186
Goethe Institute, 77
Gogol, Nikolai, 122
Gonchar, Viktor, 237
GONGOs, 78
Google, 89
Gorbachev, Mikhail, xxiii, 2, 6, 10, 101, 103,
    140; and economy, 41; era of, 21, 38, 45,
    223; frees political prisoners, 60, 227;
    and Germany, 172; and KGB, 21; putsch
    against, 31; and Russian history, 104;
    and Yeltsin, 29
Gordeev, Alexei, 224
Gordievsky, Oleg, 82
gosudarstvennik, 120
Gotland, 167
Great Fatherland War, xi
Great Patriotic War, see Second World War
Great Terror, 109
Greece, xxiv, 14, 15, 156, 178; and gas
    supplies, 165, 177, 181
Greenland, 186
Gref, German, 224
Gromov, Aleksei, 39
Grozny, ix, 25
GRU, 21, 39, 125, 142, 154, 230
Grushko, Aleksander, 83
Guam, 190
Guantánamo Bay, 3
Gulag system, 58, 103–4, 110
Gunvor, xxiii
Gusinsky, Vladimir, 41, 46–7
Gutseriyev, Mikhail, 51
Gyurcsány, Ferenc, 179
Hahn, Gordon,
    xxii
Hamas, 202–3
healthcare, 32, 38, 93, 94; in Eastern Europe,
    157
Helsinki Final Act, 136, 218
Heritage Foundation, 163
Hermitage Capital, 98
Hezbollah, 202, 203
Hiroshima, 109
history, 70, 104–16, 208; Estonian and
    Russian views of, 150; Putin and, 112;
    revisionism, 110, 116, 120, 208
Hitler, Adolf, 2, 12, 79, 104, 106, 107, 108,
    109, 111, 112, 113, 117, 152
Hitlerjugend, 79

HIV/AIDS, 228
Hochtief, 173
homosexuality, 4, 74, 157, 206, 228
Hoover, Herbert, 218
housing, 3, 31, 32, 45, 93, 94, 123
human rights, 10, 14, 58, 60–1; agreements, 4, 13, 119; German criticisms and support, 172–3; international legal redress, 73, 136; Soviet bloc signs up to, 136, 218; supported by Kremlin, 70; in Uzbekistan, 132
Human Rights Watch, 75
Hungary, xix, 15, 54, 237; and gas supplies, 165, 175, 179, 180, 244; and history, 104, 109, 115, 226; NATO membership, 131; and Pristina airfield crisis, 198
Hussein, Saddam, 191

ideology, 5, 17, 40, 100, 101–27, 199; of centralization, 122; "ideological vacuum," 116; ideological vocabulary, 120–1; and 'New Age' thinking, 124; "sovereign democracy," xv, xxii, 5, 17, 119, 124–6, 149, 204, 208
Ifanov, Vyacheslav, 65
Illarionov, Andrei, 89–90, 99
Ilves, Toomas Hendrik, 12, 63, 112, 153
Imendayev, Albert, 58
immigrants, illegal, 80, 142, 151
imperialism, 103, 212
India, 57, 87, 88, 93, 106, 191, 201, 213
Indonesia, 201
Institut Français, 77
Instituto Cervantes, 77
intellectual property laws, 231
interior ministry troops, 52, 62
Intermediate-range Nuclear Forces (INF) treaty, 197
International Atomic Energy Agency, 193
International Bar Association, 72, 229
International Commission of Jurists, 72
International Energy Agency, 170
international law, 177, 215, 240
International Monetary Fund, 84, 87
internet, 43, 150, 155
Iran, 65, 193, 208, 213; and gas supplies, 166, 176, 177, 181; and nuclear proliferation, 4, 192, 194, 203; relations with Russia, 11, 202; and SCO, 205
Iraq, xvii, 176, 191, 192, 195, 203; war in, 3, 49, 126, 177, 208
Ireland, 89
Islamic Conference Organization, 202
Islamic extremism, 55, 97, 156, 200, 202, 203
Israel, 47, 105, 107, 170, 202; Russian relations with, 203
Italy, xxiv, 8, 15, 158; and gas supplies, 165, 166, 177, 180, 181, 182
Itera, 169, 245
Itogi, 46

IT sector, 89–90, 231
Ivanov, Sergei, 39, 79
Ivanov, Viktor, 39
Ivan the Terrible, 21
Izvestiya, 4, 64, 227

Jabelia, Manana, 142
Japan, 92, 109, 111, 116, 185
Jews, 106, 109, 113, 114, 203
Jordan, Boris, 72
journalism, 1, 40, 46–7, 63–5, 77, 117
JP Morgan Chase, 180
judiciary, 10, 33, 58, 72–4, 125, 164, 170
judo, 19, 22
Just Russia party, 69

Kadyrov, Akhmed, 123
Kaliningrad, 155
Kaljurand, Marina, 153
Karachinsky, Anatoly, 89
Karelia, 54
Karimov, Islam, 132
Kartofelnikov, Aleksei, 24
Kasparov, Garry, 59, 61–2, 63, 159
Kaspersky, Yevgeny and Natalya, 89
Kasyanov, Mikhail, 63
Katowice, 112
Katsav, Moshe, 221
Katyn massacre, 104, 110, 234
Kazakhstan, 133, 135, 176–8, 204, 205, 208, 237
KazMunayGaz, 178
Kent State University, 109
Kerensky, Aleksandr, 30, 70
KGB, 3, 6, 8, 41, 59, 222, 240; increasing power, 16, 19–22; and Orthodox Church, 119; Putin's career with, 20, 246
Khakamada, Irina, 67
Khodorkovsky, Mikhail, 48, 49–51, 61, 73, 75, 95
Kholodov, Dmitry, 227
Khristenko, Victor, 224
Khrushchev, Nikita, 101
Kipling, Rudyard, 219
Kiriyenko, Sergei, 220
Klebnikov, Paul, 65
Kodori Gorge, 146
Kohl, Helmut, 172
Kokoshin, Andrei, 187
Kolerov, Modest, 150, 154
Komi, 54, 103
Komsomol, 79
Komsomolskaya Pravda, 154
Kondopoga, 81
Kosachev, Konstantin, 149
Kosovo, ix, xvii, 198, 199, 201, 203
Kostanov, Yuri, 229
Kovalchuk, Mikhail, 231
Kovalev, Sergei, 60
Kovykta gas field, 97

Kozlov, Vladimir, 76
Kozlovsky, Oleg, xiv
Kozluduy nuclear power station, 179
Krasnodar, 63
Krasnoyarsk, 228
Krasovsky, Anatoly, 237
Kross, Jaan, 114
Kryshtanovskaya, Olga, 20, 222
Kuala Lumpur, 202
Kudrin, Aleksei, xv
Kukly, 47, 63
Kurchatov Institute, 231
Kurdish separatism, 176
Kursk submarine, 37, 47, 73
Kuznetsov, Boris, 73
Kyiv, 68, 78, 145, 230, 239, 241
Kyrgyzstan, 132, 133, 135, 204, 237

Laar, Mart, 137
Lacis, Otto, 27, 223
Lake Seliger, 79
languages, 54, 76, 150–1, 219, 239
Lantos, Tom, 216
Larsson, Robert, 160, 242, 239
Latin America, 90, 109, 182; see also South
    America
Latvia, xxv, 12, 15, 115, 152, 159, 220, 226,
    237; borders, 137; citizenship and
    language policies, 150–1, 153; and gas
    supplies, 165, 171, 175; and gay rights,
    157; and history, 113–14; introduces flat
    tax, 224; and military threat, 144;
    money-laundering, 84; oil supplies, 143,
    272
Latynina, Yulia, 63, 243
Lavrov, Sergei, 187
law, rule of, 8, 30, 57–8, 62, 71–2, 84, 120,
    126, 135, 207, 213, 214; see also judiciary
Lebanon, 177, 203
Lebedev, Aleksander, 227
Lenin, Vladimir Ilyich, 16, 29, 32, 101, 103
Lesnevskaya, Irena, 64
Levitin, Igor, 160, 224
Liberal Democrat party, 83, 102
Liberal Russia party, 223
Libya, 93, 175
Lipman, Masha, 124, 228
Lithuania, xxv, 6, 12, 76, 132, 134, 219, 237;
    citizenship and language policies, 151;
    and gas supplies, 165; and history,
    113–15; introduces flat tax, 224; and
    Kaliningrad, 155; oil supplies, 209, 220;
    politicians' links with Russia, 132;
    relations with Poland, 115
Litvinenko, Aleksandr, 2, 60, 81–4, 222, 230,
    236
Lokshina, Tatyana, 227
Lomonosov Ridge, 187
London, 2, 11, 13, 40, 42, 48, 60, 64, 68, 82,
    83, 95, 207, 210; see also City of London

London Stock Exchange, 85, 99
Lowe, Norman, 233
Lubyanka, 21, 119, 236
Lucas, Edward, xi, xii
Lugovoi, Andrei, 2, 83
Lukashenka, Alyaksandr, 134–5
Lukin, Vladimir, 70
Luzhkov, Yuri, 24, 29, 46

Mabetex, 24
Macedonia, 115, 179, 237
MacKay, Peter, 187
mafia, Russian, 22, 37, 41, 45–6
Malashenko, Aleksei, 202
Malaysia, 202
mammoths, 79
Mangold, Klaus, 173
manufacturing industry, 92, 93
Mari-El, 54, 76, 103
Markelov, Leonid, 76
Markov, Sergei, 116
Marxism-Leninism, 5, 13, 101, 125
Mashal, Khaled, 202
Maskhadov, Aslan, 53
Mazõeikiai oil terminal, 159–60, 220
Me_iar, Vladimír, 131, 237
media, 9, 20, 77, 207, 213; and elections,
    67–8; and opposition, 58, 62–4; under
    Putin, 43, 46–7, 52; and rewriting of
    history, 115; and Ryazan bomb incident,
    27; and war memorial row, 152–3; under
    Yeltsin, 7, 8, 52; see also newspapers;
    radio stations; television
Mediterranean, 10, 180, 187, 191
Medvedev, Dmitri, 79, 125, 224; European
    security organization, idea of, xvii; and
    presidential election (2007), xiii
Merkel, Angela, xxi, 160, 166, 173–4, 176
Mestnye, 80
Mexico, 201
Microsoft, 166
middle class, 7, 40, 42–4, 54, 93
migration, 80, 136, 142, 149, 151, 157, 204,
    238; see also immigrants, illegal
military, Russian, 4, 5, 10, 16, 23, 133, 139,
    143, 146, 147, 155, 171, 189–99; 212;
    budget, 189; see also army, Russian; navy,
    Russian; nuclear weapons; special forces
military incursions, 146
Milo_evic, Slobodan, 131, 198, 237
Milov, Vladimir, xvii, 244
mineral water, 118, 143, 236, 238
MIRO, 243
Mir space station, 187
Milosz, Czeslaw, 40
missile defence system, American, 193–5,
    196, 205
missiles, 5, 10, 65, 143, 189–90, 190, 191,
    193, 198, 203, 239, 244
Mogilevich, Semion, 170

MOL, 180
Moldova, 137–9, 150, 199, 212; Russian withdrawal from, 196–7
Molodaya Gvardiya, 116
Molotov–Ribbentrop pact, 111, 129, 137, 168, 241
Molyakov, Igor, 58
money-laundering, 77, 84, 85, 210
Montenegro, 224
Morar, Natalia, xiv
Mordovia, 54
Moscow, 29, 46, 227, 231; airports, 43, 68, 98; anti-Americanism, 44; apartment bombings, 7, 22–4; Berezovsky's club, 48; British Council office raided, 77; cab drivers, 80; Cold War visits, 192; demonstrations, 61; Estonian embassy attacked, 153; gay rights campaigners attacked, 74; Georgians deported, 142; and Litvinenko affair, 83; and Litvinenko press conference, 82; museums, 103, 110; nationalism, 44; Nordost theatre incident, 68; prisons, 47, 50; proposed peace conference, 203; racism, 81; Red Square protests, 110, 241; and Ryazan bomb incident, 26, 222; think tanks, 116, 117, 182; as "Third Rome," 120; "White House," 29; William Browder and, 98
Moscow, River, 101
Moscow bar association, 73
Moscow Carnegie Center, 81, 116, 202, 245
Moscow Helsinki Group, 60, 75, 136, 228
Moskalenko, Karina, 73, 75
motorcades, 71
Mugabe, Robert, xix
Munich, 117
Munich Agreement, 111, 129
Murmansk, 59, 70
music piracy, 89
Muslims, ix–x, 75, 140, 156, 202, 229
Muslim world, 202–3
Mussolini, Benito, 11

Nabucco gas pipeline, 166, 175–80, 210
Naftohaz Ukrainy, 170
Nagorno-Karabakh, 110, 237
nanotechnology, 224
narcotics, 205; *see also* drug abuse
Naryshkin, Sergei, 39, 224
Nashi, 79–81, 240; and Estonian war memorial, 112, 153
nationalism, 14, 44, 53, 79, 102, 103, 118, 140, 152, 204
NATO, xvii, xxiv–xxv, 145, 197, 210; and Afghanistan, 213; and airspace violations, 10, 189–90; alternatives to, 136, 205; and Baltic states, 12, 143; and Bulgaria, 178; and Cold War, 15, 130, 157, 244; cooperation with Russia, 45;

and Estonia, 145, 197; expansion, 4, 130–1, 195, 200–1; and Georgia, 143, 145; and Germany, 172; and nuclear threat, 5; and Russian threat, 191, 198; Russian views of, 117; and Turkey, 176; and Ukraine, 78
navy, Russian, 187, 190
Nazarbayev, Nursultan, 133
"Near Abroad," x, xii
Nemtsov, Boris, xvii
newspapers, 43, 64; Mari, 76; English-language, 150; Russian-language in Israel, 203
Netherlands, the, 15, 90; and gas supplies, 165, 171, 174, 181; and history, 107;
New Testament, 5
New Times, 63–4, 227
New York, 95, 210
New York Stock Exchange, 99
NGOs, 10, 74, 78, 149, 150; *see also* voluntary organizations
Nicaragua, 112, 234
Nicholas I, Tsar, 119
Nicholas II, Tsar, 103
Nicolini, Mário, 237
Nigeria, 94
Nissan, 88
Nixon, Richard, 15
Nizhny Novgorod, 61, 227, 233
NKVD, 21, 222
Nord Stream gas pipeline, xix, 99, 158, 166–71, 175, 210, 242, 243
Norsk Hydro, 186
North America, 13
North Atlantic, 189, 193
North Caucasus, 202
Northern Fleet, 187, 190
North Korea, 4, 194, 213
North Ossetia, 52–3
North Pole, 186–7
North Sea, 164, 171, 175, 189
Norway, 77, 158, 181, 185, 186
Novatek, 183
Novaya Gazeta, 63, 68, 222, 227
Novosibirsk, 49
Novye Izvestiya, 26
NTV, 46–7, 63, 65, 165
nuclear power, 171, 179, 213
nuclear proliferation, 4, 55, 177, 192, 203
nuclear waste, 77, 102
nuclear weapons, 10, 13, 109, 126, 172, 189–91; American and NATO, 193, 198, 213; Chinese, 194; Hiroshima bomb, 109; Iran and proliferation, 192–3
Nyÿazow, Saparmyrat, 133

October Revolution, 70, 104
Office for Democratic Institutions and Human Rights (ODHIR), 136
OGPU, 21, 222

oil, 9, 12, 49, 85, 178, 182; foreign investment in, 91, 96, 165; and oligarchs' companies, 47–52; pipelines, 16, 23, 63, 143, 164, 180, 184; prices, 32, 67, 84, 87, 91, 92; revenues, 87–8, 90; state ownership, 91
Okhrana, 21, 222
oligarchs, 6, 13, 37, 41, 219; Putin and, 47–52
Olmert, Ehud, 221
Omsk, 49
ÖMV, 179
opposition parties, 28, 53, 61–4, 69, 193
Oprichniki, 21, 222
Organization for Economic Cooperation and Development (OECD), xxiv, 72, 121, 236
Organization for Security and Co-operation in Europe (OSCE), 14, 136, 138, 143, 212, 239
organized crime, 81, 86, 132, 143–4, 157, 198
ORT, 48
Orthodoxy, see Russian Orthodox Church
Orwell, George, 79, 105
Ossetians, 139–41
Ostauschuss der deutschen Wirtschaft, 173
Our Home is Russia party, 102
Oxford, 5, 49

Pacific Fleet, 190
Pacific Ocean, 190
Pakistan, 194, 201
Paksas, Rolandas, 132
Palestinian territories, 202
Pamfilova, Ella, 70
Panfilov, Oleg, xiv
Paris, 77
parliament, Russian, 7, 24, 62, 71–2, 117, 125, 149, 198; committee on ex-soviet region, 187; see also Duma; Federation Council
patriotism, 10, 20, 78, 116, 120, 153
Patrushev, Andrei, 224
Patrushev, Nikolai, 25–6
Pemex, 183
PEN, 75
pensions, 33, 44, 102
perestroika, 7, 91
Perm, 110
Peter the Great, Tsar and Emperor, 108, 114
pharmaceuticals, 89
Piebalgs, Andris, 169, 181, 182
Pinyaev, Alexei, 222
Piontkovsky, Andrei, 63–4, 206
PKN Orlen, 220
Plato, 5
Playboy, 190
Poederlee, 175
Poland, xvii, xxiv, 5, 41, 45, 134, 160, 183; abrasive diplomacy, 158; foreign investment, 92; and gas supplies, 165, 167, 168, 171; Germany and, 223; and history, 104, 107, 114–15; imposition of martial law, 109, 246; and missile defence, 193; NATO membership, xxv, 131; relations with Lithuania, 115; and "rendition," 195; support for Estonia, 153; and 'two-speed' Europe, 209
police, 24, 26, 41, 58, 59, 62, 74, 81, 95, 125, 130, 142, 153; see also secret police; tax police
Polikanov, Dmitri, 44
political freedoms, 7, 9, 13, 21, 30, 44, 67, 92, 116, 150, 169, 213
political prisoners, 60–1, 135, 153
Politkovskaya, Anna, murder of, 1–2, 53, 63, 65, 73, 218, 228
pollution, 73, 93
polonium, 2, 82, 218
Portugal, 15, 38
Pravda, 4
Presidential Council on Promoting the Development of Institutions of Civil Society and Human Rights, 70
PricewaterhouseCoopers, 88; and Yukos affair, 95–6
Prikhodko, Sergei, 224
Primakov, Yevgeny, 24, 29, 220
Pristina, 198
privatization, 33, 116
professions, 40
Prokhanov, Aleksandr, 202
Promneftestroi, 50–1
propaganda, 3, 10, 43, 79, 141, 153, 155, 195, 213; Soviet, 40, 59, 102, 130, 170
property, private, 16, 51, 84, 92, 95, 100, 207, 210
prostitutes, 38, 79
protectionism, 84, 90
protests and demonstrations, 10, 58, 61, 64, 79, 140; Soviet era, 110, 241; against welfare reforms, 123, 183
Pskov, 154
psychiatry, punitive, 17, 58–60, 70, 110, 241
Public Chamber, 70–1
public opinion, 26, 28, 45, 66, 69, 71; and anti-Westernism, 117; and Duma, 72; and justice system, 72; and Orthodox Church, 118; and Soviet Union, 70
public services, 44, 93, 94; in Eastern Europe, 157
purges, 104, 108
Pushkov, Aleksei, 201
Putin, Vladimir, ix, x, xi, xv–xvi, xvii, xxi–xxii; accented German, 220; and America, 3, 154, 200–1; bans foreigners from markets, 80; and Belarus, 134; blames others, 66; business interests, 67–8; and centralization, 123; and China, 204; and collapse of Soviet

Union, 12, 54, 106; and CSTO, 205; denounced by Litvinenko as pedophile, 82; denounces NGOs, 10, 78; and economy, 16, 91–2; and energy policy, 163–4, 177–9, 181; engages Islamic world, 202; friendship with Schröder, 168–9, 172; and Georgia, 184–5; heads FSB, 19, 34, 246; as heir to Andropov, 16, 21; and history, 106–7, 109, 114; ideology, 120–1, 124–5; KGB career, 20, 169, 246; manner of speech, 23, 37, 221; meets Bush, 238; and Merkel, 173–4; military policies, 190–2, 196–8, 200; and murder of Anna Politkovskaya, 1–2, 217–18; and Nashi, 79; personality cult, 57; personal popularity, 29, 38, 57, 69; and presidential election (2004), 67; and presidential election (2008), xiii promotes intelligence services, 154; relations with the West, 117; and religion, 118; rise to power, 7–10, 17–22; and Roman Abramovich, 228; and Samara summit, 159; support for Russian-speakers, 149; and terrorist attacks, 25, 52; and Yeltsin era, 40, 45, 47

Qatar, 82, 230
Quebec, 52

racism, 80, 106
Radio Liberty, 228
Radio Moscow, 5
radio stations, 43
Raiffeisen Bank, 170
railways, 39
Rakhman, Emomalii, 133
Rakimkulov, Megdet, 180
raw materials, 9, 16, 31, 41, 85, 163, 164, 199
Reagan, Ronald, 15, 94, 172
rearmament, 10
Red Army, 6, 106, 111, 112, 113, 114
Red Terror, 104
Reformation, 70
reformers, 6, 21, 30, 31, 37
Reiman, Leonid, 231
religion, 118–20, 141, 236
Renaissance, 70
renationalization, 91
REN-TV, 47, 63–4
research and development, 89
retail markets, 80
Revue Baltique, 113
Rhine, River, 3
Rice, Condoleezza, 83, 102
road safety, 71, 74
Rodionov, Igor, 131
Roma, 157
Roman Catholic Church, 120
Romania, xxiv, 115, 131, 158; American bases in, 196; and gas supplies, 165, 178;

and Moldova, 137–8; and "rendition," 195
Romanova, Olga, 228
Romanov family, 103
Rome, ancient, 120
Rompetrol, 178
Roosevelt, Franklin D., 109
Rosneft, 39, 91, 165, 204, 210; acquisitions, 50–1, 98–9
Rosoboronexport, 191
Rossiiskaya Gazeta, 110
RosUkrEnergo, xxii, xxiii, 170
ruble, 9, 30–1, 50, 52
Rushailo, Vladimir, 25
Russian Academy of Sciences, 20
Russian-Chechen Friendship Society, 75
Russian Orthodox Church (ROC), 118–19
Russian Research Centre on Human Rights, 75
Russneft, 51
Russophobia, 213
Ryazan bomb incident, 24–8, 47, 222
Rybkin, Ivan, 67–8
Ryzhkov, Vladimir, 71

Saakashvili, Mikheil, ix, x, 140–3
Sachs, Jeffrey, 33
Safronov, Ivan, 65
St. Petersburg, 8, 22, 88; British Council office closed, 77; demonstrations, 61; elections, 66; investment summit, 94, 201; nationalism, 44; Putin and, 19, 37, 38, 39, 49–50, 169; racism, 81
Sakhalin–2 gas project, 97, 174
Sakharov, Andrei, xv, 103, 110, 226, 232
Salzburg, 179
Samara summit, 62, 159
sanctions, 209
Saratov, 65
Sarkozy, Nicolas, 147, 176
Saudargas, Algirdas, 219
Saudi Arabia, 13, 87, 90, 94
Savitskaya, Svetlana, 58–9
Sberbank, 50, 98
Schmidt, Helmut, 243
Schmidt, Yuri, 226
Schröder, Gerhard, 99, 109, 166, 234
Sechin, Igor, 39, 99, 217, 224
Second World War, 108, 111, 157
secret police, 16, 21, 30, 103, 207
Serbia, ix, 78, 131, 159, 198–9, 200
Serdukov, Anatoly, 224
serfdom, 126
Service, Robert, 233
Sevastopol, 147, 155
sexual abuse, 59; promiscuity, 93
Shakirov, Raf, 64
Shanghai Cooperation Organization (SCO), 11, 135, 204
Shchekochikhin, Yuri, 27, 64, 223, 227

Shell, 13, 84, 97, 243
Shenderovich, Viktor, 63–4
Shevardnadze, Eduard, 140
Shevtsova, Lilia, 116, 117, 118, 122
Shkval torpedo, 189, 191
Shtokman gas field, 173, 184–6
Shunin, Ilya, xiv
Shuvalov, Igor, 224
Siberia, 49, 65, 76, 81, 97; deportations to, 113, 126, 137; gas fields, 184, 185, 234
Sibneft, 48, 49
Sikorski, Radek, 168
Silesia, 107
siloviki, 20, 22, 37, 119
Singing Together, 57
skiing, 57
Slavic languages, 54, 120
Slavophiles, 103
Slovakia, 15, 78, 131, 180, 227; and gas supplies, 165, 167
Slovenia, 165, 178
Slovnaft, 180
Smolensky, Aleksandr, 41
Snohvit gas field, 185
Sobell, Vlad, 125
software, 89
soldiers, suicide among, 5
Solidarity trade union, 5, 112
Sonatrach, 182
Soros, George, 59, 99
South America, 182; *see also* Latin America
South China Sea, 205
South Korea, 185
South Ossetia, 85, 141, 197, 199
South Stream gas pipeline, xix, 177
sovereign democracy, xv, xxii, 5, 17, 119, 124–6, 149, 204, 208
Soviet Union, 2, 3, 4; annexation of Baltic states, 12, 114–15, 137, 150, 152, 237, 238; annexation of Estonia, 110, 149–50, 179; anti-Semitism, 203; ban on pornography, 190; bases closed, 45, 200; collapse of, 6, 101, 106, 109, 116, 130, 146; constituent republics, 223; economy, 31, 32; foreign views of, 94–5; and gas infrastructure, 144, 176, 184; and history, 103–4; and ideology, 40, 101–2; industries, 30, 94; invasion of Afghanistan, 11, 104, 109–10, 138, 144–5, 202–3; life in, 4–6, 16, 38, 42–3, 101; military legacy, 192; national anthem, 104, 232; nomenklatura, 38–9; and Orthodox Church, 118; penal system, 58, 103, 104, 110; propaganda, 79, 130; Putin and, 12, 19–21; Russian pride in, 54, 103; scientific legacy, 89, 103; ties with Germany, 172; UN vetoes, 212; youth movements, 79
space race, 214
special economic zones, 90

special forces, 189
speech, freedom of, *see* political freedoms
Stalin, Josef, x, xv, 2, 16, 32, 59, 88, 101; deportation of Chechens, 222; history and, 103–5, 107–9, 111–13, 121, 130
Stasi, 20, 169
Statoil, 185, 186
Steele, Jonathan, 219
Steinmeier, Frank-Walter, 174
Stepashin, Sergei, 220
Stockholm, 242
stock market, Russian, 51, 88
Stolypin, Piotr, xvii
Stomakhin, Boris, 75
Storchak, Sergei, xv
Strabag, 173
Strasbourg, 73, 75
Strategic Arms Reduction treaties, 193
Strategic Rocket Forces, 65
Strods, Heinrihs, 115
submarines, 5, 190–1; *see also Kursk* submarine
Sudan, 191
Sudetenland, 160
Suez crisis, 109
Sukhumi, 140
Surkov, Vladislav, xxii, 120, 124–6, 217
Suslov, Mikhail, 101, 125
Sutyagin, Igor, 60, 73
Sverdlovsk, 29
SVR, 83, 154
Sweden, xxiv, 114, 143; Defense Research Institute, 160; and gas supplies, 167, 171
Switzerland, 24, 84, 158, 165, 169, 170, 200
Syria, 11, 65, 177, 191, 192, 203

Tajikistan, 11, 133, 135, 204
Taliban, 200, 203
Tallinn, 12, 151–3, 175, 234
Tatars, 54, 75, 110, 147, 156
Tatarstan, 52, 54, 69–70, 97, 192, 202
taxation, 71, 90; flat taxes, 38, 140, 224; and NGOs, 75; and Orthodox Church, 118; as proportion of GDP, 94; and renationalisation, 91; and Yukos affair, 49. 52, 95–7
tax police, 52, 77, 142
Tbilisi, 145
telecommunications, 39, 92
television, 7, 39, 46, 47, 48, 63, 64, 65; in Mari, 76; Russian-language in Israel, 203
Terentyev, Savva, xiv, 225
terrorism, 135; counter-terrorism, 205; and internet, 155; Moscow apartment bombings, 7, 22–4; Ryazan bomb incident, 24–8, 47, 222; *see also* "war on terror"
Teutonic Knights, 114
thallium, 223
Thatcher, Margaret, 94

theocracy, 102
Third World, 246
Tkachenko, Yuri, 24, 27
Tlisova, Fatima, 65
TNK, 97
tobacco, 32, 118
Tokyo, 95
Tomsk, 228
Total, 186
tourism, 43
Toyota, 88
trade unions, 12, 94–5, 106, 232
Transdniestria, 85, 110, 138–9, 147–9, 196, 238
Transparency International, 14, 72
transportation, 93, 123
Trebugova, Yelena, 64
Trenin, Dmitri, 199, 245
Trepashkin, Mikhail, xv, 27, 60, 82
Trotskyism, 232
Truman, Harry S., 109
Trutko, Marina, 58
Tsarist era, 21, 30, 103, 171
Turchynov, Oleksandr, 170
Turkestan, Chinese, 204
Turkey, 15, 43, 54, 82, 136; anti-Americanism, 201; and Armenia, 237; and gas supplies, 176–7, 180–1
Turkic peoples, 54
Turkmenistan, xix, 133–4, 135; and gas supplies, 176, 177, 204, 205
Turku, 228
TV–6, 47
TV-S, 47

Ukraine, xvi, 140, 180; and Bosnia crisis, 198; and Crimea, 110, 150; famine, 104, 108; foreign investment, 92; and gas supplies, 167–70, 185; instability in east, 241; introduces flat tax, 224; language, 239; Orange Revolution, 79; period of independence, 137; Russian influence in, 147–8; and Transdniestria, 138; withdrawal from CIS, 135
underwear, 79
unemployment, 32, 33, 33, 108
Union of Right Forces party, 228
union state, 134
United Civic Front, 59
United Nations Declaration of Human Rights, 119
United Nations Development Program, 11, 137
United Nations Human Development Index, 93
United Nations Law of the Sea Convention, 186
United Nations Security Council, xix, 199, 212
United Russia party, 66, 69, 116

United States of America, xxiv, 3, 72, 80, 124, 178, 189, 200–1; and 9/11 attacks, 3, 38; alliance with Europe, 130, 138, 199; anti-Americanism, 81, 201; and Belarus, 134; and Bulgaria, 196; and Central Asia, 132–3; and demographics, 93; economy, 92; energy independence, 180–2, 185; foreign investments, 97; and former Yugoslavia, 231; and Germany, 172, 174; and global hegemony, 126, 160, 201; and history, 106, 109–13, 117; and Kosovo, 198; Litvinenko affair, 83; military policies, 178, 196, 98; Putin and, 117; relations with Russia, 45, 49; Russian refugees in, 65; support for Educated Media Foundation, 77; think tanks, 63, 78, 172; and Turkey, 176; and Ukrainian Orange Revolution, 79; and Yukos, 50
Unity party, 232
universities, 43, 157
Urals, 29, 52, 204
uranium, 10, 81, 192
Urumqi, 204
Uspaskich, Viktor, 132
US State Department, 72
Uvarov, Count Sergei, 119
Uzbekistan, 132, 135, 204, 205

van der Veer, Jeroen, 97
Venediktov, Aleksei, 63
Venezuela, 11, 90, 181, 191, 192
Ventspils oil terminal, 143, 220
Versailles peace treaty, 116
VGTRK, 63
Vienna, 179, 197
Vienna Convention, 244
Vietnam, Russian bases in, 45, 245
Vietnam War, 106, 109–10
Vilnius, 6, 219
vlastnaya vertikal, 121
vodka, 40, 102, 164
Volga, River, 58, 73; basin, 171
Volgodonsk, 23
Volkswagen, 88
Volozh, Arkady, 89
voluntary organizations, 77–81
Vory v zakone, 225

Warnig, Matthias, 169
"war on terror," 3, 133, 195, 215
Warsaw Pact, 3, 4, 11, 131, 138, 156, 193, 200, 205
Warsaw uprising, 114
Washington, DC, 45, 64, 69, 84, 90, 109. 140, 191, 201, 202
welfare reforms, 123, 183
Western Europe, 8, 12, 14; and Eastern Europe, 148, 156, 157; energy supplies, 168; and history, 105, 110, 171; and missile defence, 194

Westerwelle, Guido, 167
Winchester College, 42
Wingas, 175
Winiecki, Jan, 31
Wintershall, 167, 175
workers, 31–3, 44, 95, 101; agricultural, 93
World Bank, 84
World Council of Russian People, 119
World Trade Organization (WTO), xxiv, 14, 84–5, 168
"WWW," 204

xenophobia, xvi, 6, 78, 80, 102, 105, 116, 120

Yabloko party, 28, 63, 66–7, 69
Yakunin, Vladimir, 39
Yamal gas field, 184
Yandarbiyev, Zelimkhan, 82
Yandex, 89
Yanukovych, Viktor, 239
Yavlinsky, Grigory, 28
Yekaterinburg, 29, 77
"Yelena," 58–9
Yeltsin, Boris, 6–9, 19, 22, 46; and Belarus, 134; and Chechnya, 221; and corruption, 31–2, 44; and economy, 30–4, 84; era of, 25, 38, 40, 64, 69, 70, 103, 204, 208; and federalism, 52–3, 55, 121; and former Yugoslavia, 198–200; and Germany, 172; and media, 47; memoirs, 223; popularity, 23–4, 29–30; Putin and, 37, 92, 107; reconciliation policy, 12; and religion, 118; and rewriting of history, 115–16; and Roman Abramovich, 221
Yevroremont, 40
youth movements, 43, 78–81, 116, 230
Yuganskneftegaz, 50, 91
Yugoslavia, former, 4, 151, 178, 180, 200; *see also* Bosnia; Croatia; Kosovo; Serbia
Yukhanova, Nadezhda, 25, 27
Yukos, 48–51, 61, 84, 91, 95–6, 99, 169, 183; Western interests and, 182, 209, 210
Yuryev, Michael, 123
Yushchenko, Viktor, 78, 230
Yushenkov, Sergei, 27, 223
Yuzhno-Russkoye gas field, 175

Zagreb, 178
Zaitsev, Gennady, 27
Zakayev, Ahmed, 82–3
Zakharenko, Yury, 237
Zavadsky, Dmitry, 237
Zavtra, 202, 245
Zdanovich, Aleksander, 25
Zeebrugge, 175
Zhdanov, Andrei, 153
Zhirinovsky, Vladimir, 102, 232
Zimin, Ilya, 65
Zorkin, Valery, 72
Zubkov, Viktor, 92
Zug, 169–70
Zyuganov, Gennady, 29, 46